THE

HISTORY

OF

GENERAL SIR CHARLES NAPIER'S

CONQUEST

OF

SCINDE

BY LIEUT.-GEN. SIR W. F. P. NAPIER

DEDICATED
TO THE BRITISH PEOPLE

The Naval & Military Press Ltd

published in association with

FIREPOWER
The Royal Artillery Museum
Woolwich

Published by
The Naval & Military Press Ltd
Unit 10 Ridgewood Industrial Park,
Uckfield, East Sussex,
TN22 5QE England
Tel: +44 (0) 1825 749494
Fax: +44 (0) 1825 765701
www.naval-military-press.com

in association with

FIREPOWER
The Royal Artillery Museum, Woolwich
www.firepower.org.uk

The Naval & Military Press

MILITARY HISTORY AT YOUR FINGERTIPS

... a unique and expanding series of reference works

Working in collaboration with the foremost regiments and institutions, as well as acknowledged experts in their field, N&MP have assembled a formidable array of titles including technologically advanced CD-ROMs and facsimile reprints of impossible-to-find rarities.

In reprinting in facsimile from the original, any imperfections are inevitably reproduced and the quality may fall short of modern type and cartographic standards.

NOTICE.

Some repetitions, and passages having a prospective reference, will be met with in the first and second portions of this work, because they were originally published separately, at long intervals. They are retained however as indicating the persevering enmity of men in power towards Sir C. Napier.

Alterations in the original text have also been made, touching the character and actions of Sir James Outram and Colonel Jacob of the Scinde horse; because subsequent knowledge has furnished proof that the merit attributed to them rested for the most part on their own assurances, which are not to be credited, inasmuch as both men have since shewn themselves to be systematic vaunters.

LIST OF PLANS.

CONQUEST OF SCINDE.

PART I.

CHAPTER I.

To the British people this work is dedicated. The conquest which it records, and the character of the conqueror, belong to the nation, which will not fail to do justice to a man who displayed such bravery in war, and such beneficent administrative wisdom in peace. But it is necessary to place him under the people's protection, because faction has designated him as one of a brood always eager to spill blood. It is true that he, and another of his name, have toppled down thrones and changed the fate of kingdoms. Don Miguel of . Portugal, and the Egyptian Ibrahim, attest Admiral Napier's vigour in war; while the fallen tyrants of Scinde, clanking their chains in the ears of sympathizing faction, attest that of General Napier. But to benefit mankind by peaceable arts has ever been the object of the man who warred so sternly at Meeanee.

In Cephalonia, where he long governed, his true tendencies were developed. For there he furrowed the lofty mountains with roads, in skilful contrivance equal, in greatness scarcely inferior to that of Mount Cenis. There he improved and adorned the harbour with fine quays, and light-houses of beautiful construction, created fisheries, and advanced agriculture. There he quelled feudal oppression, reformed the law courts, upheld justice, and honestly gained the affection of the labouring people by unceasing exertions, always evincing that benignity of purpose which renders the labours of peace glorious.

His efforts were painfully clogged by the vulgar jealousy

B

of a splenetic man in power the Lord High Commissioner Adam—with whom stupid pomp was a vital principle of government, and whose narrow intellect led him always to obstruct and finally to drive Sir C. Napier from his post with an accusation of tyranny! To this absurd and false charge Lord Ripon, the distant authority, listened; but the people, called victims of his misrule, passed their comment, and it is a precious one for those who honestly strive to aid the lowly. Thus it runs. Sir C. Napier, when iniquitously deprived of his command, possessed in Cephalonia, a piece of land so small that he took no heed of it on his departure; but the grateful Greek peasants voluntarily cultivated it and transmitted the value of the produce yearly to him, wherever he resided, without his being cognizant of their names!

Sir F. Adam could only see in the future conqueror of Scinde a person to be crushed by the leaden weight of power without equity; he could not comprehend qualities so far above his own; but they were noted by another observer of greater authority—one whose youthful genius pervaded the world while he lived, and covered it with a pall when he died: for to him, mountain and plain, lake and torrent, the seas, the skies, the earth, light and darkness yielded their poetic secrets, to be told with such harmonious melody that listening nations marvelled at the sound, and when it ceased they sorrowed. Lord Byron, writing from Cephalonia in 1823, thus expressed himself. "Of Colonel Napier's military character it were superfluous to speak; of his personal character I can say from my own knowledge, as well as from all public rumour, or private report, that it is excellent as his military; in short, a better or a braver man is not easily to be found. *He* is our man to lead a regular force, or to organize a national one for the Greeks. Ask the army; ask any one."

This eulogy, pronounced when Greece, struggling for freedom, like her own fabled Encêlädus shook the world at every throe, had reference to a design formed by Sir C. Napier to deliver the bright land of ancient days. Largely conceived it was, and many brave enthusiastic men, habituated to war, were ready with their valour, and wealth, which was not small, for they were not mere adventurers, to throw themselves, under his guidance, into the Peloponnesus, where he was advantageously known by his wise and just government of Cephalonia, and by his benevolence towards the dispossessed Suliotes. The enterprise bad fair for success, but Byron's recommendation and Napier's proffered services were alike disregarded by the Anglo-Greek committee in London—a happy neglect, seeing that the acquisition of a great kingdom, and the restoration of the British military reputation in India, shaken by previous events, were the result.

This purposed descent on Greece was not the only project formed by him against the Turkish power, which he abhorred from witnessing the great cruelties exercised on the unhappy people of the Archipelago and Peloponnesus. He had been previously employed on a secret military mission to Ali, Pacha of Yoanina, to whom, when consulted as to operations against the Porte, he said, " Give me the selection of your troops, and one of the millions in your coffers, and in six weeks I will place you in the seraglio, Sultan of Constantinople, if you will declare the Christians free." The Pacha liked the project, but would not give the treasure ! One month afterwards he offered two millions ! The reply was :—" Too late, the Turks are in the Etolian mountains ! you are lost." And the miser, Ali, gave up his life and money together !

During his forced retirement from military life, Sir C. Napier added the following works to his country's literature, —*The Roads of Cephalonia; The Colonies; Colonization, with Remarks upon small farms and overpopulation; Military Law; An Essay on the State of Ireland; Notes upon De Vigny's Lights and Shadows of Military Life.* Finally, a Historical Romance, called *William the Conqueror,* soon to be published, and evincing the Author's versatile powers.

Having become a Major-General, Lord Hill in 1839, at the recommendation of Lord Fitzroy Somerset, a man not to be swayed by calumny, which was not spared, placed him in command of the Northern District of England. It was a troubled period; but acting as an officer entrusted with the preservation of social order, he gained the approbation of the Government, without ill-will from the people, who appreciated his honest desire for their welfare, while he controlled them by military force.

Passing through Egypt, he saw amidst the false glare given by interested persons, all the weakness and oppression of Mehemet Ali's government, which he thus exposed.

"A person staying but a short time in a country has no right to suppose he can trace causes with certainty: he can, however, judge of effects when they are strongly marked. Rich land, a variety of produce with a ready market for it in Europe, and a noble people, belong to this country. Mehemet Ali has ruled it for forty years, and the result is horrible! I have not seen, nor can I hear of any deed of his, nor the result of his deeds, that has not the stamp of tyranny, of mischief, of villainy. His mind is capable of projecting clever things for his own supposed advantage, or pleasure, or renown; incapable of great works for the regeneration of a people, or even for their temporary advantage: he does not even leave the means of subsistence in their possession! His only really great work, the Canal of Mahmoudie, eighteen feet deep, ninety feet wide, and sixty miles long, cost, it is asserted here, the lives of twenty-nine thousand persons in one year, out of the hundred and fifty thousand employed: they were starved by him, and dug the canal with their hands!

"Take that as a sample of his infernal rule. A great man would have given them tools; he would not, to save expense, have slain twenty-nine thousand poor men within the year. And when his canal was finished, the commerce on it would have proved its use and his greatness; but no boat floats thereon which does not contain the Pacha's property, for no man but himself is a proprietor. This highway of two hundred miles through his dominions, for it is one with the Nile, exhibits no sign therefore that the barbarian's mind is either great or good. What encouragement has he given to his people? None! He has hired foreign men to make all things which he requires for war, and his establishments are of a size which render his government one of devilish oppression ; his monopolies no country could support ; he is living on his capital !

" To give an illustration of his system. In two districts, the rent being alike for each, some accident injures the crop on one and it becomes impossible for the people to pay more than half rent. The Pacha levies the deficiency on the other, and both are ruined ! An Abyssinian, or some merchant from the interior of Africa, arrives with merchandise, and is offered a large sum in cash. He cannot take it ! The Pacha seizes the goods and pays, when *convenient*, with articles from the Pacha's own stock of merchandise, to the amount of *half* the value ; and this robbery is so frequent as to be the rule, not the exception. The Pacha then sells the goods to the original cash purchaser, and all trade is thus checked, except that which is in the hands of Englishmen. The result of all this is a ruined miserable people.

" The troops are ill equipped, but they are the best thing one sees, except the ships of war. The men, both soldiers and peasants, are fine strong Arabs with thin faces, intellectual to the greatest degree, good-humoured, honest-looking, and resolute. The Egyptian I have not been able yet to distinguish from the Arab, but *all* appear fine looking. In five days I have seen many beaten severely by men in authority, without any apparent cause ; they all seemed disposed to resist, but the consequences were too terrible, and smothered rage was very clearly depicted. Forty years' rule should have produced better fruit, if Mehemet Ali were, as we are told, a great man : of that I see no proof, no trace ! Ibrahim beat a man to death last week in this town (Cairo). The poor fellow did not bring eggs enough ? —' How many turkeys have you got ? How much corn do they eat ? Do they lay eggs to cover that amount ? ' ' Yes ! ' ' Then you must bring so many eggs daily.' The man failed for two or three days. Ibrahim sent for the wretched creature, and with his own hands, using a club, beat him to death ! I recollect his doing the like when I was in Cephalonia.

"Ali Pacha's ' *vast improvements*,' have been to strengthen his forces, and he has done that, at ten times the cost necessary. My conviction is, that his reputation for greatness originates in the opinions and interests of silly English adventurers and speculating merchants, incapable of judging him, but whose fortunes he makes, and from no other source. The man lives upon his capital. How far this may be forced upon him I cannot tell."

Mehemet Ali's faults were not the only objects of animadversion. From a gentleman living in Egypt, and not unwilling to be quoted, Sir C. Napier heard, that the comptrollers of the British Museum had directed the engineer employed to remove objects of ancient art from Egypt, to cut the statue of Sesostris into four pieces, that it might be sent to England more cheaply! Obedience was refused.

Having reached Bombay in 1842, he took command at Poona, and in his letters from thence, forcibly depicted the vices of Lord Auckland's government, civil and military. His observations were laid before a minister of competent knowledge at home and were returned with this remark, "*Too true a picture drawn by a master hand.*" But then Lord Ellenborough came to rebuke the nepotism of the directors, to curb the jobbing tribe, to reduce newspaper editors from a governing to a reporting class, and to raise the spirit of the army, sinking under insult and the domineering influence of a hireling press. India was thus saved. .

At Poona, Sir C. Napier, desirous to exercise himself in the handling of troops, a practice necessary for the most experienced officer, if he would be a ready captain; desirous also to restore neglected discipline, in what he truly called the "*noble Indian army,*" broke the monotony of formal parades to work his troops over the neighbouring hills, arousing the latent military energies of the officers, and making all mindful that they were soldiers, not trainbands.

He disabused them also of a pernicious error, inculcated by the newspapers of India with a pertinacity of falsehood peculiarly characteristic. They said, and belief was given to them, though worthy only of unbelief, *that the matchlock of the Affghan and other enemies was superior to the British musket in range and precision.* Simply to reason against this fallacy, would, he knew, be fruitless. Promulgated with a bad motive, it had been accepted as a truth with dogged credulity, and could only be refuted practically. To draw attention he adopted this device: provoking a warm advocate for the matchlock to wage on a matchlock against a musket, he selected marksmen, practised with them until the best shooter was known, and then daily contended in person with that man. They were nearly equal: the camp became interested, bets were multiplied, and the subject occupied the soldiers' thoughts, which was the General's object. The stiffened neck of the prejudice was thus bent; for at the end of two months the reputation of the matchlock was lost at Poona. This dexterous management indicated the great captain ere the red stamp of battle made him patent; for previous to the trial a feeling was prevalent that to encounter the matchlock was to fall in useless strife. The sepoy's musket is however cumbrous for his strength, because of that strange economy which spares a pound in the expense of a soldier's weapon at the cost of the soldier himself!

Observing many errors in the organization and discipline of the Indian army, Sir C. Napier digested in his own mind alterations with respect to the artillery and baggage, some of which he afterwards effected ; and always he was sanguine in these matters, because of the willingness to learn which he found in the Company's officers. But the follies of the time were great, and one for its supreme absurdity merits notice. Every soldier was ordered to have a large box, in addition to his usual baggage; and the 22nd regiment, acting under this preposterous regulation, marched for Scinde with 1,300 boxes! A camel could carry but four, and thus 300 camels, each occupying five yards in theory, in practice ten yards, were added to the other Indian impediments of a regiment. Truly the strong hand of Lord Ellenborough was wanting to lift the Indian Government from such a slough. He came in time, and no man watched his government with more anxiety than the General at Poona. Nor was this anxiety soon relieved, for, previous to the final burst of Nott and Pollock on Cabool, no positive principle of action to guide his judgment, was evinced in the operations, and he characterized the war by one expressive phrase. " *A tragic harlequinade.*"

Meanwhile public opinion assigned him a capacity for great actions, and a vague prescience of coming glory which often foreruns victory, predisposing men to give all their energies for its attainment, prevailed in the military community. Yet he desired no active command beyond the Indus. He disliked the appearance of affairs, and dreaded the prevailing shameless system, which, having then no experience of Lord Ellenborough's energy, he could not hope to see overborne:—upheld as it was by faction and the influence of the Court of Directors in England; and in India by the most vehemently unscrupulous press that ever pandered for hire to bad men at the expense of the public interest. He had therefore no inclination to become responsible, according to his degree, for disasters he could not but anticipate from the policy of rulers, who were sure to charge their errors on the executive officers: for to make bricks without straw, and to be calumniated, is the task and fate of British generals.

An order from the Governor-General soon sent him to Scinde. Dated the 26th of August, it gave him the command of the troops in that country and in Beloochistan, with entire control over all the political agents and civil functionaries; and it peremptorily informed him that, "If the Ameers, or any one of them, should act hostilely, or evince hostile designs against the British forces, it was the Governor-General's fixed resolution never to forgive the breach of faith, and to exact a penalty which should be a warning to every chief in India."

The fierce tenure of this order, issued at a moment of great difficulty, after great disasters, bespoke in Lord Ellenborough a consciousness of danger, but magnanimous resolution; it told the General that a crisis demanding all his energy and ability was at hand, that much was expected from him, but by a ruler who would neither shrink himself, nor fail towards others. Wherefore, with a frame slight and meagre, and, though of iron hardness, furrowed by wounds, he, in his sixty-first year hastened to take command as eagerly as a young warrior : bred in camps he had been fifty years awaiting this crowning trial. It is rare to see great prudence in war tempering the heroic valour and confidence of a youthful general ; more rare to find the sanguine daring of early years untamed by age and its infirmities.

On the 3rd of September, Sir C. Napier embarked in the *Zenobia* steamer for Scinde, thus commencing his new career upon Oliver Cromwell's fortunate day, a coincidence which he noted with satisfaction. The augury was good, yet seemed at fault in the commencement; for cholera broke out, and the hideous misery of the voyage he thus described :

" In six bitter days and nights we cast fifty-four dead into the sea, just one-fourth of our companions ! One passenger, it happened, was a surgeon, and he was assisted by two native apprentices belonging to the hospitals : fortunately only two of the sailors died, or we should have been lost for want of hands. The engineer perished the third day, but happily there were amongst the passengers two others going to the steamers on the Indus. Since landing ten more soldiers have died, and one captain : making sixty-four in all ! This pulls down the spirits of men. It was the worst description of blue cholera. The agonies, the convulsions, the dreadful groans, were heart-rending : and then the screams of the poor women who lost their husbands and children !   And amidst all this, in the darkness of the night, the necessity of throwing the dead overboard the instant life was extinct to make room for the living !   Then also, added to this scene of human wretchedness, the violent effects of the disease could not be cleaned, and extreme filth increased the misery.   Well ! God be praised ! it has ceased, but more troops are on this voyage and I dread to hear of similar sufferings, for most of it has been caused by neglect.   I have made a formal complaint to Sir George Arthur, who, I am sure will stir about the matter.   The Commander of the *Zenobia*, Mr. Newman, is a noble fellow.   I believe all that were saved owe their lives to him; and we, the officers, have given him a gold snuff-box in token of our gratitude. On making the land both mates got drunk, and such a night scene of confusion I never saw. We were nearly as possible on a reef of rocks; we fired guns and rockets, but no help came; had we struck, all must have perished; at least all the sick, eighty in number: at last we cast anchor, and luckily on good holding ground."

To provide for the survivors was his first care, and then further mishap befell himself. While attending some rocket practice, one of the fiery missiles tore the calf of his right leg to the bone; but a life of temperance and a patient endurance, were repaid by a surprising cure; the hurt healed by the first intention, and the fifth day saw him travelling up the Indus towards Hydrabad.

Some superstition the human intellect seems always to lean towards; many of the greatest minds have rested thereon, and those who deal in war seldom reject predestination. Sir C. Napier's life encourages this sentiment though reason should recoil. In infancy he was snatched at the last stage of starvation from a vile nurse; when a young boy, attempting a dangerous leap, he tore the flesh from his leg in a frightful manner, and a few years later fractured the other leg. At the battle of Coruna, struggling with several French soldiers he received five terrible wounds, and but for the aid of a generous French drummer would there have been killed. At the battle of Busaco a bullet struck his face and lodged behind the ear, splintering the articulation of the jawbone, and with this dreadful hurt he made his way under a fierce sun to Lisbon, more than one hundred miles! Returning from France, after the battle of Waterloo, the ship sunk off Flushing and he saved himself by swimming to a pile, to which he clung until a boat took him off, half drowned, for the beam was too large for climbing and he was overwhelmed by each recurring surge.

Now, escaping cholera, a second shipwreck, and the rocket stroke, he was hastening to conduct with matchless energy a dangerous war. But how the spare body,

shattered in battle and worn by fifty years' service in every
variety of climate, could suffice to place him amongst the
famous captains of the world is a mystery. His star was in
the East!

Scinde was politically disturbed. The British disasters
at Cabool and Ghusni, the frequent checks given to detachments in the hills of Beloochistan, the recent repulse and
consequent retreat of Colonel England before an Affghan
force not more numerous than his own ; even the firm yet
long isolated position of General Nott at Candahar, had
abated the fear of British power in Scinde, and the Beloochees
were, princes chiefs and followers, alike disposed for war.
Colonel England was retiring from Shawl by the Bolan
passes, through hostile tribes, having with him the main
body of the troops destined to form the army in Scinde, and
the Ameers were keenly watching his progress : had another
disaster befallen him they would have commenced hostilities;
for only four thousand men were then in their country, at
Sukkur and Kurrachee, four hundred miles apart, and without
a secure communication.

This critical state of affairs was met with sagacity and
energy. " Danger from their warfare I see none" wrote the
General from Kurrachee. " I can beat all the princes of
Scinde when England joins me, for I shall then have twelve
thousand men. No cavalry however, and I should feel the
want of it if the Ameers attack me; but I shall have some
soon. My difficulty will be to act as chief political agent to
the Governor-General. I believe his intentions to be just
and honourable. I know my own are. But Hell is paved
with good intentions, and both of us may have great difficulties to encounter. Yet I feel neither diffidence nor
hesitation. My plan is formed, so is Lord Ellenborough's,
and I believe they are alike. The hill tribes threaten to fall
on England's column as it descends the Bolan pass. There
are however reasons to doubt this, and I have sent to advise
and authorize the Commander in Upper Scinde to make a
forward movement towards the pass; which I hope he will be
able to do, and thus favour England's retreat by menacing
the rear of his enemies. He has the mass of my troops with

him ; I have only four thousand in Upper Scinde. I ought to have been here two months ago. I have now to travel two hundred miles up the Indus, with a guard of only fifty men, through a hostile country. This appears foolish, but I must get to my troops. I set off to-morrow, and there will be no small interest in threading the windings of the noble river Indus."

At Hydrabad he resolved to wait on the Ameers as a mark of respect, and to make personal observation of their characters. These Princes, barbaric of race and feelings, sensual and treacherous, were yet polite of manners, and subtile to sound those depths and shallows of the human mind formed by crime and passion—they had guides thereto in their own dispositions, but for virtues they had no tests and looked not for them. They knew, having made diligent inquiry, that the General came with all political as well as military power, which had not been before even when Lord Keane menaced their capital at the head of a great army, therefore they hastened to offer suitable respect. Their palanquin was sent for his use, and this the highest honour of their court was enhanced by the presence of their sons, who met him beyond the city gates, bringing camels for his retinue.

Around them clustered the great Sirdars and nobles on horseback, with thousands of retainers, chiefs and followers, having keen heavy swords girt to their sides and large shields thrown over their shoulders. The General was at the head of his own guard of the wild horsemen of India. Thus they met, the two masses commingling, and being surrounded by a multitude on foot, shouting and screaming, moved altogether with a rushing pace towards the palace. A gorgeous disarray! All were clothed in bright colours, their splendid arms gleamed and glittered in the broad sunbeams ; and high above the crowd the giant camels swayed their huge bodies to and fro with an uneasy motion, while the fiery horses, bearing rich housings, neighed and bounded with violence from side to side, their swarthy riders writhing their bodies convulsively and tossing their sinewy hands aloft with frantic energy. And all this time the

multitude on foot were no less vehement. Wearing fine
embroidered caps, which set off their handsome eager faces,
their piercing eyes, their teeth of snowy whiteness, they
pressed forwards, fighting and crushing each other to see the
"General Saib of the Feringees." He, reclining in the open
high arched palanquin of crimson and gold, a small dark-
visaged old man with a falcon's glance, must have disappointed their expectations, for they knew not then the
heroic force of mind which was to invalidate their wild
strength and furious courage on the dreadful field of Meeanee.
Now, ignorant, proud and fierce, with barbarian pomp they
passed tumultuously along, winding in the deep shadows of
the ancient massive towers of Hydrabad, their numbers
increasing at every step, until they reached the embattled
gate of the fortress, through which the bearers of the palanquin could scarcely struggle to the palace, but when they did
the hubbub ceased.

The Ameers, having, as they said, consideration for the
General's recent hurt, held their Dhurbar in the Court below
to spare him the ascent of their great staircase. Richly
they were dressed, and their swords and shields resplendent
with gold and jewels. None were handsome, but all were
youthful save Nusseer and another, both being however
younger than their visitor. Sweetmeats and provisions were
presented, and compliments exchanged, while each party
watched keenly for indications of character by which to guide
their future intercourse. What impression the Englishman
made cannot be known, but the studied respect, the oriental
politeness, the princely pomp and display of wild military
power, by which the Ameers sought to impose on him, failed
to affect his judgment. Well knowing that with barbarians
friendship is self-interest and wisdom deceit, he kept his
mind immoveably intent upon his mission. He was in Scinde,
not to bandy compliments with Princes but to maintain the
power and influence and interests of England in all their
integrity at a moment of danger, when a slight concession
might prove fatal. With this object diplomatic cajolery had
no proper connection. His orders were to maintain the cause
of British India by a fair and just, though stern and un-

yielding policy, by force of arms if policy failed. Putting their flattering attentions aside, he gave them an austere warning that the unsteady weak policy of the political agents was ended, and international obligations would be henceforth rigidly enforced : for at Kurrachee he had obtained proof of their malpractices, and now in writing told them that he would, if they did not cease, make the Governor-General cognizant of them with a view to a forcible remedy.

This letter being delivered, he passed on to Sukkur, where he arrived the 5th of October, and forthwith commenced a policy which reduced the Ameers to choose between an honest alliance or a terrible war. They chose dishonesty and battle ; but their deceit was baffled by a superior intellect, and their swords were broken by stronger arms. Why it so happened shall be shewn in another place :—clearly it shall be shewn that the war was of the Ameers' seeking, and their heavy misfortunes were a just punishment of their folly and wickedness—misery to them, to the world a benefit. With abilities and energy placing him amongst the greatest of those famed western captains who have forced the pride of the East to stoop on the battle field, Sir C. Napier sought not strife, it was thrust upon him ! But the peculiar position of Scinde in 1842, and its connection with British Indian policy when he assumed the command at Sukkur must be first considered by those who seek the truth, and are desirous to be assured that the dreadful sword of England was not drawn in an unjust quarrel. Wherefore the next chapter shall contain a retrospective examination—for the Scindian war was no isolated event. To use the conqueror's expression, it was " *The tail of the Affghan storm.*"

CHAPTER II.

THE origin and progress of British power in the East is well known. Commencing in trade it has been magnified by arms and policy, and the glittering bubble must expand until it burst, or it will collapse. Strangers more civilized, more knowing in science and arts, more energetic of spirit, more strong of body, more warlike, more enterprising than the people among whom they settle, must necessarily extend their power until checked by natural barriers, or by a counter-civilization. The novelty of their opinions, political and religious, the cupidity of their traders, the ambition or avarice of their chiefs, the insolence of superiority, the instinct of self-preservation, all conduce to render collision with the native populations inevitable, and conquest as inevitable as collision. It is the struggle of the fertile land with the desert of Egypt, the waters of the Nile directed against the waste, the stream of civilization against barbaric ignorance.

But a reflux of barbarian power continually menaces British India, and peace cannot be till all is won. The necessity for expansion is urgent, and the more so that the subjected people's condition has not been improved in proportion to the extent of the conquest, or the greatness of the conquerors : the frame of government is not essentially just and liberal, and as it wants support of benevolent wisdom, prying people must be kept at a distance.

This inherent craving for aggrandizement has carried British India to the roots of the Himalayas on the North, menacing and menaced by the mountaineers of Nepaul ; to the Irrawaddy on the East, grating harshly with the Burman empire. It has sent fleets and armies to obtain a corner nest in China for the incubation of commerce ; but the eggs will produce the gliding serpent, the ravening kite, the soaring eagle. China will be overturned, changed in all her institutions: unless her politic people, acquiring as they are like to do the arts of European warfare, thrust the intruding strangers from the land.

The march of aggrandizement has been more rapid towards the West, because there is felt the dangerous influence of a counter-civilization, if such a term can be applied to Russia as she expands towards the East. Peril from that quarter is prospective and probably distant, but not to be despised, inasmuch as the basis of Russian strength is natural and enormous. The perception of this truth has hurried, not without policy, the British Indian frontier towards the West, where, under the name of sovereignty protection or influence, it extended before the Affghan war along the left bank of the Sutlege to the lower Indus, and from thence by the Thurr, or great Indian desert, to the run of Cutch and the ocean. From that line the bayonets of England protruded, from thence her voice of command went forth to the nations of Central Asia, and the state of those nations must be considered before the policy of invading them to forestall Russia can be judged.

In the days of Alexander, the country beyond the Sutlege contained the kingdoms of Porus and Taxiles. It is now the Punjaub, or land of the five rivers, namely, the Sutlege or Garra, formed by the junction of the ancient *Hyphasis* and *Hesudrus;* the Ravee or *Hydrastes* of the Greeks; the *Acessines* of antiquity, now the Chenaub; the Jelum, formerly the *Hydaspes,* upon the banks of which the Macedonian hero overcame the giant Indian chief; the *Indus,* which still retains its first name. These streams, descending from the Himalayas or Indian Caucasus, flow southward until they unite in one great river called the lower Indus. Their union is completed at Mittunkole, below Moultan. From thence the vast volume of their waters bears downward to the sea through an immense plain, which, commencing far above their junction, ends only at the coast : this plain is overflowed periodically in summer by the Indus, as the Nile overflows the land of Egypt.

Looking at the countries thus watered, as they confronted

the British line before the Affghan war, and in the order of their descent from the mountains, we find Cachmere at top, amongst the high branches of the five streams ; the Punjaub next ; Scinde the lowest. This may be called the *first parallel* of nations then opposed to British India.

Westward of the Indus, at a mean distance of forty or fifty miles, a majestic shoot from the Indian Caucasus goes southward to the sea, bearing many names, such as the Soolyman, the Bolan, and Hala mountains. Presenting in its whole length a natural wall of rugged strength, pierced only in a few places by roads, it closes at some points on the river, at others recedes, as in Cutch Gundava, more than a hundred miles.

These mountains, and their kindred ranges of Kojeh and Gilghie, with the elevated table lands belonging to them, form the countries of Affghanistan and Beloochistan ; the former lying to the north, bordering the Punjaub and Cachmere ; the latter lying to the south, bordering on Scinde. This vast tract, including Seestan or Segistan of the desert, formed the *second parallel* of nations opposed to the frontier of British India. It is bounded on the south by the ocean ; on the north by that continuation of the Indian Caucasus, known as the Hindoo Khosh and the Parapomisan range, as far as the city of Herat, which is the western door of Affghanistan opening into Persia : with exception of the Herat corner, it is bounded by deserts on the west.

From Herat a great spine of mountains runs to the Caspian Sea, dividing Toorkmania from Khorassan proper and Persia. The former, lying north of this spine, is separated from Affghanistan by the Hindoo Khosh and the Parapomisus. Anciently this was the Bactriana, Sogdiana, and Chorasmia of the Macedonians ; it is now known as the districts of Koondooz, Balk, Bokhara, Samarcand, and Khiva, or Orgunjé, which borders on the Caspian and Aral seas. Toorkmania, Khorassan, and Persia, formed therefore the *third parallel* of nations between the Indian frontier and the Russian base of operations.

Through Toorkmania flows the Oxus, running from the Hindoo Khosh to the Aral Sea ; it is navigable from above

c

Balk to its mouth, more than 600 miles—and it is up the
Oxus, through the barbarous nations of Toorkmania, over the
snow-clad Hindoo Khosh, and across the rugged Affghan
country that Russia must win her way, by force or policy,
to meet a British army on the Indus. Or by this route, or
through Persia and Khorassan to Herat she must move ; for
of her military colonies, planted in the countries ceded to her
by China, north of the Himalayas, little account need be
made, if indeed they exist. Her progress by Constantinople
is another question, depending upon European diplomacy and
European arms.

Such being the geographical relation of the countries of
Central Asia with British India, the political relations and
strength of those more immediately affected by the recent
wars shall be now touched upon.

The population of the Punjaub, said to be five millions,
consists of Seiks, Hindoos, and Juts, also to be found in
Scinde, Affghanistan, and Beloochistan. The first are the
ruling race, though not the most numerous ; they are
athletic, warlike, and turbulent, having a peculiar religion
and a holy book called the "*Grinth.*" Of recent date is
their power. A few years ago the Punjaub was under
the shadow of the Dooranee empire; but Runjeet Sing,
having combined the many republican communities of the
Seiks into one conquering state, wrested Cachmere and the
Peshawar district from Affghanistan, and took the fortress
of Attock on the Indus, which has ever been and probably
ever will be the entrance to India for armies coming from
the West. He also extended his power over Moultan, including some tributary dominions of the Bhawal Khan lying
between the Sutlege and the Indus. His regular force was
fifty thousand, five thousand being cavalry ; and he had three
hundred guns, half of them efficient for the field. All these
troops were well disciplined under European officers ; and he
kept eighteen thousand irregular horsemen in constant pay :
he manufactured his own arms and materials for war, his
revenue was large, and successive Governors-General sought
his friendship in person. At first he held aloof, but sagacious
to perceive that the amity of the mighty strangers, interested

though it might be, was less formidable than their enmity, he, contrary to the wishes of his nobles, accepted political engagements and maintained them until his death.

Proceeding southward, Scinde would be the next country to treat of; but as its affairs must be curiously inquired into, and their connection with those of Affghanistan, Beloochistan, and Doodpoutra shewn, the state of those nations demands previous notice.

Doodpoutra, governed by the Bhawal Khan, Bhawalpore being the capital, lies on the left of the Sutlege, between the British stations on the upper part of that river and Scinde. The Bhawal Khan's dominions extended at one time across the Sutlege and the Acessines to the Upper Indus, but he was then a tributary of the Doorance monarch, and on his refusal to pay Runjeet Sing the same tribute, the latter seized the territory between the rivers. The Ameers of Scinde also took from the Bhawal Khan a large district on the left bank of the Lower Indus, and he being thus pressed, accepted the offered protection of the British, by which his dominions were guaranteed against further encroachments.

The origin of the Affghan or Dooranee empire is of recent date. Ahmed Shah, the founder, was of the Sudoyzie family, sacred in the Dooranee tribe of Affghanistan. Taking advantage of the temporary ascendancy of the Dooranees over the Giljhies, with whom power had before resided, he constituted, in the middle of last century, one conquering nation of Affghans, in place of the ill-cemented confederacy of republican tribes, clans, and families which previously existed. Ahmed was not a mere eastern swordsman. A great commander, a statesman, and politician, he warred successfully against Persia, subdued Khorassan as far as Meschid in the west, reduced Balk and the neighbouring Uzbecks beyond the Hindoo Khosh, awed Bokhara, overrun the Punjaub, acquired Cachmere, occupied Surhind, took Delhi and Agra, and overthrew the Mahrattas. Moultan, Doodpoutra and Scinde were his tributaries; Beloochistan and Seestan of the desert were parts of his kingdom. He died in 1773, and was succeeded by his son Timour Shah, who was succeeded by his son Zeman Shah, who, blind, old, and an exile, was still living when the British entered his country.

Zeman Shah on the throne, had repeatedly menaced India, but each time Persian warfare or civil commotion stopped his invasion, and he was finally dethroned and blinded by his brother Mahmood, who was in turn dethroned, but not blinded, by another brother, Shah Sooja-ool-moolk, to restore whom the English invaded Affghanistan.

Futteh Khan, chief of the great Barrukzie family, of the Dooranee tribe, restored Mahmood, but governed under the title of Vizier, until Kamran the son of Mahmood, persuaded his father to put out the Vizier's eyes. The brothers of the blinded man took up arms, and then the barbarous Princes caused the helpless, yet stern and courageous old Vizier, to be deliberately hacked to pieces in the Dhurbar: they were, however, driven in flight to Herat, where Mahmood died, but Kamran retained the government of the city and province.

Shah Sooja was then recalled from exile, because only from the small and sacred family of the Sudoyzies could a king be chosen. On the journey, he displayed so much arrogance towards the Barrukzies, who had recalled him, that, taking timely warning, they at once raised his brother Eyoob to the throne. Sooja, whose highest merit seems to have been the forbearing to put out his dethroned brother's eyes, being thus again set aside, Azeem Khan, the eldest surviving brother of Futteh Khan, became Vizier and governed in Eyoob's name; but he soon died of grief for the loss of a battle against Runjeet Sing. Commotions followed, Eyoob and his son became exiles, and the great Dooranee empire was broken up.

During these civil wars, the Persians recovered Khorassan and menaced Herat; the King of Bokhara appropriated Balk; the neighbouring Uzbecks resumed their independence; Cachmere, Peshawar, the Punjaub, Moultan, with part of Doodpoutra, became the prey of Runjeet Sing.

Meanwhile the British conquered Tippoo Sultan, overthrew the Mahrattas, added Delhi and Surhind to their Empire, and established themselves on the Upper Sutlege, at

Loodiana. The Bhawal Khan then ceased to be a tributary of Cabool; and Merab Khan, the Brahooe-Belooch, Prince of Khelat, assumed independent sovereignty, allying himself with the Ameers of Scinde, who not only refused tribute but seized a part of Affghanistan on the right of the Indus. The hill tribes of Beloochistan also resumed their democratic independence, while the Affghans, averse to kingly rule from natural feelings, customs, and original organization, split into four great divisions, holding together as a nation only by their common religion and language. Thus, while Kamran held Herat, where, in 1837-8, he was besieged for a year by the Persians, at the instigation of Russian agents, the brothers of the Viziers, Futteh and Azeem Khan, appropriated the rest of the Kingdom. One seized Candahar, city and province; another took Peshawar, paying tribute to Runjeet Sing; a third brother, the celebrated Dost Mahomed, became chief of Cabool; his rule extending beyond the Hindoo Khosh on the north, to Herat on the west, to Jellallabad on the east, and to Ghusni, including that town, on the south.

The Affghan population, reckoning the Persian Kuzzle-bashes and other settlers, is stated to be more than five millions; that of Beloochistan at one million and a half. Dost Mahomed maintained nine thousand cavalry, two thousand infantry, and fourteen guns. The Candahar man, nine thousand cavalry, and six guns; the Peshawar chief, three thousand men, with six guns. But these numbers did not represent the force of the country, every chief had his own followers, every tribe and clan was armed and warlike.

The state of the countries bordering on Scinde, when Lord Auckland undertook the miserable Affghan war, being thus shewn, the course of Scindian affairs can be traced without interruption and a better understanding, from the first commercial connection to the final conquest.

Scinde was formerly peopled by the Mhurs and Dhurs, now called Scindees, a strong handsome race. Pagans at first, they were conquered and converted by Mahomedans from Damascus, in the seventh or eighth century, and in the beginning of the eighteenth century, the Kalloras, military fanatics from Persia, obtained rule. Ahmed Shah subjected them, yet suffered them to retain hereditary power under the title of Meahs.

In 1771, a Belooch tribe called Talpoorees, which, with others of their race, had come from the hills to settle on the plains of Scinde, possessed great influence. They held all the principal offices of state, and were the soldiers of the country, until the Kallora prince, jealous of their power, put their chief to death, whereupon the tribe dethroned him and set up his nephew. But the son of the murdered Talpoor, returning from Mecca in 1778, renewed the quarrel and killed the new Meah in battle. His brother replaced him, and peace was restored for a time ; yet soon the Meah murdered the Talpoor chief, fresh commotions ensued, and after many assassinations and crimes on all sides the Kallora prince was driven away. Aided by the Prince of Khelat, and the Affghan monarch Timour, he renewed the war, and was finally restored on certain conditions. Those he broke, and murdered the Talpoor chief who had succeeded his first victim, but the tribe then killed him in battle, and drove his son an exile to the Punjaub, where he still lives.

If the Kalloras were bad princes, the Talpoorees have been worse. The first of them, though confirmed in his sovereignty by the Dooranee monarch, was forced to share the country with his brothers ; and when he died in 1800, those brothers, known as the " *Char Yar*," again divided the power, yet unequally, calling themselves the Ameers, or Lords of Scinde. From this division sprung the Kyrpoor Ameers, or Lords of Upper Scinde; the Hydrabad Ameers, or Lords of Lower Scinde ; and the MeerpoorAmeer :—from it also sprung the anomalous order of succession, which gave the Rais, the Puggree or turban of command, in each family, to the brother instead of the son. Nevertheless, the Hydrabad Ameers were in some degree paramount.

The Char Yar soon called down more of the hill Beloochees, giving them land on military tenure, and with this aid enlarged their dominions.

On the side of Cutch they took from the Rajah of Joudpore, Omercote in the desert and Parkur beyond it, thus coming into contact with the British frontier.

South-westward, they took, from the chief of Luz, Kurrachee, the best port of Scinde.

On the north-east they took Subzulcote and Bhoong-Barra from the Bhawal Khan.

On the north-west they spread at the expense of the Affghans, from whom they took Shikarpoor, and the fortress of Bukkur, which, standing on a rock in the middle of the Indus, completely commands the navigation.

The first Ameers and their sons, whose recent fall has been so inordinately and ostentatiously lamented by factious writers, and pretended philanthropists, who think cruelty for the lucre of gain a virtue, and dealing death in defence of country a crime; by such philosophers, and by disappointed peculators in expectancy, and by political dupes, they have been proclaimed as innocent victims. But these heavily bemoaned lords were themselves usurpers of yesterday: many are alive, and notably Roostum of Kyrpoor, who were engaged in the dethronement of the Kalloras. Rapacious invaders of their neighbours also they were, and their Scindee subjects they afflicted with every kind of misery. These last, indeed, call the events which changed their rulers, the "*massacre of the Meahs.*" The Beloochees call it the "*Conquest.*" They have another conquest now to reckon from !

. To the Belooch it was a conquest, resembling that of the Norman in England when Harold fell, for each chief was lord of the soil, holding it by military tenure; yet in this differing from his Norman prototype, that the Ameers could, and often did, deprive him of his Jagheere or grant from caprice. This precarious tenure stimulated his innate rapacity, and he is habitually grasping, a fatalist without remorse, an overbearing soldier without fear, and a strong-handed robber without shame, because to rob has ever been the custom of his race. Athletic, and skilled in the use of his weapons, for to the sword only his hand clutches, he is known, says his conqueror, "by his slow rolling gait, his fierce aspect, heavy sword and broad shield, his dagger and matchlock. Labour he despises, but loves his neighbour's purse." It was, however, the Scindee and

Hindoo that he plundered, because his own race in the hills were like himself in disposition, and somewhat more robust.

Turbulent subjects, the Beloochees often coerced their princes, and always strived to sow dissension amongst them, because commotions yielded plunder and high pay. Indeed the Ameers' system led to self-destruction, and having an instinct of this they secured their persons by numerous slaves, being in the traffic of human beings, both importers and exporters. The slaves, chiefly Abyssinian blacks, were attached by manifold favours, while to all others the Ameers were brutal tyrants. Their policy, stupid in its selfishness, was to injure agriculture, impede commerce, oppress the working man, and accumulate wealth for sensual indulgence. " What are the people to us?" was the foul expression of Noor Mohamed to Lieut. Eastwick. " Poor or rich ! what do we care if they pay us our revenue !—Give us our hunting grounds and our enjoyments, that is all we require." Hence the most fertile districts were made a wilderness to form their *shikargahs*, or hunting grounds : their zenanas were filled with young girls torn from their friends, and treated with revolting barbarity. In fine, the life of an Ameer was one of gross sensuality, for which the labour and blood of men were remorselessly exacted, the honour and happiness of women savagely sacrificed !

How the British power came to bear on their affairs shall now be explained.

A commercial intercourse with Scinde was established under the Kallora prince, in 1775, through a factory established at Tatta, then a wealthy town. Fiscal vexations and civil commotions caused it to be abandoned in 1792, but in 1799 Lord Wellesley made an effort to restore it. The influence of Tippoo Sultan and the jealousy of native traders, aided by a cabal at Hydrabad averse to the British connection, overcame the favourable inclination of the Talpoor prince who then reigned, and Mr. Crowe, the superintendent, was peremptorily ordered to quit the country in 1800. This insult was not resented, and in 1809, a fear of Napoleon's policy having caused British missions to be sent to Cabool, Persia, and Scinde, the brother Ameers displayed great arrogance. They assented to a treaty indeed, but the terms were brief even to contempt. Commencing with the customary falsehood of " eternal friendship," it provided for mutual intercourse by vakeels or envoys, and the Ameers promised to exclude the French. No more.

It was renewed in 1820, with additional article to exclude Americans, and settle border disputes on the side of Cutch, where the British frontier then touched on Scinde. An army of demonstration was however required to enforce faith as to the last article. To exclude French and Americans, of whom they knew nothing and whose presence they did not desire, was for the Ameers a pleasure, but the border disputes affected their interests, and troops were necessary to enforce the treaty.

Up to this period the measures of the Anglo-Indian Government with respect to Scinde were merely efforts to open commerce ; but soon the inevitable concomitant, a disposition to profit from superior knowledge and power, became perceptible, and its progress and effects must be traced to shew *when* it broke the bonds of justice and true policy, which are inseparable.

An enlightened desire to open commerce by the Indus, induced Lord Ellenborough, when president of the Board of Control, to employ Sir Alexander Burnes, then a lieutenant, for the exploration of that river in 1831; and under pretence of conveying presents to Runjeet Sing, the navigation of the Indus was effected; an important step, the consequences of which were immediately foreseen and predicted by two poor ignorant but prescient men.

" *The mischief is done, you have seen our country,*" cried a rude Beloochee soldier when Burnes first entered the river.

"*Alas ! Scinde is now gone, since the English have seen the river which is the high road to its conquest,*" was the observation of a Syud near Tatta.

Twelve years afterwards their sagacity was justified !

In 1832, Lord W. Bentinck sent Colonel Pottinger to Scinde, to effect a new treaty, and to survey the course of the Lower Indus, which was done by Lieutenant Del Hoste, while Pottinger negotiated. At this time the lower country was governed by the Ameers of Hydrabad, whose chief was Ali Moorad, one of the *Char Yar*. His brethren were dead, and their sons yielded to him as the *Rais*, or presiding Ameer, which gave the right of negotiation, and certain possessions which went with the turban.

In Kyrpoor, the capital of Upper Scinde, Meer Roostum, the nephew of Ali, was *Rais*, with like advantages, holding that government independently, though the superiority of the Hydrabad family was faintly acknowledged ; hence duplicate treaties were necessary, one with Ali, the other with Roostum, and the following conditions were agreed upon.

1°. A free passage for travellers and merchants through Scinde, and the use of the Indus for commercial pursuits ; but no vessel of war was to float on that river, nor military stores to be conveyed by it.

2°. No merchant was to settle in Scinde, and travellers and visitors were to have passports.

3°. A tariff was to be proclaimed, and no arbitrary dues or tolls exacted.

4°. The old treaties were confirmed, and the friendly intercourse by vakeels enlarged.

5°. The Ameers bound themselves to alter the tariff, if found too high ; and also to put down, in concert with the Rajah of Joudpoor, the robber borderers of Cutch.

This was the first treaty giving the Anglo-Indian Government positive and specific rights as to Scinde. It was obtained by negotiation, without menace, and framed with a policy tending to general good. But in 1834, another commercial treaty was negotiated, by which the tariff was fixed, and the tolls on the Indus arranged.

Colonel Pottinger was made political agent in Scinde, having a native commercial agent at the bunder or port of the Indus, where all tolls were to be collected, no transit duties on vessels or goods being allowed, unless the latter were landed. The main point of the treaty was the division of the money received. The Anglo-Indian frontier touched the Upper Sutlege, and the Government justly claimed a right to navigate it to the sea, because it is an injury to have a river sealed by a nation nearer to the sea. But to profit from geographical position by reasonable tolls, is no more than to profit from climate or soil. Wherefore this treaty provided, that tolls should be taken only at the mouths of the Indus, and the gross amount divided amongst the Governments having territory on the banks—namely: the Ameers, the Bhawal Khan, the Maharajah, and the Anglo-Indian.

High tolls and the robber habits of the Beloochee tribes on the Upper Indus rendered this treaty unavailing for trade, and the Ameers soon drove the English native agent away from the port. The coast and the lower branches of the river had however been meanwhile surveyed, and in 1835 a steamboat floated on the Indus, but this, the only fruit of the negotiation, was a private enterprise by Aga Mohamed Rahim, a mogul merchant of Bombay.

Declaration of irrevocable friendship headed every treaty, yet bad faith and jealousy were constantly evinced by the Ameers, and in 1836 the Anglo-Indian Government peremptorily meddled with the political affairs of Scinde. This was caused by the increasing influence of Russia in Central Asia, where her agents were assiduously impressing a notion of Russian greatness, seemingly to prepare for an invasion of India. Lord Auckland was alarmed, and went about to obtain a counteracting influence over the Affghans. The ruler of the Punjaub was too wary and powerful to be coerced in furtherance of this plan; but the weakness of Scinde offered facilities not to be overlooked, and to increase and consolidate British influence in that country was a necessary preliminary. This was an approach to the abuse of superior power, yet founded on the instinct of self-preservation, and so far legitimate if the means involved no direct oppression. But when did a powerful nation ever scrupulously regard the rights of a weak one? On this occasion the first proceedings were, externally, moderate as the attainment of the object would admit, and with a plausible gentleness relentless power enforced its behests.

Runjeet Sing had been long intent to spoil the Ameers, and now, under pretext of chastising the Mazarees, a predatory tribe nominally subject to Scinde, commenced hostilities by

seizing the town of Rohjan, and capturing a fort on the
north-west frontier close to the Indus. From that point he
menaced a regular invasion; yet, considering the great
courage and barbaric skill of the Scindian Beloochees, it is by
no means certain that he would have succeeded; and it is
certain the Ameers neither desired nor asked for foreign aid.
" We have vanquished the Seik, and we will do so again,"
was their confident delaration. But the Seik monarch, by
a singular coincidence, demanded at this moment from the
Anglo-Indian Government a supply of arms, to be sent to
him up the Indus! that is to say, through the heart of the
country he was going to invade; and this opportunity for
meddling was seized by Lord Auckland. The Maharajah
was reminded of an article in the Scindian treaty of 1821,
by which the transit of military stores on the Indus was
interdicted, and he was admonished not to trouble his
neighbours unjustly. The British political resident at Lahore
was also directed to employ every resource, short of menace,
to deter Runjeet Sing from hostilities; and at the same time,
Colonel Pottinger, who had hitherto remained in Cutch, was
sent to Hydrabad to offer what was designated a closer
alliance with the Ameers; he promising the protection of
the Anglo-Indian Government against the Seiks, in consideration of which it was hoped they would receive, and
themselves pay a British force to be stationed in their
capital! And this force was actually assembled by the
Bombay Government.

Soon a doubt that mere professions of amity would not
induce the Ameers to let their dominions be thus taken
possession of caused a modification of this proposal, and
Pottinger was empowered, if a demur occurred, to offer the
mediation of the British instead of a close alliance, provided
a political resident was admitted at Hydrabad, through
whom all intercourse with Runjeet Sing was to be carried
on—a British force to sustain this mediation, to be tempo-
rarily quartered in Scinde at the expense of the Ameers!
He was also to negotiate for the surveying of the coast, the
fixing of buoys and land-marks, the re-establishment of the
native agent, the warehousing of goods without payment of

duties, the establishment of fairs in Scinde, the repression of the Mazaree robbers, and the clearing of jungle, that is to say, cutting down the Ameers' shikargahs or hunting grounds to facilitate tracking up the Indus : finally, the appointment of a British superintendent-general. The diplomatic subtilty of the Ameers was thus provoked, and as their mode of dealing was always the same, the history of one affair will serve as a guide to all. But first the anomalous nature of their sovereignty must be treated of, because it really influenced their policy and actions, while it also served as a cover for their hollowness.

When the first of the Talpoor sovereigns died, his brothers had divided the country unequally, and excluded his son Sobdar from power, though not from his private patrimony. Their names were Ghoolam, Moorad, and Kereem, of Hydrabad; Tharou of Meerpoor : Sorab of Kyrpoor. All were dead at this period; Kereem without issue, and Ghoolam leaving one son, who was treated as Sobdar had been treated.

Moorad left two sons, Noor Mohamed and Nusseer Khan, who were at this time the ruling Ameers of Hydrabad; Noor, because he was *Rais* and wore the turban:—Nusseer, because he governed Noor.

Tharou left a son, Ali Morad, who succeeded to the Ameeree of Meerpoor; but he also died, and was succeeded by Shere Mohamed, called the Lion.

In Upper Scinde, Roostum, the eldest son of Sorab, was *Rais* of the Kyrpoor Ameers, but he had many brothers.

The superiority of the Hydrabad branch was faintly acknowledged by the Ameers of Kyrpoor and Meerpoor; but by all the law of primogeniture was discarded—the brother, not the son, succeeded to the turban. This system, springing from the original usurpation, occasioned constant jealousies and disputes; for though the three seats of government were distinct, the territories were dovetailed in a strange and tangled fashion, and each Ameer was absolute in his own hereditary domains; each had armed followers, purchased slaves, and hired the hill tribes according to his means. Discord therefore prevailed, fear was prevalent amongst high and low, and the labouring people were plundered and oppressed to a degree, says Pottinger, "*possibly unequalled in the world.*" Moreover, the tribes knowing that in civil commotions pay would be high for military services, and plunder abundant, always encouraged, and at times forced the princes into domestic wars.

Thus influenced, the policy of the Ameers could not fail to be tortuous and vacillating even though their natural dispositions had been frank and honest, which was not the case. Falsehood, cajolery and delays, were their diplomatic resources, and forgery was common with them. Shrewdly polite of manners they invariably paid extravagant attentions to the British political agents, proffering entertainments and presents with prodigal liberality, flattery still more profusely; and judging from the official correspondence published, they seem never to have failed in gaining the friendship of the different agents, and not seldom to have blinded them.

The chief Ameers would accept, with all appearance of joy and gratitude any proposition, and promise abundantly; yet rarely did performance follow promise, and constant evasions or direct violations of every article attended the conclusion of every treaty. If pressed they would plead the difficulty, real or pretended, of obtaining the assent of the inferior Ameers; and always one of these last seems to have been designedly in opposition, playing the refractory part. Forged letters, false seals, with secret and unusual forms of correspondence, were employed to lead, or mislead the recipients of them, and these were accompanied by false assertions as to promises which never had been made, and nefarious assumptions of evil intended where all had been fair and honest—such were the means sedulously, systematically, and not unskilfully employed by the Ameers at all times in their intercourse with the British political agents.

Pottinger reached Hydrabad in September, and in December told Lord Auckland that his negotiation was successful; but he had only pressed the modified mediation; and to obtain that, had exceeded his powers in promising corresponding services. His report was premature. The treaty was not ratified until 1838, and then only because significant hints were given that Runjeet Sing would be let loose, perhaps aided, to work his pleasure in Scinde. That ambitious Prince had frankly accepted the British mediation, and his connection with the Anglo-Indian Government was cemented by a public personal interview with the Governor-General ; his troops also still occupied Rohjan, and fear of his warfare procured the treaty. It contained but two articles, providing for the mediation and the residence of a political agent at Hydrabad, who was to move where he chose, attended by an escort of British troops of any number deemed suitable by his own Government !

All this was done under pretence of a friendly interest ; but it is impossible to deny the injustice. Analyze the negotiation. The Seik monarch menaced with invasion ; the Anglo-Indian Government seized that moment to offer protection, on condition of permanently occupying the capital with troops, to be paid by the Ameers ! That was simply, an impudent attempt to steal away their country ; and the modified proposal to mediate, which followed, was only more subtil, not less immoral—the intent in both cases was profit, covered with a sickening declamation about friendship, justice, and love of peace. Lord Auckland, while thus instructing his envoy, declared his conviction, arising from long experience, that Runjeet Sing would not act against the Ameers in opposition to the wishes of the British authorities ; hence, to mediate, there was no need for the admission of troops into Scinde, and the threat of letting the Seik monarch loose was a consistent termination to such diplomacy.

This treaty, by which a loaded shell was placed in the palace of the Ameers to explode at pleasure for their destruction, was abstractedly an unjust oppressive action. Was it also a wanton aggression ? Great interests, even self-preservation, was involved according to the views of the Anglo-Indian Government, and men can only act according to their light. Was that light good ? Was the view taken of affairs a sane one by statesmen of reach and policy ; or was it the offspring of weak distempered minds, actuated by a groundless terror clouding the judgment, and by a shallow ambition ? If the intrigues of Russia appeared to menace the stability of the British-Indian Empire, it was undoubtedly the duty of Lord Auckland and his council to counteract them; yet wisely and justly, without degrading their country's reputation by violence and incapacity :—for surely public men may not with impunity undertake the government of millions, sport with their happiness and misery, mar or make their fortunes as chance guides, with profound ignorance of principles, and a reckless contempt for details.

There were two modes by which Russia could attempt an invasion of India. Directly with a regular army, or by influencing Persia and the other nations of Central Asia to pour their wild hordes upon Hindostan. The first had been effected by Alexander the Great, and he was deified for the exploit. No man else has done the like : for the irruptions of Ghengis, Tamerlane, and Nadir, were the wars of Asiatic princes, and though Russia is half Asiatic of dominion, her regular armies are European of organization. To lead a great and conquering force to India from Europe after the manner of Alexander, requires an Alexander, who shall be at the head of troops prepared by previous discipline, and by political as well as military organization. He must be of a fierce genius, untameable will, and consummate knowledge of war; he must have the confidence of his soldiers, and choose a proper conjuncture of affairs in Europe for his enterprise, for that also is necessary to success. But such a man, and so situated, if a subject, would be as likely to march on Moscow as Delhi : the leader must therefore be a Czar, or the son of a Czar, and the adverse chances are thus immeasurably increased.

Russia wants a man. If she find him his views will hardly be turned eastward; Europe will have more to fear than India. But is Russia really to be feared in Europe? The profound falsehood of her government, her barbarous corruption, her artificial pretensions, the eye-glitter of her regular armies, shining only from the putrescence of national feeling, would lead to the negative. Her surprising progress in acquisition of territory within the last hundred years would lead to the affirmative. If we believe those writers who have described the ramifications of the one huge falsehood of pretension, which, they say, pervades Russia, her barbarity, using the word in its full signification, would appear more terrible than her strength. Nor can I question their accuracy, having, in 1815, when the reputation of the Russian troops was highest, detected the same falsehood of display without real strength. At the Imperial parades on the Boulevards of Paris, oiled, bandaged, and clothed to look like men whom British soldiers would be proud to charge on a field of battle, the Muscovite was admired. I followed him to his billet, where, stripped of disguise, he appeared short of stature, squalid and meagre, his face rigid with misery, shocking sight and feeling—a British soldier would have offered him bread rather than the bayonet.

Nevertheless, some innate expanding and dangerous strength must belong to a nation, which, during long contests with the most warlike people of continental Europe led by Frederick and Napoleon, has steadily advanced with arms and policy, until her Cossacks may encamp on her own territory within a few marches of Vienna, Berlin, Stockholm and Constantinople. Her regular armies may be bad, her fleets in the Baltic and the Black Sea may be worse; but they are there, and she can send half a million of wild horsemen, who, without pay, would invade Europe for plunder, and, sustained by regular armies on the Russian frontier, make such ravage as half a century could not repair. The chances of revolution have been spoken of as a remedy for the Muscovite power; yet who can predict that revolution will not augment her warlike strength and ambition. Her policy is national, and it menaces freedom and happiness and civilization. Poland was the first error of Europe in respect to Russia; Circassia may be the second; Constantinople the last and the greatest.

Had Russia a man capable of invading the East when Lord Auckland fell into such fear? Was the conjuncture of affairs in Europe favourable to the enterprise? Was there a suitable army ready? By what line was it to operate? Was it through Persia to Herat? or, starting from the Caspian, to march up the Oxus to the Hindoo Khosh?

Was it to overrun Affghanistan, or win over that country by policy as a new base of operation, previous to crossing the Indus? Were the wild Toorkmans of Orgunjé, the settled people of Bokhara, the fierce Uzbecks of Balk, to be conquered or gained over as friends? Were not these questions of weight in this matter? Could the solution of them leave doubt, that a regular invasion of Hindostan by a Russian army was then a chimera?

But Persia! Through Persia the tide of war might be poured! Yes! when Russia has broken that country down to a province, and that she cannot do while the gallant tribes of Circassia maintain their independence: it was in the western not the eastern Caucasus, therefore, that the security of India was to be sought. Had Russia even possessed a Macedonian Alexander, the policy of the Grecian Memnon would still have been again effectual, for slow would have been that hero's progress if the wise Persian General had lived. There was provocation for meddling with Circassian affairs, modern Persia was as open to British as to Russian influence, and by the Persian Gulf she could be reached more easily than by Circassia. But the only effort made by the Whigs to conciliate the Shah, was a miserable abortive mission, stinted in presents with a ridiculous parsimony, which made Mr. Ellis, the able, clear-headed gentleman employed, ashamed of his task.

To combine by an active astute policy the nations of Central Asia against the British Empire in the East, remained for Russia; and Lord Auckland asserted that she was busily, though secretly, engaged therein; that her agents were every where; that the Persians were besieging Herat with her assistance, at her instigation, and for her profit. How was this secret hostility to be wisely met? Surely by cultivating the good will of the high-spirited Affghans, the wild Toorkmans, the keen-witted Persians. To speak to their self-interests by commerce and by presents, to their sagacity by missions, and to trust their instinct of self-preservation for the rest: that would have been an intelligible policy. The reverse appeared wisdom to Lord Auckland's advisers, and his proceedings bore at once the stamps of incapacity and injustice. He undertook a gigantic enterprise of war without a knowledge of guiding principles; and as he did not employ those who understood war a direful calamity terminated the folly.

Affghanistan had just been broken down from a great and domineering state to a weak confederacy of democratic communities; and this new organization was in unison with the habits and feelings of that courageous and strong-bodied people. Dost Mohamed, their principal chief and the head of the most powerful family of the most powerful tribe, was comparatively an enlightened man, vigorous and well disposed towards British interests. Yet he, and his nation, whose welfare could have been promoted and its good-will secured, it was resolved to invade, and in the manner most offensive. That is to say, forcing on them a native prince twice before driven from supreme power by the nation; thus combining the most deadly of political offences and injuries, a foreign yoke and a hateful native monarch. Shah Sooja, the exiled king, chosen as the instrument for this occasion, was without talent, and vigorous only in cruelty; his executions, his vengeance, are well known, his exploits in battle unknown. He was thrust forward in the preposterous hope, that he, who had been unable to keep his throne when placed on it by his own countrymen, would remain firm when restored by strangers offensive to the Affghans as invaders and oppressors; still more offensive as infidels: and he was thus to reconstitute his kingdom in unity and strength, so as to form an efficient barrier for India towards the west!

What kind of policy was that which sought a war in Central Asia, a thousand miles from England's true basis of power, the sea. Central Asia! where from remotest times the people have been organized for irregular warfare, which the nature of their country and their own wild habits render peculiarly appropriate. The military strength of England lies in her discipline, in her great resources of money and materials for war, in the strong knit massive organization of her troops, in her power of combining fleets and armies together. She, of all nations, is least calculated from her customs and morals, to meet irregular warfare on a great scale. Yet here we find a collision provoked with Russia on the steppes of Tartary, a trial of strength in Central Asia with a nation more powerful in irregular troops than all the rest of the world together : and that trial preceded by an odious aggression, sure to render all the barbarous nations inimical to England, if not friendly to Russia.

This wild conception, concocted and urged by the Whig Government at home ; this conception, so nearly allied to madness, was executed with consistent absurdity. Shah Sooja was proclaimed King, and troops, commanded by British officers, paid from the Calcutta treasury, were called the King's National Army, though not an Affghan was in the ranks,—and for this King was claimed all the lost rights of the Dooranee monarchy, with tribute and obedience from the nations formerly subject to it. To place him on the throne, a strong army was gathered with great stores on the upper Sutlege; but Cabool was to be reached, and between that city and the Sutlege was the Punjaub, under a monarch, wily and powerful, a proclaimed friend and ally. It would have been consistent with the claims of Shah Sooja, to have demanded from Runjeet Sing the restoration of the Dooranee provinces, which he had recently got possession of by force of arms. For in this he differed from the other powers who had broken from the Affghan monarchy ; they merely asserted their independence, if exception be made for the small district of Cutch-Gundava, seized by the Ameers ; whereas Runjeet conquered largely after establishing the Seik kingdom. But he was too fierce, too strong, too useful, to be roughly dealt with. It was safer to give than to take with him ; and, therefore, a tripartite treaty was concocted, as if it were a voluntary compact between equal and independent powers understanding their own interests and able to maintain them—the contracting parties being Runjeet, the Anglo-Indian Government, and Shah Sooja !

Pretending to be a renewal of ancient engagements, this treaty bound Shah Sooja to relinquish his claims on Cachmere, Peshawar, Attock, and some smaller dominions ravished by Runjeet Sing from the Dooranee monarchy; and he was also, when re-established on his throne, to make presents, and in other ways practically admit the supremacy of the Maharajah, though in the treaty they were styled equals. If the Shah called for the aid of Seik troops, they were to share in the "plunder" of the great Barrukzie family, which contained sixty thousand heads of the noblest houses of Affghanistan—an article unwise and shameful, lowering the British policy to the level of barbarism.

The invasion of Affghanistan being resolved upon, military principles required, that the shortest lines of operations should be adopted, and those were in the Punjaub. The Maharajah had just concluded a treaty, advantageous to himself, at the expense of the King, who was under the influence of the Governor-General; and it was but reasonable that he should grant in return a free passage through the ceded territory acquired by that treaty; that is to say, through Peshawar and the Kyber passes, which was the best route to Cabool. There was no reason either, if he had faith in his British allies, why the Punjaub should not be made the base of operations, and the invading army assembled on the Indus, to penetrate by the Kyber to Cabool, and by Deera Ishmael Khan, not a difficult route, to Ghusni and Candahar.

When a great point, technically so called, is to be made in war, there are only two modes of effecting it recognized by military art. By the first, an army should march with all its military means, compact and strong, to bear down opposition, trusting to its leader for an establishment in the country where it is to halt. Such was Hannibal's invasion of Italy. Success depends upon sagacious calculation of power and resistance, moral and physical; in fine, upon the leader's genius. This is the highest effort of a general. The second mode is to trust the communications to allies, or to nations subjugated on the march, increasing the army by levies from those nations as it advances. Such was the Macedonian Alexander's method of approaching India.

There was no Hannibal to invade Affghanistan, but the method of Alexander might have been adopted without his genius. Runjeet Sing was an ally to whom the communications should have been entrusted; and to ensure his fidelity, an army of reserve should have been assembled on the Sut-lege. If he refused consent, his alliance was hollow, and policy dictated the forcing him to acquiesce, or the subju-gation of his kingdom as a preliminary step to the invasion of Affghanistan. Not so did Lord Auckland reason. Dis-regarding military principles, of which his advisers seem to have been as profoundly ignorant as they were disdainful of equity in their policy, he resolved to perpetrate against the helpless Ameers of Scinde in the form of aggression, that which he dared not even propose in the way of friendship to the powerful Maharajah. With this view articles were inserted in the Tripartite Treaty, under which Runjeet accepted the British mediation for his dispute with Scinde; and the Shah, who had resigned without an equivalent his richest provinces to Runjeet, also agreed to relinquish his sovereign rights on Scinde, on condition of receiving the arrears of tribute.

The object of all this machinery was to obtain a pretence for seizing so much of the Ameers' territory as would secure a line of operations against Affghanistan through Scinde—a line so defective, that military considerations alone should have stopped the invasion if no better could be found. But the Kyber passes offered one of only five hundred miles, reckoning from Loodiana to Cabool, and only three hundred, if a base had been first established at Attock. Moreover, by Ishmael dera Khan and the Gomul pass, taking the Punjaub as a base, would have been only three hundred miles to Can-dahar, and two hundred to Ghusni. Instead of taking these lines the one adopted run from Loodiana to Roree on the Indus, crossed that great river, and went through Cutch-Gundava, a country fatal from heat to European troops in summer, to penetrate by the terrific defiles of Bolan, amidst hostile predatory tribes, to the sterile highlands of Affghan-istan, where sepoys could not live in winter from the cold. Then, passing by Candahar and Ghusni, fortresses of no mean repute, to reach Cabool: the whole distance not less than fifteen hundred miles, exposed to the operations of the incensed Ameers, the hostile Belooch tribes of the hills, the doubtful faith of Runjeet Sing and his discontented nobles. And with what object? To plunder and spoil the most powerful and popular family of the most powerful tribe in a nation of five millions,—a people whose fathers had within man's memory conquered from Delhi to the Caspian, from the Oxus to the Ocean! It was to force a hateful monarch upon a hardy courageous people, democratic from customs and institutions, and despising the religion of the strangers who thus sought to control them. They were to accept him also with this stigma, that to recover his crown he had resigned a third of the tribes to their inveterate enemies the Seiks!

Sir John Hobhouse, in a turgid speech upon this enterprise, said, the line of the Bolan pass was chosen because Shah Sooja's adherents were in that quarter—a puerile reason, yet shewing that the King was not desired by the nation at large. However, under the weight of this policy, Affghanistan, that great military point, was to be made by a general of no military repute, with troops for the most part physically unfitted to sustain the climate, with unsafe communications, and without moral or political resources. He was to advance in the wild hope that a weak arrogant prince would rally an adverse people, reconstitute a great nation which had before fallen to pieces in his hands, and form with it a bulwark for India against Persia and the wild populations of Central Asia, stimulated to hostility, and supported by Russia! The genius and sagacity of Wellington were not needed to predict misfortune, but his remark was—" *The troops will force their way through a wild disunited people, only to find the commencement of their difficulties.*"

The passage through Scinde and the Bolan pass nearly wrecked the army. It is said Lord Keane lost many hundred soldiers, thousands of camp followers, and forty thousand camels on the march ; that want of promptness and combination amongst the tribes alone enabled him to reach Candahar; and that at Ghusni his progress would have terminated but for the engineer Thomson's ready genius, and the fiery courage of Colonel Dennie, who, breaking through the only weak part of the barbarian's defence, won a peerage for the General. Shah Sooja thus regained his throne, and fools gaped at him while the Affghan men of spirit pondered revenge. For a time success seemed to attend the unjust aggression, sustained by the vigour of the brilliant, ill-requited Dennie; but when he and the intrepid Sale marched to Jellallabad, error succeeded error, not unaccompanied by crime, with fearful rapidity, until an entire destruction of the invaders closed " *the tragic Harlequinade*." The system of " making smart young men, who could speak Persian, political agents, and supposing them generals and statesmen," failed. England lost an army by the experiment : and Lord Auckland gained a new coronet—but clotted and stiff with the blood of British soldiers, shed in an unjust war, it must be uneasy to wear.

CHAPTER III.

CONNECTED with the Affghan war were some peculiar negotiations most discreditable to the Anglo-Indian Government.

The tripartite treaty of June 1838 was in July sent to Colonel Pottinger, preparatory to a new course of diplomacy with the Ameers, modelled on that which led to the treaty of two articles, in virtue of which he was a political agent in Scinde. This time the project was more artfully conducted. Shah Sooja, recognized as King, and a contracting person in the tripartite treaty, and having an army raised, paid, and officered by the Anglo-Indian Government, was thrust forward as an independent sovereign. He agreed to relinquish all claim to supremacy and tribute from Scinde, on condition of receiving a large sum of money, the amount to be determined under the mediation of the Anglo-Indian Government, which thus constituted itself umpire in an old quarrel, revived by itself to suit its own projects, without the knowledge of the party most interested. But war is costly : the King's army required pay, the Ameers had treasure, and to reach their gold, and lay grounds for more important demands, was the real object. Pottinger's instructions, shamelessly explicit, ran in substance thus :—" Tell the Ameers, a crisis menacing British India has arrived. The Western Powers have combined to work evil. The Governor-General has projected a counter-combination. He calls on his friends for aid. The King has ancient claims on Scinde, but he will accept money in discharge of them, and makes the Governor-General arbitrator of the amount. Great is the benefit thus conferred on the Ameers. They will gain undisturbed possession of their territory and immunity from farther claims. Warm is the Governor-General's friendship for the Ameers, and in return he demands ostensible proof of their attachment. The

King will arrive at Shikarpoor in November; he will be supported by a British army. The Ameers must therefore agree to pay him the money or abide the consequences, one of which will be, to take military possession of their town and district of Shikarpoor. Meanwhile, the article of the former treaty which forbids the transmission of military stores up the Indus must be suspended." Yet to maintain that article intact had been the very ground of interference with Runjeet Sing in the former negotiation!

So far all was in friendship; but the Persians were besieging Herat, and, though no war had been declared, and England was by treaty bound not to interfere between Persia and the Affghans, the former were designated as opponents of the Governor-General's projects, and the Ameers were supposed to have formed engagements with them. If so, it was to be construed as an act of hostility, and a British army from Bombay would immediately enter their capital; yet, if any inferior Ameer, popular in Scinde, was inclined to side with the British, he was to be separately supported and advanced to power! The amount of the King's money claim was left undetermined, but it was significantly observed, " *the Ameers must be wealthy.*"

Noor Mohamed, the chief Ameer of Hydrabad, had indeed written to the Persian, yet more, as Colonel Pottinger judged, from religious zeal than political views; for the Ameer was a "*Shea*," or believer in Ali, as the Persians are; whereas Sobdar, the person contemplated by the instructions as likely to side with the British, was a "*Soonee*," or believer in Omar. There was however a Persian agent hovering about Hydrabad, and there was ground for believing that an intercourse unfriendly to British interests was maintained. Nor can this excite wonder. The previous negotiations had left the Ameer in no doubt as to the ultimate object of the Governor-General, and he naturally looked around for support.

Pottinger assured Lord Auckland, " he would not fail to tell the Ameers, that the day they connected themselves with any other power than England would be the last of their independence, if not of their rule—and neither the ready

power to crush and annihilate them, nor the will to call it
into action were wanting, if it appeared requisite, however
remotely, for the safety or integrity of the Anglo-Indian
empire or frontier." The disclosure of his instructions was
however to be delayed until the armies destined to support
them approached Scinde, and meanwhile, the Ameers of
Hydrabad obtained some knowledge of the tripartite treaty.
Their indignation was great, and their first thought a resort
to arms; but they heard the Persians had failed in an assault
on Herat, with great loss, and being themselves embarrassed
by civil contention with the Lugaree tribe, they exchanged
the design of fighting for their usual diplomacy of falsehood,
flattery, menaces and cajolery. And it is not to be supposed
they had given no reasonable ground for complaint in respect
of the commercial treaties: they had violated them systematically, with as little scruple as Lord Auckland now set aside
the article forbidding the transit of military stores by the
Indus.

Pottinger warned his Government that obstacles would
arise; but he treated one of the Ameers' arguments with
such ill-founded contempt, as to create a suspicion that he
was launching a bitter sarcasm at his own employers.—
" Sobdar and his party, will," said he, " probably even go
so far as to declare the demand for money a breach of the
late agreement, on the principle, that without our assistance,
Shah Sooja had no means to exact a rea from them, and the
demand may be considered as our own. I do not, by pointing
out this argument, mean for an instant to uphold its correctness, but it is one just suited to the capacity and feelings of
the individuals with whom I have to negotiate."

Aye! and to the capacity and feelings of every man
capable of reasoning at all! And the Ameers did afterwards
urge it with homely but irresistible force.

" *It is a joke,*" they exclaimed, " *to call it a demand from
the King. You have given him bread for the last five-and-twenty
years, and any strength he has now, or may have hereafter, is
from you. The demand is yours!*"

Pottinger thus continued:—

" Had our present connection existed some years, and our

Resident thereby had time, by constant kindly intercourse with the chiefs and people, to have removed the strong and universal impression that exists throughout Scinde as to our grasping policy, the case might have been widely different; but I enter on my new duties without any thing to offer, and with a proposal, that will only strengthen the above impressions, *for many besides the Scindees will believe at the onset that we are making a mere use of Shah Sooja's name* to revive a claim which has long been esteemed obsolete."

Noor Mohamed's letter to the Persian Shah, treated lightly by Pottinger, was by Lord Auckland, with strained construction the hyperbolic compliments of the East considered, construed as a tender of allegiance, offered when the opposition of the British Government to the Shah's designs was notorious: it implied hostility, and the Ameer had thus forfeited all friendly consideration. Energetic measures must be adopted, and as Meer Sobdar appeared faithful, it might be advisable to give him the turban under British supremacy.

This indignation was a masque, the mode of proceeding had been previously decided. Five thousand men had been assembled at Bombay to invade Scinde; a Bengal army was coming down the Sutlege to occupy Shikarpoor, contrary to treaty and without even the form of asking leave, and Pottinger was empowered to use the Bombay force to back his negotiation. This requires short comment. Springing from a predetermined plan to seize Scinde, it would have been better to have spared expressions of friendship and love of justice. The motives were the extraction of money for the King's army, and to plant a subsidiary force in the country, with a view to its final subjection.

Lord Auckland was desirous to fasten first on Upper Scinde, because there the passage of the Indus was to be made by the Bengal army, and the line of communication for the Affghan invasion established. Wherefore Sir A. Burnes, then on a mission to the Prince of Khelat, was ordered to turn aside and negotiate a treaty with the Kyrpoor Ameers as he passed. He was to demand money, and what was called, a *loan* of the rock fortress of Bukkur, standing in mid

stream of the Indus, where it was purposed to cast a bridge
that the Bengal army might pass and unite with the King's
force at Shikarpoor. If asked for a remuneration, Sir Alexander was to give an evasive answer; but he was to obtain
stores and military transport, and though under the control
of Pottinger was to present himself rather as a confidential
friend than a political agent!

Meanwhile the Ameers of Hydrabad, whose rule extended up the right bank of the Indus to Shikarpoor, far
from assenting to the occupation of that place by the King,
who intimated in general terms his design of going there,
replied to him, in substance, thus : " *The Beloochees are not
pleased, you must not come to Shikarpoor. The power of Dost
Mohamed is well known. The Shah of Persia is before Herat;
he is supported by the Russians : you cannot come by Shikarpoor.
If Runjeet Sing and the British support you, there is a direct
road to Khorassan* (their name for Affghanistan) *from Loodiana : go that way and we will assist you.*" This biting
sarcasm on the strange mixture of fear, folly, and audacity
which had dictated the line of operation through Scinde, was
deemed insolent; and Pottinger, now changing his opinion
as to the nature of the Ameers' correspondence with the
Persian, exclaimed against their duplicity, and advised the
immediate employment of the troops at Bombay.

During these negotiations an undercurrent of complaint
run strongly against the Ameers for violations of the commercial treaties, which they were required to respect while
the Governor-General unhesitatingly cast them aside. It is
however remarkable, that even at this time, Ali Moorad, the
younger brother of Roostum of Kyrpoor, he who has been so
vilely slandered by the Indian press, remained firm to his
engagements and punished all transgressors of the commercial
treaties.

Political shame being now laid aside, and occasion rife,
Lord Auckland, pretending a virtuous indignation at the
duplicity of the Ameers, and their unwarrantable enmity
and jealousy of the British !—moved with pity also for the
distracted state of their government, a state which his envoy
was expressly instructed to foment, declared that five thou-

sand troops should instantly seize Shikarpoor, and such
other parts of Scinde as might be deemed eligible to facilitate the invasion of Affghanistan and give effect to the
tripartite treaty. All the Ameers who were inimical to the
British, even those who had simply evinced unwillingness to
aid the invasion of the Affghans, with whom they had no
quarrel, were to be displaced from power; and this violence
was offered to independent governments, over which no
rights had been established save by treaties, not sought for
by them and both in letter and spirit opposed to these
aggressions! But to make amends, the Ameers were assured, that the seizure of their territories by a British army
meaned nothing injurious to their interests!

Pottinger, while admitting that Noor Mohamed's Persian
correspondence had not been proved, was yet disposed at
first, to bring the Bombay troops at once to Scinde, and
proposed to encourage informers against the Ameers to
strengthen the case! But he soon found that the Ameers,
if driven to war, could seriously embarrass the advance on
Affghanistan, and that camels, grain, money, boats, and
storehouses, could be more easily got under the masque of
friendship. Hence he advised delay, but Lord Auckland
ordered immediate action. The Ameers then menaced the
envoy with personal violence, and failing to intimidate him
offered abject apologies, which he disregarded and called for
the troops. One demand however he recoiled from. The
Ameers produced formal discharges from the King of all
sovereign claims on Scinde—how then could money for
another relinquishment be honestly required? His scruples
were spared by an order not to trouble himself about that, it
would be settled by others!

In an angry discussion with the Ameers, they declared
that the army coming to Bukkur should not cross the Indus
there. That said Pottinger depends on the Governor-
General's orders. "Those are not the decrees of the Al-
mighty! they can, and shall be altered," was the rejoinder
of Noor Mohamed. But an iron screw was upon him, and
each day a fresh turn taught him that resistance was vain.
And while the Hydrabad Prince was thus writhing under

Pottinger's grasp, Burnes laid as strong, though a more courtly hand upon the Rais of Kyrpoor.

It was now declared that all the Ameers designed to march on Candahar if the Persians had taken Herat, and Roostum of Kyrpoor, weaker than Noor of Hydrabad, and more exposed to the Seiks and the King's army, trembled. Befooled also by hints of complete independence if he quietly yielded Bukkur, he became infinitely conciliating with Burnes. Yet secret discontent was rife, and his brother Moobarick openly opposed concession. Roostum's outward conduct was however so agreeable that it drew forth the following exquisite specimen of diplomatic jargon from the Governor-General,— " The favourable temper of that chief has been already noted ; this feeling Captain Burnes has been instructed to cultivate, and for its mainte- nance, in connection with the great importance of the tem- porary cession of Bukkur, I have informed Captain Burnes, that I am not unprepared to receive propositions for admitting the guaranteed independence of Kyrpoor as an additional arrangement, dependent to a certain degree on contingent events at Hydrabad."

But Roostum's submissive behaviour did not save him from the humiliating assurance, that the sins of the Hydra- bad Ameers would be visited on him also; and that the advance of the armies to Affghanistan would not free Scinde from British troops until the King was firmly fixed on his throne.

Earnestly then the Kyrpoor Ameers offered new treaties, and to cast themselves generally on the British protection ; but this would have saved them from the peculiar protection designed for them, namely, entire obedience to the Anglo- Indian Government. Yet so unreserved did their desire to be received as friends appear to Burnes, that he observed, " With such an adherence, I am quite at a loss to know how we can either ask money or any favour of this family."

Pottinger, with more penetration, judged this submission to be as doubtful as that of the Ameers of Hydrabad, and said so. Whereupon, Burnes explained, that he only meaned to say they were guided by interest at Kyrpoor, while fear

would best succeed at Hydrabad, and " Scinde might thus
be laid prostrate at the mercy of the Governor-General."
This was stripping Lord Auckland's policy of all disguise, a
policy so painful, that both Burnes and Pottinger, at different periods, advised open war instead.

A new influence was now employed. The Meah of the
Kallora dynasty lived as an exile in the Punjaub, and his
claims were put forward by the British negotiators ; yet the
Ameers still struggled, and Pottinger, apparently tired of the
lengthened contest, advised the cessation of diplomacy, a demand for Kurrachee, or tribute as a step to future supremacy,
and the enforcement of that demand by an army !   Burnes,
also, speaking of military measures against the Hydrabad
Princes, declared that " *nothing on the records of Indian
history was more justifiable :* " a dreadful avowal for Anglo-
Indian political morality.

The King's force, and the troops from Bengal were now
descending the Sutlege, the Bombay army reached the
mouths of the Indus, and though negotiations were continued, the establishing of a subsidiary force in Scinde was
resolved upon : Pottinger even urged the seizure of all the
country between the Hala mountains and the lower Indus,
from above Tatta down to the sea, to give " *a compact territory, complete command of the river, and the only sea port ;*
when, Sukkur and Bukkur being occupied by British troops
on the upper Indus, and British agents placed in Kyrpoor
and Hydrabad, British supremacy would be as fully established in Scinde, as though it had been entirely subjugated."   Burnes urged personal humiliation in addition, yet
strongly objected to the seizure of territory, as likely " to
tarnish the national honour throughout Asia, and the
Ameers, though rancorous and hostile in feeling, had been
guilty of no act to justify such a measure.   The intention
to injure was not injury."   But what honour was there
to tarnish, if nothing in the records of Anglo-Indian history
was more justifiable than the aggression now being perpetrated?

Shrinking from Pottinger's proposal, on the score of
expediency, not that of morality, the Governor-General de-

clared, he would not "incur the jealousy and distrust of States hitherto friendly or neutral," alluding to the powerful Runjeet, and to the Khelat prince, whose hostility would have endangered the march upon Affghanistan. He however persisted as to the subsidiary force, Sir John Keane had arrived with the Bombay army at Vikkur on the Indus, no leave asked, and the means of coercing the Ameers were therefore at hand. Those of Hydrabad then assembled their warriors to fight; but distracted between fear and anger could take no firm resolution. Meanwhile Roostum, after a sore mental struggle which led him even to contemplate suicide, gave up Bukkur, he phrased it "the heart of his country," and admitted that Upper Scinde was a British dependency.

The treaty now imposed was called the treaty of nine articles; though dated the 24th of December, 1838, it was not ratified until January 1839.

Thus far the course of injustice was unchecked. But now some of the Affghan difficulties were felt, and Lord Auckland, dreading the embarrassments which the Ameers of the Lower Scinde could still create, abated for the moment his demands; yet in secret only, to Pottinger, who had joined General Keane at Vikkur, leaving a sub-political agent at the residency of Hydrabad. Soon, however, Sir Henry Fane reached Roree with the Bengal army, the King arrived at Shikarpoor, and then the three armies, simultaneously, made hostile demonstrations. The King advanced towards Larkaana by the right bank of the Indus; the vanguard of the Bengal troops menaced Kyrpoor on the left bank; Keane moved up that river, and a reserve previously assembled at Bombay received orders to embark. The Ameers then plundered the British stores collected at Hydrabad, and drove Lieut. Eastwick the sub-agent, who they justly despised, with contumely from the residency. Assembling twenty thousand fighting men, they excited a general commotion, and it was discovered that to trample on Scinde involved great military and political questions. The cry of war was every where heard, Kurrachee was forcibly seized by the British, and Hydrabad was menaced with destruction.

E

Sir J. Keane, contemplating a battle, designated it as *a pretty piece of practice for the army;* and the Ameers were awed by the fierce aspect of his troops, who were eager to storm their capital. After announcing a horrid resolution to put their wives and children to death and fight to the last, they quailed at the muttering of the tempest, and ere it broke signed a new treaty presented by Pottinger—but for that indulgence were forced to pay two hundred thousand pounds, half on the instant. Dated February the 5th, this new instrument bound them to accept a subsidiary force, and contribute three lacs yearly for its support; to guarantee the good behaviour of the Beloochee chiefs; to contract no engagement with foreign states unknown to the Anglo-Indian Government, to provide storeroom at Kurrachee for military supplies; to abolish all tolls on the Indus, and to furnish an auxiliary force for the Affghan war if called upon to do so.

In return, the Anglo-British Government pledged itself not to meddle with the internal rule of the Ameers either generally or in respect of their separate possessions, and to disregard complaints from their subjects; but reserved a right to interfere and mediate in quarrels between the different Ameers, and to put down refractory chiefs. It promised to protect Scinde from foreign aggression, and bound itself not to make engagements with external powers affecting the Ameers' interests without their concurrence— thus virtually admitting the injustice of the tripartite treaty, though it was the basis of all their proceedings. This stringent document did not however satisfy the Governor-General. It granted too much. Kurrachee had been conquered during the negotiation, and he retained it, regardless of the treaty, which was immediately altered and ratified without asking the Ameers' consent to the changes! They were commanded to accept it in its new form.

The first document had been made in the names of the Hydrabad and Anglo-Indian Governments; but that implied a chief, and the Auckland's policy was to weaken by dividing. The altered treaty was therefore made quadruplicate, one for each Ameer, alike in all things save the payment of money, on which point Sobdar was favoured as a recompense for his amity during the negotiations. So also in the treaty with the Kyrpoor man, a distinction was made; but there the exception was to exact a penalty from Mooba-rick, in expiation of his previous enmity. Thus a nice discrimination marked every step of the oppression, and the amended treaty was, after many writhings, fastened round the lower Ameers' necks; and in conjunction with that imposed on Roostum became a text for the political obligations of all the Scindian rulers, for Shere Mohamed, of Meerpoor, subsequently sought to be admitted to the same terms as Sobdar. The efforts of the Ameers to ameliorate the pressure continued however until July: and it is characteristic of the negotiations, that Kurrachee was retained as a conquest, though war had not been declared. Pottinger urged its restoration on the ground that no act of hostility had been committed by the Ameers, though the firing of a signal gun, unshotted, had been made a pretext for destroying their fort with broadsides from a line-of-battle-ship, the *Wellesley!*

The affairs of Scinde being now brought to a remarkable epoch, it is fitting to give exactly the substance of those treaties which guided the intercourse between the Ameers and the British authorities, up to the war which ended the reign of the former.

First stands the treaty with Roostum.

Defensive and offensive, it engaged the British Government to protect the territory of Kyrpoor. In return, Roostum and his successors were to act in subordinate co-operation with the Anglo-Indian Government, and acknowledge its supremacy. They were to have no connection with other chiefs or states nor to negotiate without the sanction of the British; were to commit no aggression on any one; and if by accident disputes arose, were to accept the arbitration and award of the Anglo-Indian Government. At the requisition of the Governor-General, Roostum was to furnish auxiliary troops according to his means, and render all aid during the Affghan war. - He was bound to approve of all the defensive preparations in Scinde which might be deemed fitting, while the security of the countries beyond the Indus should be threatened.

On the other hand, the Anglo-Indian Government declared it would not covet " a drain or a dam of Roostum's territory, nor his fortresses on this bank or that bank of the Indus." He and his successors were to be absolute and independent in their possessions as rulers, and no complaint by their subjects was to be listened to. But he was to co-operate in all measures necessary to extend and facilitate the commerce and navigation of the Indus; and to facilitate amity and peace, resident ministers were to be accredited to and from each of the contracting powers : but the British Resident might change his abode at will, attended by an escort whose strength was to be determined by his own Government. A supplementary article gave the British power, in time of war, to occupy Bukkur, which was in the middle of the stream commanding the navigation !

This treaty was followed by the Hydrabad quadruplicate treaties, of fourteen articles, concluded with Noor, his brother Nusseer, and his nephews Sobdar and Mohamed, each separately. Bearing date the 11th of March, 1839, it provided :—

1°. Lasting friendship and unity of interest between the contracting parties.

2°. A British force, its strength determined by the Governor-General, should quarter in Scinde.

3°. Noor, Nusseer, and Mohamed, were each to pay one lac of rupees yearly towards the cost of the subsidiary force, but Sobdar was exempted as a reward for previous friendship.

4°. The Ameers' territories were placed under British protection.

5°. The Ameers were to be absolute as rulers, each in his own possessions, and no complaint made by their subjects to be listened to by the British.

6°. Disputes between independent Ameers were to be referred, with the sanction of the Governor-General, to the Resident for mediation.

7°. If the subjects, that is to say, tribe chiefs under one Ameer were aggressive towards another Ameer, and the latter was unable to check them, the British Government might interfere with force.

8°. Negotiations with foreign states, unless sanctioned by the Indian Government, were forbidden to the Ameers.

9°. An auxiliary force was to be furnished when required for purposes of defence.

10°. The Timooree rupee current in Scinde being of the same value as the Company's rupee, the latter was to pass as lawful money in that country ; but if the British authorities coined Timooree rupees in Scinde, a seignorage was to be paid to the Ameers, yet not during the Affghan war.

11°. No tolls were to be paid for trading boats passing up or down the Indus.

12°. Merchandise landed from such boats and sold, was to pay the usual duties, excepting always those sold in a British camp or cantonment.

13°. Goods of all kinds brought to the mouth of the Indus were to be kept there, at the owner's pleasure, until the best period for sending them up the river arrived; but if any were sold at the mouth, or other parts, always excepting British camps or cantonments, they were to pay duty.

14°. The treaty was to be binding on all succeeding Governors of India, and upon the Ameers and their successors for ever ; and all former treaties not rescinded by this, were to remain in full force.

Noor Mohamed, now convinced of the inexorable injustice of his oppressors, thought to turn the general injury to his peculiar profit, and secretly advised Pottinger to retain Kurrachee as a means of impressing the subordinate chiefs with the power of the British, in which he only anticipated Lord Auckland's resolution by a few days : his real object was to pass himself off with the chiefs as a man favoured by the powerful British Government, and thus keep them submissive under his exactions. His friendly tone was soon imitated by the other Ameers of Hydrabad; yet the grace with which they resigned themselves to their wrongs, did not save them from the cruel mockery of being asked by Pottinger, if they had " the slightest cause to question British faith during the last six months." And the farther mortification of being told that "henceforth they must consider Scinde to be, as it was in reality, a portion of Hindostan, in which the British were paramount and entitled to act as they considered best and fittest for the general good of the whole Empire." To this the humbled Ameers replied with helpless irony, "That their eyes were opened. They had found it difficult to overcome the prejudice and apprehension of their tribes, who had always been led to think the only object of the British was to extend their dominion. Now they had been taught by experience English strength and good faith."

Having concluded his long course of negotiations, Pottinger thought "the world would acknowledge, that if the English-Indian Government's power was great, its good faith and forbearance was still more to be wondered at!" And then "distinctly recorded his opinion, though anticipating no such event, that if ever the British military strength was to be again exerted in Scinde, it must be carried to subjugating the country."

To accord a good faith and forbearance to these negotiations is impossible. Palliation on the score of necessity is the utmost that can be asked, and that but faintly.

Can even that be justly conceded?

Pottinger said, Lord Auckland must be fatigued with the perusal of Noor Mohamed's barefaced falsehoods, and unblushing assertions of firm devoted friendship. It was certainly necessary to name the Ameer, lest doubt should arise as to which side the words were applicable; for was it not with constant assurances of friendship that Lord Auckland gave the Ameers a right to address him thus.

You besought us to make treaties of amity and commerce. We did so, and you have broken them.

You asked for our alliance, we did not seek yours. We yielded to your solicitations, and you have used our kindness to our ruin.

You declared yourself, without our knowledge or desire, our protector against a man we did not fear, our mediator in a quarrel which did not concern you. In return for this,

which you termed a favour, you demanded permanent possession of our capital, military occupation of our country, and
even payment for the cost of thus destroying our independence under the masques of friendship! mediation! protection!

You peremptorily demanded our aid to ruin Dost Mohamed, who was not our enemy. And our backwardness thus
to damage, against justice and against the interest of our
religion, him and his nation with whom we were at peace,
you made a cause of deadly quarrel.

To molify your wrath, we gave your armies a passage
through our dominions contrary to the terms of our commercial treaties. In return, you have, with those armies, reduced
us to a state of miserable dependence.

Can these undeniable facts be justified with reference to
national honour? Can they be called forbearing, generous,
moderate? Can they be justified on the ground of international law, of self-preservation—on that necessity which sets
all common rules aside? Can they even be justified by that
necessity for aggrandizement which has been supposed inherent to the peculiar nature of the British position in the
East.

Lord Auckland said Russia and the western Asiatic
powers were combined to destroy British India, that the
invasion of Affghanistan enjoined the contingent aggression
on Scinde; and if the latter was pushed too far the fault
was with the Ameers, who were jointly hostile, perfidious,
insolent and obstinate.

But the invasion of Affghanistan was itself unwarranted
by policy. Founded on doubtful anticipation of danger, it
was unjust and ill-judged, was commenced on false principles,
political and military, executed with incredible absurdity,
and terminated in a dreadful calamity which went nigh to
shake in pieces that Indian empire it was designed to secure.
It was not founded on any real necessity, or the danger it
was intended to obviate would have augmented on its failure.
It was not the result of any inherent force of circumstances
beyond the ordinary foresight of man; no extraordinary
genius, no far-reaching sagacity was requisite to detect the

fallacy of the conception, and the warning voice of England's great captain, whose words on such a subject should have had oracular weight, was raised in hope to stay the mischief. It was the offspring of vanity and ignorance, devoid of expediency and public morality. And if this, the principal action, was neither just nor necessary, the accessory action against Scinde was an oppression, indefensible even though it had presented less odious phases during its progress.

If the secret engagements of the Ameers with the Persians; if their confederation with the Affghan chiefs of Candahar; if their repeated violations of the commercial treaties; if their violent insulting conduct towards the British Resident; if their arrogance, their duplicity, their perfidious intentions deserved chastisement, they should so have been proclaimed, and war declared. This might have been a stern procedure, but not a treacherous oppression. It would have been politic also on military considerations to have first warred down Scinde: a subdued enemy would have been less dangerous on the communications, than a forced ally, incensed by injustice and of unbroken strength.

Why were the Ameers' territories fastened on to have a long, circuitous, unsafe line, when short and safe lines were to be had in the Punjaub? Runjeet Sing profited largely by the tripartite treaty, and was to have share of the spoil anticipated from the plunder of the Barrukzies. Hence it would have been nothing unreasonable to have demanded a base of operations in his dominions. If he refused, a quarrel would have been legitimate, and more profitable than with the Ameers—but Runjeet was wily, and powerful enough to give trouble; the Ameers were despised, and supposed to be rich. Fear and cupidity! these were the springs of action. Sir Alexander Burnes had said their treasury contained twenty millions sterling.—" The Ameers may be supposed wealthy," was one of the earliest intimations given by Lord Auckland to Pottinger.

The armies passed onwards to Affghanistan, the subsidiary force entered Scinde, and the political obligations of its rulers became totally changed. The original injustice remained in all its deformity; but when sanctioned by a treaty, without public protest or stroke in battle, became patent as the rule of policy, and new combinations involving great national interests were thus imposed on Lord Auckland's successor, demanding a different measure of right from that which existed previously. For amongst the many evils attendant on national injustice is the necessity of sustaining a wrongful policy, thus implicating honest men in transactions the origin of which they condemn. Some abstract moralists inculcate indeed, that governments stand in the same relation to each other that private persons do in a community; and as leaders and guides of nations, should be governed by the same rules as leaders and guides of families. It would be well for the world were this practicable. But when private persons wrong each other there are tribunals to enforce reparation; or they may voluntarily amend the wrong. Apply this to nations. Their tribunal is war. Every conquest, every treaty, places them on a new basis of intercourse. The first injustice remains a stigma on the government perpetrating it; but for succeeding governments new combinations are presented, which may and generally do make it absolute for self-preservation, and therefore justifiable, not only to uphold but to extend what was at first to be condemned.

Scinde is a striking illustration of this truth. The Affghan invasion being perpetrated, the safety of the troops engaged imperatively required that Scinde should continue to be occupied, and the treaties with the Ameers enforced. Say the Affghan armies ought rather to have been withdrawn, and two scores of injustice wiped off together. Was it possible? If possible, would it not have been imputed to fear, to weakness, to any thing but an abstract sense of justice? Nations, especially in the East, are neither so pure nor so frank as to greet virtue in a state garb. Wrong they are ever ready to offer to others, wrong they ever expect; and when it fails to arrive, opportunity favourable, they despise the forbearance as a folly. To have abandoned Affghanistan without redeeming the character of British strength, would have been the signal for universal commotion, if not of insurrection, throughout India. The having

abandoned it at all led to the Scindian war, which was an
inevitable consequence of the flagitious folly of the first
enterprise.

One alleviation for this otherwise unmitigated trans-
gression against Scinde remains, and it is a great one. It
was not perpetrated against a people but their rulers, and
they were bad, indescribably bad. Oppressors themselves
they were oppressed by stronger power. They were tyrants,
without pity or remorse, and without pity their fall should
be recorded. Their people gained as they lost; the honour
of England suffered, yet humanity profited; the British
camps and stations offered asylums to thousands who would
otherwise have led a life of misery. Yet this palliation,
amidst so much to condemn, was incidental, and cannot be
pleaded by Lord Auckland, because the treaties expressly
resigned the people to the cruelty of their rulers.

The invasion of Affghanistan presents no such redeeming
accompaniment. It was undertaken to force a proud tyrant
on a people who detested him; and being conducted without
ability, terminated in disaster so dire as to fill the mind with
horror—enforcing what cannot be too often repeated, that
incapacity and vanity are, in great enterprises of war,
tantamount to wickedness.

Colonel Pottinger, created a baronet, continued Resident
in Scinde until the beginning of 1840. He was then replaced in the lower country by Major Outram, having been
previously relieved in the upper country by Mr. Ross Bell.
His negotiations offer noticeable points of character. His
natural feelings of justice, breaking out at the sight of Shah
Sooja's receipts for a debt which he was again demanding at
the head of an army; his reprobation of the *Wellesley's* attack
on Kurrachee, and his frequent exhortations to treat the
people gently, are in strong contrast with his assertions as to
British loyalty and forbearance, good faith, and moderation
in political acts, which no sophistry can palliate. Nor is
the deference he recommended for the tyrannical pleasures
of the Ameers, while he took away their real rights, less
curious. Treating of their *Shikargahs,* or hunting preserves,
he acknowledged they had formed them by turning, within

a few years, a fourth of the fertile peopled land into a wilderness; and that they were still persistent in that devastating career, one of them having recently destroyed two large villages to make a *Shikargah* for his son, only eight years old! and all declaring that their hunting was dearer to them than their wives and children—acknowledging all this, he nevertheless desired that their hunting might be respected, because the ancient forest laws of the Normans were equally pernicious! And while thus recurring to the most cruel oppression of the worst period of English history, as a guide for Lord Auckland and an excuse for the Ameers, he recommended a conciliating and protective policy towards the people!

CHAPTER IV.

THE mutations of the Affghan war, and the hostility of
Merab, Prince of Khelat, encouraged the Ameers to intrigue
secretly against the British; the death of Merab, whose
capital was stormed, and himself killed by General Wiltshire,
coupled with internal dissensions in Scinde, forbad any open
effort in 1839. But in 1840, the Brahooes rose for the son
of Merab and defeated several British detachments; the
Murrees, a tribe of the Cutchee hills, were also driven by
British injustice to insurrection; the son and grandson of
Runjeet Sing died in quick succession, the Punjaub was in
wild commotion, and then the Ameers thus spoke in their
secret councils.

"It is good to combine with other powers, because the
British Government is surrounded by enemies, because it
fears insurrection in India, and is lax in its rule over neighbouring states; but it is difficult, because its rule is rigid in
Scinde, and we are divided and quarrelling. If we could all
unite it would be well."

At the time these councils were held, Dost Mohamed
returned to Affghanistan at the head of an Usbeg army;
British detachments had been cut off in the Cutchee hills,
and the general aspect of affairs was menacing. But
then Shere Mohamed of Meerpoor was at enmity with the
Hydrabad Ameers about a boundary line, and was anxious
for a treaty with the British on the same terms as Sobdar, who was his friend. In Upper Scinde, Moobarick
had died, disputes arose about his possessions, and union
amongst the Ameers was impossible. Soon Colonel Dennie
won the battle of Bamean, the Dost surrendered himself, and
it became known that a Russian expedition against Khiva had
totally failed. Reinforcements then entered Scinde, and a
strong British force was gathered on the Upper Sutlege to

watch the Punjaub. In this state of affairs the Ameers, seeing ten thousand men at their palace gate avoided open offence.

Noor Mohamed died towards the end of the year, his last act being to claim the British protection for his brother Nusseer, and his youngest son Hoossein, against the machinations of his eldest son Shadad, a man incredibly brutal and wicked. He protested also in his last moments that his friendship and alliance with the English, since the treaty, had been sincere. This declaration was certainly a legitimate ratification of that treaty, and the other Ameers confirmed it soon after his death by seeking the arbitration of the Governor-General on the boundary dispute with Shere Mohamed. This last named Prince's desire to treat would have been another confirmation, if it had been frankly met; but the Anglo-Indian Government, and its agent Major Outram, true to the spoliating policy of the first negotiations, rendered that which might have borne the grace of a voluntary contract on one side and a favour on the other, a rapacious injustice.

Shere Mohamed asked to be treated as Sobdar had been, but a heavy fine was demanded for the alliance; and when he sought to lessen the sum by undervaluing his possessions, it was called a crime! Hitherto he had enjoyed a nominal independence; now Major Outram, while admitting that possession and right were with Mohamed in the boundary dispute, recommended that a fixed tribute should be demanded by the British, under pain of letting the Hydrabad Ameers loose, with an intimation, that if he proved too strong they would be aided, and his losses would not be confined to the disputed territory. And this expressly to lower his opinion of his own importance! Such a compendious negotiation produced immediate acquiescence, and was called able diplomacy! Shere Mohamed paid fifty thousand rupees yearly for the favour of British arbitration and protection. The arbitration then went on, and at the same time the chiefs of tribes were assured of their feudal possessions.

Every governing power having now in turn voluntarily accepted the treaties, by demanding protection against native

opponents, the legal force of those instruments increased;
they had lasted two years, and furnishing, as they did, asylums in the British stations to oppressed multitudes, they had
also acquired that secondary moral force which belongs to
utility, irrespective of abstract justice. But the Ameers,
while apparently submissive sought to evade their tribute,
and Lord Auckland, thinking cession of territory more sure
and profitable, coveted Shikarpoor, the largest city of Scinde,
decayed indeed from the tyranny of the Ameers but promising with better government to recover its former importance: and it was advantageously placed on the line of
communication with Affghanistàn. The Ameers assented to
the cession in discharge of tribute, and the British thus gained
three permanent military stations in Upper Scinde; namely,
Sukkur, Bukkur, and Shikarpoor. The first, having an
entrenched camp, was on the right bank of the Indus; the
second, on a rock in the middle of that river; the third,
twenty miles to the north-west of Sukkur, on the high road
to the Bolan pass. In Lower Scinde they also held Kurrachee, the only good port: thus the Ameers' candle was
burning at both ends.

About the middle of 1841, died Mr. Ross Bell, who as
political agent, had governed Upper Scinde and Beloochistan
with unbounded power; but under his sway insurrections
had occurred amongst the Booghtees and Murree tribes,
occasioned, it is said, by his grinding oppression, accompanied
with acts of particular and of general treachery, followed by
military execution, bloody and desolating, involving whole
districts in ruin. He was in constant dispute with the military officers, and has been described as a man of vigorous
talent, resolute, unhesitating, devoid of public morality, and
vindictive; of domineering pride, and such luxurious pomp,
that seven hundred camels, taken from the public service,
were required to carry his personal baggage. That his conduct was neither wise nor just, seems a correct inference from
the results of his administration, but Lord Auckland approved
of it, and regretted his loss; the story of the camels is an
exaggerated statement, and the general accusations have been
principally promulgated by Dr. Buist, of the *Bombay Times,*

whose word, for praise or blame, is generally false and always despicable.

Mr. Bell's functions were transferred to Major Outram, who thus became political agent for the whole of Scinde and Beloochistan. Tranquillity in the latter country was obtained by the cessation of oppression. Lord Auckland restored the son of Merab to his father's dignity, which contented the Brahooes, and allayed the excitement of the Ameers, who were connected by marriage with Merab's family : not that his misfortunes had been deeply felt by them, but the termination of hostilities in Beloochistan released a large British force for action in Scinde.

This quietude continued until the Cabool calamity, in the beginning of 1842, shook the reputation of British power throughout the neighbouring nations, disturbed all India, and excited the smouldering fire of revenge with the Ameers. Nusseer Khan was now considered the head of that fraternity. Secret communications between him and Sawan Mull, the Seik chief of Moultan, were detected by the political agents, and the suspicion thus awakened, was increased by like communications between Roostum of Kyrpoor, and Shere Sing, then Maharajah of the Punjaub, and falsely supposed to be less friendly to the British alliance than his predecessor Runjeet. The Ameer's officers behaved vexatiously, a sure sign, and Roostum repelled remonstrance haughtily, assuming an unusual tone of independence as to the cession of Shikarpoor, for which no treaty had yet been executed: the delay being however with the British authorities. Outram accused the Ameer of mean shuffling on this occasion, yet himself directed his assistant, Postans, to give Roostum hopes of keeping Shikarpoor by the use of ambiguous language, such as would leave the Governor-General a right to reject or insist on the agreement, according to the profit which it might promise ! But a new era was now commencing, Lord Auckland quitted India, leaving it in all the confusion, terror, and danger, necessarily flowing from the political immorality and astounding incapacity which had marked his mischievous government. And if any man, not blinded by party prejudices, shall doubt the correctness of the picture of Whig oppression and folly painted in the foregoing pages, let him read and compare all the Parliamentary papers on the subject and he will doubt no longer.

Lord Ellenborough, the new Governor-General, arrived too late to prevent, yet in time to remedy the most dangerous evils menacing India from his predecessor's impolicy, which he denounced in a vigorous proclamation designed as a warning to future governors. The beacon burned bright, and the flame spreading wide scorched some whose cries have never ceased. Previous to his coming, the ship was rocking in the shallows, but when his strong hand was felt she ceased to strike, and answering to the helm was steered into deep water. Nevertheless, those men whose political iniquity brought India to the verge of ruin, are now, with incredible effrontery, imputing their own crimes and absurdities to him, especially in what relates to Scinde. His share in the subsequent transactions in that country shall therefore be exactly stated, and judgment left to the common sense of mankind.

He found the public mind confused with terror by the Cabool catastrophe, the surrender of Ghusni, the blockade of Candahar, and the seeming inability of General Pollock to relieve Jellallabad. Colonel England was, soon afterwards, defeated by an inferior force at Hykulzie and fell back to Quettah, leaving General Nott, as it was supposed, to certain destruction.

He found the finances embarrassed, the civil and political services infested with men greedy of gain, gorged with insolence, disdaining work, and intimately connected with the infamous press of India, which they supplied with official secrets, receiving in return shameful and shameless support: for, thus combining, they thought to control the Governor-General and turn the resources of the State to their sordid profit.

He found the military depressed in spirit, and deprived of their just allowances ; the hard-working soldier oppressed, the idle vapourer encouraged, discipline attainted, and the military correspondents of the newspapers, assuming, falsely it is to be hoped, the title of officers, constantly proclaiming sentiments without an indication of honour or patriotism.

Amidst these difficulties he steered as became a brave man, conscious of danger and of his own resources to meet it. His first effort was to stay fear on one side and rising hopes on the other, by a manifesto of his views, in which a vigorous determination was apparent. This proclamation of silence as it were, suspended the general confusion, and gave time to combine military operations, for teaching exulting frontier nations that England's strength was not to be safely measured by recent misfortunes. Lord Auckland's policy had been unjust, wicked, and foolish towards those nations! But was Lord Ellenborough therefore in the very crisis of evil, nicely to weigh the oppressions of his predecessor? Was he to set aside all combinations flowing from that predecessor's impolicy? Was he who had undertaken to save the Indian empire to bend before victorious barbarians, deprecate their wrath, cheer them in their dreadful career by acknowledging their anger to be legitimate? Was he to encourage their revengeful passions, and foment the hopes of other powers eager for war, by a humility which could only appear to them weakness? The safety of the empire was to be secured: England was not to sink because Lord Auckland was unwise.

Lord Ellenborough saw clearly and struck boldly; but widely different was his method from that of his predecessor. In Scinde rapacity had hitherto been masked with professions of friendship—the tongue was soothing, the hand furtive and grasping. With Lord Ellenborough the tongue spake no deceit, but the hand was shewn in sinewy strength as a warning.

Let Pottinger's instructions from Lord Auckland be compared with the following, given to Outram by Lord Ellenborough—bearing in mind, that the one had no right to meddle with the Ameers, whereas the other stood on treaties acknowledged and acted upon for three years: that the first was ministering to an insane aggressive policy; the second stimulated by the lofty ambition of saving India.

" The Governor-General is led to think you may have seen reason to doubt the fidelity of one or more of the Ameers of Scinde. He therefore forwards three similar letters to be

F

addressed according to circumstances, and at your discretion,
to those of the Ameers whom you may have ground for suspecting of hostile designs against the British Government.
And you will distinctly understand, that the threat contained
is no idle threat intended only to alarm, but a declaration of
the Governor-General's fixed determination to punish, cost
what it may, the first chief who shall prove faithless, by the
confiscation of his dominions. But there must be clear
proof of such faithlessness, and it must not be provoked by
the conduct of British agents, producing in the minds of any
chief a belief that the British Government entertains designs
inconsistent with its interests and honour."

Nor were his letters to the Ameers less explicit: running
thus : —

" While I am resolved to respect treaties myself, and to
exercise the power with which I am intrusted, for the general
good of the subjects of the British Government and of the
several States of India, I am equally resolved to make others
respect the engagements into which they have entered, and
to exercise their power without injury to their neighbours.
I should be most reluctant to believe that you had deviated
from the course which is dictated by your engagements ; I
will confide in your fidelity and in your friendship, until I
have proof of your faithlessness and of your hostility in my
hands : but be assured, if I should obtain such proofs, no
consideration shall induce me to permit you to exercise any
longer a power you will have abused. On the day on which
you shall be faithless to the British Government sovereignty
will have passed from you ; your dominions will be given to
others, and in your destitution all India will see, that the
British Government will not pardon an injury received from
one it believed to be its friend."

This declaration, by which he was guided in commencing
the Scindian war, and by which its justice and policy must
be measured, is not to be taken in a political sense alone.
Commercial interests affecting the whole civilized world were
at stake. The Indus had been by the treaties with the
Ameers and with Runjeet Sing, made the high road of
nations ; those treaties, preceding the political engagements,

had been freely conceded, were just in themselves, obtained justly, and with a beneficent object: they were for the interest of mankind at large, and were not abrogated by the political treaties, save in the one point of not transmitting military stores by the Indus.

But Lord Ellenborough's singleness of purpose was evinced in several ways. Outram at this period announced that "he had it in his power to expose the hostile intrigues of the Ameers to such an extent as might be deemed sufficient to authorize the dictation of any terms to those chiefs, or any measure necessary to place British power on a secure footing;" and he advised the assuming the entire management of the Shikarpoor and Sukkur districts to render British power over the Indus invulnerable. This was quite in the spirit of aggressive policy, which was never distasteful to Major Outram until Lord Ellenborough deprived him of his political situation. This proposal was rejected: Lord Ellenborough looked only to future loyalty in the Ameers, and offered them a renewed intercourse on well-understood grounds.

The great operations for restoring the British military reputation in Affghanistan, previous to abandoning that country, were now in full progress. Jellallabad had been succoured, the armies of Nott and Pollock directed by a combined movement on Cabool, and the Governor-General's hands being thus freed from the military fetters fastened by Lord Auckland, were instantly employed in choking off the civil and political leeches sucking the public. He broke the connection between official men and newspaper editors; and, defying the blatant fury of the latter and the secret enmity of the former, he drove the unclean people from the administration. He restored the drooping spirit of the army by a vigorous protection of its honour and interests, and he put to flight the political agents and their assistants, who, numerous as locusts, had settled on the countries beyond the Indus, in numbers equalling the whole of the salaried officers employed for the diplomacy of all Europe! Their vanity, uncontrolled power, pomp, and incapacity had contributed more than all other things to the recent misfortunes.

Wild was the uproar these reforms occasioned. All the rage of faction broke loose. No calumny that sordid falsehood could invent or cowardly anger dictate was spared: and when malice was at fault, folly stepped in with such charges as, that the Governor-General's state harness was of red leather! he wore gold lace on his pantaloons! But while such matters were dwelt upon, the incessant activity, the assiduity, the energy, the magnanimity of the man were overlooked. The moral courage and fortitude, which could, in the midst of disaster and abasement of public spirit, at once direct the armies to victory and purify the administration, which could confide in military honour while defying the vituperation of the Indian press, re-echoed by the scarcely more scrupulous press of England—these great and generous qualities were overlooked or sneered at, as well as the complete success they procured for the country. But newspapers are not history, and Lord Ellenborough's well-earned reputation, as an able, victorious, and honest Governor-General, will outlive faction, its falsehoods, and malignant press.

Outram withheld the Governor-General's warning letter to the Ameers, lest, as he said, fear should drive them and the chiefs of tribes to extremities, all being alike conscious of treasonable designs. This view of the matter was accepted by Lord Ellenborough, and was a convincing proof that his object was tranquillity, not subjugation; yet it seems an error, inasmuch as he should have been careful to keep his own manly policy clear of the crooked paths of his predecessor's. To declare oblivion for the past, to look only to the future, acting on a necessity which he found existing to bind him would have been a better course: but the error was one adverse to violence, a view confirmed by the tenor of his first dispatches.

" The recent engagements attendant on the restoration of the young Prince of Khelat, and the uncertain state of the war, imposed he said, the necessity of maintaining a strong position on the Indus in Scinde, and the power of acting on both sides of that river; consequently, the continued occupation of Kurrachee to communicate with Bombay, and the

occupation of Bukkur and Sukkur to insure a passage over
the Indus, were requisite for safe intercourse with the
British stations on the Sutlege on one side, and with the army
at Candahar by the Bolan pass on the other. The supporting of commerce by the Indus was another great obligation; and as his desire was to put an end, at any financial
loss, to the system of taking tribute for protection, he proposed to exchange that to which the Ameers were liable
by their treaties, for permanent possession of Kurrachee,
Bukkur and Sukkur. Protection was in most cases as much
the interest of the British Government to afford, as it was
the interest of the protected state to receive; but however
equable in principle the bargain might be in practice, it
could not fail to affect amity, to raise disagreeable discussions, and to make the British officers employed appear
odious extortioners in the eyes of the people, who were taxed
to pay the tribute, and oppressed by other exactions made
under pretence of that tribute. Territory, therefore, he
desired instead, or in place of territory, the abolition of
duties burthensome to commerce. He was aware that, regard
being had for the former treaties and the reciprocal obligation imposed by them, difficulties might arise, and much
time elapse before his object could be attained, but this was
to be the governing principle of his policy."

Assuredly there was nothing here oppressive or unjust.
Roostum had already consented to cede Shikarpoor to Lord
Auckland, who had certainly contemplated the permanent
occupation of Scinde, and no qualms of conscience then disturbed the East Indian Directors, though they have since so
strongly expressed their disapproval of the same thing when
done by Lord Ellenborough in a crisis which justified the
act. It would thus appear that injustice is essential to
render acquisition of territory palatable to the statesmen of
Leadenhall Street; or that they are not statesmen, but
sordid, trading, prating persons, who adopt the amount of
dividend, or personal irritation, as guides for the government
of a great empire. Lord Ellenborough's policy was wider.
He sought to remove incentives to collision amongst the
Ameers, to protect the oppressed people, to raise the British

character, and to forward the general interests of commerce by opening the navigation of the Indus—and those objects he sought by fair negotiations without menace.

Meanwhile Outram, acting at this time with strained partisan zeal against the Ameers, and declaring that he " should not be sorry to afford Government grounds for making an example of Nusseer," diligently gathered proofs, direct and indirect, of the hostility of the Ameers, and grounded on them a proposal for a new treaty; saying that they gave Lord Ellenborough a right to dictate his own terms: and in truth they were numerous and strong.

1°. Intercepted letters, addressed by Nusseer of Hydrabad, to the Moultan chief, and by Roostum of Kyrpoor to the Maharajah, Shere Sing. These he designated treasonable, a term difficult to understand as applied to sovereign princes; but they were in violation of the eighth article of the treaty of 1839, which forbad the Ameers to negotiate with foreign chiefs or states, unless sanctioned by the British Government: moreover the Moultan man had collected a large force on the frontier of Upper Scinde under false pretences.

2°. A secret confederation of the Bráhooes and other Beloochee tribes, encouraged by the Ameers with a view to a general revolt against the British supremacy, if new reverses in Affghanistan, which were expected, should furnish a favourable opportunity. The names of the chiefs and the plan of revolt were obtained, and the rising was to be a religious one. " *The sword was to be drawn for Islam.*" Indeed, Colonel England's defeat at Hykulzie had so excited the hopes and confidence of the tribes that every thing was ready for a general outburst, when the relief of Jellallabad by General Pollock checked the movement.

3°. Nusseer of Hydrabad and Roostum of Kyrpoor, formerly enemies, were become fast friends, both being governed alike by one Futteh Mohamed Ghoree, the minister of Roostum, well known as a man of talent, intriguing, bigotted, and bitterly hating the British. Nusseer also, had endeavoured by a false accusation to have Sobdar, who appeared friendly and loyal, made to pay tribute contrary to

the treaty: doing this with a view to force him by such
injustice into the general confederacy.

4°. Nusseer had, during the previous year, proposed to
the Seiks to drive the British away, as the Affghans had
done, offering to assist them.

5°. Lieutenant Gordon, employed to survey the lower
country and the coast, discovered that several chiefs, owing
no homage to the Ameers, had recently gone to Hydrabad
with their followers, pretending fear of the Affghans. At
the same time obstacles were raised to hinder the execution
of his survey, and throughout the lower country he found a
decided hostile spirit amongst the Beloochees—a native even
informed him that he was to be either driven from the
country where he could observe their preparations, or killed.
It was known also that the hill tribes and those of the plain
were alike ready to attack the camp at Kurrachee, when
news of reverses in Affghanistan should arrive.

6°. Shere Mohamed of Meerpoor, had secret intercourse
with the Seiks, and was confederate with the Moultan
man. Sobdar of Hydrabad and Ali Moorad of Kyrpoor,
were the only persons supposed to be faithful to their engagements.

7°. The plan of the hostile Ameers, was to get pos-
session of Bukkur, as all the fighting would be, they said, in
Upper Scinde, where the Kyrpoor Princes were to attack
Ali Moorad's villages if he did not join the confederacy ; the
British would of course interfere, and then the Hydrabad
troops would move up and unite to give battle.

8°. A Persian had come with secret messages from the
Shah to Nusseer.

9°. There was backwardness in the payment of tribute,
with a view to the intended outbreak, and tolls and duties
were levied contrary to the treaties.

Outram, grounding his proposed treaty on these hostile
demonstrations, recommended also the taking permanent
possession of Shikarpoor, and the overthrow of Lord Auckland's policy with respect to the equality of the Ameers ;
arguing, very justly on this point, that each Ameer evaded
responsibility, charging it on others ; that the negotiations

were necessarily complicate, and every petty dispute was referred to the British Government when it ought to be settled among themselves. His proposed treaty, the preamble to which he worded very offensively for the Ameers, involved the cession of Bukkur, the site of the ancient Sukkur, and an intrenched cantonment there, in perpetuity; the cession of Kurrachee in perpetuity; free passage and communication for commerce between Kurrachee and the Indus at Tatta; the old articles against tolls, and the right to cut fuel for steam navigation on each side of the river to a certain extent. This was the first direct proposition for interfering with the Ameers' " *Shikargahs,*" for Pottinger's proposal was merely to cut a way for tracking. It gave them infinite offence; for they loved them better than their wives and children, better than their subjects' lives, better than their country's prosperity, better than the commerce of the world!

In return, he proposed to exonerate the Ameers from all arrears of debt, and from all future tribute; a boon amounting altogether to nearly half a million of rupees of annual tribute, and a million of arrears of debt.

Now, if Outram and his subordinates did not forge these accusations, it follows that violations of the treaties, and a wide-spread conspiracy to destroy the British troops in Scinde, gave Lord Ellenborough a right to dictate new terms, calculated to secure the public interest. And if the grasping policy which has been attributed to him, really influenced his proceedings, the opportunity was favourable; the cause of offence given of major importance, and the means at hand; for Colonel England was then returning from Candahar, and a great army of reserve was assembling on the Sutlege.

Here it is fitting to shew why that army of reserve was assembled. Vehemently ridiculed at the time by the Indian press, it was at once a proof of Lord Ellenborough's prudence and of the infamy of that press, which was then vociferously devoted to the support of peculation and the depression of the military spirit: calumniating every man who displayed patriotism or useful talent, it urged the

sepoys to mutiny, and incited and taught the enemy how
and where to assail the troops with most advantage.

When Lord Ellenborough arrived in India, there were
30,000 Seik troops at Peshawar, and only 4000 British
troops, of whom 1800 were in hospital. The presence of
these Seiks gave great anxiety; and when 5000 of them advanced, unasked and unwished for, towards Jellallabad,
General Pollock, directed by Lord Ellenborough, persuaded
those half hostile, turbulent men to pass to the left bank of
the Cabool river, leaving the resources of the right bank to
the British, with clear communications, from Jellallabad to
Peshawar; but when the army returned from Cabool 20,000
Seiks followed it closely, and it was to awe them the reserve was assembled on the Sutlege. For though Shere Sing
was friendly to the British his Sirdars were hostile, and notably so those of the Sindhawalla family, by whom he was afterwards assassinated. Dhian Sing, his minister, urged him to
fall on Pollock while traversing the Punjaub, and that expressly *"because the Indian press had told him the British
meaned to attack the Seiks."* Shere Sing, relying on Lord
Ellenborough's good faith, was by the presence of the army
of reserve enabled to resist Dhian's proposal, but he afterwards strongly stated to the foreign secretary, who visited
him at Lahore, the great embarrassments caused in dealing
with his chiefs and soldiers by the unprincipled falsehood
of the Anglo-Indian press.

Outram's counsel and proposed treaty were rejected by
Lord Ellenborough, who condemned the offensive tone assumed by that agent, and rejected the cession of Shikarpoor:
but repeating his determination to punish faithlessness, he
intimated his wish to restore the district of Subzulcote and
Bhoong-Barra to the Bhawal Khan, from whom they had
been wrested forcibly thirty years before by Roostum and
his brother Ameers. He did not however, put forward any
pretence of abstract justice to overrule the speciality of the
case; but simply to give effect to his avowed resolution to
punish bad faith and reward fidelity. Yet he did not positively decide that it should be so, and disclaimed any desire
for hasty change in the political relations with the Ameers;

for he had then hope that the operations of Nott and
Pollock, and the return of Col. England's column, would
restrain their disposition to be hostile.

Fresh offences dissipated this hope, and shewed the mischief of Outram's meddling as to the warning letters: their
delivery would certainly have checked the Ameers, and could
not as Outram supposed have hastened an outbreak, because, although their resolution was fixed to regain independence, their preparations varied as the mutations of the
Affghan war gave them hopes or fears.   Now, unwarned,
they pushed their secret practices, and one Mohamed Shurreef, a Syud, acting in their views, and conjoined with
Mohamed Sadig, an Affghan, were stirring up the Cutchee
hill tribes to war on the British communications with Candahar; but the capture of Shurreef by stratagem caused
Sadig to fly, and stopped the outbreak. The expectation of
it had however, excited all the hopes and arrogance of the
Ameers.   They interrupted the navigation of the Indus,
fired on traffic boats, exacted tolls contrary to treaty, and
even sentenced merchants and traders who had built houses
and established shops in the British cantonment of Kurrachee to have their goods.confiscated, and their houses pulled
down.   This was barbarous as well as hostile, for all the
British stations were crowded with persons flying from the
Ameers' tyranny. The reviving commerce of the country
was indeed odious to them when thus protected from their
exactions—" We do not choose to let our subjects trade with
the British, and the fifth article of treaty forbids any interference between us."

This was a subtle plea, yet fallacious, because it was not
a dispute between the Ameers and their subjects, but an act
of hostility against the British, who were thus isolated like
an infected people : indeed, the Ameers designated them as
a " *pestilence in the land.*"

Shurreef's capture and Sadig's flight only checked the
Ameers for a moment, and they were again excited by
Nott's advance from Candahar, considered by them a forced
abandonment of that important place.   And though he
afterwards destroyed Ghusni, and in conjunction with Pol-

lock ruined Istalif and Cabool, the apparently hurried retreat from Affghanistan which followed, bore for these
misjudging people the character of a flight. The Scindian
Beloochees and Brahooes became then more confident, and
the Ameers of Upper and Lower Scinde consulted how best
to league against the Feringees. Seik vakeels were at
Kyrpoor, ready to start for Lahore loaded with presents for
the Maharajah; and at the same time letters came from the
victorious Affghans to remind the Ameers they were feudatories of the Dooranee Empire, and exhorting them to act
boldly in the common cause.

Outram's political agency now ceased. It was not Lord
Ellenborough's policy to divide power between military and
political chiefs; nor to place the former lowest when war was
at hand—hence the removal of Outram was a consequence
of Scinde being under a general. But there were other
causes for dismissing him. His capacity was found to be
mean, and the Governor-General had been compelled to
withdraw all confidence from him for a specific offence affecting the public honour. He was also offensive from his
habitual pertinacious urgency of his own views and opinions
without any supporting ability to recommend them. He was
dismissed, and Sir C. Napier took the entire charge of Scinde
and its troubled affairs. The clamour of many tongues
was immediately raised, as if a man of incredible genius
and unmatched services had been removed from a country
where he alone could guide events to a happy conclusion.

Outram himself publicly declared that his policy in
Scinde was productive of beneficial results, and that his
removal would produce deplorable consequences; but no
facts bore out this announcement; his superior genius was
nowhere to be found except in the columns of a despicable
Indian newspaper, to whose proprietors it was said he owed
money. Sir C. Napier indeed, misled at first by his vaunting
tales of his own exploits, offered him a glowing compliment
at a public dinner when he quitted Scinde, and generously
obtained permission to recall him to service there; but these
things were only the measure of the General's liberality, not
of Outram's ability, and they were responded to by gross
public follies, private treachery, and persevering calumny.

CHAPTER V.

AT Sukkur Sir C. Napier found the following instructions, reiterating Lord Ellenborough's policy.

" Should any Ameer or chief, with whom we have a treaty of alliance and friendship, have evinced hostile designs against us during the late events, which may have induced them to doubt the continuance of our power, it is the present intention of the Governor-General to inflict upon the treachery of such ally and friend so signal a punishment as shall effectually deter others from similar conduct ; but the Governor-General would not proceed in this course without the most complete and convincing evidence of guilt in the person accused. The Governor-General relies entirely on your sense of justice, and is convinced that whatever reports you may make upon the subject, after full investigation, will be such as he may safely act upon."

Written in September, four months after the warning letter to the Ameers, and after receiving Outram's reports of their hostile proceedings with his opinion that the Governor-General might dictate any terms, this dispatch shews how entirely adverse Lord Ellenborough was to violent procedure against the rulers of Scinde. Necessity forced him to be stern in maintenance of actual engagements, but his desire was to forward by peaceful means a mutually beneficial intercourse ; his ultimate object being, as he said in another place, " the establishment of unrestricted trade between all the countries of the Indus the sea and the Himalayas." He threw the moral responsibility of military action upon the General, and not unreasonably. Deep therefore is the feeling of truth with which the proofs of that General's unsullied honour and humanity are now recorded ; for he went not to work shackled and bound as a mere executive officer ; he had a wide discretion, and an awful charge upon his conscience from a confiding superior to do what was right and just according to the light afforded him. Whether he responded with a worthy spirit, or disclosed sordid sanguinary feelings as prating politicians and writers infamous in their declamation have asserted, let mankind decide upon the facts now to be related—and the deity he will be found invoking aloud from the midst of the dead after battle will decide hereafter.

It has been shewn how, amidst their splendid flattery at Hydrabad, Sir C. Napier warned the Ameers that it would thenceforth be unsafe to break their engagements. The offences he specified were, the levying of duties at the port on goods going to the British cantonment; of tolls on the river, of the isolating the British station by driving their subjects from the bazaar. The first was a violation of the XII and XIII articles of the treaty of 1839. The second an infraction of ·XI article. The last was a breach of the first article, of the preamble, and of the whole spirit of the treaty, which professed amity and free intercourse, and was of deep interest. The Ameers justified this by reference to article V, which forbad the British Government to receive complaints from the Ameers' subjects. The General met the subterfuge, by shewing that the charge came from the British authorities, not from the Ameers' subjects. To this they could not reply, but as to the tolls they drew a nice distinction. It was true, tolls were not to be levied, yet that applied only to foreigners. And when the words of the article, precise and positive, making no such distinction, were shewn to them they answered, we did not understand it so or we should have opposed an article depriving us of revenue without any explanation.

·Practically they had levied those tolls without hindrance up to 1840, and though Outram then opposed the practice, he advocated the Ameers' view of the matter with Lord Auckland, in opposition to Pottinger who made the treaty, and had, through the native agent and the English assistants, insisted on the text of the treaty being the rule. Mr. Ross Bell also had denied the Ameers' interpretation. Outram indeed discovered, or rather said he had discovered, that the native political agent had intercepted Pottinger's communications: he therefore pertinaciously urged the Ameers' view; supporting his arguments with Benjamin Franklin's authority, viz.—" *That no objects of trade warranted the spilling of blood,—that commerce is to be extended by the cheapness and goodness of commodities,—that the profit of no trade could equal the expense of compelling it by fleets and armies.*" Sound maxims curiously miscomprehended. There was no forcing of commerce; it was a simple question of duties under treaty. Franklin meaned that nations cannot be forced to trade; nor to abandon trade, and that to use force is wicked and foolish. Here some four or five barbarous despots were to be restrained from injuring trade. Outram's pedantry and logic were misapplied.

But the most notable circumstance attending this dispute was the glaring inutility of the political agents. Largely paid, numerous, and lauded for some occult masonic knowledge of Eastern people, which only the initiated could understand, they were deceived, baffled, laughed at by their own native agent, and by the barbarian Ameers alike—not once, or for a moment, but constantly, and upon an important article of a treaty negotiated by themselves: a treaty affecting the commerce of the Indus, the main object of their diplomacy! At the end of three years this vital point was still a subject of dispute! To write long letters in self-praise; to describe the dress of one Prince, the compliments of another, the feasts of a third; to be the hero of a newspaper, to have innumerable clerks for writing nonsense; to employ hundreds of camels to carry personal baggage, to let the real business of the state slip from their hands, and then call for an army to pick it up—this was to be a political agent: one who " *knew the people.*"

Lord Ellenborough was more than justified in his sweeping reform: and it was the mischievous effect of the loose diplomacy employed, that induced Sir C. Napier to assume a frank and stern tone of remonstrance from the first, as more befitting the dignity of such a powerful Government as the Anglo-Indian. He knew that though morals and customs differ, man is intrinsically the same and governed by his passions: wherefore he held it shameful to tempt

the Ameers by infirmity of purpose to display arrogance
when the Governor-General was ready to bare the sword in
vengeance.

They had however been excited by an unsteady diplomacy to offensive acts, and he was to make a faithful report
of their misdeeds. This he effected twelve days after his
arrival at Sukkur; sending a list of overt acts more or less
grave, but all proving a design for war when opportunity
should offer. Supported by evidence, as good as could be
obtained where the secret machinations of princes who had
the power and the will to destroy those who informed against
them were to be laid open, this list amply warranted the
imposition of a fresh treaty.

Against Roostum of Kyrpoor was proved—secret intercourse with foreign states, contrary to treaty and hostile to
the British; maltreatment of British public servants; obstructing the navigation of the Indus; illegal imprisonment
of British subjects, and by the agency of his minister, aid-
ing the escape of Mohamed Shurreef, a public enemy.

Against Nusseer of Hydrabad—the assembling of troops
to attack Shere Mohamed of Meerpoor, upon a boundary
dispute which had been referred to the British arbitration;
perfidiously inveigling the assistant political agent to meddle
privately in a dispute between the Ameer and his subjects,
and then charging this, his own act, against the British
Government as a breach of treaty; repeated wilful violations
of the eleventh article of the treaty, with an avowed determination to set it aside; delaying the transfer of Shikarpoor when he heard of the disasters in Affghanistan;
secretly coining base money to defraud the British Government in the payment of tribute; exacting illegal tolls,
refusing to refund, and obstructing the navigation and commerce of the Indus; opposing the free supply of the bazaar
at Kurrachee, and preventing his subjects from settling and
trading in the British cantonment; employing troops to
menace the possession of another Ameer when the dispute
had been referred to the British authorities, thus violating
the third article of the treaty, which guaranteed to each
Ameer his separate dominions—neglect of tribute, and

finally exciting by letter, Beebruck, the chief of the Booghtee tribe, to take up arms against the British troops, who were he said, retreating worsted from *Khorassan*, the Persian name for Affghanistan.

These offences had been continued from early in 1841, up to September 1842, shewing a settled enmity; and at the very moment of Sir C. Napier's arrival at Sukkur, Nusseer and Roostum, contracted a secret alliance and confederacy, offensive and defensive, against the British power. They sought to draw Ali Moorad into their views, they prepared to send away their wives and children, they collected troops, enlisted many of the Affghans who had followed England's column from Quettah, issued instructions to all their feudatory chiefs to be in readiness to take the field, and held councils with the chiefs of the Murrees and other tribes. The English troops, they said, were so weak miserable and sickly they could not resist: and if they were healthy, " had they not been driven from Affghanistan! Let the priests therefore, proclaim a religious war against the Feringee caffirs! When they went against Khorassan and Cabool, they made us promise three lacs of rupees yearly for tribute. Now they have been driven from thence, and we have an answer ready when the money is demanded! "

Here were ample grounds for a resort to force. Did Lord Ellenborough seize the opportunity? Did his General advise him to do so? The answer to these questions will place their conduct in a true light, each on its own pedestal, for their distinct position must always be kept in view.

Lord Ellenborough knew all the odious process by which the treaties, giving him the right to resent these hostile measures of the Ameers were obtained. The General knew nothing of them, the official correspondence explaining them was not then published; he could not suspect its nature; he could not ask for it, nor would it have been given to him if he had. He could only look at the treaties as contracts voluntarily made, and which he was in Scinde to uphold, both as a political agent and as a military officer. He saw friendship, alliance, and protection accepted by the weaker power; with the promotion of trade, commerce and navigation, and the improvement of the people's condition. He saw those people, of all classes, crowding into the British cantonments to avoid the grinding exactions and barbarous tyranny of rulers, who, debauched and ignorant, were trampling down with the hoofs of wild beasts one fourth of the fertile land which should have fed starving multitudes. It was with this suffering and wickedness on one side, this promise of remedy on the other before his eyes, that Sir C. Napier made that report to Lord Ellenborough which was to determine the latter's course of action.

But Lord Ellenborough's right to act must be considered, or there can be no just judgment. It was the right of necessity, the right of self-preservation, a necessity he had not produced, but had found. In that consists the justice of his course, which would otherwise have been but a continuation of Lord Auckland's aggressive policy : with this palliation, that Lord Ellenborough sought no aggrandisement, put forth no mocking pretensions of friendship to cover injustice. Standing on treaties concluded, he pursued the general interests of humanity, disregarding only the conventional rights of besotted tyrants, men who themselves trampled upon all rights, and were ever ready, sword in hand, to take from their neighbours.

The origin of the Scindian war being thus placed on a sound basis for fair discussion, the following view taken by Sir C. Napier will be more readily appreciated.

"It is not for me to consider how we came to occupy Scinde, but to consider the subject as it now stands. We are here by right of treaties entered into by the Ameers, and therefore stand on the same footing as themselves; for rights held under treaty are as sacred as the right which sanctions that treaty. There does not appear any public protest registered against the treaties by the Ameers, they are therefore to be considered as free expressions of the will of the contracting parties.

"The English occupy Shikarpoor, Bukkur, and Kurrachee by treaties, 'which, if rigidly adhered to by the Ameers, would render those Princes more rich and powerful, and their subjects more happy than they now are. If stick-

G

lers for abstract right maintain—as no doubt they will—that
to prevent a man from doing mischief is to enslave him, then
it may be called hard to enforce a rigid observance of these
treaties.   But the evident object of the treaties is to favour
our Indian interests, by abolishing barbarism and amelio-
rating the condition of society, by obliging the Ameers to do,
in compliance with those treaties, that which honourable and
civilized rulers would do of their own accord. It is necessary
to keep this in view, because though the desire to do good
would not sanction a breach of treaty, it does sanction the
exacting a rigid adherence to the treaties by the Ameers;
and the more so that their infractions of them evinces the
barbarism of those Princes, their total want of feeling for their
subjects, and their own unfitness to govern a country. These
things must be kept in mind, or what I am about to say will
appear unjust, which is not the case.

" By treaty, the time for which we may occupy our
present camps is unlimited; but there is such hostility to us
on the part of the Ameers, such a hatred of the treaties,
such a resolution to break them in every way—there is
amongst their people such a growing attachment to British
rule, that the question arises, whether we shall abandon the
interests of humanity and those of the British Government,
which in this case are one, and at once evacuate Scinde, or
take advantage of existing treaties and maintain our camps
permanently ?

" If we evacuate the country, future events will inevitably
bring us back to the banks of the Indus.   If we remain, our
camps will soon be filled with the Ameers' subjects flying
from oppression. These camps will quickly grow into towns,
and the people within them will carry on a transit trade along
the Indus, to the exclusion of the subjects of the Ameers
without.   Among the latter misery and poverty will sojourn,
for the exactions of the Ameers will in a great measure
destroy both commerce and agriculture among their people.

" This produces another question : can such a state of
things long continue ?   A government hated by its subjects,
despotic, hostile alike to the interests of the English and of
its own people; a government of low intrigue, and so con-

stituted that it must in a few years fall to pieces by the vice of its construction—will not such a government maintain an incessant petty hostility against us? Will it not incessantly commit breaches of treaties, those treaties by which alone we have any right to remain in this country and must therefore rigidly uphold? I conceive such a state of political relations cannot last, the more powerful government will at no distant period swallow up the weaker. Would it not be better to come to the results at once? I think it would be better, *if it can be done with honesty.* Let me then consider how we might go. to work on a matter so critical, and whether the facts to which I have called your attention will bear me out in what I propose.

" Several Ameers have broken treaty in the various instances stated in the accompanying ' *Return of Complaints.*' I have maintained that we want only a fair pretext to coerce the Ameers; and I think these various acts recorded give abundant reason to take Kurrachee, Sukkur, Bukkur, Shikarpoor, and Subzulcote for our own, and for obliging the Ameers to leave a track way along both banks of the Indus. Stipulating for a supply of wood, but at the same time remitting all tribute, and arrears of tribute, in favour of those Ameers whose conduct has been correct; and finally, entering into a fresh treaty with one of those Princes alone as chief. I cannot think such a procedure would be dishonourable or harsh. I am sure it would be humane. The refractory Ameers break the treaty to gratify their avarice, and we punish that breach. I perceive no injustice.

" If it be determined to keep Sukkur and Bukkur, I think it would not be politic to give up Shikarpoor. The town of Sukkur stands on an elbow of the Indus, which surrounds the town on two sides; on the other two, at about four miles distance, it is closed in by a large jungle, through which passes the road to Shikarpoor where the jungle finishes. If we evacuate Shikarpoor, the robber tribes will descend from the hills and establish themselves in the jungle, Sukkur will be blockaded, and no one be able to move beyond the chain of sentries without being murdered. To clear this jungle with infantry will be impossible; the robbers will retreat,

and when the troops retire again occupy the jungle. But if
Shikarpoor is occupied, a body of cavalry stationed there
could spread along the outskirts of the jungle, while infantry
would by concert push from Sukkur through the wood. The
robbers, thus cut off from the hills, would receive such a terrible punishment as to deter other tribes from trying the
same experiment.

"As a commercial point, Shikarpoor is of considerable
importance. It offers a depôt for goods from the north and
west, with the countries of which it has long possessed channels of communication. Adverse circumstances may for a
while interrupt these, but under a firm protecting government
they would soon be re-opened. Shikarpoor goods would be
then sent to Sukkur, there to be shipped on the Indus; and
they would also be passed by land to Larkaana, and thence
to Kurrachee. These seem to have been formerly the lines
of trade; they are geographically and naturally so, and will
therefore quickly revive. But if Shikarpoor be left to the
mercy of the surrounding freebooters commerce cannot thrive;
nor, without Shikarpoor be strongly guarded, can it pass
through the jungle to Sukkur. These two towns naturally
support each other in commerce.

"In a political view Shikarpoor has the advantage of
being chiefly inhabited by a Hindoo population, tolerated for
ages by the Mussulmans, and consequently forming a pacific
link of intercourse between us and the nations north and west.
Through Shikarpoor these Hindoos will gradually filter the
stream of commerce, and be the means of social intercourse
between the Mahomedans and ourselves, in time uniting those
who will not abruptly amalgamate. Shikarpoor contains
many rich banking houses, which is a sure evidence of its
being a central point of communication between surrounding
countries, and, consequently, one where the British Government would learn what was going on in Asia. The money
market is generally the best political barometer.

"The robber tribes in the neighbourhood have kept down
this town in despite of its natural and acquired advantages;
in fact, the robber is every where the master, therefore all
around is barbarous; and barbarous must continue to be till

civilization gradually encroaches on these lawless people, and
I think Shikarpoor is precisely one of those grand positions
which ought to be seized in that view. I have therefore
directed Major-General England not to evacuate that town
till further instructions are received from the Governor-
General.

" I have drawn up this memorandum entirely on my own
consideration of the subject; but since Major Outram's arrival,
which took place when I had finished the last paragraph, he
has given me every possible assistance. He concurs in all I
have said, but, at the same time, he has added much to my
local knowledge, and in justice to the Ameers I must, with
this increase of information, enlarge upon what I have stated.

" The Ameers say, they did not understand article XI of
the treaty to prohibit the levying of tolls on their own subjects. They urge, in proof of this misconception, that they
resisted the treaty because of other articles less important,
yet never objected to article XI because they relied on
article V. This may be, and I would willingly, if possible,
suppose that they really did conceive the treaty gave them
tolls on their own subjects; but they have attempted to levy
tolls on the boats of the Khan of Bhawalpore, which the treaty
assuredly does not give them a right to do; and they have
fired into the boats of merchants from Bhawalpore. The
treaty could not have been misconstrued on these points, and
therefore I do not believe they misconstrued article XI, but
broke it purposely. The treaty has also been broken by
treasonable correspondence, and other vexatious acts, as set
forth in the return of complaints.

" Now, what punishment do I propose for their misconduct? Injury to their family? No! Injury to their
subjects? No! What then? The reduction of their territory by four places, two of which, Sukkur and Bukkur are
barren spots, yielding no revenue; the other two, Kurrachee
and Shikarpoor, towns nearly ruined by their tyranny, and
for one of which, Shikarpoor, we have negotiations pending.
To obtain these places in seignorage, it is proposed to remit
all tribute in arrear, and for the future withdraw our resident
from Hydrabad, ensure the amelioration of the impoverished

state in which their subjects languish, and, in time, add to the power and wealth of the Ameers themselves by opening the commerce of the river. To their selfish feelings, their avarice and love of hunting, ought such great general interests to be sacrificed? I think not. The real interests of the Ameers themselves demand that their puerile pursuits and blind avaricious proceedings should be subject to a wholesome control, which their breaches of treaties and our power give us at this moment a lawful right to exercise, and the means of peaceably enforcing. If any civilized man were asked this question: 'Were you the ruler of Scinde, what would you do?' His answer would be: 'I would abolish the tolls on the rivers, make Kurrachee a free port, protect Shikarpoor from robbers, make Sukkur a mart for trade on the Indus. I would make a track-way along its banks, I would get steamboats.' Yet all this is what the Ameers dread.

"They have broken treaties, they have given a pretext, and I have a full conviction, perhaps erroneously, that what I propose is just and humane. I will go farther, and say, as Nusseer Khan of Hydrabad has openly broken the treaty, if the Governor-General chooses to punish him, he may justly seize the district of Subzulcote and give it to the Khan of Bhawalpore, as I have understood there was some intention of doing.

"The second point to which Major Outram has drawn my attention is a very strong one. He tells me, the tribes on the river, above that part possessed by the Ameers of Scinde, do levy tolls, and that there is no treaty or public document forthcoming, in virtue of which we can call upon the Ameers even of Upper Scinde not to levy tolls upon their own subjects. It is therefore evident that to call upon the Ameers of Hydrabad to desist from levying tolls and to allow the tribes above them on the river to do so, would be unjust; that is to say, it would be unjust to allow the others to levy tolls, but not unjust to prevent the Ameers from doing so. The answer to the argument: 'That tolls are levied on the Northern Indus' is just this. Say to those Northern tribes, 'We have, with great trouble secured to your boats a free passage on the river through Scinde; we are resolved to open the com-

merce of that great highway of nations, and you, who receive
benefit thereby, must join in this measure leading to the good
of all and to the loss of none.' Wherefore to excuse the
Ameers upon the ground that others are not equally coerced,
is answered by coercing the others.

"Having thus given the best view I can take of this
intricate subject, I shall accompany this report by various
documents, among which there is one giving a kind of return,
if I may so call it, of the accusations against the Ameers,
upon which accusations, (relative to which I have read every
paper,) I have founded my opinion of their conduct; and by
referring to this return, it will be seen whether I have justly
estimated the complaints made against them by the political
agents. I have also added the documents verifying each
transaction. I have caused Major Outram to give me a
memorandum of the state in which the treaty with the
Ameers for the purchase of Shikarpoor remains, as it has
been in abeyance since last year. From this memorandum
it would appear, that in addition to the great advantages for
Sukkur which would attend the occupation of Shikarpoor,
this district would be a very valuable acquisition in point of
revenue in time; and would with the aid of Kurrachee cover
the expense of guarding our newly-acquired towns on the
banks of the Indus. Should it hereafter be deemed proper to
make the proposed arrangements with the Ameers so as to
punish those who have broken the treaty, the details of such
arrangements can be easily made. The transfer of tribute
due, would adequately repay whatever portions of the districts
in question belong to the Ameers whose conduct has been
loyal."

Appended to this memoir was a table of the value of each
town to be taken from the Ameers, the amount of tribute, to
be remitted, being balanced against the gross sum, which
gave a money gain to those Princes of more than thirty thousand rupees yearly; an overplus to be offered as an equivalent
for the right of cutting fuel along the banks of the river, the
wood to be paid for besides.

The view of affairs thus taken was transmitted to the
Governor-General before a knowledge of the recent confede-

racy and warlike measures of the Ameers had placed them
in a worse position; and for a man seeking occasion to
war, those last furnished ample reasons to draw the sword.
But never did Sir C. Napier desire aught but peace and
justice. Calmly he had reasoned on general grounds, and
reached conclusions with a full conviction of their honesty
and humanity; hence the hostile confederacy of the Ameers
disturbed him not. He knew them to be debauched men,
habitually intoxicated with "*bhang;*" saw that their measures though hasty and violent were adopted more in defence
than offence, as thinking their dominions were to be wrested
from them, and thus laconically noticed them. "*The Ameers
are nervous, and these ebullitions are the result.*" But though
the confederacy was an ebullition, it was only one of many
springing from a fixed resolution to throw off the yoke imposed by Lord Auckland, and such ebullitions became more
frequent and violent as the state of affairs in Affghanistan
became more or less favourable to the British.

The nature of the Ameers' rule of sovereignty and
succession was another source of mischief.

At every death possessions were split, each portion
carrying with it sovereign power, to be exercised in the
worst spirit of cruelty and rapacity. Hence jealousies,
hatreds, and civil dissensions, were added to horrible debauchery, and ignorance among the rulers; and under the
combined action of evil and hateful influences the whole
race of Scindees were being exterminated. The land was
becoming a wilderness, a few years would have inevitably
terminated the Talpoor dynasty, and the occupation of the
ruined country by the wild robber tribes would have been
certain. Their vicinity to the Anglo-Indian frontier would
have produced collisions, and provoked conquest at a later
date. These considerations made Lord Ellenborough's resolution just, necessary, and praiseworthy; nothing being
opposed, save a past wrong offered to sensual tyrants, by a
former Governor-General. Taking therefore his General's
report as a basis, he proceeded to punish bad faith, and
reward good faith; yet cautiously and with a marked anxiety
to be just, and even merciful.

Roostum's letter to the Maharajah, and the part taken by his minister, Mohamed Ghoree, in the escape of Shurreef, affixed the character of an enemy on that Ameer. Nusseer of Hydrabad's letter to Beebruck Booghtee, placed him in the same category. But, said the Governor-General, these acts must be clearly traced home to the Ameers ere any demand in reparation can be justly made. Wherefore repeating his former reasons for obtaining territory rather than tribute, he proposed to base the new arrangements upon that principle. Referring also to a great scheme he was revolving for establishing uniformity of money throughout India, he resolved to bring Scinde within its operation; but in deference to the importance which all native Princes attached to the right of coinage as a mark of sovereignty, he purposed to unite the device of the Scindian rulers with the device of England, the latter bearing the expense.

The cutting of fuel for the steamers along the banks of the Indus he insisted upon, yet directed that in practice the Ameers' feeling about their *Shikargahs* should be respected as much as possible.

As to territory he had no wish, he said, to obtain more than was absolutely necessary to secure the command of the Indus, and therefore, whatever surplus might be taken from the Ameers in the way of penalty, or in exchange for tribute, would be given to the Khan of Bhawalpore, as a reward for his unvarying friendship. A gift peculiarly fitting, as restoring territory unjustly wrested from him by the offending Ameers; which restoration would also give an uninterrupted line of communication through friendly states, from the British Station at Ferozepore to that in Upper Scinde.

For the military command of the Indus, he required Sukkur, Roree and Bukkur in Upper Scinde, Tatta and Kurrachee in Lower Scinde; most of them, as Sir C. Napier had observed, sterile places, and for which tribute to a greater amount than their worth was to be remitted.

" My ultimate object, said Lord Ellenborough, is the entire freedom of internal trade throughout the whole territory between the Hindoo Khosh, the Indus and the sea; and I only await the favourable occasion for effecting this purpose, and for introducing uniformity of currency within the same limits. To these great benefits, to be enjoyed equally by 140 millions of people, I desire ultimately to add the abolition of all tributes payable by one state to another, and the substitution of cessions of territory, so made by means of mutual exchanges, as to bring together in masses the dominions of the several sovereigns and chiefs."

Such changes, if effected without shocking the national feelings of the different people transferred, would have been a noble scheme to benefit a fifth part of the human race, and would alone have warranted a revision of the treaties with the Ameers by the force of negotiation ; but the justice of a revision by force of arms, could only rest on the violations of existing contracts. The demand for territory was a punishment, to be inflicted on proof of secret negotiations for an armed confederacy against the British ; and to obtain that proof the General was exhorted to use his utmost diligence. Meanwhile the draft of a new treaty, embodying the Governor-General's views, was sent to him, in which a distinction was made in favour of Sobdar, whose supposed unvarying faith, he not being under any tribute which could be remitted, was to be repaid by an accession of territory equal to 50,000 rupees yearly.

The required proofs were soon obtained, yet by a most rigid process. The General, taking an acknowledged seal of Nusseer, compared it with that attached to the intercepted letter to Beebruck ; they appeared similar, but when with a minute earnestness he measured each letter and their distances in both, with a pair of compasses, a difference was perceptible. He was however assured that to have two seals, thus differing to deceive, was notoriously the custom of the Ameers, and therefore desired the persons who had intercepted the letter, to procure for him also the secret seal of the Prince. This they tried but could not do, and thus removed all suspicion of treachery, seeing, that a second forgery would have secured the object of the first. No person, English or native, cognizant of the Ameer's signet, doubted the authenticity of the intercepted seal; but their assertions the General would not accept as proof, and thus delayed his decision. At last he obtained an authentic paper with the secret signet seal of Nusseer attached, and it was precisely the same as that on the intercepted letter, the writing accompanying the undoubted seal being known as that of the Ameer's favourite moonshee or scribe. The proof was therefore complete that the Ameer had urged Beebruck Booghtee to fall on the British; he had also urged the Moultan man, though less openly, to the same course, and with effect, for he raised troops and diligently fortified his capital.

Roostum's intercourse with the Maharajah was likewise proved by his seal, the authenticity of which was never questioned, and by the concurrent testimony of persons conversant with such matters as to the style and verisimilitude of thought; but the writing was that of his minister, and Roostum was old, and nearly imbecile from debauchery; wherefore Outram suggested that the minister might have affixed the seal of the Ameer without his knowledge. This fastidious delicacy of doubt, by a man who had so recently assured the Governor-General that the Ameer's conduct would justify the imposition of any terms, was put aside by this question from the General, " *If a Prince blindly gives his power and his signet to his minister, is such folly to excuse him from the consequences ?* " Subsequently, Roostum's culpable knowledge was established, and the General, who had been charged by Lord Ellenborough to draw up and present the new treaty to the Ameers when the proofs of delinquency were complete, was now empowered to choose his own commissioner to conduct the details of the negotiation. And such was the confidence reposed in his judgment to carry through this affair by diplomacy or arms, that the Governor-General left him master of both, observing only, " that he could make no concession before a native power which was collecting troops, nominally for defensive purposes, but which the least wavering would direct to purposes of aggression."

Sir C. Napier thus became arbiter of peace and war; on his head rested the responsibility, moral and political, of enforcing the treaty; in his hands were life and death for thousands; the fate of Scinde depended on his word, the fate of India perhaps on the stroke of his sword. He was an untried general, but what his friends had always known him to be he shewed himself to the world—a man of strong heart and subtile genius, sagacious in perception, ready in expedients, and of heroic daring: his fiery courage supported by a pure conscience was tempered by the gentlest feelings, and a generous spirit which spurned dishonour in whatever garb it came. " I will," he wrote to the man who had so confidingly placed him in this post of difficulty and danger, " *I will present your treaty to the Ameers. I will spare no pains to convince them, that neither injury nor injustice are meditated, and that by accepting the treaty they will become more rich, and more secure of power than they now are. If they refuse to listen to reason, if they persist in sacrificing every thing to their avarice and their hunting grounds, they must even have their way, and try the force of arms at their peril if they are so resolved.*"

With what an insane fury they did rush to arms shall be shewn hereafter.

CHAPTER VI.

SIR Charles Napier had early applied himself to the organization and discipline of his troops, for they were generally inexperienced. He drew them out frequently, and accustomed them to move in masses; he taught them by counsel also, and exhorted them to a subordinate and modest conduct towards the people. Nor was he sparing of a quaint humour which no danger or suffering has ever abated. Broad at times the stream of that humour flowed, yet never sunk to buffoonery, being always illustrative, conveying instruction and even rebuke in a laughing guise: with a jest he won the soldiers' hearts, for they felt their General regarded them as comrades and not as slaves. Thus, when some insolent and silly young men persisted, insubordinately, to ride violently through the camp and the bazaars, causing frequent accidents, he issued the following characteristic order, bringing ridicule and fear at once to bear on the offenders.

" Gentlemen as well as beggars, if they like, may ride to the devil when they get on horseback; but neither gentlemen nor beggars have a right to send other people to the devil, which will be the case if furious riding be allowed in the bazaar. The Major-General has placed a detachment of horse at the disposal of Captain Pope, who will arrest offenders and punish them, as far as the regulations permit. And Captain Pope is not empowered to let any one escape punishment, because, when orders have been repeated and are not obeyed it is time to enforce them—without obedience an army becomes a mob and a cantonment a bear garden: the enforcement of obedience is like physic, not agreeable but necessary."

He had now eight thousand fighting men; but some were

at Kurrachee, and from the Sukkur force the Bengal troops
were to be detached to Ferozepore. Lord Ellenborough empowered him to retain these last, and even offered reinforcements, but he refused them, keeping the Bengal people
back however for a time. He was also charged with a new
organization of the political establishment in Scinde, having
authority to regulate both numbers and salaries, and he
made a great reduction in both. Outram then returned to
Bombay, telling the General that with the reduced establishment he would not be able to conduct the public business:
yet he did conduct it, and most successfully, when it was ten-
fold greater than any which had fallen under Outram's direction. This reduction excited all the brutish violence of
the editors of Indian newspapers, and their obstreperous
cries deafened the Eastern community, Doctor Buist, of
the *Bombay Times*, being the most dissonant and shrill.

During these transactions, the excitement of the Ameers
increased, and the cessation of Outram's functions alarmed and
offended those of Lower Scinde. They called it a slight,
and pretended to view it as a preliminary for transferring
their country to the Affghans—the real objection being that
they judged the evacuation of Affghanistan by Pollock,
Nott, and Colonel England, to be the result of weakness;
thence conceiving new hopes, and having gauged Outram's
capacity and vanity, they thought it easier to dupe him than
the General, of whose temper they had made trial by sending
him a present of six thousand pounds, which he returned by
the bearer.

Futteh Mohamed Ghoree for Roostum and his sons; Ali
Moorad for himself, and a vakeel for Nusseer of Hydrabad,
now separately demanded conferences with the General. He
acceded to Roostum's request, desiring him to fix the day
most agreeable to himself, and even offered to cross the
Indus and meet him in his own gardens away from the
troops and unattended. Unable to appreciate this frankness,
the Ameer thought it a scheme to entrap him, and instead
of keeping tryst held a general council, where their real
feelings were disclosed. The sons and nephews of Roostum,
jealous of the Ghoree's influence, reproached the old Ameer

for offering to meet the Feringee at all, saying, Futteh's
counsel would destroy him. Even Ali Moorad here acted
with the others, and being the ablest and boldest assumed
the ascendant. He declared he would send a separate vakeel
to ascertain what the General desired; if it were money or
territory he would refuse both, and place the country in
keeping of the Beloochees—in other words declare war, for
the Beloochees were feudatory troops, eager for pay and
commotion, it being their custom in times of trouble to
despoil the labouring and mercantile people.

When the council broke up Roostum's sons took Patan
horsemen into pay, and wrote to the Boordees and other
plundering tribes to get ready for war; at the same time
the Brahooe Prince, Newaz Khan, who had been deposed in
favour of Merab's son, and was living on the bounty of the
Anglo-Indian Government at Shikarpoor, resigned his allowance and rejoined his tribe. Futteh Ghoree made a fruitless
attempt to recover his influence over Roostum when the
sons had separated, but was finally fain to accept a mission
to Roree as the agent of Ali Moorad, whose voice was now
to decide on peace or war. Letters also came from Nusseer
of Hydrabad, encouraging Roostum, and promising the aid
of troops under the command of his son and nephew, the
two Hoosseins. At the same time Shere Mohamed of Meerpoor was constituted commander of the forces in Lower
Scinde, and he promised to add sixteen thousand fighting
men of his own to the general levy.

Roostum, thus swayed, not only avoided the conference,
but assigned fear of treachery as his reason. He also wrote
to the Hydrabad Ameers, reproaching them for delay in
collecting forces, and warned all the fighting men of his own
villages to take arms. His revenue was then collected with
unusual rigour and violence; Sadig the accomplice of Shurreef was invited to Kyrpoor, and Patans, that is Affghan
horsemen, continued to reinforce the younger Ameers, who
held vaunting language about the British. In fine the
whole country was in commotion, the hill tribes assembled,
and the Moultan man continued his warlike preparations,
having no ostensible reason. Soon Roostum and his family

gathered two thousand men as a guard, and then again demanded a conference with the General, to take place four miles from Roree, down the river. This, seeing their condition, and resentful of the former failure, he refused. The Ameer proposed to hold it as before arranged in his garden, but was thus answered, " I will not go. I will not suffer you to treat me with this rudeness and as a treacherous person."

Now the general agitation augmented, and the Ameers were heard to say—" *We have eat and drunk well for many years, and have enjoyed our Ameeree ; if it is the intention of the English to fight with us, without a doubt they shall find us ready for them.*" And one sanguinary monster advised that the throats of all their wives and children should be cut if the British advanced.

It is not difficult to trace the cause of these violent convulsive movements. The aggression of Lord Auckland had left a deep feeling of anger, and the disasters of the British at Cabool had awakened hopes of revenge and independence. The evacuation of Affghanistan seemed to them weakness, and Lord Ellenborough's policy, so publicly proclaimed, alarmed them, conscious as they were of secret feelings, as well as acts of hostility. Outram's plan of withholding the warning letters had therefore failed, because the Governor-General's resolution had been proclaimed to the world as his fixed policy ; meanwhile his secret instructions were guessed at, and magnified as usual by fear and hope. Territory or money they thought must be demanded, and the arrival of England's troops at Sukkur led them to imagine the demand would be large. While thus excited, they heard from their spies that the British troops were too sickly to take the field. Then with that sudden heat so common in barbarian councils they resolved on war ; but debauched, nervous, and cowardly—many of them being also habitually intoxicated with opium or bhang—their fears o'ermastered pride and anger, and they could take no firm resolution. They were nevertheless impelled forward by their feudatories, men of iron hardihood, fatalists, and delighting in war. Against this influence they had no counter-weight save their avarice ;

for the Beloochee fighting men were very costly and insatiable.

These antagonistic impulses rendered the Ameers' policy variable, and vacillating according to the prevailing influence of the hour. Hence their alternate arrogance and humbleness; their falsehood, their complaints, excuses and secret alliances, their cry of war one day, of peace the next. And with all this they had quarrels amongst themselves, and no general plan could well be agreed upon.

Ali Moorad and Sobdar of Hydrabad, being from policy averse to break off from the British alliance, soon made known their desires. Ali obtained a conference with the General, and at once asked if the English would secure the Turban of supremacy for him?

" We will adhere to treaties," was the reply. " They bind us to protect each Ameer in his rights. The Turban of the Talpoors is Roostum's, unless he forfeits it by hostility, and he shall keep it until he dies, when it will become yours if you continue to be a friend, because such is the order of succession, and such is the treaty."

" But will you protect Roostum if he seeks to give the Turban during his life to his son?"

" No! that will be against the treaty. We shall not do so."

Feeling satisfied with this, Ali Moorad asked if he and Sobdar, being of one mind, might make a secret treaty to support the British.

" Be faithful to the British! Yes! it is your duty, but openly. Make no secret compact. You have the existing treaties, adhere to them. The English are powerful enough to make all parties conform to them."

From this conference the English General drew these advantages. He displayed his resolution to act justly; he detached the most able and formidable of the Ameers from the family league, and thus diminished the chances of bloodshed; and he made a step towards reversing Lord Auckland's policy, by having only one responsible chief with whom to negotiate. He foresaw also that the numerous minor Ameers, those petty despots would thus be reduced to

H

the rank of rich noblemen, when Shikarpoor, then daily increasing in size and wealth under British protection, should become a great city.

During these demonstrations by the Ameers, he studied their characters, coming to the conclusion, that a steady policy, appearing not to see settled hostility yet checking all violations of existing treaties, would induce them to accept the new treaty which he had peremptory orders to present, when the proofs of past misconduct justified its enforcement. This also accorded with his military precautions, for he could not calculate on peace without being prepared for war. Hence he resolved to give time, and circumstances, which were hourly changing, their chances ere he bared a sword whose edge he desired to withhold.

" Nothing," he wrote to the Governor-General, " is lost by delay. We cannot be too cautious in securing firm moral ground on which to rest the defence of whatever events may arise. The Ameers also grow weaker, delay exhausts their treasury, and then they cheat their soldiers, who of course leave them. This also is the season of fevers on the banks of the Indus. Were hostilities to commence now, I should lose many men and have a large hospital. To move on Hydrabad I must go by the river or by the desert. To supply the sick by the last would be difficult if not impossible. To go by the river would augment the hospital. The Indus is falling, and when it is at the lowest the fevers will cease. Meanwhile I have a sickly camp, and I should have regretted if the Ameers had called me out before; now they are welcome. But all these considerations have made me hitherto avoid pressing them hard on any point.

" If I am forced to take the field, I will cross the Indus and march upon Hydrabad by land, for there are objections to dropping down the river. The water is low, boats go with difficulty when lightly laden; I cannot float more than a thousand men with guns and stores, and the vessels would even then be overladen, and ground perhaps for days on the mud within reach of matchlocks. Nothing can be gained by rapidity. The enemy has no position to fortify, no works to strengthen, no stronger place to retire upon; three or thir-

teen days' movement will therefore be the same; but by
land we go compact, to beat or be beaten altogether, whereas
crowded in boats straggling for miles along the river, and
half of them grounded in the shallows under matchlock-fire,
would lead to disaster. ' Slow and sure,' is an adage suited
to my position. Moving by land I shall take Kyrpoor at
once, and thus throw myself between the northern and
southern Ameers, for there need be no slowness when once
we take the field, if unfortunately the folly of the Ameers
goes that length."

Acting on these views he endeavoured to dissipate two
errors which buoyed these Princes up. These were the supposed helpless state of the troops, and the belief that the
greatest part of those fit for duty had been recalled to
Ferozepore for the army of reserve; which their imperfect
information and judgment led them to think was gathered
in fear to defend India, instead of being the prompt action
of a prudent man to awe the Punjaub. It is thus that
barbarians, however brave and naturally gifted, always shew
themselves incapable of great combinations in war. They
have neither the patience nor the knowledge to class the
parts of an extensive military plan of operation : they see
quickly, feel intensely and strike from impulse, vehemently
and even mightily at times, but against civilization it is
only the surge of waters scourging rocks.

Sir C. Napier, as before said, had stopped the march
of the Bengal troops, and now exhibited to Ali Moorad
more than 6000 fighting men of all arms, moving with
that precision and rapidity which barbarian commanders,
used only to irregular multitudes, can scarcely understand while they see its power. Lord Ellenborough also,
desirous to avoid bloodshed by an imposing display of
force, offered to reinforce the army with all the Bombay
troops under General Nott, which were however declined as
unnecessary.

But now continued infractions of treaty as to tolls in
Upper Scinde, accompanied with insult and violence, forced
the General to vindicate his own and Lord Ellenborough's

avowed policy, and he sent a staff officer with the following letter to Roostum:—

"A merchant has been made to pay toll by your Kardar, named Kaymah, at Dowlatpore. This is a breach of the VIII article of your treaty. It has taken place several times, although this is the first complaint laid before me. I would not have suffered the breach of a treaty in a single instance had I been aware of it, and every man who makes a well-founded complaint to me shall have redress. The sufferers in the present case accompany the bearer of this letter, who is one of my aides-de-camp, and he has my orders to insist upon your Highness' repaying the toll levied by your Kardar, and also all the expenses to which the sufferers have been exposed, amounting to the sum of 238 rupees. I further insist upon the offending Kardar being sent a prisoner to my head-quarters at Sukkur within the space of five days, to be dealt with as I shall determine. Unless your Highness does immediately comply with these demands, I shall consider the various and insulting violations of treaty have been committed with your sanction, and I shall treat you as an enemy. These are the orders of the Governor-General."

The money was instantly paid, and promise given to send the Kardar to Sukkur. But the imbecile Ameer, excited by false reports, and constantly intoxicated with "bhang," immediately held a great council with his feudatory chiefs, and his words proclaimed the disorder of his mind: "See," he exclaimed, "the English having been turned out of Affghanistan and eaten dirt, have been killed so far on their return to India. Their force is large, and if they will but leave Scinde I shall meet all demands for money, even to the jewellery of our women. If they do not leave Sukkur and Scinde, if they advance to Kyrpoor, we must fight them."

His warlike hearers placed their hands on the Koran in token of obedience to his orders.

After this council messengers were sent to raise the Boordees, a powerful tribe; but the General's recent menace had evidently shaken the Ameer's resolution; for in his former council neither land nor money was to be yielded, whereas money was now freely offered, and points of honour only spoken of. There was also dissension. Roostum avowed a design to give the Turban to his son Hoossein, in violation of Ali Moorad's right, and the latter's resolution to adhere to the English was, as the General expected, fixed. He went off to his fortress of Dejee-ka-kote, not far from Kyrpoor, and disbanded the fighting men in his pay. They were instantly hired by Hoossein, who told his imbecile father Roostum to retire from state affairs. Then increasing his own armed followers he gave orders to rob and slay all British stragglers, and made loud vaunts.

In this state of things, the favourable season for acting having set in, the General, who had finished his military preparations, and completed the proofs of the Ameers' previous hostility, without reference to their recent conduct, judged it time to present the new treaty, which he had been again peremptorily commanded to enforce. It was delivered in form to the Ameers of Upper Scinde on the 4th of December, and to the Ameers of Lower Scinde on the 6th of that month, together with official notes from Lord Ellenborough, marking the estimation in which the conduct of each Ameer was separately held by the Governor-General.

To the inferior Hydrabad Princes he expressed his dissatisfaction at their conduct, and required their assent to the treaty generally; yet he called their attention particularly to the remission of tribute, as proof of his desire to establish peace and friendship. To Nusseer he sent a distinct communication, enumerating his offences and interdicting all friendship until atonement was made.

The tone adopted towards Roostum was one of sorrow, that he, formerly well disposed, should now have been led by evil counsels to a secret hostile engagement with the Maharajah, and to aid the escape of the Syud Shurreef, whose object he knew was to war upon the British. These were violations of the old treaty, too serious to be entirely pardoned, and therefore he must accept the new treaty.

Sobdar of Hydrabad was favoured throughout, because he constantly leaned to the British alliance, and condemned his brother Ameers. But his conduct sprung from discontent at being deprived of his father's dignity by the anomalous law of succession; when the crisis came he was found more perfidious than any, and anxiously striving to betray both sides. The favour shewn to him proved that no unjust pretext for hostilities was sought : moreover the Meerpoor man was unmolested, because he had not acted offensively, though his sentiments were avowedly inimical.

The Ameers now displayed all their crooked diplomacy. Denying that they had violated the old treaty, they invited further investigation, knowing it could not be openly conducted, as the death of any person daring to appear against them would be prompt. They recurred, with force also because with truth, to the original wrong inflicted by Lord Auckland, yet with feigned humility professed submission to Lord Ellenborough. But they increased their forces, and ordered the tax-gatherers to extort from the districts which were to be ceded, not only the revenue of that year but of the next; their armed Beloochees plundered all the country between Sukkur and Shikarpoor ; their spies entered the British camp, and in their councils they arranged a general plan of campaign, to be noticed hereafter.

In Nusseer's protest, a remarkable assertion, characteristic of Scindian cunning merits particular notice, as shewing how little reliance could be placed on any statement of that Ameer. " I and Noor Mohamed," he said, " saw the advantage of seeking the protection of the wisest and most powerful nation on the earth, and therefore urged Sir Henry Pottinger, during two whole years, to come into the country, after which we finally succeeded in introducing a British force." Had this been true it would have justified the Auckland aggression, and, more forcibly, Lord Ellenborough's policy; but with such a display of falsehood how could the General believe in the profession of submission? He received it indeed with seeming satisfaction ; but though Roostum's assent to the new treaty, more humble and entire than Nusseer's, specifically acknowledged British supremacy, Sir C. Napier found the measures of both at variance with their protestations, and his position became painfully difficult. The Governor-General's orders were peremptory and reiterated. But passionate violent men were to be dealt with; who were neither masters of their own senses from habitual intoxication; nor masters of their actions from the rough influence of their armed feudatories, whose attendance they had invoked, but whose desire for war and plunder they could neither check nor control. His aversion to shed blood was intense, his sense of duty to his country equally so; yet he was responsible for the moral, political, and military results of the highest order at a crisis when the slightest error might lead to a battle, perhaps to a great disaster; when each hour brought change, for the vacillation of the Ameers was surprising. A strong head and brave heart carried him with a clear conscience through the trial.

Having sent the Bengal troops across the Indus, he was preparing to pass over another body, when he was told the Ameers only awaited this separation of his forces to assail his lines at Sukkur by night; and their constant intoxication rendered the intelligence probable. Wherefore he wrote to Roostum thus:—

"Your submission to the order of the Governor-General, and your friendship for our nation should be beyond doubt, because you have solemnly assured me of the same. We are friends. It is therefore right to inform you of strange rumours that reach me. Your subjects, it is said, propose to attack my camp in the night time. This would of course be without your knowledge, and also be very foolish, because my soldiers would slay those who attack them; and when day dawned I would march to Kyrpoor, transplant the inhabitants to Sukkur, and destroy your capital city, with the exception of your Highness's palace, which I would leave standing alone as a mark of my respect for your Highness, and of my conviction that you have no authority over your subjects. I should also so far entrench on your Highness's treasury as to defray the expenses of this operation, because it is just that all governments should pay for the mischief which their subjects inflict upon their neighbours. I therefore advertise your Highness of the destruction which such an attempt on my camp would inevitably draw down upon Kyrpoor, in order that you may warn your people against committing any such act of hostility."

This warning was effectual, and vakeels from Upper and Lower Scinde reached him with assurances from their masters that the new treaty should be accepted. These messages from Sobdar and Hoossein Ali of Hydrabad were cordially expressed; Nusseer and Meer Khan employed only general terms. But the General's secret intelligence still contradicted all their declarations. Ali Moorad was loyal: the others of Upper Scinde were daily augmenting their forces; their women had been sent from Kyrpoor; councils were continually held; and a communication from Nusseer was discovered, which disclosed their real views.

He complained to Roostum that " Sobdar and Hoossein were, like Ali Moorad, in the British interest, but all the chiefs of tribes and of the armed men were with him, Nusseer, and if Roostum was ready the sword should be drawn." That ancient Ameer also rebuked his sons for precipitation in sending off the women, saying, "the vakeels are at Sukkur to deceive. When the British regain confidence, and weaken their forces, the torch shall be lighted to consume them." The *däks*, or mails, were at the same time robbed, disorders were everywhere rife, and the Boordees promised to harass the Bengal troops if they marched towards Ferozepore. These furious proceedings and wild councils did not disturb the General's judgment. Infirmity of purpose and intoxication were to him apparent in them, and he anticipated no military opposition in Upper Scinde; but the verbal submission of the Ameers authorized, and the orders of the Governor-General enjoined him, to take possession of Subzulcote and Bhoong-Barra, which lay in his rear on the left bank of the Indus. Wherefore he passed that river with a considerable body of troops, sent the Bengal column to occupy those districts, and publicly proclaimed the policy of Lord Ellenborough, according to the terms of the treaty.

This passage of the river, effected in the middle of December, was an operation of some difficulty, and it was the first military measure in execution of Lord Ellenborough's

avowed policy. It was also a decisive one, rendering the
negotiation an armed parley. It remained to be seen, who
would strike who succumb. On one side was the strong
warrior armed in steel, brandishing a heavy but sheathed
weapon in warning, for his desire was peace — on the other
a crouching savage, urged by fury and hatred, troubled by
fear and doubt, yet constantly creeping forward knife in
hand.

A slight topographical notice is here necessary to render
the operations intelligible: wherefore, taking the British
stations in Upper Scinde as a point of departure, the march
of an army down the Indus on either bank shall be sketched.

Those stations were Shikarpoor and Sukkur on the right
bank; Roree on the left bank; and Bukkur between them
in the middle of the stream.

Shikarpoor, situated about twenty miles from the river,
in a plain, was on the high road to the Bolan pass.

Sukkur was on the bank of the Indus, and protected by
an entrenched cantonment.

Bukkur was a fortress.

Sir C. Napier's army, occupying Sukkur and Roree, had
the whole of the Ameer's country before it, except Shikarpoor
which was behind his right flanks, and the districts of Subzulcote and Bhoong-Barra which were behind his left flank.

Advancing by the right bank of the river he would pass
over an immense alluvial plain, bounded on the right by
the Hala mountains, on the left by the Indus, and intersected with canals, and smaller water-courses called nullahs,
some artificial, the most part formed by the annual inunda-
tions.

Sixty miles from Sukkur they would come upon Larkaana, a city near a minor river, or rather a canal, connected
with the Indus, called the Aral.

Marching onwards they would reach Sehwan, the site of
an ancient fortress, about one hundred miles from Larkaana,
where the Lukhee hills, shooting from the Hala range, close
in upon the river and form a pass. which renders Sehwan a
post of strategic importance, confirming the notion that it
was one of Alexander's stations.

From this pass the plain gradually opens out again by the continued divergence of the mountains from the course of the river, until it reaches the ocean, and gently spreads with a low and placid front, assuaging rather than opposing the fury of the waters.

Passing over this second plain the troops would have to their left Hydrabad, which lies on the other bank of the Indus some eighty miles below Sehwan, they would then reach Tatta, fifty miles below Hydrabad.

Near Tatta, formerly celebrated for its manufactures, but then, like all places under the abominable rule of the Ameers, sunk to ruin, the Indus, opening out like a fan, runs in many branches to the sea, forming a delta, intricate, swampy and unwholesome. The march of the troops to avoid this tangled country, would be to the right, leading through Garra, a town of some consequence, to Kurrachee, which lies close under the Hala range, and is the only safe and commodious port of Scinde—its distance from Tatta being about eighty miles.

From Roree, an army advancing down the left bank, would also pass over an immense plain, spotted with shikargahs and intersected with nullahs from one to sixty feet deep.

On their right would be the Indus, which makes however a wide sweep from Sukkur to Hydrabad, the convex towards the mountains, offering the chord for a march upon the latter town. Along this chord the main road run, but there were several routes, one following the winding of the river.

On the left was the great desert, which flowing as it were from the Punjaub hems in a narrow strip of fertile land, including Subzulcote and Bhoong-Barra, as far as Hydrabad, where it eases off gradually towards the east, leaving a wide space between it and the delta.

Fifteen miles from Roree the army would come upon Kyrpoor, the capital of Upper Scinde. At twenty-five miles it would confront the strong fortress of Dejee-ka-kote, crowning an isolated rock belonging to Ali Moorad, and supposed by the Beloochees to be impregnable.

At seventy or eighty miles from Roree it would enter
Nowshera, the last town possessed by that Ameer to the
south, bordering on Lower Scinde. From thence a march of
one hundred and twenty miles would bring it to Hydrabad,
the fortified capital of Lower Scinde, when, on its left, would
be Meerpoor, the fortified capital of Shere Mohamed.

There are several Meerpoors, but this capital is on the
very edge of the desert, at the distance of forty miles on a
right line drawn from Hydrabad eastward, which being
prolonged for fifty miles more falls on Omercote of the
desert, a strongly fortified town forming a post of connection between Meerpoor and the Bombay frontier.

It will now be understood, that by occupying Roree,
his left resting on the desert, Sir C. Napier barred the
Ameers of Kyrpoor from Subzulcote and Bhoong-Barra
while his Bengal troops seized those narrow districts behind
his position; thus he obtained the object of the treaty with
Roostum, without quitting the defensive, or provoking a
war, and exactly obeying the Governor-General's orders.
The Beloochees dared not attack him in this position, which
could be reinforced by the Bengal troops; they could not
pass his flank save by the desert, where with a short movement he could intercept them. They were indeed strong at
Larkaana on the right of the Indus, and might assail Sukkur which was hemmed in with jungle; but he had there
an entrenched pivot of movement, and relying on its strength
sought to quiet the Ameers by reason.

Lord Ellenborough had allowed him to choose a Commissioner for conducting the details of the new treaties, and
with a generous impulse he asked for Outram, thus risking
the Governor-General's displeasure. Lord Ellenborough,
acceded, reluctantly indeed, but, discarding personal feeling,
was unwilling to deprive the General of the supposed advantage of Outram's local experience: thus the latter was in
an evil hour recalled to Scinde. This act of kindness was
seized by newspapers in Outram's interest and under his
dictation, to extol his superior genius and capacity, and to
abase the reputations of Lord Ellenborough and Sir C.
Napier. The first was described as having basely driven a

remarkable man from his former political duties in Scinde; the second as presumptuously and ignorantly undertaking those duties without ability for the task; both as having plunged headlong into difficulties which they could no way escape from save by recalling their able victim. This absurd insolence, so characteristic of Indian newspapers, is best exposed by the following letter from the General to Lord Ellenborough on the occasion.

"*I have no intention of waiting for Major Outram's arrival, because till we get into the details of the treaty I do not want assistance; and as your Lordship has been so good as not to give me a colleague, I mean to consult no one. I see my way clearly.*"

Soon after this letter was written Outram arrived, with the newspaper reputation of having consummate knowledge of men and things in Scinde, knowledge acquired by experience and sustained by great natural capacity: yet he committed error upon error. With a dull, perverted perception of character, his experience did not prevent him from becoming a dupe to the Ameers' gross diplomacy; on no occasion did he display capacity, on many he displayed great ignorance, and on all great presumption. His pertinacity and vanity led to deplorable loss of life, and he would have caused the entire destruction of the army but for the superior intellect and resolution of his General, who he then tried to deceive and has ever since calumniated.

While passing the Indus Sir C. Napier discovered that Roostum's vakeels had brought money to corrupt the soldiers, had delayed the delivery of the Ameer's letters, and given all those Princes false hopes. This mischief he vigorously checked, writing thus to the Ameer. "The men you sent to Roree are robbing you. They will tell you that they are bribing my soldiers, and they extract money from your Highness under that pretext. If they were really bribing my soldiers to desert I would punish them, but they are doing no such thing—your Highness is robbed by your servants. However, if you are not robbed, and that, as they pretend, they were bribing my soldiers, it was high time to turn them out of Roree, which I have done, and if I find them attempting to disturb the loyalty of my troops it will be worse for them. Ameer, I have received my orders and will obey them. I laugh at your preparations for war. I want to prevent blood being shed : listen to my words— consult with your brother, his Highness Ali Moorad. Your own blood will not deceive you—your servants will. These men were four days in Roree, and did not deliver your letters to me; had I not sent for them, they would still have kept them from me to gain time that they might rob you. Eight days have passed, and I have not heard that your Highness has nominated a commissioner of rank to arrange the details of the treaty. I expect to have in writing your full acceptance of the draft thereof, by the return of the bearer. Your Highness is collecting troops in all directions, I must therefore have your acceptance of the treaty immediately—yea or nay. I will not lose the cold weather. You must be prompt, or I shall act without consulting your Highness ; my time is measured, and I cannot waste it in long negotiations.

" Your Highness' letter is full of discussion ; but as there are two sides of your river, so are there two sides to your arguments. Now the Governor-General has occupied both sides of your Highness' river, because he has considered both sides of your Highness' arguments. Many of your family have taken the same view of the case that the Governor-General has ; and the respect which they have shewn to the British Government is repaid to them by the Governor-General. But I cannot go into the argument—I am not Governor-General; I am only one of his commanders. I will forward your letter to him, if you wish me to do so ; but, in the mean time, I will occupy the territories which he has commanded me to occupy. You think I am your enemy—why should I be so? I gain nothing for myself; I take no gifts, I receive no Jagheers. What is it to me whether your Highness, or any other person, occupies the land? The Governor-General has given to you his reasons and to me his orders : they shall be obeyed."

This drew from Roostum an unmeaning public reply, but covering a secret message, to the effect, that being eighty-five years old he was oppressed by the younger members of his family and desired to take refuge in the British camp. It was an embarrassing proposition. Too favourable for a peaceful termination of the disputes to be rejected, it had however this drawback, that every proceeding of the Ameer would be imputed to coercion. The General therefore prevailed on Ali Moorad, who was then with him, to carry back the following written response :—" Your Highness is, I believe, personally a friend, but you are helpless amongst your ill-judging family. I send this by your brother. Listen to his advice, trust to his care : you are too old for war, and if battle begin how can I protect you ? If you go with your brother, you may either remain with him or I will send an escort to bring you to my camp, where you will be safe. Follow my advice, it is that of a friend. Why should I be your enemy ? If I was, why should I take this trouble to save you ? I think you will believe me, but do as you please."

It is plain the Ameer was left by this letter master of his movements, though invited to a step promising peace, and that was the only wish of the General. But meanwhile the British däks had been intercepted, and there were two parties to deal with in the same house—Roostum and his sons. Wherefore, resolute to suffer no secret hostility, while he soothed the old man in private he publicly menaced through him his turbulent family. " My letters," he wrote, " have been stopped near Kyrpoor. This has been done without your consent, or it has been done by your orders. If by your orders you are guilty. If without your consent you cannot command your people. In either case I order you to disband your armed followers instantly; and I will go to Kyrpoor to see this order obeyed." Thus with skilful appliance of gentleness and sternness, according to the need of the moment, he gradually approached a peace compatible with the Governor-General's orders.

Necessary it is that Sir C. Napier's intercourse with Roostum on this occasion should be well understood, because the Ameers of Hydrabad did afterwards, and so likewise did Roostum, contrary to all truth and reason, and

honour, represent it as the hinge upon which war turned.
And every assertion of the Ameers, however foolish and
false, found its echo in Bombay and in England. Their
complaints, foul as their hearts, were adopted and proclaimed in Parliament and out of it, as truths; as truths when
truth was the only thing they wanted; by some with factious
motives, by some in ignorance, the ignorance that will not
inquire lest it should be enlightened against its will: by
others merely to " bestow their tediousness upon the public,"
being as intent as ever was Dogberry, that the *word* not
written down should be remembered.

Roostum, adopting the General's recommendation, fled
with his wives and attendants to Ali Moorad's strong fort
of Dejee, and there resigned to that chief the Turban, with
all the rights and lands attached.

When Sir C. Napier heard of this cession he thus advised Ali Moorad. " I think your Highness will do well
not to assume the Turban, for the following reasons. People
will say the English put it on your head against the will of
Meer Roostum. But do as you please. I only give you my
advice as a friend who wishes to see you great and powerful in Scinde. This is the wish of my Government. The
Governor-General has approved of all that I have said to
you. If to be the chieftain gives you power, I should say,
assume the Turban. But it gives you none. You are
strong without it. No one in Scinde can oppose you, no one
out of Scinde can oppose you. The British Government will
secure you against all enemies. It is not true that we want
to injure the Ameers. You know, and I know, that the
Ameers have tried to form a conspiracy against the English,
and for this the Governor-General has punished those who
were guilty. His Highness Meer Roostum has been betrayed by Futteh Mohamed Ghoree; but if a ruler gives
his power to another he must bear the consequence. The
chief has now given his seal to your Highness, who will not
betray him, because his honour must be your honour; for
you are both Talpoors, and the family of the Talpoors will
grow great and powerful in Scinde under your auspices.
Look at Sattara and others; have we taken their territories,

though we surround them on all sides? No! But we do
not surround Scinde. It is our frontier; we wish to see it
great and rich, and strong against those on the other bank
of the Indus that they may not attack, but for this we must
have friendly rulers like yourself and Meer Sobdar. Woe
attend those who conspire against the powerful arms of the
Company. Behold the fate of Tippoo Sultan and the
Peishwa, and the Emperor of China. Highness, you will
rule Upper Scinde with glory and power if you are true to
the treaty made with the Company. You know, for I had
it from your own lips, that the Ameers of Upper and Lower
Scinde were in league against us, all, except his Highness
Meer Sobdar and yourself, therefore have they suffered."

Ali Moorad replied, that the cession had been voluntary,
the act solemn, complete in form and recorded by the holy
men in the Koran. It was therefore a perfect document, and
irrevocable according to the Mahomedan law and the custom
of the Talpoors. And this was true. The event however was
unexpected; to use the General's expression it burst like a
bomb-shell upon Roostum's family and followers; they all fled
in a south-easterly direction by the desert, and the chance of
war in Upper Scinde ceased. But Lord Ellenborough's
orders had been peremptory to disperse all the armed bands
menacing the British station, as well as to enforce the new
treaty, and the General was actually in march on Kyrpoor
with that object when Roostum's resignation happened.
Wherefore, being close to Dejee and feeling it important that
the aged Ameer's abdication should be not only spontaneous
but publicly known to be so, he proposed to visit Roostum,
with the intent to restore him if he had been coerced.

Instead of accepting this friendly proposal Roostum fled
into the desert with his treasure, two guns and several thousand followers, thus ungraciously proving his entire freedom
of action. All the Ameers of Upper Scinde inimical to the
British were then also in flight, and no organized force
remained in that province, save that under Ali Moorad, who
was friendly from disposition and interest. The difficult
question of tranquilizing Upper Scinde without an appeal to
arms was thus satisfactorily solved.

Roostum when flying from Dejee, wrote such a letter to excuse his sudden departure as marks the profound falseness of his character. "The General," he said, "had advised him to be guided by his brother Ali Moorad, and Ali had told him to fly lest he should be made captive by the British : therefore he fled." This was denied by Ali Moorad, and the old man's duplicity was apparent, seeing that when he sought an asylum in the British camp the General had advised him to go to Dejee, proof that to capture him was not an object. He also disavowed ceding the Turban : yet the act had been done in presence of the holy men and all the Dhurbar; and the document recording it, being afterwards shewn to the doctors of the Mahomedan law in Calcutta, was by them recognized as authentic and irrevocable. Moreover Roostum had thousands of armed followers with him when he fled to join his sons, who were then in arms, and closely allied with the Ameers of Lower Scinde. Ali Moorad therefore could not coerce him without a battle, and it was not for his interest that Roostum should fly, denying his abdication.

That Sir C. Napier desired to have but one governing chief in each province is true, and a proof that no evil was designed; for to divide power, with a view to conquest is an old and sure policy. It is also true, that Ali Moorad being in the vigour of manhood next in succession to the Turban, and friendly to the British connexion, was the man he wished to make chief of Upper Scinde. But to desire a reasonable advantage and to obtain it by foul means are things widely apart. A true summary of transactions in Upper Scinde would run thus.

The Ameers had violated treaties. Lord Ellenborough, placed in a dangerous position by the Affghan disasters, proposed a new treaty as security for the future, but containing also a demand of territory as a punishment for past transgressions. The conditions were not onerous in a pecuniary view to the Ameers, and were most beneficial for their oppressed subjects and the general interest of mankind. The Ameers professed submission, accepted the treaty, and promised to sign it, but prepared for war. Then the British General took forcible possession of the districts to be ceded by the accepted treaty; yet without bloodshed, and not before

I

the Ameers had gathered forces to fight; not before they had
formed hostile combinations, menaced the camp at Sukkur,
sought to debauch the soldiers, and stirred up the Boordee
tribe to attack the Bengal division on its march to Ferozepore:
moreover he could not have delayed longer without operating
in the hot season—a dreadful chance where the mercury rises
above 130 degrees in the shade!

The justice or injustice of the first treaties could not affect
Sir C. Napier's proceedings. He was sent to Scinde, not as
a lecturer to discuss the morality of a former Governor-
General's negotiations, but as an executive officer to uphold
the interests of England at a moment of great difficulty. This
duty he was executing faithfully when, in the heat and crisis
of the transactions, the chief Ameer Roostum, frightened by
the approach of a war he was hourly provoking at the instigation of his sons and nephews, proposed to seek an asylum
in the British camp, thus providing for his own safety while
his family were carrying on hostilities. This was in itself a
virtual renunciation of the Turban, and a step towards the
introduction of one friendly and vigorous-minded chieftain,
instead of an oligarchy of princes with whom nothing could
be permanently or satisfactorily adjusted. But far from
seizing with an aggressive spirit this occasion, the General,
stedfast in justice and fair dealing, gave the Ameer advice
tending to his safety and honour, leaving him free to act, with
assurance of protection and safety. " *Remain with your own
brother, you are too old for war.*" " *Come to me and I will
protect you.*" " *Choose for yourself.*" These frank expressions could not be misunderstood, and cannot be perverted,
they are patent in words and meaning. Roostum was not
misled nor misused by the English General, but by his own
falsehood and folly; the transaction was as honourable to
Sir C. Napier as any part of his glorious career in Scinde;
and the efforts of Lord Howick and other persons in the
House of Commons to give it another character only confirmed this truth: futile even to ridicule they were laughed
at and pitied.

From the flight of Roostum may be dated the commencement of the Scindian war. The sword had been taken from

the Ameers of Upper Scinde, as it were by sleight, but they
fled to the desert and to Lower Scinde, there to raise in conjunction with their cousins of Hydrabad the standard of
battle. They trusted in their sandy wastes, their strong and
numerous fortresses, their deadly sun—in the numbers,
courage, strength, and fierceness of their wild Beloochee
swordsmen, and braver barbarians never gave themselves to
slaughter. In these things they trusted, and not without
reason. But they were opposed to what they could not understand, having no previous experience of his like—a man
of fiery yet vigilant valour, skilled in war, daring as the
boldest chieftain of their hills and more mighty in fight: they
found him so when their thousands went down before the
bayonets of his valiant soldiers, wallowing in blood : but never
was he cruel or ferocious, for he loved peace and justice with
a true heart, and strove hard to avoid the clash of arms. The
Ameers would have war, and in the shock were broken like
potsherds, it was they who sought the strife. No Etruscan
fecial ever cast his spear across a boundary, invoking his gods
to attest the justice of a war, with a purer conscience than
Charles Napier marched to battle. Now it shall be my task
to shew how victoriously he bore the banner of England, how
widely he has since spread England's fame for justice and
gentleness, how the Beloochees reverence and the Scindians
bless him, though the Ameers mourn.

Whether he is to live for more glory, or to die an over-
laboured man beneath that flaming sun, whose fiery aspect
withers the principle of life, casting men dead to the earth
by hundreds as quickly as the malignant ray descends, is in
the darkness of futurity. If he lives, he will display all the
resources of a mind capacious to regenerate and govern as
well as to conquer. If he dies in harness he will leave a
spotless reputation. Living or dead his place is amongst the
greatest of England's captains.

This anticipation, written when he had conquered at
Meeanee and Hydrabad, is now in 1857 being again acknowledged by the nation, as when the public voice sent him
back to India. Living and dead the people recognize his
genius and virtue.

CONQUEST OF SCINDE.

FIRST PUBLISHED IN 1845.

PART II.

CHAPTER I.

In the first portion of this work it has been shewn, that the English General had to deal with complicated political matters, pitiful in character yet pregnant with terrible consequences. His second course of diplomacy was combined with military operations, for he had to meet the mixed negotiation and warfare of the three sovereign families of Kyrpoor, Hydrabad, and Meerpoor, in the aggregate and separately; and also the intrigues of each member of those families, all of whom claimed, and by Lord Auckland's treaties were entitled to independent power.

Frequently at war with each other, these petty Sovereigns could from the number of their Beloochee followers, and the treasures extorted from the miserable Scindian and Hindoo, easily raise serious commotions: and often they did so. Hence the Ameers of Hydrabad, and those of Kyrpoor, were neither united amongst themselves, nor together; nor as public bodies could they be said to be at peace or war with the British Government. All professed amity, and even boasted of their attachment to the Auckland treaties; yet daily violated those treaties on essential points. When rebuked for infractions they boldly denied them; and some members of each family always urged their particular good

faith, designing to profit either way; yet experience proved
that they, like the others, secretly cursed the subjection they
publicly acknowledged. The Ameers most remarkable for
this double dealing were, Roostum of Upper Scinde, Sobdar
and Mohamed Khan of Lower Scinde and young Hoossein
of Hydrabad, but he was a boy under Sobdar's tutelage.

All were at this time gathering troops without ostensible
cause; and though at enmity with each other willing to
unite against the intruded supremacy of England. Their
policy was however mutable in the extreme, being influenced
by fear, anger, hope, and drunkenness, alternately. Their
proceedings were therefore fantastic; and with such a medley
of interests that the General could scarcely decide whether
he was to negotiate or to fight, how or with whom to treat,
where to menace, where to soothe, when to strike, who to
support. " Their system," he said, " leaves no one responsible; their professions are so mixed, that if I were to
throw a shell into Hydrabad, it would be as likely to fall on
the head of a friend as an enemy." In fine, the policy of
dividing· power among many—effectual when, as in the
Auckland policy, the design was to encroach and oppress,
became burdensome when justice and tranquillity were
sought.

To the embarrassments thus created were added an undercurrent of personal intrigues, plots and quarrels, which in
the East especially, always disturbs the main stream of
affairs. Sir C. Napier indeed, peremptorily refused from
the first to meddle with this turbid flow of vice and folly;
but he was compelled to sound its depths as an aid for his
judgment in doubtful matters.

This entanglement of affairs enabled Lord Howick, Lord
Ashley, and others of less note, to confuse and darken the
true story of the General's negotiations with the Ameers;
their object being to sustain an ungenerous but impotent opposition to the vote of thanks in the House of Commons.
But the taint is in the blood, the conceit hereditary. Lord
Grey of old assailed the conduct of the Duke of Wellington in the Peninsula; his son that of Sir C. Napier in
Scinde.

To purge the public mind of credulity in the spurious humanity, the puerile political philosophy put forward by those men with all the peevishness of faction, this work is written. The obscurity produced by calumniators shall be dispelled, and with it the dream of patriarchal, fallen Princes, bending beneath the blood-stained sword of a fierce soldier, for whom military glory was as God, justice as nothing! Instead of this, will be found a brave and generous British officer, who in nearly fifty years' service, struggling against climate, wounds, wrongs, and poverty, was never swayed a hair's breadth in his noble career, by fear or self-interest or false glory. Sir C. Napier never did a base or sordid action.

When the Ameer Roostum fled from Ali Moorad's fort of Dejee-ka-kote, the affairs of Scinde had reached a crisis requiring intrepidity, enterprise and judgment, to determine it in favour of British interests. But the full play of the two first qualities was restrained by anxiety to avoid slaughter. "If I can prevent blood being shed, and do not do so, I shall be a murderer," was his language at the time. "The General is the only man in the army who does not wish for a battle, was the language of the camp." And so intent was he to protect the people from suffering, that when at Roree, exposed to and expecting an attack, he detached the Bengal troops to occupy the ceded districts behind him, lest the Bhawal Khan, to whom they were given, should first take possession with his wild horsemen and ravage the villages.

Nor was Lord Ellenborough's aversion to violence less unequivocal. His instructions are on record. They inculcate the moral obligation of avoiding war by all means, save the sacrifice of British honour and the supremacy absolutely necessary at the time for the safety of British India. And it is fitting again to advert to the real situation of that Empire, when this wise and vigilant statesman, so potent from his knowledge of affairs and laborious energy, came to restore the reputation and strength of England in the East.

He found the first tarnished by bad faith and defeat, the second sapped by folly and corruption. The disaster of Cabool was recent and terrible; the subsequent surrender of

Ghusni augmented the general terror, and directed the public fears to the isolated position of General Nott's army at Candahar, where, blockaded by the Affghans, it was without money or medicine, or means of transport for a march. Then came the unsuccessful attempt of General England at Hykulzie to succour Nott; the dangerous siege sustained by Sale in Jellallabad, and General Pollock's long protracted inability to aid him. Pollock's own army, dispirited and precariously supplied with provisions, was wholly dependent on the Seiks, who, irritated by the falsehoods of the Anglo-Indian press, were stubborn, moody, and with double his numbers infesting the communications rather than protecting them.

In the interior of India universal despondency prevailed, and such a terror of the Affghans pervaded the population, it was scarcely possible to find resources for succouring the Generals: of three hundred and fifty camels, sent in one convoy to Pollock, three hundred and twenty were carried off in a single night by their drivers, one day's march from Peshawar. Meanwhile the Governor-General's secret plans were given to the newspapers by men in office; and a mischievous, ignoble spirit, the natural consequence of making editors and money-seekers the directors of statesmen and generals, degraded the public mind and shed a baneful influence over the army. In Scinde deep-laid plans of hostility were on the point of execution. At Madras several sepoy regiments, smarting under a sordid economy, were discontented if not in absolute mutiny. Actual insurrection existed at Saugur, and was spreading on one side to Bundelcund; on the other, along the Nerbudda to Boorampoor. The ancient fear of England's power, and that confidence in her strength which upholds her sway, were nearly extinguished—the Indian population, whether subjects of England or of her allies and feudatories, especially the Mussulman portion, desired and expected the downfall of her Empire.

Such was the terrible state of affairs, and but an outline of them is here given, when Lord Ellenborough assumed the government of the East. In one year, with incredible activity and labour he checked internal abuses, put down insur-

rection, restored confidence to the public, and military pride
to the army. Succouring the isolated forces in Affghanistan,
he enabled the Generals to win glorious victories, to daunt
external enemies, to repair past disasters, and add the great
and rich province of Scinde to the British Empire. And
none of those Generals could truly assert that success was
not insured, according to their genius, by the Governor-
General's magnanimous confidence and support—his letter of
the 4th of July to General Nott, giving him a discretion to
move forward or retreat, was a model of fine feeling, and
fine discrimination of character.

These great results were not obtained under the advice of
old Indian counsellors, but in despite of them and their mischievous habits. Lord Ellenborough's correspondence with
Nott and Pollock, from the letter just noticed to the re-
capture of Cabool, was withheld carefully from the usual
official channels of communication, and even from the Council
at Calcutta. Had it not been so, the intended operations
would soon have become publicly known, according to custom,
and so have reached the enemy; Ghusni would have been
prepared for defence against Nott; Pollock would have been
more strongly encountered; and though success might still
have been attained, great loss would have been sustained and
the effect felt throughout India.

This secrecy was the first offence of Lord Ellenborough,
and, with few exceptions, the persons holding political situations immediately commenced an intriguing hostility
against him, for thus rolling up their vanity and official consequence while he moved onward. That he should have
completely succeeded was the second offence: it rendered the
first inexpiable. And when, with a just indignation, he
suspended a civil servant of the Company for calumniating
the army, the Court of Directors also became inimical to
him, and made every effort to weaken, thwart, and oppose
his Government: at last, finding his energy too great for
their evil influence, with malignant desperation they re-called
the man who had just saved their empire, because he would
not sacrifice the interests of England and the welfare of
India to their silly pride and sordid nepotism.

But the public voice now, and the judgment of posterity hereafter will do him justice. History bears an avenging rod. She will tell, and it will be a tale to wonder at and execrate, that what great statesmen and noble armies gained and defended in the East with matchless vigour, the base cupidity and pitiful wilfulness of their merchant princes endangered—that there was a constant struggle between enlightened policy and groping avarice, between real greatness and conceit. That the Court of Directors, powerless as they should be when a man of knowledge and energy presides at the Board of Control, sought the semblance of authority and dignity, by ostentatious communications and correspondence with particular officers in India; heading, as it were, an opposition to the Government carried on in its own name—that, acting as a political agitator, it encouraged intrigues and malversations where it could not command, and in all ways augmented the difficulties of ruling that immense empire—that the public press of India, so false, so noisy and base, was not the organ of the many but of the few; not of the governed people but of the governing Europeans, who sought their own profit apart from the general good. Finally, that a foul complicated system, odious to honourable minds, pervaded the Anglo-Indian policy; and when a Governor-General of great ability, untiring energy and unbending firmness, attempted to check its evil influence, the Directors with puerile vanity and selfish passion recalled him, substituting calumny for reason in excuse.

The Ameers' resolution to thrust the English out of Scinde was not one of a day, it was a deep-rooted feeling in accord with the sentiments of their Beloochee subjects; and all the mountain tribes of that fierce race beyond the frontier were willing to aid. Being zealous Mahomedans, a religious sympathy as well as the ties of kindred made them rejoice in the Affghans' success, and led them to desire a repetition of that triumph in Scinde; but heads of greater ability, and hearts of greater courage than the Ameers possessed planned the means. Roostum's Vizier, Futteh Mohamed Ghoree, a wilely man, was one of these. In conjunction with other designing persons, Affghans and Seiks as well as Beloochees,

he concerted a general combination of those nations to fall on
the British stations with two hundred thousand fighting
men, and of this number the Ameers could furnish seventy
thousand.

To destroy Colonel England's column on its return from
Candahar to Sukkur, when Nott moved against Cabool, was
part of this scheme; its success was to be the signal for a
gathering of the nations to fall on the British force, which
would then have been weak and isolated at Sukkur and
Kurrachee. Some default of concert, and the unexpected
strength of England's column, far more numerous than the
one he led up to Candahar, for he had been reinforced by
Lord Ellenborough, prevented the meditated attack on that
officer, and Scinde was thus strongly occupied. This checked
the Ameers, and the Ghoree's policy was then thwarted by
the vigorous diplomacy of Sir C. Napier, which was founded
on their mutual jealousies and disputes, and their vacillating inebriate habits. Yet secret negotiations amongst
themselves and with foreign chiefs, confused plans, infractions of treaty, and the latent hatred manifested from time to
time in their speeches and councils, indicated that the general
plot was only deferred, not abandoned. It was national with
the Affghans and Beloochees; but the Seiks were deluded
by the falsehoods of the Anglo-Indian press, and their better-
informed Prince, Shere Sing, could hardly restrain them
from falling on the British troops when retiring through the
Punjaub. The assembly of an army of reserve on the Sutlege was therefore imposed upon the Governor-General,
principally by editorial falsehoods; and as it was useful the
editors ridiculed it, after their nature, in which folly strives
hard with villainy for pre-eminence.

But if the Ameers of both Scindes had been then united
for the war so long contemplated, the Seiks could not have
been controlled by their Prince, and a great commotion, extending probably to Nepaul and Gwalior, to Bundelcund
and the districts south of the Nerbudda, would have shaken
India to its centre: the army of reserve would have been its
only support. Most essential was it also that Sir C. Napier
should during that critical period keep the Ameers in a state

of irresolution; and he did so by his adroit diplomacy and
imposing military attitude, the unreserved confidence of the
Governor-General enabling him to act without fear of responsibility. "I felt," he said, "that under Lord Ellenborough
I might go headlong, if I saw my own way clearly." Every
thing he required, and even more, was given to him. The
Bengal division was placed at his disposal, he was offered
more cavalry and guns, and all the Bombay sepoys of Nott's
army: his command also was extended to the troops of the
Bombay Presidency in Cutch.

The first result of this freedom in counsel and action was
the passage of the Indus. The Ameers had then only the
option of letting him take possession of the ceded districts, or
of attacking him in a strong position with a part only of their
army. The first would have been a practical acknowledgment
of the treaty, which it was never their intention to make; the
last, a dangerous experiment and a premature disclosure of
their hostility. This skilful politico-military movement therefore greatly perplexed them, and gave the General Government
another respiration under the pressure of its difficulties. Yet,
if Roostum had not at that moment fled from his turbulent
sons and nephews to give the Turban to his brother, the war
would have begun in Upper Scinde; for the Ameers of the
lower province were certainly preparing to take the field, and
Ali Moorad, doubtful of the result, would probably have been
inclined to act with the others. Some time would have been
required indeed to bring all their forces together; but that
was in their policy, which was not to call the British troops
into the field until the hot season.'

Roostum's movement, the impulse of an old man's selfishness, was therefore a great event; and it was by the ready
sagacity of the English General rendered a decisive one. It
secured the alliance of Ali Moorad, and forcing the younger
Princes to a premature display of hostility compelled them to
abandon Upper Scinde without a blow. This was an irrefragable proof of their sinister designs; yet Roostum's cession of
the Turban has been with stupid malignity denounced as the
result of coercion and the cause of war, when in truth it prevented a war in Upper Scinde. That old Ameer soon saw his

error and sought to retrieve it by low cunning which failed:
but had he remained united with his own family and with the
Hydrabad Ameers he would have been very dangerous.

The General had now to disperse the armed bands in
Upper Scinde: he had refrained from attempting it when at
Sukkur, well knowing, as he said, that it would be to chase a
" *Will-o'-the-wisp.* " His first object was to combine his
military and political measures solidly—" I can put them all
into the Indus, they are barbarians, yet I act as if they were
all French." When he had fixed his base securely at Roree
and covered the ceded districts, he resolved to execute his
orders. Had Roostum been still Rais, he and his family would
have secretly caused the bands to disperse, with orders to re-
assemble again later, and then openly, with oaths and lamen-
tations and reproaches, would have declared their innocence,
and protested against the injustice of suspecting them! Thus
time would have been gained for the coming of the deadly
sun, when they would have laughed alike at their oaths and
at the General, and aided by the Ameers of Lower Scinde,
have commenced war with the advantages of numbers, union,
and climate.

The passage of the Indus, leaving the cantonment of
Sukkur to its own resources against the Belooch force assembled at Larkaana was not an ordinary matter. It placed
the active force on the true line of operations, put the political and military measures in harmony, and insured the
occupation of the ceded districts while it gave the army a
menacing position with a secure base. The passage was
however in itself no easy operation; for though the fighting
men were few the followers were nearly twenty thousand, and
the baggage enormous. "I have not plagued your Lordship
with difficulties unavoidable and not insuperable, but the
baggage of an Indian army is an awful affair,"—such was the
simple note of the General at the time: those who have commanded will feel its force. And war involves indeed so many
combinations, so many details, so much preparation, that
there is no surer indication of a great commander than
bringing the multifarious parts of an army to work well
together in a compact form. Simple the matter seems then,

but what energy of genius is required to bring it to that simplicity! The steam-engine with its small whirling balls at top governing the giant's complicated iron skeleton below, is the type of a well-conducted army.

Sir C. Napier's diplomacy was now successful. By detaching the legal heir to the Turban from the family policy, and by alternately soothing and menacing the old Rais and his turbulent relations, he had brought Moorad's courage and ambition, Roostum's fears and cunning, and the arrogance of his unruly sons and nephews into collision, and all opposed to the able Futteh Ghoree's policy—a matter of great moment, for he had been the foe of Moorad, the secret director of Roostum, and the sound adviser of all the other Ameers, even those of Hydrabad when their passions would let them listen to his counsels. This disunion retarded that junction of the forces of Upper and Lower Scinde which was to be the preliminary to hostility, the clouds of war gathered in the former were conjured and dissipated; and when the wavering Roostum fled from Dejee again to join his sons the farce of the Kyrpoor troubles terminated. But then new actors of a sterner aspect appeared, giving notice that a dreadful tragedy was preparing.

From that time every movement of the English General became critical, involving terrible results; and it is essential to a right understanding of his character to shew, step by step, how exactly he ruled his conduct by the principles of honour and the rights of treaties—obeying his orders rigidly, yet making every effort to preserve peace, ere his sharp sword cut away the Talpoor dynasty from the land it afflicted. Cautiously and justly he proceeded towards the Ameers, and benevolently towards their people, while he supported the dignity of his own country, and the honour of her arms. Meeting low arts with fair dealing, baffling cunning with superior calculation, he steadily approached his object with an earnest desire to avoid spilling blood; but when the waving of weapons forbad this, with incredible energy and daring he broke through their innumerable hosts as a plough-share breaks through the earth. A full harvest of happiness for Scinde has blessed the glorious labour.

After occupying Roree and the ceded districts he could
no longer delay executing the Governor-General's orders to
disperse the armed bands. He had repeatedly warned the
Ameers that his orders were to that effect, and the constant
answer was—" There are no bands, we are all submission."
Nevertheless the bands were there, strong in number and
violence, and increasing. They exacted the revenue in advance; they robbed the people and the merchants; they drove
from the country all the camels to prevent the British troops
obtaining any; they stopped the däks coming to Sukkur, and
intercepted the communications of the army. There was no
remedy but force, and the General, seeing it would be useless
to send moveable columns in pursuit through so large and
intricate a country, resolved to strike at their head-quarters.
This was Kyrpoor, the capital, which being then filled
with fighting men he resolved to storm. He marched
in December, at the head of two thousand infantry, nine
hundred cavalry and twelve field pieces, besides a battery of
24lb. howitzers drawn by camels. Roostum was however
then in Ali Moorad's fort, and Ali himself being acknowledged as Rais and in alliance with the British, the General
had strong hopes that the other Ameers, perplexed and dismayed by Roostum's conduct, would not risk an assault, and
before he moved, sent them this warning letter:—

" Ameers, I have to request your Highnesses will protect
our post coming through your country. Two of our mails
have been stopped in the territory of Kyrpoor, and I am
going to inquire into this matter, and put a stop to such
aggressions. Wherever my posts are stopped there will I
march with my troops; and your Highnesses will have to
pay the expense if this happens within your territory."

His right to act thus was undoubted. For if the Ameers
had called up the bands and directed their operations, as
indeed they had, it was war; and if the bands acted without
orders, they were common enemies, being also robbers, plunderers and murderers, who filled the whole country with
terror and wailing. But in reality the Ameers had brought
them together, had paid them, and were quite unable to restrain them if they had desired to do so. To disperse such

mischievous bodies was not only a social right but a duty, even though orders to do so had not been received.   It was also in strict accordance with Roostum's original treaty, which gave the Anglo-Indian Government a right to repress the aggression of one Ameer against another, and, more strongly to restrain violence against itself.

The 26th of December the General reached Mungaree, a fort near Kyrpoor, where he encamped, because, as he expected, the sons and nephews of Roostum, dismayed and perplexed by the cession of the Turban, had gone off to the south with their fighting men, treasures and families.   On the 28th however Roostum, once more changing sides, had followed them from Dejee, with his troops and money, and then the Beloochee forces assembled at Larkaana crossed to the right bank of the Indus and made for Hydrabad, thinking that some of the Ameers would surely hire them for battle. Thus no armed men remained in Upper Scinde, save those under Ali Moorad. The Governor-General's orders were thus fulfilled without bloodshed. Then arose the Scindian labourer with a shout of exultation, and the trafficking Hindoo clapped his lean hands in joy at the flight of the oppressors. Relieved from the swordsmen whose sharp blades cut short remonstrance against robbery, both husbandmen and traders flocked to the British camp with provisions, cowering joyfully under the protection of the " *just Feringee General.*"

With a vigorous hand he guarded their rights of life and property.   Inflexible to marauders, he was ever on horseback watching and enforcing obedience to orders—no light task, for the abolition of flogging in the sepoy army left him only the choice of death or imprisonment for plunderers; but death could not be often resorted to, and confinement required guards, weakening the force in the field, while the culprit enjoyed the great pleasure, according to Eastern habits, of doing nothing.   To remedy this defect in the military code, he multiplied his provost-marshals, thus placing plunderers in the hands of functionaries who were not restricted as to corporal chastisement.   Exhorting his officers to vigilance he warned them, that straggling and marauding were the greatest evils for an army, quoting the Duke of Wellington's authority for the importance of having the peasants for or against the troops. He thus saved the people from violence, and the army from destruction; but with characteristic villainy the editors of the Indian press denounced his conduct; calling upon the sepoys at the most critical period—" to rise and put an end to the fellow's breach of law." And these exhortations to mutiny and murder were unpunished, because they came from a faction supported by the Directors and the Bombay Government!

The Indian Government is weak, and it will never be strong, until the official persons are compelled to support the Governor-General in preference to courting the Leadenhall trading politicians. Despicable as the editors of Indian newspapers are however, there is no wisdom in despising their efforts to produce evil; their falsehoods nearly caused the destruction of Pollock's and Nott's armies, while traversing the Punjaub on their return from Cabool, and they actually produced the first Seik war.

At Mungaree Sir C. Napier was detained several days by heavy rain, an unusual occurrence in Scinde. During this forced halt he visited Ali Moorad at Kyrpoor, to concert measures for maintaining tranquillity in Upper Scinde, when the army should descend on the lower province, according to the Governor-General's orders—for the difficulties which had just been terminated in Upper Scinde still existed with the Ameers of Lower Scinde, and time pressed. Hydrabad was one hundred and fifty miles distant, it was then the beginning of January, and beyond the middle of March military operations could not be carried on without great risk from the heat. The Ameers knew this, and their intrigues, their falsehoods, and pretended submissions, their promises to accept the new treaty, and the negotiation they had commenced by their vakeels, were all designed to waste the cool season unprofitably for the British.

Correct intelligence of their movements and numbers it was very difficult to obtain in a country where lying is the natural order of intercourse, and truth-telling the exception; yet, many emissaries being employed and much pains bestowed, the obscurity gradually cleared up. The constant

K

afflux of armed men from the hills, the plains, and the desert, was ascertained; and it was certain the Ameers, if they united and freely dispensed their treasures, could, time being allowed, bring into the field from seventy to eighty thousand fighting men of most robust bodies and courageous spirits, well armed, and well exercised in arms after their fashion — a fashion not contemptible.   The Beloochees knew well the difficulties the country presented to an enemy, planned their defence with great intelligence, chose their positions well, and, unlike other Asiatics, prided themselves on their infantry in preference to their cavalry.

Sir C. Napier had not at this time more than eight thousand troops, widely distributed, at Sukkur, at Kurrachee, and in the field.   The 41st British regiment was below Hydrabad in march to embark for Bombay; the Bengal division was within a march or two, but occupying the ceded districts till the Bhawal Khan took possession, when it was to move to Ferozepore.   Three thousand fighting men were in the field; yet only brought there by the exercise of an overbearing will, and incessant pains-taking to overcome obstacles of a serious nature; for Scinde had been nearly exhausted by Lord Keane's army of carriage, which in Indian parlance means camels and other beasts of burden, and it had not yet recovered: moreover, the Ameers secretly menaced the contractors, and the principal one forfeited his deposit rather than risk their vengeance.   They had also, caused all the camels to be driven away, an act of war in itself, and sufficiently indicative of their ultimate object.

Only six hundred miserable worn-out animals, the refuse of Lord Keane's commissariat, were available for the field force.   The delirious invasion of Affghanistan had therefore entailed a dangerous war in Scinde, and nearly deprived the army of means to support that war with success.   Folly begets mischief.

Of the three thousand men in the field, many of the sepoys had been, during the three years of the Affghan contest, placed in difficult situations; and some had suffered severe defeats from the brave barbarians of the hills. The moral effect of this had been dispiriting; but now finding themselves under an able commander, past disasters were only so far remembered as to produce respect for their enemy's courage, and that is not the worst cast of mind for soldiers in dangerous operations.

Soon the emissaries' reports enabled the General to scan the military horizon. Two thousand men, under Mohamed Ali, Roostum's nephew, had thrown themselves into Shah Ghur, a desert fort to the east, on the borders of Jessulmere; his design being to gather a larger force there to operate against Roree and the ceded districts. But Shah Ghur was an appurtenance of the Turban; wherefore this movement of Mohamed was an act of war against Ali Moorad, as Rais, giving the English General a right under the treaty of nine articles to interfere.

Roostum had seven thousand men and several pieces of cannon within the borders of the desert, to the south, hanging on the cultivated district for the sake of water, but with the desert at hand for a retreat. He was in direct communication with his sons and nephews, most of whom were at Dingee, a large fortress some forty-five miles south of Dejee, and just on the line of demarcation between Upper and Lower Scinde. To that point the Beloochees from Larkaana, and other places, were hastening in arms; and from thence the Princes concerted with the Hydrabad Ameers a new plan of warfare.

Mohamed, or Hoossein Khan, Roostum's son, had thrown himself with two thousand men and all his treasure into Emaum Ghur, another desert fortress, which he had previously stored with grain and gunpowder. This place, was by the Beloochees accounted impregnable, and to Europeans inaccessible as being in the very heart of the waste. They designed it as a place of arms for the forces of Upper Scinde, and its seizure was another act of war against Ali Moorad, for it also belonged to the Turban. There were reports besides of several numerous bodies of Beloochee cavalry wandering in the waste, but the destination of all was said Emaum Ghur. (Plan 3.) The Hydrabad Ameer, and the Meerpoor man, were likewise collecting troops, though less ostentatiously; and all had agreed to

act with the Princes of Upper Scinde, on a plan arranged
with a skill and intelligence that had nothing barbarous in
conception. Subsequent intelligence made known that it
was the work of the purchased Abyssinian and Arab slaves
of the Ameers, called " *Seedees*," amongst whom one Hoche,
a black, was conspicuous for his ability, greatness of mind,
and heroic courage.

Expecting that their opponent, so prompt and resolute as
they had found him in all his proceedings, would not fail to
attack Kyrpoor, as indeed he designed, the first arrangement of the Ameers had been that the Beloochees of Upper
Scinde should fall back fighting from that capital to Dingee, where they were to be reinforced to the amount of
fifteen thousand men : those stationed at Larkaana, of equal
force, being to assail the camp at Sukkur, while the retreat
upon Dingee was effected. If the attack from Larkaana
succeeded, the British field force would be isolated · they
thought, and was to be immediately opposed by the great
mass of the Upper Scinde army, reinforced by the Hydrabad and Meerpoor forces, which were promptly to unite at
Dingee and give battle.

The foresight of the General in forming a new base
at Roree vitiated this military plan ; and his detection of
their schemes, for delaying the campaign by false negotiations until the hot season, vitiated their policy.   Roostum's secession completed their confusion ; they fled to
Dingee as shewn, drawing after them from Larkaana the
force which was to have stormed Sukkur.   However at
Dingee they prepared to execute the second part of the
original plan, modified by the course of events : that was
to inveigle the British troops, whose numbers they well knew,
amongst the nullahs and swamps on the left bank of the
Indus, and to keep them stationary there by fresh negotiations and intrigues, until the inundation should flood the
camp and the fierce sun strike the soldiers down—" then
blades were to be drawn," and the Beloochee, as they expressed themselves in their Dhurbars, were " *To make the
Caffirs, as they fell beneath their swords, cry out, Oh, God !
what have we done, that you let these devils loose upon us ?* "

" If we fail to keep him on the river bank, if he attacks, and that we are defeated," thus they reasoned, " we will retreat in two bodies on different lines. The Kyrpoor Ameers, with the force of Upper Scinde, must strike into the desert to rally at Emaum Ghur, where there are provisions, powder and treasure. The Ameers of Lower Scinde will fall back on Hydrabad, and that is a strong fortress. Whichever body the British General pursues, the other must close on his rear.

" No European has ever seen Emaum Ghur ; it is built in the heart of the wilderness, it is only to be approached by vague uncertain tracks, not known to strangers, and in some places without water for several marches. He cannot reach us there.

" If he halts and encamps after his victory on the river's bank, late in the season, pestilence will destroy his troops. If he enters the waste in pursuit of the Upper Scinde forces, those of Lower Scinde will cut his communication with the cultivated district and the river, and his troops will perish from heat and thirst on the burning sands.

" If he marches upon Hydrabad he will encounter the armies of Lower Scinde well based on that strong fortress, and having the sultry swamps of the Delta to retire upon in the south if again defeated; or they shall make for Meerpoor eastward, another strong fortress on the edge of the desert, having Omercote behind them in the heart of the waste. Meanwhile the force of Upper Scinde, returning from Emaum Ghur, shall emerge upon his rear and cut his communications with Roree.

" If he sees his danger and endeavours to fall back on Roree, we will all unite to pursue him with harassing attacks night and day. He will never be able to reach Sukkur !"

They counted on having nearly seventy thousand fighting men, and thirty pieces of cannon for this warfare, and knew, if they gained any marked advantage or even sustained the first shock without utter ruin, the Affghans and Seiks, the Brahooe-Beloochees, and the Moultan man, it might be the Bhawal Khan's people also, would take part in the war. Then internal commotions would shake India, the native army of Gwalior would take the field, and the British empire in the East be rocked to its foundations.

Such was the formidable warfare the English General had to deal with; such were the terrible results to be expected from an error in judgment, or a misfortune, where the adverse chances of climate, of intrigue, and of the sword, were arrayed to confuse his perception by a sense of responsibility as much as by the sense of danger. Did he tremble? Let his actions reply.

That such a plan might be adopted had not escaped his comprehension, and with a counterstroke he was prepared to put it aside, and so shake their confidence as to render them amenable without fighting.

He had at first opposed Ali Moorad's assumption of the Turban, thinking it would augment the chances of hostilities: that opinion was now changed. Roostum's restless cunning would have baffled Ali Moorad's government : he would have equally fled from Dejee, bearing with him the dignity and influence of Rais; an advantage lost by ceding the Turban, for the Beloochees obey the wearer of the Puggree, no matter how acquired. It is indeed a most ancient Asiatic maxim, that to the throne, not the man, belongs dignity and power. The cession was therefore an advantage which he now turned to account.

To retire again to Roree, or to delay his own advance, was not to be thought of; to beat the force at Dingee, and, then, lumbered as he was with baggage and followers, to pursue into the waste men without incumbrance and sun-proof, would end in disaster. To advance on Hydrabad involved a siege, which, as his communication with Sukkur would be cut by the people from Emaum Ghur, must be tedious and bring him into the hot season. That was the stay and hope of the Ameers. Their desert they thought inaccessible to him. He thought that an illusion, and resolved to dispel it before the cool season passed. In this view he resolved to strike at Emaum Ghur — an enterprise as hardy as any of which military records tell. Similar it was in design but more dangerous, more daring, than that of Marius against Jugurtha's city of Capsa. Like Capsa,

Emaum Ghur was accounted impregnable, as well as inaccessible. It was in the heart of the desert, eight long marches distant, the exact site unknown, the tracks leading to it and the wells were but vaguely indicated by the native informist: indeed few knew them, and those might be traitors. Some marches must be made without finding water, and all the springs were capricious, bubbling up at times freely, at other times disappearing to rise again at a distance, never certain as to locality or abundance: and the rolling sands governed by the winds always menaced entire destruction to man and beast.

This hidden fortress, Charles Napier resolved to seek out and assail, though he knew it was garrisoned by two thousand of the best Beloochee warriors, for none but the best would encounter the privations of the desert when necessity did not urge them. Many thousand horsemen also were on the skirts of the wilderness, knowing the water pits, able to fill them up or poison their waters and then fall on the fainting soldiers!

It was an enterprise worthy of Alexander and his Agrians, but well reasoned. Success would first deprive the Beloochees of a moral confidence, and a material resource suiting their superior power to sustain heat; then their chosen position of battle at Dingee would be turned, rendered useless, by the march to Emaum Ghur and the return, which last was designed by a way different from the advance. Their whole plan of operations would thus be frustrated, and their united forces thrown upon one line to the south, where, crowded and embarrassed, they must disperse or accept battle to cover Hydrabad, without time for preparation. This last trial however he expected to be spared. The taking of Emaum Ghur, thought by the Ameers stronger than Hydrabad, would he hoped intimidate those inebriate, luxurious Princes.

But the enterprise involved political considerations. To move against Emaum Ghur, and Shah Ghur, which he also contemplated, would be hostile acts against the two Princes who had seized them; not so, necessarily, against the Ameers generally, though designed to influence them. It would be a continuance of his operations against the armed

bands he had been ordered to disperse, for it was with those
bands the two fortresses were garrisoned. The right to attack
them was under the treaty of nine articles, reinforced by the
authority of Ali Moorad, whose property as Rais they now were.
Originally they belonged to Roostum, but only as Rais and,
ceding the Turban, he ceded them. Roostum did not dispute
this law but denied the valid cession of the Turban, saying,
he had previously given it to his son, who therefore held
Emaum Ghur of right. This was however notoriously contrary to the Talpoor law, and to complete the confusion,
he now offered his own authority as Rais, which he had
twice ceded, to remove Hoossein and Ali from Emaum Ghur
and Shah Ghur.

This was one of Roostum's many intrigues to gain time
for the general plan of campaign : yet it proved the absolute
authority of the Rais over the forts, and Ali Moorad was the
lawful Rais. He was so even without Roostum's cession :
for when that Ameer resigned the Turban to his son, he legally divested himself but could not legally give it to another
—it fell by law to Ali Moorad. Hoossein and Ali Mohamed
were thus brought under article V, which gave the British a
right to interpose in any dispute between two Ameers. Ali
Moorad was indeed averse to the British entering the desert,
saying he would reduce Emaum Ghur himself. This was
futile. He had formally complained that his nephews resisted the authority of the Rais, and by article III he was
bound, as Roostum's successor, to act in subordinate co-operation with the British. It followed that Mohamed was a rebel
and an outlaw. No declaration of war was therefore necessary, and policy forbad delay. Ali Moorad's presence was
however desirable, to give an appearance as well as the
quality of right to the enterprise. His knowledge of the
waste and of the fortress would be useful ; and it was also
essential—to teach him who had wavered in his alliance at
first, and now showed a dislike to have the British penetrate
the waste, that he could no longer choose his part, having to
deal with a man his over-match in policy, who thus described
his views.

" I had discovered long ago that the Ameers put implicit faith in their deserts, and feel confident we can never reach them there; and therefore, when negotiations and delays and lying and intrigues of all kinds fail, they can at last declare their entire obedience, their innocence, their humility, and retire beyond our reach to their deserts, and from thence launch their wild bands against us, so as to cut off all our communications and render Scinde more hot than nature has already done. So circumstanced, and after all the consideration I could give the subject, and after drawing all I could from Ali Moorad, whom I saw last night at Kyrpoor, I made up my mind, that, although war was not declared nor is it necessary to declare it, I would at once march upon Emaum Ghur, and prove to the Talpoor families, both of Kyrpoor and Hydrabad, that neither their deserts nor their negotiations can protect them from the British troops; for while they imagine they can fly with security to the deserts, they never will be quiet.

"I told Ali Moorad I would place his Killedar in Emaum Ghur; that your Lordship was determined to support the family chief, as bound by treaty; that those people who fled with armed men to Emaum Ghur, and refused to obey their chief, Meer Roostum, were in fact rebels, and I was resolved to follow them. His reply was, 'He would take Emaum Ghur himself.' I answered, 'I knew he could do so, and his readiness to save my troops the trouble was praiseworthy, and I was much obliged to him.' However, I was determined to shew the Ameers of Hydrabad their deserts were of no avail; that I could and would follow them everywhere, whether it was to the deserts of Scinde or to the mountains of Beloochistan; that following his cousins to Emaum Ghur was, perhaps, the most difficult of any operation of the kind, and therefore would have the most effect.

"I thought it not amiss to lift up the curtain, and let my friend Ali Moorad look into futurity; it is well for him to feel that he is wholly dependent on our power; that everything he can honestly wish for is his, as our faithful ally, but, that should he be a traitor he has no refuge. He is vigorous minded, ambitious, and, I suspect, a cunning man, but apparently generous and bold; in short, as good as barbarians can be, and better than most. Sheik Ali Nusseer, his minister, is very clever; he has lived in Bengal, knows our power, and has, I believe, convinced his master that it is not to be resisted; besides, he sees that while he keeps his master good friends with us, his own fortune must thrive : he is therefore our own."

Ali Moorad was now declared Rais by the following manifesto.

"Ameers and people of Scinde. His Highness the Ameer Roostum Khan sent a secret messenger to me, saying, he was in the hands of his family and could not act as his feelings of friendship for the English nation prompted him to do; and if I would receive him, he would escape and come to my camp. I answered his Highness I would certainly receive him, but my advice was, for him to consult with his brother, the Ameer Ali Moorad Khan. He took my advice. He went to the fort of Dejee, to his brother. When I heard of this I was glad, for I thought that Scinde would be tranquil; that his Highness would spend his last days in honour and in peace. I moved with my troops towards Kyrpoor, to force his violent family to disperse the wild bands they had collected. I sent his Highness word I should visit him; I wanted to ask his advice as to the arrangements for the new treaty. I thought he had again become the friend of the Government I serve. That night I heard he had solemnly conferred upon his brother, the Ameer Ali Moorad, the Turban of command over the Talpoor family, which brother is the lawful heir to that honour. I thought this a very wise proceeding, and it added to my desire to meet his Highness, that I might hear from his own lips all about these things and report the same to the Governor-General, being assured that these acts would recover for him the good opinion and friendship of the Governor-General of India.

" My feelings towards his Highness were those of friendship, honour and peace. I even advised his Highness' brother, the Ameer Ali Moorad, not to accept the Turban, but to assist his brother, the Chief, in the cares of government. I laboured for the honour of the Talpoor family.

What then was my astonishment to find, that when I expected to meet the Ameer Roostum Khan his Highness had departed from the roof of his brother, thus insulting and defying the Governor-General, whose commander I am. But my surprise is greatly increased, by hearing that his Highness has joined his family and the armed bands who have cut off our communications and stopped our mails. These things have surprised me; but my course is plain, and I thus publish it to the country, that all may know it, and conduct themselves accordingly. I will, according to the existing treaty, protect the chief Ameer, Ali Moorad, in his right as the justly constituted chief of the Talpoor family. God willing, I mean to march into the desert. I will disperse the armed bands that have stopped our mails. I will place the Killedars of the chief, Ali Moorad, in command of every fort; and I will act towards the Ameers of Hydrabad as I shall find their conduct deserves."

Scarcely had this been published, when a letter from Roostum arrived, in which he denied having voluntarily ceded the Turban, and intimated that the English General had betrayed him into Ali Moorad's hands, designing to make him a captive. At the same time a letter of an equally false character came from Nusseer of Hydrabad, professing obedience indeed, but only to obtain time for the assembling of the tribes.

These artifices were too gross.

" Ameer," said the General, in reply to Nusseer, " I have received your letter. When a man's actions and his words do not accord, I am greatly distressed to know how to act. The Government of the Ameers is one of many heads. All speak and act after a different, and a very strange manner. I cannot judge afar off. I came to Kyrpoor to see how matters stand, and I mean to go to Hydrabad to do the same. I cannot distinguish friends from enemies at two hundred miles' distance, and as you say you are the friend of the Company and Governor-General you will rejoice to see me. I hear of troops collecting in the south, armed men shall not cross the Indus, therefore I take troops."

To Roostum he wrote in a sterner manner, for he was indignant at his falsehood, and the accusation of treachery.

" Your Highness's letter obliges me to speak with a language I regret, but the honour of my country, and the interest of yours, leaves me no alternative.   The gist of your Highness's letter is this.   That I advised you to be guided by your brother, the Ameer Ali Moorad ; and that he advised you to fly from a meeting with me, as a conspirator who wished to make you a captive.

" Ameer, such a subterfuge is unworthy of your Highness's rank.   You know it is not truth.   You know that you offered to come to my camp, and that I advised you to go to your brother's fortress instead of coming to my camp ; you therefore well know that I had no desire to capture you, nor to interfere with your family arrangements.   Yet you now pretend that when I asked you to meet me, you flew from me, not from any desire to avoid a meeting with me but because I advised you to be guided by your brother's advice, and he advised you to fly !   I will not suffer your Highness to take shelter under such misrepresentations. You made submission to me as the representative of the Governor-General ; you have solemnly resigned the Turban, and you now avow that you look upon this, the most solemn and important act of your life, as a farce and a mockery !

" Ameer, I do not understand such double conduct : I hold you to your words and deeds ; I no longer consider you to be the chief of the Talpoors, nor will I treat with you as such, nor with those who consider you to be Rais."

While thus occupied at Mungaree, Ali Moorad's Vizier, Sheik Nusseer, told him, that Futteh Mohamed Ghoree, the prime mover of all mischief, had come disguised to Dejee-ka-kote, and corrupted two thousand of the Rais' troops, intending to carry them off to the sons and nephews of Roostum. The Sheik had therefore seized him, and asked significantly, " What shall be done with him ? "   " Keep him captive, but do him no hurt," was the reply.   It was a fortunate event, and a good omen.

During the fall of rain the army could not move, because the camels slip in the wet and dislocate their hips ; thus the

Bengal division, under Colonel Wallace, having moved contrary to orders in bad weather, lost ninety in one day ! Soon however the return of a serene sky enabled the General to advance on Dejee, where he was desirous to confer with Ali Moorad again, and to receive the latest reports of his emissaries before he plunged into the unknown waste. He reached it the 4th of January, and was then joined by Outram from Bombay. The reports from the emissaries also arrived. The Belooch forces at Dingee were said to have gone to the desert, on the skirts of which Roostum hovered with his troops; all were bound, it was supposed, for Emaum Ghur, and not less than twenty thousand fighting men, besides the garrison of that fort, were in the waste.

No exact intelligence could be obtained of the tracks to Emaum Ghur, or of the situation and copiousness of the waters; and it was evident that Ali Moorad was still averse to strangers going there. The English General was not to be turned from his resolution but his difficulties augmented. He had now made four marches with his whole disposable force, the two last actually within the precincts of the desert; his next move was to be into the wilderness, without sure guides, without any well-grounded expectation of finding water and forage, and with almost a certainty of being met and fought with, or at the least harassed by the Beloochees in great numbers. He desired therefore to await the Governor-General's approval before he made the attempt, but the recent heavy rains, unusual in Scinde, had so facilitated the execution of the design, that he would not lose the opportunity by delay.

His first notion was to march upon Emaum Ghur with his whole force, by the road of Laloo, a place considered to be in the desert, though near the edge of the cultivated district. This line would still turn the recusant Ameers' position at Dingee, and cut their communication with the fortresses in the waste; he could then choose, whether to wheel suddenly on his right and fall on them at Dingee; or to his left and march on Emaum Ghur. For with a nice generalship, knowing how war changes its face day by day, he designed to steer so as to be ready for any accidental

advantage which might offer; hoping always to alarm the
Beloochees at Dingee, and again cause them to disperse or
retreat. In either case he could gain time to make his point
in the desert, without being troubled by them during that
perilous march; and if, as his spies reported, the Dingee
force had already gone to Emaum Ghur, his resolution was
to follow them and fight a decisive battle at its gates, before
the Hydrabad army could collect to harass his rear. If they
retreated confusedly on Hydrabad, his intention was, to relinquish the desert march and strike at them beneath the
walls of that capital.

New events changed these views. The Belooch movement
into the waste from Dingee had been prematurely reported;
the Ameers had attempted it, but their men soon revolted
at the difficulties, and returned, preferring battle to privations. Meanwhile, a native agent sent to explore and
note the state of the wells, came back with such a tale of
arid sands and dried up pits, that the General resigned all
hope of being able to march with the whole army. Then
with surpassing hardihood he selected two hundred irregular
cavalry, put three hundred and fifty of the 22nd Queen's
regiment on camels, loaded ten more of those animals with
provisions, eighty with water, and resolved with these five
hundred men to essay that enterprise for which only the day
before he had allotted three thousand, thinking it even then
most hazardous as in truth it was. The guide might be
false, Ali Moorad might prove a traitor, the wells might be
poisoned, the water-skins might be cut in the night by a
prowling emissary; the skirts of the waste were swarming
with thousands of horsemen, who might surround him on the
march, and the Ameers had many more and better camels
than he had, upon which to mount their infantry: finally
Emaum Ghur was strong, well provided, and the garrison
alone four times his number! To look at all these dangers
with a steady eye, to neglect no precautions, to discard fear
and brave the privations of the unknown wilderness, was the
work of a master spirit in war, or the men of ancient days
have been idly called great.

Compelling Ali Moorad and the native guide to go with

him, he warned them in his quaint mode to beware of foul
play, saying, such was his anxiety for their subsistence, they
should only eat and drink at the wells with his soldiers, for
thus only could he be sure they were not suffering—then
he started, having organized a body of camel-riders to
maintain his communications with his army. The weight
of nearly fifty years' service had not bent his head, the drain
of many wounds had not chilled the fiery current of his
blood; refusing no labour, enduring every privation equally
with the youngest and most robust of his troops, he led his
small band into the heart of the trackless waste, not in pride
and arrogance of daring, but to strike at the vital parts of
the Ameers' strength, and to find peace where they had
prepared only war.

His march could not be concealed, but relying on the
weak nature of the Ameers he, with infinite sagacity, sent
them formal notice, saying—" I am not going to plunder or
to slay, if you make no resistance. If you do, abide the
consequences!" Thus he considered and provided for every
chance in this desperate trial, with a coolness of calculation
that gained for him the unrestricted commendation of that
great general, whose genius is imperial England's pride;
and now it will be understood why the man who won Assaye,
he who commenced the passage of the Douro with a single
boat and twenty-five men, why he, the Duke of Wellington,
speaking in the House of Lords with that elevated simplicity,
which is the peculiar characteristic of his mind, thus described
the exploit :—" *Sir Charles Napier's march upon Emaum
Ghur, is one of the most curious military feats which I have
ever known to be performed, or have ever perused an account of
in my life. He moved his troops through the desert against
hostile forces; he had his guns transported under circumstances
of extreme difficulty, and in a manner the most extraordinary,
and he cut off a retreat of the enemy which rendered it impossible for them ever to regain their positions.*"

On the evening of the 5th he began this march; the
night was dark, the sand deep, the guide lost the track; yet
the troops made nearly twenty-five miles before they halted.
The second day's journey was somewhat less, but forage

failed, water became scarce, and he sent back three-fourths
of his cavalry, retaining only fifty of the best, and hoping
rather than expecting to retain even those beyond another
day.   Yet he was resolute to proceed while a hundred men
could be kept together.

Roostum with seven thousand armed followers, ten times
the number of the British, was now suddenly found on the
flank: but treating him as one who must be submissive, the
General sent Outram to his camp, still pushing on himself
with his fifty wild horsemen, his two howitzers, and his three
hundred Irish infantry, whose Guebre blood, bounding in
their veins, seemed to recognize the divinity of that Eastern
sun which their forefathers had worshipped two thousand
years before.

A wild and singular waste was that they were penetrat-
ing.   Sand-hills, north and south, stretched for hundreds of
miles in parallel ridges, symmetrically plaited like the ripple
of a placid tide.   Varying in height, breadth and steepness,
they presented one uniform surface.   Some were only a
mile broad, others more than ten miles across; many were of
gentle slopes and low, others lofty, and so steep the howitzers
could only be dragged up by men.   The sand, mingled with
shells, run in great streams resembling numerous rivers,
skirted on each side by parallel streaks of soil, which
nourished jungle, yet thinly and scattered.   The tracks of the
hyena and wild boar, and the prints of small deers' footsteps
were seen at first, yet they soon disappeared, and the solitude
of the waste became unbroken.

For eight days these intrepid soldiers traversed this
gloomy region, living from hand to mouth, uncertain each
morning if water could be found in the evening; and at
times it was not found; they were not even sure of their
right course, yet with fiery valour and untiring strength they
continued their dreary dangerous way.   The camels found
little food and got weak, but the stout infantry helped to
drag the heavy howitzers up the sandy steeps, and all the
troops, despising the danger of an attack, worked with a
power and will that overcame every obstacle.   On the eighth
day they reached Emaum Ghur, eager to strike and storm,

and then was seen how truly laid down is Napoleon's great maxim, that in war, moral power is to physical force as four to one.

Mohamed Khan had a fortress, with a garrison four times stronger than his coming enemies, yet he fled when they were two marches distant, by tracks known only to his people, taking with him his treasure but leaving his stores of grain and powder behind!

Emaum Ghur, never before seen by Europeans, was square and of considerable size. The centre was a tower, also square, and fifty feet high, built of well-burned bricks; it was encompassed by walls forty feet high, with eight round towers constructed of unburned bricks. This citadel was surrounded by another strong wall fifteen feet high, recently erected, and also of unburned bricks, which offer a peculiar resistance to artillery, for the shot penetrates yet brings nothing down. The howitzers were ineffectual, and recourse was had to mines, for the General resolved to destroy the place. Ali Moorad was averse to this, but finally consented, firing the first gun himself.

This was no wanton act. " Princes," wrote the General to Lord Ellenborough, " are not always faithful, and if Ali Moorad should fall off from our alliance, this stronghold in the desert might prove vexatious, and require another perilous march to retake it. Meanwhile its existence fosters a false confidence in all the other Ameers, and its sudden destruction will tell on them with stunning effect." Such were his principal motives, but he had observed that the Ameers perpetrated their intolerable oppression with impunity from the strength of their castles, and he thought to destroy even one of those was a gain for humanity.

The place was full of gunpowder and grain, the last was distributed among the troops, the price being first paid to Ali Moorad. The powder loaded twenty-four mines to blow up the fortress. This was effected on the 15th, with the following singular display of zeal and firmness on the part of the chief engineer, Major Waddington. The matches of all the mines having been lighted, an assistant engineer took refuge behind some accidental cover at a short distance to

L

await the explosions; from thence he perceived his chief still bending over the train of one mine. Eagerly he called upon him to run, for " the other mines are going to burst." " That may be, but this mine must burst also," was the calm reply. Having deliberately arranged the match, Waddington walked away, holding up his hands as if to guard his head from the huge hurling fragments, which successive bursting mines sent into the air to fall in showers around him. It was a grand action! He would have done better to have reserved his heroism for a greater occasion—but it was a grand action!

A choice of new operations was now to be made. The Beloochees in Shah Ghur, the other desert fort, refused to yield it to Ali Moorad. The place was distant, and the General had no guides; yet he was going, when one of his camel riders came from Dejee, with news that the tribes were gathering fast at Dingee. This decided him to gain the Indus and rejoin the bulk of his army; but he chose a new route, more to the southward, because his object of causing them to disperse had not been attained, and he thus designed to pour upon their flank, not as in retreat, but with war and terror. Hence, with unmitigated hardihood he made a fresh sweep through the unknown wilderness, seeking, as chance guided, uncertain tracks and springs, but trusting to the water skins, replenished at Emaum Ghur.

Again his gallant soldiers marched with equal vigour and fortune, for on the second day they struck Tugull, from whence two known tracks led, one to Hydrabad the other to Dingee. There another camel rider met him with intelligence that Roostum had quitted the waste; that the force at Dingee was broken up, and the Hydrabad Ameers were terrified. Thus a second time the lowering cloud of war seemed dissipated without a life lost. Nevertheless the treaty was not signed, and, following up his threat the General resolved to visit Hydrabad. Wherefore ordering supplies to be sent down the Indus, he called the main body of his troops down from Dejee to Abu-Bekr.

The first three days of his return march had been very trying; on the fourth water and forage was found: on the eighth day, January 23rd, he reached Peer Abu-Bekr. Here his whole force being united, he halted. Eighteen days he had been wandering in the waste, suffering privations and risking dangers demanding the greatest mental energy to face unappalled: yet he came back without the loss of a man, having taken a fortress, dispersed an army, and baffled the Ameers' plan of campaign.

CHAPTER II.

NEW combinations, military and political, now produced an unexpected course of action, and it is necessary so to recapitulate the past policy, that each step in the conquest may be understood, and that the foul charges of injustice and violence may be dispelled by facts.

The first period of Sir C. Napier's assumption of the political duties was marked by his quick perception of the grievous vacillating weakness and vanity of the political agents, and his own frank firm intercourse with the Ameers.

The second period was marked by his precise, vigorous analysis of the proofs furnished by Outram as to the hostile designs of the Ameers: this analysis being made under the following just and discriminating instructions from Lord Ellenborough.

" Your first political duty will be, to hear all that Major Outram and other political agents may have to allege against the Ameers of Hydrabad and Kyrpoor, tending to prove the intention, on the part of any of them, to act hostilely against the British army. That they may have hostile feelings there can be no doubt; it would be impossible to believe they could entertain friendly feelings; but we should not be justified in inflicting punishment for their thoughts."

The third period was marked by negotiations to induce the Ameers quietly to accept the new treaty, imposed to punish their infractions of the old treaties and their underhand hostility. Upon this hostility the question of justice hinged, and it has been shewn with what caution, pains and acuteness the Ameers' delinquency was ascertained. Acting then on the policy previously proclaimed to all India, Lord Ellenborough insisted on the new treaty, which did but slightly punish past sins, and was in truth framed rather to benefit civilization than to hurt the Ameers. Its unaggressive character was shewn by restoring to the Bhawal Khan the districts taken from him by the Ameers.

Lord Ellenborough could not with any safety recede at this critical period from his avowed policy. The armies of Pollock and Nott were then dangerously situated, and any weakness leading to disaster in Scinde, would be sure, aided by the treason of the newspaper editors to produce wide-spreading mischief.

This third period was terminated by the vakeels from Lower Scinde accepting the new treaty in the name of their masters; and a like acceptance by Roostum with the addition of his seal in confirmation.

To the fourth period belongs the passage of the Indus, the occupation of the ceded districts, and the march on Kyrpoor against the armed bands; but none of these things were attempted until Roostum and the Ameers of Hydrabad gave warrant by accepting the new treaties—nor until their menacing language, stoppage of däks, anticipation of revenue, discrepancy of words and acts, and the unvarying reports of emissaries proved that a secret plan of hostility was in progress. Ali Moorad's defection from the family policy, the cession of the Turban, and the flight of the younger Princes terminated this period.

The fifth period was marked by the efforts of Roostum and his sons to maintain a footing in Upper Scinde, their sudden occupation of Emaum Ghur and Shah Ghur, and the entrenching of a position at Dingee; and this military holding of Upper Scinde, while they were in close connection with the Ameers of Lower Scinde, indicated plainly their original design as to war. For while holding ground in the upper province, they were more in connection with the Seiks of Moultan, the Brahooe-Beloochees and the Affghans of Candahar. The astonishing desert march and rapid return baffled all their calculations, and terminated the troubles of Upper Scinde. But during that march happened a course of diplomacy which led to a terrible contest, wherein Sir C. Napier vindicated his double armorial legend—" *Ready aye Ready,*" " *Sans tache.*"

It has been shewn how, on the second day's march against

Emaum Ghur, the General came suddenly upon Roostum's camp. The Ameer greatly alarmed sent a message to say he was submissive, which alone would prove hostile intentions. Outram, at his own desire was permitted to confer with Roostum, for the General thought Ali Moorad might have frightened the old man and caused him thus to flee into the waste : hence he desired to reassure him ; yet forbad Outram to give him hope of any thing beyond the quiet enjoyment of his private possessions, for no concession would reinstate him as Rais.

Outram returned with a son of Roostum, to whom the General explained his views, telling him his father might return to Kyrpoor, or live where he pleased, with the assured protection of the British Government. The Prince seemed satisfied, and went back accompanied by Outram, who now, with the General's consent, invited Roostum to come to the British camp. He agreed to do so, yet pleaded present fatigue, and having thereby deceived Outram decamped in the night and fled, thus re-enacting the same false part he had played at Dejec-ka-kote : for he could not now suspect any foul design, seeing, that force might have been used to bring him to the camp.

When Emaum Ghur fell, the General, thinking to profit by that event despatched Outram to Kyrpoor, as his Commissioner. He was to invite by proclamation all the Ameers of both Scindes to meet him there on the 20th of January, either in person or by vakeels, to complete the new treaty. The Hydrabad Ameers did not refuse, but did not obey: those of Upper Scinde were entirely contumacious. On his journey, Outram again came on Roostum in his old camp, and proposed that they should proceed together to Kyrpoor. Roostum had seven thousand armed men and seven guns at this time, with which he was going to reinforce his sons and nephews at Dingee ; these he kept out of sight, pleaded fatigue as before, begged of Outram to go on, promised to be at Kyrpoor next day, laughed at the simplicity of his dupe, and then marched to the south.

This deceit was, with an inconceivable logic, ascribed by Outram to the evil influence of Ali Moorad, who was then far distant with Sir C. Napier, while Roostum was surrounded by his own friends and guided by an army! But at this time Major Outram's mind was singularly disturbed, and his views, pertinaciously urged, were marvellously wild and inconsistent. He had, on quitting Scinde when deprived of political employment, repeatedly advised Sir C. Napier to trust Ali Moorad as a man of superior ability, confirmed honour, and unvarying friendship for the British. At the same time he denounced Futteh Mohamed Ghoree, Roostum's Vizier, as an unprincipled man, hostile to the British and dangerous in every way.

With these sentiments on his lips he went to Bombay, and in six weeks came back as the General's Commissioner. During that time he had no means for further judgment of men or affairs, and the two men's actions had, during the interval quite justified his character of them. Yet now, after only two interviews with Roostum, both marked by that old man's deceit, Outram with astounding mutability became the vehement vituperator of Ali Moorad, and by desire of Roostum, recommended at this most critical period, that Mohamed Ghoree, who had recently added to his other offences that of corrupting Ali Moorad's troops, should be released! To assign any motive beyond vanity and ignorance for this conduct would point to crime.

A positive refusal to release the Ghoree, should have taught Outram caution as to any after display of such meddling folly; and this first exhibition of it should have taught the General to doubt Outram's capacity: it amazed and shocked him, yet did not destroy his first favourable impressions of the man, which he retained until insensate propositions, involving the safety of the army, brought a painful conviction that he had relied on a person of little talent but of extraordinary activity and pertinacity in error.

Previous to the march on Emaum Ghur, Roostum, knowing that enterprise was in contemplation, urged the Ameers of Hydrabad to persevere in their warlike preparations, saying the British could not penetrate the waste and would return suffering and dispirited. This counsel had caused the position at Dingee to be maintained, contrary to the General's expectation : but when Roostum heard Emaum Ghur was taken, and the troops returning with that haughty resolution which success confers, he advised the Princes to retreat on Khoonhera, a fort skirting Lower Scinde, within the waste yet well watered. To that place, after deceiving Outram, he went himself, to be in closer connection with the Ameers of Hydrabad and Meerpoor, hoping to remain in safety until the fighting men of Lower Scinde assembled.

With a better military head he would have met and overwhelmed the troops on their return through the waste; and it was to avoid that danger the General came back by a different route. Roostum however judged well, thus to relinquish Upper Scinde altogether, and bring the influence of his now powerful armed force to bear on the councils of the Hydrabad Princes; for dismayed at the fall of Emaum Ghur, and wanting still three weeks to gather all their feudatories for battle, they now called the Ameers of Upper Scinde madmen, forbade their entering Lower Scinde, and sent vakeels to Kyrpoor, which they had previously avoided.

The Upper Scinde Princes were not so to be shaken off. They had quitted their palaces and luxurious gardens to make hurried journeys with their zenanas, and had expended much treasure in collecting forces. Hence, inflamed with fury, and backed up by the hardy plunder-loving Beloochees who had gathered under them, they would not hear of peace. The Hydrabad Princes were told, that willing or unwilling they must make common cause; and then they swore, and with them swore all the Belooch Chiefs of both provinces who had assembled, that they would "fight the accursed Feringees and destroy Ali Moorad."

In this crisis the Hydrabad Ameers played, as usual, a double game: assenting to war, they hastened the gathering of their feudatories, but also sent deputies to the British camp. These men came with the credentials of ambassadors, the instructions of spies, and vocation of military commissaries, bearing secret orders for the northern tribes on the right of the Indus, to come with all their warriors to Hydrabad.

When they first came Sir C. Napier thought it was in fear, and that he should in Lower, as in Upper Scinde, arrive at a peaceable termination. He was mistaken. He did not then know the haughty character, the fierce courage of the Beloochee race, nor their influence over the feeble minds of their Princes. This error he the more readily fell into, because he wished it so; and because Outram with preposterous vanity was continually asserting that he could easily procure the submission of the Ameers. Cautious however to test their real inclination he issued a proclamation, calling on them once more, to meet his Commissioner and frankly settle the dispute, or manfully take the field.

This produced no effect. Pressed by the antagonistic fears of the British army and their own wild chiefs, they yielded to the last as more nearly dangerous : but also their feelings were for war. They only yielded in appearance, dreading an immediate conflict while many of their feudatories were still distant : as these came in their pride arose.

Such was the state of affairs when Sir C. Napier, issuing from the waste, rejoined his army at Peer Abu-Bekr the latter end of January. He had then nearly three thousand men, whose right touched the broad waters of the Indus, on which floated his armed steamers and supplies. Their left rested on the waste where there was no longer an enemy. The Ameers might indeed again launch troops on that side, and by a wide movement turn his flank to fall on Ali Moorad, who had returned to Kyrpoor; but that Prince had his own forces, and was supported by British troops left at Sukkur. He was prepared also for hostilities, because many Killedars on the right of the Indus, trusting to the forts which covered the country, resisted his tax-gatherers; in the event of his being overpowered, the Bengal division could descend from Subzulcote to aid : nor could the Ameers send the tribes on the right bank of Indus against Sukkur with advantage, because of its strength. The line of operations was therefore simple ; the right flank was secured on the river, by which the steamers could turn the enemy; the left was indeed uncovered, to the desert, but the Scinde irregular horsemen under Capt. Jacob were there to prevent surprise.

No sure intelligence of the Ameers' numbers or designs could now be obtained ; yet it was evident those of Lower Scinde were seeking to gain time, and those of Upper Scinde bent on war ; for the proclamation inviting them to a conference, had declared that each vakeel must come with full powers under pain of exclusion, and his master being treated as an enemy. The 20th of January was fixed for assembling. This was afterwards extended to the 25th, yet from the Ameers of Upper Scinde no person came ; and of the vakeels from Hydrabad only Sobdar's had full powers. Wherefore, after halting two days at Peer Abu-Bekr, Sir C. Napier moved slowly towards the south, hoping for rather than expecting peace, and reasoning thus :—

" I cannot lose time, the hot season approaches, and these barbarians must not treat the British power with contempt. Their intentions are doubtful, their conduct suspicious ; armed men are hastening to them from every quarter ; it is necessary to approach near to ascertain their real position and views. If, as it is said, the Ameers of Lower Scinde have refused to make common cause with those of Upper Scinde, or to let them enter their country, the latter will be found on the frontier, where they may be attacked in front, while Jacob turns their right from the desert. The steam-boats will be on their left, Hydrabad closed against them, they must win the battle, or be destroyed, or submit and sign the treaty. If they fly to the desert, no place of refuge is there, Emaum Ghur is destroyed. They must go northward, where they will meet Ali Moorad and other British troops : the Bengal division is now on its march to Ferozepore, but the Bhawal Khan's cavalry are in the ceded districts and available as allies."

This view was comprehensive, and the General feeling strong, sent the Hydrabad vakeels back with compliments, accepting their presence as a mark of amity ; and to omit nothing which could conduce to peace, he extended the period for treating to the 1st of February. Outram also, at his own urgent request, was suffered to go to Hydrabad, because he persisted to say he could bring the Ameers to submission. Nevertheless the General continued his march : for though he unwisely yielded to Outram's silly vanity he doubted the effect of his diplomacy.

" I have now," he wrote to him, " waited long enough for the authorized vakeels, and I think you may proceed to Hydrabad, if you think so doing likely to prevent bloodshed and reconcile the Ameers to the draft treaty, so far as being amenable to it can be called reconciliation. I am most anxious they should not resist. I am sure they will not resist by force of arms, but I would omit no one step that you, or any one thinks, can prevent that chance. I think you may probably do good, and not the less for my movements in that direction."—" I wish you would write to Roostum, to say that I will receive him at any time with every attention to his comfort if he comes to my camp."

This was written on the 28th of January, and on the 30th he again extended the time for treating to the 6th of February, writing thus again to Outram.

" I have seen the Hydrabad deputies. I have ordered them to meet you there on the 6th of February, and you are to tell me directly, whether or not they have brought the deputies of Meer Roostum and the others, with the prescribed powers. If they have, I wait the result of negotiations. If not, I march against them as enemies on the 6th, but I am willing to do all I can to save the mischief that will fall upon these Ameers, if they will not meet you."

To the Ameers of Lower Scinde he wrote at the same time, in conciliatory terms, praising their apparent desire for peace ; but to those of Upper Scinde he had, on the 27th, addressed the following proclamation, which very exactly epitomized the past transactions with those Princes.

" Ameers, I was ordered to make a new treaty with you. Your Highnesses agreed to the draft of that treaty in words, while you raised troops to oppose it by deeds. You were ordered to disperse your troops, you did not disperse them : you hoped to deceive me by a pretended agreement to the draft treaty. You thought you could procrastinate until the hot weather should prevent any military operations by the British troops : you imagined you could then assail us on all sides with impunity. If we marched against you before the heat came, you thought our march would be late, and you resolved to resist with arms : if worsted in fight, you looked to the desert as a certain refuge. You were right, had we abided your time and marched by the road you expected. But we preferred our own time, and our own road ; we marched into your desert, we destroyed your magazines of powder and of grain, we destroyed also the fortress in which they were lodged, safely, as you vainly supposed ; we have returned from the desert, and we have yet three months of weather fit for war.

" But I want to prevent war. I therefore desired you to meet Major Outram at Kyrpoor on the 25th instant, there to discuss and arrange the details of the draft treaty, to accept or reject them as seemed best to your Highnesses. What is the result ? Your Highnesses have neither replied to my letter, nor sent delegates invested with authority to meet my Commissioner. This conduct is insulting to the Government I serve. I told you that if you so acted I would take possession of your territories, but my object is to avoid hostilities while I obey the orders of the Governor-General. I therefore will still give you to the 1st of February to send your vakeels to my head-quarters, in hope that you may correct the imprudence with which you have hitherto acted, and which I deeply regret. My military operations must go forward, but your persons shall be respected, you shall be considered as friends up to the first day of February : after that day I shall treat all as enemies who do not send vakeels to meet me.

" Ameers, you imagine you can procrastinate till your fierce sun drives the British troops out of the field, and forces them to seek shelter in Sukkur. You trusted to your desert and were deceived. You trust to your deadly sun and may again be deceived. I will not write a second letter to you, nor a second time expose the authority which I represent to indignity ; but this proclamation will, I hope, induce you to adopt a manly instead of an insidious course."

The 31st of January the army reached Nowshera, belonging to Ali Moorad, on the southern border of Upper Scinde, and then it was said the Ameers of that province were at last willing to submit. The tale was false, yet so ready was the General to save them, that he seized the occasion to urge on Lord Ellenborough a mitigation of the draft treaty, where he thought it pressed hardly on their pecuniary interests : nor would he have been refused, if the events which immediately followed had not ended their reign altogether.

At Nowshera he halted five days, partly to bring up supplies, principally to give time for Outram's negotiation at Hydrabad : thus a third time extending the period for a peaceable termination, although then on the verge of the hot season. Soon repentance came. Outram's conduct at Kyrpoor had become a subject of amazement : at Hydrabad it passed the bounds of sanity.

It has been shewn how at Kyrpoor he proposed to release the mischievous Ghoree, using the most abusive language against Ali Moorad, as if that Ameer's adherence to the British alliance was in his eyes a heinous crime. His next step was, without authority, to grant the Ameers a longer day for treating than had been proclaimed : that was approved of ; but he forgot to fix a day, which gave an opening for indefinite procrastination until the General amended the error. Then he proposed to alter one of the principal articles of the draft treaty, which had been deliberately drawn up by Lord Ellenborough, thus stepping beyond the line of his mission, which was to arrange details, not to reform.

Corrected on those points by Sir C. Napier, he, seeing that only the Lower Scinde Ameers had sent vakeels, proposed as before said to proceed alone to Hydrabad as a negotiator, saying all would be easily arranged. The General, more prescient and suspecting treachery, sent the light company of the 22nd Queen's regiment after him, and one hundred convalescents would have followed but for some misunderstanding of orders : this foresight saved Outram's life. But his consent to Outram's going at all was given reluctantly and it proved very detrimental, as did all the counsels of Outram which were assented to : those which were rejected would have caused the destruction of the army.

The five days of grace now accorded to the Ameers was
a magnanimous display of generous intrepidity; and the
gross imputation that Sir C. Napier sought battle ferociously
is thus negatived. He never sought battle at all; it was
forced upon him: but faction has neither eyes nor ears for
truth; nor any sense save for malice. He saw through the
falsehood and shifts of the Ameers to prolong diplomacy
until the sun should become deadly: he had but six weeks
safe for field operations, and already the heat was oppressive; yet, without being blind to their arts and solely
from his strong desire for peace, he gave those deceitful
people five days which he could have used with the utmost
advantage in war. What was to hinder him from making
forced marches, attended by steamers which would have
picked up his weakly men and carried his provisions, and
thus fall like a thunderbolt in the midst of the Ameers' half-
collected army under the walls of Hydrabad? What but
his earnest desire for peace, and his contempt of false glory!
Strong in his sense of justice and humanity, secure in the
consciousness of genius, firm in moral resolution, he delayed
the blow to his own risk, rising above the consideration of
danger though it was of a nature to chill the stoutest heart,
combining a fearful responsibility to his own Government
with the risks of war.

All the Ameers' proceedings were deceitful. They had
no thought save to gain time for the assembling of their
whole army, which they calculated could not be before the
middle of February; and to delay the war until that period,
no falsehood or intrigue, no fraud or daring violence, was
spared. By their agents the General's correspondence with
Outram was stolen from the latter; and meanwhile Roostum
and his sons were writing ridiculous statements to Outram
designed to mislead, and which did mislead him. The
General's spies however, gave clear and positive information, all contradicting Outram's and the Ameers' statements,
which were nearly alike. The emissaries all spoke thus:

" The warriors of the different tribes, however distant,
are in march on Hydrabad. All the Princes of both Scindes
are in close alliance. The people of the country universally

declare, that if the Ameers stand against the British, a great commotion will happen all over Scinde."

But soon an incontrovertible proof was obtained. Sobdar, exceeding all others in villainy, secretly sent a vakeel to say he had joined the other Ameers to betray them; that he was still the fast friend of the British, and when the battle took place his five thousand warriors should fall on their unsuspecting countrymen. "Tell him," said the indignant General, "that my army fears no Beloochee force. I want no help, I despise traitors, and if I find his men in the field I will fall on them. I love not traitors!"

The last day of grace was the 6th of January, and on the 5th the Hydrabad vakeels sent word, that Roostum had promised to meet Outram in that city. Sir C. Napier answered that the Ameers' promises, and especially Roostum's, were too well known to be now regarded. Next day he marched, but only eight miles still hoping to prevail peaceably.

Now rapidly the heat came on, and the signs of war augmented. From a spy he learned that Roostum had indeed gone to Hydrabad; but his sons remained at Khoonhera with seven guns and fifteen hundred men; the rest had gone to their homes, but under an engagement to return at a moment's notice. It was also reported that the Meerpoor man would receive them, and give them Omercote in the desert as a place of arms.

"This will not do," the General wrote to Outram. "This will not do: the Governor-General's orders to disperse the armed bands with these Princes are positive. I have no time to lose; my troops must soon disperse from the heat, I will not lose the cool weather. Say then to the Ameers of Kyrpoor thus—You were told in December 1842, to disperse your armed bands, yet you have kept, and still keep them together. Disperse them instantly or I will fall on them.

"To the Ameers of Hydrabad say thus:—

"If you permit the bands of Upper Scinde to assemble in your territory I will treat you also as enemies. And if you let them go to your fortress of Omercote in the desert, I

will first assault Hydrabad, and then Omercote. You may
receive your relations of Upper Scinde as guests, but not as
enemies of the British."

Owing to some difficulty of navigation, Outram did not
reach Hydrabad until the 8th of February, having only
thirty sepoys under Captain Wells, for the light company of
the 22nd did not arrive until three days later. His first
despatch gave a positive opinion that the Ameers had no
hostile designs ; yet he admitted they were storing Omercote with grain, and were very blustering. On this it was
well observed by the General, When men bully and bluster
at the head of sixty thousand men, it is no joke for three
thousand who are within their reach.

At a long conference with Outram, the first day of his
arrival, the Ameers, Roostum being present, made loud lamen-
tations, denied all the obnoxious acts, proved against them
before the new treaty had been proposed. Pretending great
amity still, they demanded the restoration of the Turban to
Roostum, saying that was the only obstacle to signing the
treaty : this could not legally be done, but it furnished
ground for procrastination. They were earnest to delay the
General's march, saying they could not otherwise restrain
their Beloochees, who would plunder far and wide, friends
and foes alike : thus admitting that they had collected a
large force, which they had previously denied.

Then they protested against the new treaty, again denied the charges on which it was founded : all of which had
been furnished by Outram himself — but they added we will
sign if you, Outram, advise us so to do : thus asserting and
sacrificing Roostum's claims with the same breath ! Sobdar
still the most hypocritical, declared himself ready to sign
the treaty at once. Finally, all promised that vakeels should
go next day to the Residency and accept the treaty.

The next day, 9th, was however occupied with messages.
No vakeels came, and time was thus wasted until evening.
Then the Ameers who had meanwhile corrupted Outram's
moonshee sent the vakeels to the Residency, which was four
miles from their Palace, but only to give a promise to accept
it, having affixed their seals to this promise. This was

precisely what Roostum had before done at Kyrpoor. The
Ameers had at that moment a large force assembled in a
camp four miles northward of Hydrabad, and it had been
there since the 6th, yet Outram knew nothing of it though
so close to him! He disregarded all the indications of
hostility pointed out by his officers, and asserted that no
warlike designs were entertained. The Ameers had measured
his capacity.

They were now sure that all their fighting men, even
the most distant, those of the hills above Shikarpoor in the
north and those near Kurrachee in the south, were in movement, and confident in their numbers and prowess thought
only of blood and revenge. The masks of gentleness and
submission were no longer necessary, and in their pride and
cruelty, they resolved, with a horrid violation of hospitality
and the laws of nations, to murder the Commissioner, his
officers, and escort : then to throw down the assassin's knife,
and give battle with sixty thousand ferocious warriors, skilled
in the use of their weapons and to whom fear was unknown.
" *How could they fail of victory ? There were less than three
thousand to fight with, and only five hundred of those Europeans ! The Affghans had with twenty thousand destroyed
a greater number of English, and the Affghans were not to be
compared to the Beloochees. How could they fail ?* "

By previous intrigues, much falsehood, and feigned
dispersions of their followers, they had, as they thought,
adroitly drawn the small British army into an isolated
position, far from its reserves. It was at their mercy. And
what mercy theirs would have been is known. They had
ordained, that, after the victory, every man woman and
child belonging to the British Government in Scinde should
be collected and have their throats cut on the field of battle!
" *so shall we make it famous.*" The General alone was to be
spared, that they might put a ring in his nose, and lead
him with a chain in triumph to their Dhurbar. Against the
walls of their palace he was to be thus fastened, a spectacle
and a signal example while life lasted of their power and
vengeance ! Nusseer alone opposed this dire ferocity, and
when his remonstrances were unheeded, he suggested a ring

M

of gold as less dishonourable. " No!" exclaimed the savage Shahdad with an oath. " Of iron, and a heavy one!"

In this frame of mind they invited Outram and all his officers to attend a Dhurbar in the evening of the 12th, to see them affix their seals and signatures to the draft treaty, in ratification of the assent given by their vakeels at the Residency. This Dhurbar was the final snare. They had arranged to have all their fighting men assembled on the 9th; but the religious feast of the Moharem, which they observed rigidly, intervened and delayed many of the tribes. The plan was something confused thereby, for it was intended to slay the Commissioner and go forth to battle at once; but the Moharem did not end until the 11th, and the Ameers, impatient for treachery and blood, would not, by waiting for the assembly of the whole army let this favourable opportunity of killing the Commissioner pass: moreover the light company of the 22nd had now arrived, and more troops might follow. Wherefore they appointed the Dhurbar to be held on the 12th, being all prepared for murder, and out of thirty thousand warriors already assembled told off eight thousand to attack the Residency.

Blindly went Outram to the slaughter-house, and if he escaped it was because the Ameers, thinking the General as silly as his Commissioner, hoped for a greater victim. To aid their hope Outram laboured with implacable active stupidity: his own statements will elucidate this.

He arrived to negotiate with Princes who he had, only sixteen days before, thus described: " It is my intention to discuss every matter in future, in the presence of both parties, thereby to check in some measure, the bare-faced lying they have recourse to behind each others' backs."—" I am positively sick, and doubtless you are tired of those petty intrigues, brother against brother, and son against father, and sorry that we should be in any way the instruments to be worked upon by such blackguards; for, in whatever way we may act, we must play into the hands of one party or the other, unless we take the whole country to ourselves."

With these sentiments, so recently expressed, he gave implicit credence to the Ameers' protestations of peaceable intentions; and to their assurance, that they had ordered their bands to disperse, though he was at the moment surrounded by them. He knew they had commenced storing Omercote, and given other signs of hostility, but that he called blustering. Roostum's declarations, that the General had ordered him to obey Ali Moorad, and that he had not voluntarily resigned the Turban, he in some measure supported, accompanying the statement with his usual abuse of Ali Moorad, and suggesting a change of policy with re-- gard to that Prince. Yet one irrefragable proof of Roostum's falsehood he entirely passed over, namely, that the General had by Outram's own mouth told the old man, if he had been unjustly or harshly used by Ali Moorad he would right him, and protect him if he would come to the British camp. The Ameer, knowing the truth would then be discovered, always avoided that test.

In this credulous state of mind, Outram continued on the 9th, though the Ameers had failed in their promise to give him camel-riders and guides for his despatches; failed in their promise to send their vakeels in the morning to accept the treaty: and had, as he knew, corrupted his moonshee and stolen his papers. Nor was he shaken by the refusal of the Kyrpoor Ameers to send vakeels, unless it could be done without prejudice to Roostum's claim on the Turban. Finally he promised to use his influence for check- ing the advance of the army, which was their real object, as the Moharem feast had delayed the assembling of all their forces.

It was a fearful thing to see a man, entrusted with such great interests, thus entirely beguiled by Princes whose falsehood and treachery he had himself so recently and strongly described. At this time the Belooch villages, throughout the whole country, between Hydrabad and the British troops, were filled with warriors awaiting the signal for battle. Tribes were in march from the most distant points: the men of the desert from Omercote in the east; the Jockeas from near Kurrachee in the south; the Murrees, Dhoomkees, Booghtees and Chandians, from the hills above Shikarpoor in the north. All these tribes whose abodes were hundreds of miles distant from each other, who had no common bond save the name of Beloochee and the pay of the Ameers, were hastening to one central point, where an army was already collected, and all openly proclaiming their resolution to fight the Feringees. Yet Outram assured the General no hostile designs were entertained by the Ameers; they had dismissed their men, and had no armed followers beyond their usual retinue! But those Princes avaricious and luxurious, were notoriously afraid of the fierce men assembled around them; how then could it be supposed they would expend so much money, endure such inconvenience, submit to such control, unless with the object of driving the British from Scinde, a previous plan for which Outram had himself detected only a few months before!

The General had now reached Sukkurunda, on the Indus, sixty miles from Hydrabad, and there halted at Outram's desire; not that he agreed to his views, but was to the last moment willing to adopt any suggestion tending to prevent war, consistent with the safety of his army. Military exigencies also accorded with this desire for peace. The camels, worn out beasts, had fallen behind, and a three days' halt was convenient to get them up and prepare for a fight, if battle could not be avoided. Nevertheless he would not yield to Outram's pleading in favour of the Ameers, and against Ali Moorad. " I have no power," he said, " to discuss former treaties, yet I will state to Lord Ellenborough all the Ameers say, because it is fair to them; but I am sure we should not tell them so now, because they would build interminable discussions thereon. Tell them therefore, that their plea of not being able to control the Beloochees is sufficient excuse for any Government to overthrow theirs."

At the same time, having received a letter from Shere Mohamed of Meerpoor, who pretended to be disquieted, he thus wrote to him—" No hostility has to my knowledge been committed by you. There is no mention of your name in the treaty; nor is there any intention of dispossessing you of any of your land, or doing anything displeasing to you. The British Government makes war on its enemies, not on its friends."

On the 10th Outram reported that the Kyrpoor Ameers, after promising to sign the draft treaty had deferred it on account of the Moharem, until the 11th—that he had accepted that excuse, and again desired that the army should halt, because he was sure the treaty would be finally executed by Roostum and his family. And now, in the extravagance of his credulity, the Commissioner urged the General to quit his army and come alone to Hydrabad! Urged him to come into the midst of twenty thousand warriors, eight thousand of whom were in the city, and all turbulent and menacing! and for what purpose? that he might thus be convinced how superior the Commissioner's judgment was to his own!

On the 11th he again wrote that the Kyrpoor Ameers were to sign and seal an acceptance of the treaty by vakeels that day; as if it were a step forwards, when Roostum had actually performed that ceremony more than two months before. He recommended also new arrangements, argued in favour of Roostum, and employed language injurious to Ali Moorad, which was his constant habit. To this he added, that the armed Beloochees under Roostum's sons and nephews at Khoonhera, were, as that Ameer told him, only their necessary attendants, about twelve hundred; that all others had been dismissed, and those remaining had no hostile designs against any one. Further, that the Hydrabad Ameers assured him, they had again sent orders for their bands to disperse, although they did not imagine any remained toge- ther after the former orders. And this strange letter, con- taining matter most offensive to Ali Moorad's feelings and interests, he purposed to send by a servant of Roostum, though he had, only a fortnight before, declared that Ameer to be surrounded and controlled by spies and blackguards in Ali Moorad's pay! thus very directly enabling them to pre- sent to Ali, instead of the General, a missive calculated to drive him in fear from the British alliance!

Accident alone prevented this letter being given to Roos- tum's servant; but so intent was Outram to enforce his absur- dities, that he wrote a second and a third letter the same day, repeating them. Roostum's anxiety to have it believed that there was no army at Khoonhera was well-founded.

That place was sixty miles from Hydrabad north-east; Sukkúrunda was the same distance north. The British could therefore have fallen by a rush on Khoonhera and destroyed the seven thousand men there: Roostum would then be desolate. Meanwhile the armed men said to be disbanded by the Ameers of Hydrabad were encamped, to the number of twenty thousand, at Meeanee, north of the city, and there entrenching a position, with the expectation of being reinforced by twenty-five thousand more in eight days. Never was a civilized man so beguiled, so mocked, so befooled by barbarians as Outram, since the days of Crassus.

During this course of folly events at the British camp curiously contradicted his assertions. The villages in the vicinity were filled with armed men, who menaced and insulted the British officers; and hundreds more daily passed on the left of the army by the desert, making for Meeanee. The General thinking he might find information of the Ameers' designs on some of these people, ordered Jacob to arrest all armed men passing his position. Soon twenty-five chiefs had the insolence to ride through the camp; they were stopped, but refused to give up their arms or go to head-quarters: the General sent a squadron to bring them in. They were of the Murree tribe, whose mountain abode was north-west of Shikarpoor hundreds of miles distant. Hyat Khan chief of the tribe was one. He pretended a mission to demand wages due from the Ameers for former services: yet he exclaimed when brought to the General "Why do you stop me? There are six hundred armed Beloochees in a village only two coss from you, there are plenty everywhere!"

On searching him however, letters were found from Mohamed Khan of Hydrabad, an Ameer who always professing entire submission and friendship for the British, and who, in conjunction with Nusseer and Sobdar, had only one week before sent letters by deputies to assure the General, "they had no part in Roostum's movement towards their territory—that his forces at Khoonhera were only necessary attendants—that they deprecated the advance of the British troops as improper, and claimed the fulfilment of the General's *promise* to remain at Nowshera till the 9th of February."

No promise had been given, but the 9th was the day originally fixed by the Ameers for the concentration of their forces, and they would have been so but for the Moharem feast, which had been forgotten in their calculation. Hence Mohamed's letter was to cover the deputies from suspicion in the English camp, while they forwarded the letters now found on Hyat.

In the first of these Mohamed Khan told the Murree Chief, that on the 9th it was designed to advance northward; but a halt would take place at Meeanee, and there Hyat must come with every man of his tribe who could carry sword, shield, or matchlock. The second letter exhorted him to be firm and faithful and obedient to the orders of Gholam Shah, his deputy, who thus united, following the General's expression, the characters of spy, plenipotentiary, and recruiting officer. The real designs of the Ameers could no longer be doubted, yet Outram continued incredulous.

On the 12th, having to meet the whole of the Ameers, and see the treaty formally executed, he wrote in the morning previous to the holding of the Dhurbar thus:—

"These fools are in the utmost alarm in consequence of the continued progress of your troops towards Hydrabad, notwithstanding their acceptance of the treaty, which they hoped would have caused you to stop. If you come beyond Halla, if so far, I fear they will be impelled by their fears to assemble their rabble, with a view to defend themselves and their families, in the idea that we are determined to destroy them, notwithstanding their submission. I do hope, therefore, you may not consider it necessary to bring the troops any further in this direction; for I fear it may drive the Ameers to act contrary to your orders to disperse their troops, or rather not to assemble them, for they were all dispersed yesterday; and thus compel us to quarrel with them."

How could it be believed that thousands of poor, rapacious, warlike men, who had come from abodes hundreds of miles distant, seeking prey and plunder, fanatics also, could be dispersed and sent back, and recalled again with a wave of the hand; that powerful and arrogant chiefs were thus to be dealt with by effeminate Princes! And if the latter did not mean to fight, what was the meaning of Sobdar's previous proposal to make his men fall on their comrades in the battle ? Moreover, at the moment Outram was writing, Hyat Khan was taken, with the letters mentioned on his person; the plain of Meeanee was swarming with warriors, preparing it for battle with mattock and spade; and eight thousand of the Lugaree tribe were only waiting for the murder of the Commissioner in Dhurbar, to fall on his escort.

Outram's statement was inaccurate as to facts as well as opinions. The whole of the Ameers had not accepted the treaty; and those who had, were supplying the troops of the Upper Scinde Princes who had not. The British force had not advanced.

This foolish letter was despatched on the 12th at noon, and at three o'clock he wrote again, to say the coming of the 22nd light company had added to the general disquietude —he desired authority for assuring the Ameers that the British army would not advance further, and to them he had expressed his hope that it would not. He intimated also an intention to pledge himself that no harm was designed by the General: and complained that he was not left free to pledge himself positively to all he conceived fitting: in other words that he had not the sole direction of this great matter, when every hour exposed his incapacity to conduct any part with judgment.

And now, again, he urged the strange counsel that Sir C. Napier should come alone to Hydrabad! "It would remove all doubts." "Unquestionably" replied the caustic General, "*It would remove all doubt, and my head from my shoulders.*" But again Outram's facts were false. The Ameers had not complied with all the terms; they had not disbanded their troops—sixty thousand were actually on the front, flank, and rear of the British; the latter had not moved forward; the Upper Scinde Ameers had not subscribed the new treaty, they had only promised to do so.

After despatching the last of these letters, Outram, attended by his officers went to the Dhurbar, where the Ameers signed and sealed the new treaty with all formalities. Nusseer of Kyrpoor was absent, but his seal was promised. Roostum's griefs against Ali Moorad were, as usual, made the principal topic of conversation and remonstrance, and Outram in his report again advocated his cause with the same pertinacious abuse of Ali Moorad.

On the 13th he thus described the state of affairs. " From what I saw yesterday of the spirit of the people, it appears to me the Ameers are now execrated for their dastardly submission, as they consider it, to what they style robbery. For the first time, since I came to Scinde in an official capacity, I was received last night by a dense crowd on emerging from the fort, after leaving the Dhurbar. Shouts expressive of detestation of the British, and a particular cry in which the whole population joined as in chorus, the meaning of which I could not make out at the time, but which I have since ascertained was an appeal to their Saint against the Feringees.

" Although the Dhurbar and streets of the fort were densely crowded, the Ameers' officers kept such a vigilant look-out that no evidence of the popular feeling was permitted ; but in passing through the city it could not be restrained ; and had we not been guarded by a numerous body of horse, headed by some of the most influential chiefs, I dare say the mob would have proceeded to violence ; as it was, a stone was thrown, which struck Captain Wells, but being quite dark, in the shade of the gateway he could not see by whom. This I was not aware of until we got home, and I have taken no notice of it to the Dhurbar, as it is evident the Government did its utmost to protect us, as was shewn by the escort refusing to go back after clearing the city ; whereas, heretofore, I had always dismissed it ; saying they had strict orders to accompany us the whole way. In fact the Ameers had reason to fear that their Beloochees might attempt mischief, having been the whole day engaged in paying off and dismissing those who had flocked to the city since the night before last, on hearing of the continued advance of your troops.

" Before I went to Dhurbar they had got the city quite clear, but after dark great numbers had flocked in again. I am anxiously looking out in the hopes you will come down in the steamer and stop the troops ! ! "

The cry to the Saint might alone have awakened Outram to some sense, seeing he had himself in the previous year, said the Ameers intended a religious war, which was confirmed by the spies in September 1842. Yet neither that coincidence, nor the violence displayed, prevented him from again urging the General to put himself in the power of the Ameers! Nor did he desist from this advice, even when writing a postscript to say he had discovered the design was to murder himself and his officers; and that Nusseer of Kyrpoor, the Ameer whose signature was wanting, had gone off for a plundering warfare in Upper Scinde, which would draw all the Beloochees to that quarter!

His comprehension of the Dhurbar plot was very different from that of Captain Wells, whose view of it after knowledge proved to be correct. On entering the Dhurbar, Wells saw at once that mischief was designed, because the armed men instantly clustered around each officer's chair, separating them. This made him fix his eyes on the young son of Nusseer, a fat luxurious boy, resolving to seize him as a shield and hostage: the boy, conscious of the intended treachery, slunk away.

In this gloomy way the Dhurbar was prolonged, until Outram told the Ameers he had despatched a steamer for the General and expected him at Hydrabad immediately; then their aspects changed, and they left the assembly suddenly, an action affronting and indecent, according to eastern customs. It was to deliberate, as Captain Wells thought at the time, upon the question of murdering those who were in their power at once, or sparing them that day to entrap the General; for in their barbarous pride they thought his judgment and penetration no greater than Outram's. Deciding on the last, they suffered all to depart unhurt and countermanded an attack ordered against the Residency; but having little time to ensure obedience, sent a guard with the Commissioner to prevent mistakes, which he accepted as a compliment and a kindness!

On all points Outram was wrong. Nusseer Khan of Kyrpoor had not gone to the north; nor was there any thought of a partisan warfare. Haughty and brave, the

Beloochees had resolved on a pitched battle, trusting to their sharp swords and bold hearts for victory. Outram's diplomacy may thus be measured: while assuming to know the Ameers' most secret policy he was entirely unobservant of their actions perpetrated as it were under his windows.

Sir C. Napier's judgment was disturbed neither by the deceit of the Ameers, nor by the credulity of his Commissioner, nor by the inaccuracy of the reports sent to him. On the 13th, while Outram was giving full scope to his hallucinations, the General gave him a full exposition of their falsehood, and said he would march next day, finishing thus—" The troops have Lord Ellenborough's orders on their side, and I have delayed, from first to last, at risk of their lives, and my own character as an officer till, *not the eleventh but the twelfth hour.* If men die in consequence of my delay, their blood may be justly charged to my account." Outram continued, however, to press his peculiar opinions. On the 13th he wrote a second letter, saying the Ameers had just told him their Beloochees were uncontrollable; they had taken an oath to become " *yageo*" *rebellious*, unless Roostum was righted, and they would not obey the Ameers. Armed men, he said, were flocking into the city, and all the sheep and bullocks had been driven away from the vicinity; yet he was resolved to stay, and again prayed the army might not advance, expressing his confidence that the Ameers were doing all they could to disperse the Beloochees, and send them out of Hydrabad. And this was true—they were sending them to the field of Meeanee!

Outram's monoculous diplomacy was now characterized by a proposition so extravagant, as to excite painful conjectures for a motive.

The army was on the left bank of the Indus, with a direct line of operations by that river upon Hydrabad, and all the supplies came down from Roree and Sukkur by water.

On its left was the desert, and a line perpendicular to the Indus, drawn eastward from Hydrabad, would fall on Meerpoor first, and then on Omercote. These towns belonged to Shere Mohamed. The first was on the edge of the waste, the second in the heart, and both were fortified. This was the Ameers' principal line of retreat, because to have fallen back south would have exposed them to an attack from Kurrachee.

Outram knew Omercote had been recently supplied with stores; that Sir C. Napier had no connection with Meerpoor, and could have none until after a battle; yet, having twice in vain pressed that General to quit his troops and come alone to Hydrabad, he now urged it a third time with this astounding addition, that he should also send his army to Meerpoor! thus at once depriving the troops of their General, whose death was certain at Hydrabad, and of all communication, supplies, or means of retreat! A mad house, or a scaffold should have been the answer!

The Beloochees of Lower Scinde, thirty thousand strong, were then assembled on the plain of Meeanee; the Princes of Upper Scinde had seven thousand at Khoonhera; the Chandians, more than ten thousand strong, had crossed the Indus in rear of the British camp on that river; Shere Mohamed had ten thousand at Meerpoor. Omercote was garrisoned, and thousands of the hill tribes were coming down to the Indus. The British army, only two thousand eight hundred strong, would therefore have been placed, without a General, on the edge of the wilderness, forty miles from its true line of supply, having a fortified town and an army and the waste in front, and fifty thousand fierce warriors on its rear. Beaten, it would have been pushed into the desert to have perished there. Victorious, it would equally have perished; because, reduced in numbers, without ammunition, and encumbered with wounded men and camp followers, it could never have regained Roree, a distance of two hundred miles, harassed by swarming multitudes who would have renewed the action the moment it retreated. And in this desperate state it was to be placed, in mere wantonness of folly, without any conceivable object, political or military!

This was the advice of a man who afterwards caused himself to be represented in the newspapers as the guide and controller of an incapable General. This was an illus-

tration of that knowledge of eastern affairs and eastern
people; of that wondrous talent which, it was said, distinguished the political agents of Lord Auckland; those smart
youths, empowered to direct generals and armies as well as
to manage negotiations, and the suppression of whom has
drawn upon Lord Ellenborough the foulest calumnies, and
never-ceasing vituperation. Such is the value of newspaper
reputation. The disaster of Cabool was in the ordinary
course of things!

The diplomacy at Hydrabad was not yet terminated.
At three o'clock on the 13th, two deputies from the Ameers
waited on Outram to say that, after he had quitted the
Dhurbar the evening before all the Sirdars met; and because he had given no pledge to restore Roostum to the
Turban, swore on the Koran to fight the British army, and
not sheathe the sword until they had restored him: they
would march that night, and the Ameers could no longer
restrain them. On this statement the deputies founded new
remonstrances, and reiterated their former griefs and arguments, finishing by a desire that he would pledge himself to
obtain redress for their masters. This was refused.

Then they asked if the British would let them fall on
Ali Moorad? No! "It is hard," they replied, "that
you will neither promise restoration of what has been taken
by Ali Moorad, nor allow us to right ourselves." At last
they exclaimed: "The Kyrpoor Ameers then must fight
for their own bread, which Ali Moorad has taken: and why
should the Ameers of Hydrabad be answerable for that?"
You will not be answerable if you do not let them fight in
your territory, and do not assist them.

Outram was here compelled to answer according to his
instructions, which were rigid. Nothing had been taken
from the Kyrpoor Ameers, except by the new treaty, which
they had accepted, and the justice of which has been placed
beyond question. Nothing had been given to Ali Moorad,
save the Turban and its rights, and that was a voluntary
gift from his brother Roostum. The British General had
no part in it, he had even opposed it; but once done, it was
irrevocable by their own laws. That it was really a free

gift is beyond doubt. It was witnessed by a Syud or Peer, a religious man of great reputation, who dared not lower his own fame for piety by lending his sanction to Ali Moorad's injustice. Advantageous it was also to Scindian and British interests. Neither did the Ameers care for it save as a pretence : they were resolved to war on much better grounds, namely the recovery of their independent sovereignty, which had been deceitfully and forcibly filched from them by Lord Auckland. That independence was however injurious to British interests and to humanity. New interests had sprung up, connected with an advancing civilization and not really hurtful to the Ameers, though restrainful of their hellish tyranny, which rendered them objects of horror not of sympathy.

Now once more Outram wrote warmly in favour of their views, as stated in the conference, and reiterated, as an acknowledged fact, that lands belonging to the other Ameers had been given to Ali Moorad by the General! This was utterly false : nothing had been given to him save the Turban, and that by Roostum!

This curious despatch had a more curious postscript. At ten o'clock in the night he added " he was told the Beloochees were next morning to march and fall on the British, and the Residency was to be attacked in the night : but this was all boast and vanity, and he had not even placed a sentinel—it would end in smoke." How unfit he was for his employment, may be judged from the close-following events, and from after acquired information.

The Ameers were then all prepared for battle ; some were in the camp, and their ferocious Beloochees, from Sehwan to the mouth of the Indus, were, under orders, butchering every man woman and child belonging to the British on whom they could lay hands. Many were destroyed, some only escaped by extraordinary courage, fighting for their safety, and others with great sufferings gained refuge by flight. Amongst those killed was Captain Innes, when going down the river sick.

On the 14th the Ameers commanded Outram to begone ; for they saw the hope of getting the General into their hands was illusive, and designed to attack the troops at the Residency in the confusion of an embarkation. They feared also that they might entrench themselves and await reinforcements by water. He took no heed of this order, speaking of it as " bluster ;" and then hearing of Hyat Murree being seized, treated it as confirming his own ridiculous misconceptions. " The capture of that chief," he said, " would make the Beloochees commence plundering ; it would implicate the other chiefs, and hostilities would thus occur, he therefore had sent orders to stop the 41st regiment, then on its way to Kurrachee to embark for Bombay ; thus taking upon himself to interfere with a positive order of the Governor-General, which directed that regiment to embark immediately. The letters found on Hyat he spoke of with contempt, as opposed to his own opinion, which he now for the tenth time advanced. " The Ameers had no hostile intentions, they only sought to gain some benefit for Roostum by an appearance of fermentation amongst their Beloochees; but that fermentation would become real because of the detention of the Murree chiefs."

Previous to this event being known at Hydrabad, the Ameers, through the corrupted moonshee, got back the treaties they had so recently signed and sealed in the Dhurbar, and in the same place tore them to pieces and trampled the fragments under foot !

Let the extravagance of Outram's reasoning now be considered.

All the fighting men of both Scindes, some seventy or eighty thousand, had been put in motion at enormous cost merely to reinstate Roostum. The Ameers, so jealous of each other, so avaricious, so luxurious and selfish, had wasted their treasures, abandoned their debaucheries, and endangered their existence as Sovereigns, to serve an old man for whom they cared so little, that they will be found a month later refusing him a morsel of bread, and the loan of a cloak to keep his white head from the raging sun !

Outram now desired the Hydrabad Ameers to send those of Kyrpoor away, lest destruction should fall on both, pledging himself to bear them harmless through the crisis ;

and having thus, as he phrased it, made a last attempt to save them, he claimed credit for the act, as one likely to prevent their warriors falling on the British with large numbers.—" Not that they would venture a battle, but would annoy the line of march, cut off foragers, and harass the camp at night." He also thought the Kyrpoor Ameers would fly to Omercote.

It was his fate to be always wrong. The Beloochees were in no manner influenced by his " last attempt to save;" they did not infest the line of march; they did not cut off foragers, or insult the camp at night; the Kyrpoor Ameers did not fly to Omercote; the Belooch army went forth to battle, as they had always designed, and most gallantly and terribly they fought.

While Outram was thus floundering, the General was calm, prescient and decided. He was willing to risk much for peace, more for his country's honour. He had been patient while sufferance was wise, but when it became folly to bear more he shook wide the English banner, and drew a sword as sharp as ever struck beneath that honoured symbol!

CHAPTER III.

OUTRAM'S peevish voice of folly was now stifled by the sound of gathering armies, a sound heard by all but him: it caused such terror that guides and villagers who had hitherto been zealous in the British interests fled dismayed; they knew what a strength of battle was pouring down, and being ignorant of the power which genius and discipline conferred, fled from what they thought a doomed force.

The signing of the treaty on the 12th was by the General regarded as a mockery, even as the Ameers did when they got it back to tear in pieces. War was certain. But the universal terror made it difficult to discover what he was to fight. He knew that Roostum's seven thousand men were moving from Khoonhera, on the left, to unite in his rear with ten thousand Chandians who had recently crossed the Indus. Many thousands of the Rins, a very powerful tribe, were said to be following the Chandians; the Murrees and other hill tribes were also coming down; and Shere Mohamed of Meerpoor, though in no manner menaced or even mentioned in the new treaty, was advancing towards Hydrabad with ten thousand warriors. The Ameers, he knew, counted on having sixty thousand fighting-men on the field of battle by the morning of the 18th, but where that field of battle was, or by what roads the men were to be brought together he had not yet ascertained.

Should he yield to the disproportion of force and, breaking through the Chandians and Khoonhera people, regain Roree? He would be followed by the whole of the Belooch army, harassed day and night, and perhaps forced to fight at last on unfavourable ground, and with a retreating dispirited force; he might also, as Indian Princes' faith was not proverbial, then find Ali Moorad's army before him as enemies! But he had read Wellington's observations on Colonel

N

Monson's disastrous retreat before the Mahrattas, and drawn
the conclusion, never to give way before barbarians! Let
the Beloochees then be sixty or a hundred thousand, was his
magnanimous observation, I will fight.

But how fight? Should he attack whatever might be in
front? or, making only one march in advance, gain Halla, a
steam-boat station, and there entrench with his back to the
river, awaiting reinforcements by water? I can do both he
thought. If I fight and win all will be smooth. If I lose I
may still fall back on Halla to entrench. In this mood, resolved to dare, yet neglecting no precaution, he ordered
Colonel Roberts, commanding at Sukkur, to dispatch two
regiments down the river, with all the stores and provisions
he could stow in country boats and two steamers, which were
immediately sent up. Then putting his sick men and treasure on board the remaining steamers, he commenced his
march; but the enormous train of baggage and followers
embarrassed him, because the country offered no walled
village for temporary deposit. In this difficulty, with the
readiness of genius, he made that which was a weight and
hindrance become a part of his order of battle, adding to his
strength—how shall be shewn further on. Now hoping to
surprise the Ameers he rapidly moved on Hydrabad; and
seeing Outram's tendency to go beyond his credentials wrote
thus :—

"Do not pledge yourself to anything; I am in march,
I will make no peace with the Ameers, but attack them
wherever I can come up with their troops. They need send
no more proposals, the time has passed and I will not receive
their messengers : there must be no pledges. Come away if
possible, if you have not boats entrench your house for defence; your men have provisions for a month, and I will be
with you the day after to-morrow. Hold no intercourse with
the Ameers. Send a messenger to the 41st regiment to
hurry it on for embarkation, it should not have been stopped;
both the Governor-General and the Government of Bombay
have written letters upon letters to insure that regiment
being at Kurrachee by the 18th, and are so anxious about
it they have sent up a steamer to hurry the embarkation."

This was written on the 15th, and the storm of war so long impending was then bursting at Hydrabad.

On the 11th the Ameer Shahdad, whose savage nature made him prone to deeds of treachery and blood, either designing to lull suspicion, or hoping to obtain some advantage, sent his interpreter to the Residency with a declaration of friendship, and to say, his people would not mix in the coming disturbances: he would even go in person to the Residency and remain there to protect it. His offer was fortunately rejected, yet from recklessness, for so safe did Outram think himself, that even on the morning of the 15th, when Captain Wells pointed out many indications of preparation for an attack, he would not heed him.

This offer of Shahdad was a curious illustration of the habitual treachery and falsehood of the Ameers. At the very moment he made it, Nusseer had gone forth of the city to take the command of the Beloochee army at Meeanee, fixing his quarters in a pleasant garden, two or three miles from that position. There he was holding council with his chiefs and the brave slaves of his household, having previously arranged with Shahdad and Sobdar, who remained behind, that they and their cousin Mohamed Khan, some other Ameers, and Ahmed Khan the Lugaree chief, should with that tribe, eight thousand in number, storm the Residency, and on the 15th this was done. Sobdar gave orders, yet remained close in his palace, while Shahdad, all armed for war and surrounded by friends, led the column of attack; not however into fire; cowardly as he was cruel, he stopped on horseback beneath a clump of trees, out of shot, while the brave Lugaree led his warriors to the assault.

Sir C. Napier, anticipating such an attack, had on the 14th ordered a steamer with fifty men and a supply of ammunition to drop down to the Residency; by some accident the steamer went without the men or stores, and the assault of eight thousand Beloochees with six guns, was to be sustained by one hundred having only forty rounds each. They had however a stone house, a low wall and the support of two armed steamers; and when were British soldiers, well led, ever appalled by disproportion of numbers?

About nine o'clock, cavalry and infantry were seen to take post on three sides of the compound, or enclosed ground, of the Residency. The 22nd men, under Captain Conway, immediately lined the low wall of the enclosure on the land fronts; the rear, though open to the river, was swept by the guns of the *Planet* and *Satellite* steamers. These vessels were moored in the Indus, some four hundred yards from the house. The Beloochees, occupying the houses and gardens around the compound, opened a matchlock fire on the British, whose covering wall was scarcely five feet high.

Captain Conway, having under him Lieut. Hardinge and Ensign Pennefather of that regiment, was aided by Captains Green and Wells of the Company's service. He made his men reply to the fire slowly, and only when good opportunity offered, preserving their ammunition for the rush which he momentarily expected. Meanwhile Captain Brown of the Bengal Engineers, who had come down with the General's last letter, directed the guns of one steamer. Thus prepared the British met the attack, and when the Lugarees, gathering to make a rush, exposed their masses, the sudden fire, striking them down in heaps, broke their assault and the soldiers slowly sinking again behind the wall, awaited with stern content the next provocation to slaughter.

Bravely and constantly did the Lugarees fight, and though their efforts were vain against discipline and courage combined, the want of ammunition rendered it impossible to maintain the post permanently. Hence, when the matchlock fire had been sustained for three hours it was resolved to withdraw while there was still left ammunition to fight a way to the river. At this moment the enemy brought up guns, which they forced John Howel, an Englishman in their service, to direct, but he pointed too high, and the troops still held the wall while the baggage and property in the house were being removed.

The last operation was soon ended: the camp followers and servants being exposed to a cross fire, on the open space leading to the river, would not return for a second load. Then the troops, after four hours' fighting, seeing no more could be done, suddenly run together, and covering their rear with skirmishers, retreated to the water, from whence the steamers, well placed by the captains, Miller and Cole, swept the flanks with their guns and kept the pursuers on one line.

The *Satellite* worked up the river at once, under fire from the Belooch guns, until one of the latter was dismounted. The *Planet* stopped to take off a large transport boat, and then the whole proceeded in search of the army, being followed and assailed with shot from both banks. The loss was however only three killed, ten wounded, and four missing; one of the dead, two of the wounded, and all the missing being camp followers. The Lugarees were said to have had sixty slain and many wounded; amongst the latter Mohamed Khan. This was a fine prelude to the astonishing exploit that was to follow.

Outram, during the action, had remained safe within the stone house, and did not appear until the troops were embarking; yet he had the effrontery afterwards to claim the merit of the defence; and the musketry had scarcely ceased when he wrote a despatch commencing with the startling assertion, that "his letters for several days back must have led Sir C. Napier to expect the negotiations would fail!" Whereas, besides constant assurances that the Ameers were not hostile, and calling their menaces *bluster*, he had on the 13th announced the formal acceptance of and signing of the treaty in full Dhurbar!

He joined the army at Muttaree, not, as might be expected, downcast at his political failure, but with a more inflated notion of his own sagacity, and still forward to thrust pernicious counsels on the General. Thus, despite of the attack, and his despatch above quoted, he persisted to say the innocent Ameers desired peace, and urged another day's halt! Then, finding Sir Charles fixed in his resolution to advance, he proceeded to meddle with the military dispositions, displaying an incapacity truly remarkable.

First he desired, as shewn, that the march might be delayed a day, which would have given the enemy twenty-five thousand additional men at Meeanee; then he proposed sending a detachment to Tatta, as if the disparity of

numbers was not already sufficiently great; and with ignorant presumption, he spoke of the Beloochees' mode of
warfare, and the places where they would be found, as if war
was a thing of conjecture instead of fact: finally, assuming
that the enemy would only harass the line of march and
would not fight, he asked for a detachment to drop down the
river and burn a shikargah, to deprive the Beloochees of
cover! He urged this so pertinaciously, that the General
yielded; and then Outram demanded the best of the Europeans and native troops: he would thus have caused the
destruction of the army next day: being restricted to two
hundred sepoys he with them quitted the army at the
moment it was marching to battle! It was a great fault to
give him so many; ten would have furnished him with an
excuse for going away as well as two hundred.

War is a series of facts; imagination has no place in the
art: he who would admit conjectures instead of conclusions
from realities, will never be a great general, though he may
be a fortunate one. A commander should be always prepared, but only act upon what is, not on what may be.
Outram here conjectured that the Beloochees would occupy
a wood near the Indus, and in the night they moved eight
miles off. War is however never made without errors, and
the permitting Outram to go to Hydrabad at all was the first
of a series made by Sir C. Napier. Delaying five days at
Sukkurunda was the second. Permitting Outram's shikargah
expedition was the third. The two first were made, knowing
them to be errors, but were sacrifices of military advantages
to humanity. The last was a violation of the rule which
forbids detachments on the eve of battle. There is no impunity for mistakes in war; and thrice, and again, this truth
rushed next day upon the General' mind, when his line bent
inwards before the hurricane of Belooch warfare.

Quitting Sukkurunda the 14th, the army had reached
Muttaree the 16th, being then sixteen miles from Hydrabad,
and towards evening the spies brought reports, afterwards
found to be generally correct. They said the Ameers' troops
were ten miles off, entrenched in the bed of the Fullaillee, a
river flowing strong and large during the inundation time

but then dry, some parts excepted, where deep muddy pools remained. Only fifteen thousand men were actually entrenched, but twenty-five or thirty thousand others would certainly be found there on the 18th, and there were as many more on the flanks and rear of the British.

This was a formidable state of affairs: the army was reduced to two thousand six hundred of all arms fit for duty, and from those the two hundred under Outram were to be deducted. The attack on the Residency had shewn the Beloochees to be brave and persevering fighters, and their numbers were overwhelming. Sir C. Napier thus questioned himself—" Shall I attack or await their assault? If the latter, I must entrench myself on the Indus, and await reinforcements. This will have the appearance of fear, and pestilence may pervade the camp; accidents may detain the reinforcements, and the enemy's immense numbers may abate the courage of the sepoys, many of whom have been formerly defeated by these savage foes, and still feel the influence of those disasters. I will not await, I will attack." Such were his written notes on this occasion.

He knew the gathering of the tribes had been retarded by the Moharem, and having ascertained their distances and rate of movement, judged that the whole could not assemble before the 18th, which coincided with the statements of his spies; wherefore he resolved to fight next day, hoping to find only fifteen thousand in position. But subsequent to the emissaries' last reports, twenty thousand Beloochees had suddenly crossed the Indus, and thirty-six thousand men were really in order of battle. This great army had been passing the river since the 14th within a few miles of Outram, while he was vehemently asserting that the whole had been disbanded, and the fermentation only feigned to support Roostum's restoration to the Turban!

Late in the evening of the 16th the General heard of the formidable accession of strength, yet only vaguely, and with different versions, but his resolution was unshaken, and thus avowed in a letter, written after receiving the intelligence.

" The Beloochees are robbers, inspired by a feeling of enthusiasm against us, and because of our protecting the

poor *Scindian people.* They have sworn on the Koran to destroy the English General and his army ! I, being ready for the trial, march at midnight, and I shall be within a few miles of them by six o'clock: perhaps I may make a forced march and begin the battle sooner than they expect. Various matters will decide this between now and the morning."—
" Their cavalry is ten thousand strong, and in a vast plain of smooth, hard, clayey sand; my cavalry about eight hundred ! These are long odds, more than ten to one; however, to-morrow or the day after, we shall know each other's value."

Marching in the night of the 16th, his advanced guard discovered the enemy at eight o'clock next morning, and at nine o'clock the British line of battle was formed. Thirty-six thousand enemies were in front: the best spy said forty thousand, but the cavalry were only five thousand. Their position was twelve hundred yards wide, along the bed of the Fullaillee, whose high bank, sloping towards the plain in front, furnished a rampart.

Eighteen guns massed on the flank in advance of the bank, poured their shot on the troops while forming the line, and the Beloochee wings rested on shikargahs, which lined the plain so far as to flank the advance on both sides. They were very large and dense, and that on the Beloochee right intersected with nullahs of different sizes, but all deep, carefully scarped, and defended by matchlock men. Behind this shikargah the Fullaillee made a sudden bend to the rear, forming a loop in which the Ameers' cavalry was placed.

The shikargah on the enemy's left was more extensive, and though free from nullahs very strong. It was covered towards the plain by a wall having one opening, not very wide, about half way between the two armies. Behind this wall five or six thousand men were posted, evidently designed to rush out through the opening upon the flank and rear of the British when the latter advanced.

To force the shikargah on his own left and assail that flank, the General thought impracticable; to turn it would waste the day, and only bring the army on to the Fullaillee again at the bend, where it furnished the Ameers with an equally good defence. To turn the other shikargah on his own right was more difficult, and would also bring him on to the Fullaillee where it had water and deep mud; he would then have to make bridges and force a passage, having the Beloochees in the shikargah still on his flank: the time thus lost would bring twenty-five thousand more enemies into position; and meanwhile the sight of such numbers might break down the confidence of the sepoys, none of whom he had proved in danger.

To fall on hardily remained, but thirty-six thousand foes were in front, and the British force was reduced by the detachment under Outram to twenty-four hundred! And from that number a strong baggage guard was to be furnished, lest the enemy should during the battle strike at the camp followers and animals, whose numbers made the fighting men appear a mere handful. There was no village with walls near; and the embarrassment was great; but with a happy adaptation of the ancient German and Hunnish method, the General cast the mass into a circle close in his rear, surrounding it with camels, which were made to lie down with their heads inwards, having their bales placed between them for the armed followers to fire over. Thus he presented a fortress not easy to storm, and assigning two hundred and fifty Poona horsemen and four companies of infantry as a guard, under Captain Tait, proceeded with less than two thousand to fall on thirty-six thousand at the lowest, for his best spy still asserted that there were forty thousand before him.

His order of battle was soon framed.

Twelve guns under Major Lloyd, flanked by fifty Madras sappers, under Captain Henderson, were on the right.

On Lloyd's left stood the 22nd Queen's regiment, under Colonel Pennefather. Less than five hundred they were, half Irishmen, all strong of body, high blooded soldiers, who saw nothing but victory. On the left were the swarthy sepoys of Bombay; small men of low caste, yet hardy, brave and willing; as good in fire and more docile out of it than the high caste soldiers, having fewer prejudices and less pride. Of these the 25th regiment were immediately on the left of the 22nd, and next to them the 12th under Major Reid. Finally came the 1st grenadiers under Major Clibborne—the whole in the echellon order of battle.

Closing the extreme left, but somewhat held back, rode the 9th Bengal cavalry under Colonel Pattle, men of high caste, stern and proud.

In front of the right infantry, skirmishers were thrown out, and on the left the Scinde horsemen, under Captain Jacob, fierce eastern troops, were pushed forward. This was to make the Beloochees shew their position and numbers; for it is the habit of the latter to ensconce themselves in holes and nullahs, resting their matchlocks on the edge and firing until the mark is close, when, throwing down that weapon they leap out with sword and shield : and strong and courageous must be the man who stands before them.

Between the two armies the plain was about a thousand yards, and for the first seven hundred was covered with low jungle which impeded the march; but three hundred yards in front of the Beloochees' line had been cleared to give free play for their matchlocks, with which they fired long shots at times, without shewing themselves. The order to advance was given, and the General rode forward attended by his staff; and by his moonshee Ali Ackbar, an Arab gentleman of high race and courage who never left his chief in danger. Constant and heavy was the fire from the Beloochee guns, and though few men could be discerned, the rapid play of the matchlocks indicated the presence of numbers, and marked the position.

A village called Kottree covered the enemy's right and was filled with matchlock men; there was no weak point there, but on their left a flaw was detected. Observing the wall enclosing the shikargah, the General rode near, and saw it was about ten feet high, and that some matchlock men who were astride on it disappeared suddenly. Riding nearer he found there were no loopholes, and still approaching the opening he looked behind and saw there was no scaffolding. Then with the inspiration of genius he instantly thrust a company of the 22nd into the space, telling their captain, Tew, to block the gap and die there if necessary: his orders were obeyed, Tew died, but the gap was maintained, and thus six thousand enemies were paralyzed by only eighty! It was, on a smaller scale as to numbers, Marlborough's game at Blenheim repeated.

The main body advanced in columns of regiments, the right, passing securely under the wall, were cheered and elated by the rattling of Tew's musketry, now reinforced by a gun. The left was meanwhile refused, to avoid a fire from the village of Kottree, which Clibborne's grenadiers were directed to storm. During the march the dead level was swept by the Beloochee guns and matchlocks, which were at times answered by Lloyd's battery, but not frequently, for rapidly and eagerly did the troops press on to close with their hidden foes.

The 22nd when within a hundred yards of the Fullaillee opened into line, and all the columns formed in succession, each company as it arrived throwing its fire at the top of the bank, where the faces of the Beloochees could just be seen, bending with fiery glances over their levelled matchlocks. But the British front was still incomplete, when the voice of the General, shrill and clear, was heard, commanding the charge. Then arose the British shout, four guns were run forward, and the infantry at full speed closed on the Fullaillee and rushed up the sloping bank. The Beloochees, sternly quiescent, with matchlocks resting on the summit, let their assailants come within fifteen yards before they delivered their fire, but the steepness of the slope inside, which rendered their footing unsteady, and the rapid pace of the British falsified their aim, the execution was not very great. The next moment the 22nd were on the top of the bank thinking to bear down all before them, but staggered back at the forest of swords waving in their front.

Thick as standing corn, and gorgeous as a field of flowers were the Beloochees in their many coloured garments and turbans. They filled the broad deep bed of the Fullaillee; they were clustered on both banks, and covered the plain beyond. Guarding their heads with large dark shields they shook their sharp swords, gleaming in the sun, and their

shouts rolled like a peal of thunder as with frantic might
and gestures they dashed against the front of the 22nd. But
with shrieks as wild and fierce, and hearts as big, and arms
as strong, the British soldiers met them with the queen of
weapons and laid their foremost warriors wallowing in blood.
Then also the few guns that could be placed in position on
the right of the 22nd, flanked by Henderson's small band
of Madras sappers, swept diagonally the bed of the river,
tearing the rushing masses with a horrible carnage. Soon
the sepoy regiments, 12th and 25th, prolonged the line of
fire to the left, coming into action successively, in the same
terrible manner.   Clibborne's grenadiers were distant, skirmishing with the matchlock men in Kottree when they
should have charged them : but that was their commander's
fault.

Now the Beloochees closed in denser masses, and the
dreadful rush of their swordsmen was felt, and their shouts,
answered by the pealing musketry, were heard along the
line, and such a fight ensued as has seldom been told of in
the records of war. For ever those wild fierce warriors, with
shields held high and blades drawn back, strove with might
and valour to break through the British ranks.   No fire of
small arms, no sweeping discharges of grape, no push of
bayonets could drive them back; they gave their breasts to
the shot, their shields to the bayonets, and leaping at the
guns were blown away by twenties at a time, their dead
rolled down the steep slope by hundreds : but the gaps were
continually filled from the rear, the survivors pressed forward with unabated fury, and the bayonet and sword clashed
in full and frequent conflict.

Thus they fought, never more than five yards apart,
often intermingled, and several times the different regiments
were violently forced backwards, staggering under the might
and passion of the swordsmen. But always their General
was there to rally and cheer them.   At his voice their
strength returned, and they recovered ground, though nearly
all their regimental leaders were down : for fast those leaders
had fallen, dying as British officers always will do when they
cannot win.

"The noble soldier Pennefather" fell on the top of the bank, deeply, it was thought at first mortally, wounded, but his place was instantly taken by Major Poole.

Major Teasdale, animating the sepoys of the 25th regiment, rode violently down a gap into the midst of the Beloochees, and there was killed by shot and sabre, dying with a glorious devotion.

Major Jackson, of the 12th, coming up with his regiment, the next in line, followed the heroic example as if the succession of death had been also in his orders. Two brave Havildars kept close to him, all three in advance of their regiment, and all fell dead together covered with wounds; not passively: several of the fiercest swordsmen were seen to sink beneath the strong arm and whirling blade of Jackson, as crowding around him they tore his body with their griding weapons.

Nearly all the European officers were now slain or wounded, and several times the sepoys, wanting leaders, slowly receded; but the General, a skilful horseman and conspicuous from his dress, was always at the point of greatest pressure, and then manfully his swarthy soldiers recovered their ground. Once he was assailed by a chief, and his danger was great, for his right hand had been maimed before the battle; but Lieutenant Marston of the 25th native regiment sprung to his side and slew the Sirdar, whose tomb has been raised by his tribe since on the spot where he fell. At another period he was alone for several minutes in the midst of the enemy; they stalked around him with raised shields and scowling eyes, but whether from something affecting their minds, for the Beloochees are very superstitious, none lifted sword against him, and the 22nd soldiers seeing him thus emerge called to him by name, and gave him a cheer, heard distinctly above the general din of the battle! And there are men who think the murmur of their factious calumnies can stifle that heroic sound!

More than three hours this storm of war continued without abatement, and still the Beloochees, undismayed, pressed onwards with furious force, their number seeming to augment instead of decreasing. Then painfully the General

felt the absence of the brave men carried off by Outram:
and that the British were not trampled under foot was to be
attributed to their rapid firing ; they tumbled their foremost
enemies down the steep bank so thickly, that the followers
could never get clear of the carcases before the muskets
were again ready to deal death, and the bayonet sufficed for
those unharmed by shot.

During this struggle Tew's company secured the opening
in the shikargah wall, and even advanced : he fell but the
gap was defended, and the right flank and rear of the men
fighting on the Fullaillee were covered. But on the left
flank, Clibborne, though not deficient in courage or talent, was
unable to grasp the points of battle, and instead of storming
Kottree withdrew his grenadiers nearly out of fire ! Thus
a fourth of the fighting men were rendered useless.

Such, at the end of three hours, was the state of the
field, when that inevitable crisis of every battle which offers
victory to the ablest general arrived at Meeanee. Clibborne's
error was grave, the right was sorely pressed, and there
was no reserve save the cavalry, which was in a manner paralyzed by the village of Kottree : yet the battle must be
won or lost within twenty minutes ! Jacob had previously
endeavoured to penetrate the shikargah on the left with the
Scinde horse, designing to turn the village and gain the
flank of the enemy's position; but the frequent scarped
nullahs, the thick jungle and the appearance of matchlock
men, soon forced him to return. The General could not
quit the right, so thick and heavily the Beloochees pressed
on, so stern and dreadful was their fighting, so wearied and
exhausted were his men ; but his eye caught the whole field,
and on his left he saw victory beckoning to him. Wherefore,
urging his men by his voice and example firmly to sustain
the increasing fury of their foes, he sent Colonel Pattle
orders to charge with the whole body of Bengal and Scinde
horsemen on the enemy's right.

It was the command of a master spirit, and with fiery
courage obeyed. Spurring hard the eastern horsemen
passed the matchlock-men in the village of Kottree, and
galloped unchecked across the small nullahs and ditches

about it, which were, however, so numerous and difficult,
that fifty of the troopers were cast from their saddles
at once by the leaps. But dashing through the Beloochee
guns on that flank, and riding over the high bank of the Fullaillee the mass crossed the deep bed, gained the plain
beyond, and charged with irresistible fury. Major Storey
with his Bengal troopers, turning to his left fell on the
enemy's infantry in the loop of the upper Fullaillee; while
the Scindian horse led, though not commanded, by Lieutenant Fitzgerald, wheeling to their right, fell on the camp,
thus spreading confusion along the rear of the masses opposed to the British infantry. Then the barbarian swordsmen, whose fury could scarcely be resisted before, abated
their fighting and looked behind them.· The 22nd perceived
this, and leaping forward with the shout of victory pushed
them backwards into the deep ravine, there closing in
combat again. The Madras sappers and the other sepoys
followed the glorious example; but the Beloochee multitude
in the shikargah then abandoned that cover to join battle
in the Fullaillee, and how fiercely the brave barbarians still
fought may be gathered from this. A soldier of the 22nd
regiment, bounding forward, drove his bayonet into the
breast of a Beloochee; instead of falling, the rugged warrior
cast away his shield, seized the musket with his left hand,
writhed his body forwards on the bayonet, and with one
sweep of his keen blade avenged himself: both fell dead
together!

The battle was now lost for the Ameers, and slowly their
gallant swordsmen retired, not in dispersion, nor with fear,
but in heavy masses, their broad shields slung over their
backs, their heads half turned and their eyes glaring with
fury. The victors followed closely, pouring in volley after
volley. Yet those stern implacable warriors still preserved
their habitual swinging stride, and would not quicken it to a
run though death was at their heels! Two or three thousand
on the extreme right, who had been passed by the cavalry,
kept their position, and seemed disposed to make another
rush, but the whole of the British guns were turned upon
them with such heavy discharges of grape and shells, that

they also went off. All were now in retreat, but so doggedly did they move, and seemed so inclined to renew the conflict on the level ground where the British flanks were unprotected, that the General, unwilling to provoke a second trial, recalled his cavalry and formed a large square, placing his baggage and followers in the centre.

Such was the battle of Meeanee, fought on the 17th of February, 1843, with less than two thousand men against thirty-six thousand. It was in fine arrangement, in all that depended on the commander, a model of skill and intrepidity combined; and in its details fell nothing short of any recorded deeds of arms. The front of battle was a chain of single combats where no quarter was given, none called for, none expected; Sepoys and Europeans and Beloochees were alike bloody and remorseless, taking life for life, giving death for death. The ferocity was unbounded, the carnage horrible. The General, seeing a 22nd soldier going to kill an exhausted Belooch chief, called to him to spare, but the man drove his bayonet deep, and then turning, justified the act with an expression, terrible in its homely truthfulness, accompanying such a deed: " *This day, General, the shambles have it all to themselves.*"

Feats of personal daring and prowess as well as ferocity were rife.

Lieutenant McMurdo, a young staff-officer, riding, like Teasdale and Jackson, into the bed of the Fullaillee, had his horse killed and fell; regaining his feet he met and slew Jehan Mohamed a great chief and a hardy warrior, in the midst of his tribe. Several of Jehan's followers then engaged him in front, while one struck at him fiercely from behind, but was by a sergeant of the 22nd so instantaneously killed that the blow fell harmless. McMurdo turned and repaid the service by cleaving to the brow a swordsman who was aiming at his preserver's back; another fell beneath his whirling blade, and then the two champions broke from the hostile press. The tomb of Jehan, a great one, has since been raised by his people, not where he fell in the nullah, but with an excusable martial vanity, sixty yards beyond the British lines where he never penetrated.

McMurdo was even surpassed in prowess by Fitzgerald of the Scinde horse, whose exploits made all who saw him in fight marvel. Three or four Beloochees had fallen beneath his tempestuous hand, when one, crouching, as their custom is, beneath a broad shield, suddenly stepped up on the bridle hand, and with a single stroke brought down the horse. Fitzgerald's leg was beneath the animal, and twice did the elated swordsman drive his keen blade at the prostrate champion; but each time the blow was parried, and then, clearing himself from the dead horse, the strong man rose. The barbarian, warned by the herculean form and countenance, instantly cast his shield over a thickly rolled turban of many folds, but the descending weapon went through all, and cleft his skull!

Lieutenant Harding, of the 22nd was the first to leap upon the bank, his legs were cut by the swordsmen and he fell; but rose again instantly, and waving his cap cheered his men to the charge; a shot went through his lungs and again he fell, receiving another sword cut that maimed his right hand, yet still he urged the men forward.

Such was the fighting of Meeanee, and it was no slight glory that those men of iron limbs and heroic hearts acknowledged their General to be worthy of them.

Twenty European gentlemen, including four field-officers, went down in this battle—six killed—and with them two hundred and fifty sergeants and privates, of whom more than fifty were slain outright; hence, as the sepoy grenadiers were very slightly engaged, this was nearly a sixth of the fighting force. The loss of the Beloochees was enormous, almost exceeding belief. A careful computation on the field gave six thousand, but the Ameers said eight thousand; and as no quarter was given, only those whose wounds did not disable them could have escaped: seventeen hundred bodies were heaped in the bed of the Fullaillee alone, and thus in four hours two thousand men struck down six thousand! At Salamanca, one hundred thousand men, with a hundred and thirty pieces of artillery were engaged for seven or eight hours, and the loss of the British scarcely exceeded five thousand!

o

When the English General had fixed his camp for the night, he rode alone in darkness to the scene of carnage, and in the midst of the dead, raising his hands to Heaven, thus questioned himself aloud " Am I guilty of this slaughter?" His conscience answered No!

He returned to sleep, and so soundly, that Outram, coming back from his silly expedition, could only arouse him by force. A false alarm had disturbed the camp, and fearing a night attack, orders were given to fire the enemy's camp.

At daybreak the victor sent this message to the Ameers— " Surrender or Hydrabad shall be stormed." Vakeels came to ask for terms. " Life! and you must decide before twelve o'clock, because the dead will then be reckoned and my soldiers have had their breakfasts."

Then came forth Nusseer, Roostum, and Mohamed of Upper Scinde ; Nusseer, Shahdad, and young Hoossein of Lower Scinde. Entering the camp on horseback, they yielded their fortress and laid their rich swords at the General's feet. These last were worth many thousand pounds, his lawful spoil, of which none could claim a share, and it would have been no small honour to a private gentleman to place the swords of so many sovereign princes in his armoury. He however returned them, making this simple report to the Governor-General " Their misfortunes are of their own creation, but as they were great I gave them back their swords.".

Richly ornamented things of state they were, but the Ameers had always been curious in the collection of celebrated swords, and three of the most famous in Asia had been picked up on the field, covered with blood—not thrown there by any Ameer for they did not enter the fight ; but probably dropt by their brave slaves who died for them in crowds, lying stark and grim at Meeanee. Mohamed Khan and Sobdar never left the fortress. The former was detained by his wound, the latter by cunning and cowardice. If the British won, he had not been in the field ; if they lost, his followers had fought with the rest!. Hoossein, the youth who, under the tutelage of Sobdar and Mohamed, had professed such

amity for the British was, when the crisis came, sent by his
mother, clothed in a curious coat of mail to the battle, with
this Spartan admonition—" Fight for your race and your
religion." He was amongst the foremost until the cannonade
commenced, but then fled, casting off his armour, which is in
the General's possession.

The Ameers were cowardly, but their chiefs and warriors
signally brave; and full honour and praise their conqueror
gave them in his public despatches and private letters.
Every respect and indulgence consistent with the public
interests he has shewn to them since, letting them know,
that courage in an enemy was no bar to his favour. This
mode of dealing, springing partly from a fine policy, partly
from his natural feelings, has deeply stirred those rough
men's hearts, for they have strong though rude notions of
honour.

Praise also he gave to his own gallant troops, with a
profound sense of what he and their country owed to them.
And for the first time in English despatches, the names of
private soldiers who had distinguished themselves were made
known—an innovation perceived and hailed by those who
never served under him : it has rendered his name dear to
thousands who never saw and never will see him, for the
British soldier is keenly sensitive to honour. His despatch
also proved how little desire for military glory influenced his
actions. It commenced with an apology for having gained a
great victory. To the Duke of Wellington he wrote thus,
modestly, as became him when addressing so great a man ; but
when Sir Jasper Nichols, the Indian Commander-in-Chief,
thought fit to criticise and censure his generalship, he, with
the rebound of genius, thus repelled the assumption of
superiority.

To Sir Jasper Nichols, Commander-in-Chief.

" 25th June, 1843.

" I have just had the honour to receive your Excellency's
note of the 9th of March, in which you say—' But I see you
made that an arduous struggle which might have been an easy

success, had you detained the 41*st regiment, and some part of
Colonel Wallace's detachment.'*

" This is a serious charge. Whether you will think it
justly founded when you hear my defence, I cannot say ; but
you will I am sure excuse my desire to stand higher in your
opinion as an officer than I appear to do.

" To begin with the 41st. Versed as your Excellency is
in Indian warfare, I need not tell you that an European regiment cannot march, especially in hot weather, without
' *carriage.*' The 41st had none—they were on the Indus in
boats. I had not, and could not obtain sufficient carriage for
the force with me ; much less could I assist the 41st. The
want of carriage compelled me to leave the 8th N.I. at
Roree. The 41st must therefore have joined me, if it could
have joined me at all, without carriage for sick, for ammunition, for water, for tents, for provisions. How could it have
joined me ? Impossible !

" But this was not all, though sufficient. Up to the 15th
the Ameers of Hydrabad had loudly declared their perfect
submission to the will of the British Government; and they
disclaimed all union with the Ameers of Kyrpoor. The latter
had not an army that my force was not fully equal to cope
with ; and the Governor-General and the Government of
Bombay, had *reiterated* their positive orders to me to have the
41st ready to embark at Kurrachee on the 20th of February.
I knew the cause of their anxiety, and that it was very
important the 41st should embark on the 20th. Was it
for me in January, when all the Ameers had declared their
acceptance of the new treaty, to write to Sukkur, in the
face of superior authority, and order the 41st to halt?
Not to join my force, for that was impossible, but to halt !
I suspect the Governor-General and the Bombay Government would not have been much satisfied with my conduct
if I had done so. The 41st therefore arrived at Sukkur
the 4th of February, found orders to proceed instantly on
its voyage, and passed Hydrabad the 10th of February,
five days before the Ameers declared war, and when Major
Outram, an accredited agent of mine, was by their own invitation living in their capital, and assuring me of their

earnest desire for peace—he being the person *supposed* to know more of Scinde than any other Englishman ; and more of the Ameers personally.

" On the day of the action the 41st were at Kurrachee. I being inland, and my letters being constantly intercepted, could not know where the 41st was, except that it was somewhere on the Indus—that is somewhere or other in a range of *three hundred miles !* I did not hear of its arrival at Sukkur, until it was past my reach, had I supposed it would be required, which I did not. How could I suppose so ? On reference to my journal, I find that on the 13th of February, being then at Syndabad, I received no less than two expresses from Major Outram to say and impress upon me, that " *there were no armed men at Hydrabad ! !* " At that moment however the town was *full* and 25,800 men were in position at Meeanee six miles off ! Short miles—for the battle was seen from the walls. I think after the above statement, your Excellency will acquit me of having the power to reinforce my army with the 41st regiment ; but this, and more, shall become public if any enquiry be necessary.

" Now for the second part of your Excellency's charge viz. ' *That I might have had an easy success, had some part of Colonel Wallace's detachment been with me.*'

" In the first place the whole brigade under Colonel Wallace, as far as I recollect, and my memory is tolerably strong, could not turn out fifteen hundred rank and file. It must therefore have been a *large* portion to have made the battle of Meeanee an ' *easy success.*' However, say that I had five hundred ; assuredly that number would not have changed the character of the engagement. It would have brought a larger force of the enemy into action very possibly, and consequently their loss and ours would have been greater in that proportion, but the action would not have been ' an easy success.' No ! nor an *easier success.* But what excuse had I to weaken Wallace, who, apparently, at the time we separated, was in more danger than I was ? He was about to seize an extensive district, and if any resistance were to be made, assuredly *there* it might be expected.

" Suppose me to have made the military error of sending

a feeble force to execute what was expected to be a perilous operation, and that I had brought a thousand men down with me to the south; what would have been the result? Water was everywhere scarce, and oftentimes I had scarcely sufficient for the small force with me. Had I had the Bengal column also, or a large portion of it, I must have marched in two columns with the interval of a day between, to let the wells fill after being emptied by the first column. The result would have been that I should have been unable to have given battle till the 19th of February, before which time the Chandians under Wullee Chandia; seven thousand under Meer Mohamed Hoossein; and ten thousand under Shere Mohamed would have joined the enemy at Meeanee! When the victory was decided all these men were within six or eight hours of the field of battle—an additional thousand on my side, an additional twenty-seven thousand on that of the enemy, would not have rendered my success more ' *easy*.'

" Your Excellency will say these things were not known to me at Roree when I first marched south. *All* were not, but enough were. 1°. I knew there was a great want of water. 2°. I knew I could carry spare provisions with me if the country refused supplies; but I should not have had carriage for this if the Bengal division was with me. The additional baggage would have been nearly as great as our own baggage, and all the wells would have been drunk dry. The Bengals had carriage for their own baggage but not for additional water and spare provisions, independent of wells and their own bazaar.

" Suppose I could have conveniently brought down the Bengal troops, and left the north unguarded. Still men are not prophets. The Ameers of Hydrabad were at peace with us, I was only marching against those of Kyrpoor. The latter had not ten thousand men, and I wanted no increase of numbers to encounter them—nor did any man believe they intended to fight: nor the Ameers of Hydrabad neither. Even on the 12th of February, Major Outram, then in Hydrabad, wrote me two letters assuring me the Ameers of Kyrpoor and Hydrabad had not a single soldier—so little did he even then apprehend hostilities.

"The Belooch army suddenly assembled, as if by magic!
I saw nothing but disgrace and destruction in an attempt to
retreat, and I resolved to attack, confident in the courage of
the soldiers.   My confidence was not misplaced: neither will
it be now, I hope, when I trust this letter will satisfy you
that I brought every man into action that was at my
disposal."

CHAPTER IV.

SIR Charles Napier now took possession of Hydrabad.
His first design had been to fall on Shere Mohamed of
Meerpoor, who was, with ten thousand men, only six miles
from Meeanee during the battle, and it was to combine that
attack with the instant gain of Hydrabad that he sent the
stern message to the Ameers, thinking it would succeed during
the terror of defeat. It did so, and Shere Mohamed would
have been surprised, if Outram, the evil principle, the Ari-
manes of the army, had not been in camp. He had burned
a wood ten miles off, where there was nobody to oppose him,
and it is possible the smoke might have been discerned, after
the fight—not while it lasted, for none were then in a mood
to look for distant objects : but with his usual intolerable
boasting he affirmed that it had essentially contributed to the
success ; whereas it had only enabled Outram to avoid the
battle and deprive the army of two hundred better men than
himself. And now, seeing that another battle was at hand,
he implored the General not to fall on Shere Mohamed,
saying he knew the man, his views, his temper, his general
policy, his disposition. He would never fight. His march
was a mere menace, he would be too glad to submit and
obtain peace ; he would hurry to that conclusion if his present
aggression was unnoticed. Write to him and he would be
pliant, march against him, and all would be mischief and
bloodshed. Such were the arguments—to which in an evil
hour the General assented, saying, " Write then what you
like and I will sign it."

Unhappy was that presumptuous counsel. Had the army
marched, Shere Mohamed would have been defeated and his
capital taken in three days. He knew this, and in his first
fear, on learning the result of the battle, wrote that he had
no part in the late fight, had not even crossed his own

frontier. This false excuse was accepted, Outram's advice adopted in all its extent, and the Ameer having thus gained time to place himself in safety by a retrograde march, immediately commenced rallying the warriors who had escaped from the battle. In a few days he was at the head of twenty-five or thirty thousand fighting men more fierce than ever. Meerpoor, his fortified capital, gave him a base and Omercote a refuge in retreat. Sir C. Napier here made the greatest error of the campaign: he should have spurned Outram. His army scarcely escaped destruction, but his desire was to spare blood, and standing amidst the carnage of Meeanee who shall blame him?

On the 19th Hydrabad was entered, the citadel was occupied the next day: then the Ameers' cowardice became manifest. Apparently built of soft bricks the fortress seemed weak; but the heaviest shot would penetrate without causing vibration, and beneath was the solid rock which could not be breached. Sir Alexander Burnes describes it as a weak place: he was in error, it was too lofty for escalade, too solid to breach, and could only be taken by mines and storm, for which its want of flanking defence gave facilities. Now the Belooch warriors were undismayed by the battle, and they were still in overwhelming force, for ten thousand fresh men had joined during the retreat from Meeanee: they were urgent for defending fortress and city, house by house, and the thick walls of the dwellings were well adapted for such a warfare. The Ameers would not fight, and their warriors went off in disgust to Shere Mohamed. The Princes rode to the British camp: thus terminating a long course of hideous cruelty and brutal enjoyment by an act of miserable cowardice.

The terrible sun of Scinde was now felt, the thermometer marked 112° in the shade, yet Sir C. Napier, who knew of the butchery contemplated by the Ameers, if they had been victorious, and of the horrible fate designed for himself; he who had before returned their swords, because their misfortunes were great, now left them full enjoyment of their luxurious palace and gardens, remaining himself in a common field tent; a generosity which, though known to Lord Howick and Lord Ashley, did not stay them from the baseness of asserting

in Parliament, that he had treated the fallen Princes with
harshness and outrage. The strong sense of an English
House of Commons rejected the foul charge with contempt.

The victor's situation now became hourly more complicated; a result of Outram's counsel. The force was greatly
reduced, unendurable heat was rapidly approaching, and
Hydrabad was too distant from the Indus, now his only line
of supply, to serve as a base, or even a depôt, seeing he had
not carriage to convey the stores from the river, a distance of
four miles. He was however compelled to put five hundred
men in the fortress, and meanwhile Shere Mohamed's army
was hourly increasing. To move in the heat with reduced
strength against him, who could retire to the desert if beaten,
would be risking all hitherto won with little hope of success.
But he knew that Ameer thought himself, and justly, the best
soldier of the Talpoor race ; and that he had not much wealth ;
wherefore he resolved to let him raise a new army, which
would augment his pride and diminish his money, because
thus doubly stimulated to action he was likely to seek the
camp, perhaps attempt to storm it, and so spare the army long
marches in the heat. This would enable the British to fight
with a refuge at hand in case of disaster, and an asylum for
the wounded in any circumstances.

In this view the General remained tranquil, but sent to
Kurrachee for every spare man there ; and judging that while
the terror of the battle was rife he might be daring, he not
only sent to Sukkur to hasten the troops he had called for
when at Sukkurunda, but also desired Colonel Roberts to send
another column of all arms by land. He had before refused
the aid of men from the Upper Sutlege, he now asked for them ;
but in this was anticipated. Rumours of the battle had
reached Lord Ellenborough before the despatch, and with
sagacious vigilance, he instantly ordered three regiments to
Scinde ; adding a camel battery, with three hundred and fifty
of Chamberlayne's irregular horsemen. Soon afterwards he
also sent the 3rd Bombay cavalry, taken from General Nott's
force, which had then passed the Sutlege, coming from
Cabool.

Meanwhile Sir C. Napier entrenched a camp close to the

Indus, thus protecting his steamer station, which he farther covered by a fort, on the opposite bank, from the hostile tribes at that side. In this camp he placed his hospitals and stores; and then, he so enterprising before suddenly, in all outward appearance, became timid and forbearing. Changing as circumstances demanded, he patiently awaited the moment when he might break forth again the fiery General of Meeanee; and for this wariness also he obtained the unstinted praise of the great captain who could best appreciate such conduct.

"*Sir C. Napier gained the camp of the enemy, got possession of his guns, and obtained the most complete victory, taking up a position in which he was not again likely to be attacked. Not only did he secure Hydrabad, and the portion of the Indus which lay in his rear; he brought up a reinforcement, and placed himself at the head of a stronger army than that which he commanded before the battle. He manifested all the discretion and ability of an officer familiar with the most difficult operations of war.*"

Such was the Duke of Wellington's criticism. And yet one stroke of ability, indicating the great commander as clearly as any act of this eventful campaign, was unknown to him. While the General encouraged Shere Mohamed's presumption, by professing, and giving all outward signs that he dreaded that Ameer's force, he guarded carefully against the influence of such conduct on his own soldiers; making them pitch their tents outside the strong camp, on an open plain, and giving them to understand he did so in contempt of the enemy.

Fame had extravagantly magnified the treasures of Hydrabad, or the Ameers' expenses had been prodigious since Sir A. Burnes announced that twenty millions sterling were in their coffers. Gold and jewels together did not much exceed half-a-million, but probably much was undiscovered. Bernier, Aurungzebe's French physician, says, the Scindian rulers of his day had secret vaults for their treasure, very difficult to discover. But in truth the women of the zenanas had the greater part; for no man was permitted to enter their apartments, and their property was so scrupulously respected, that when the slaves handed from the door females' ornaments the prize agents sent them back. The ladies, when quitting the palace were not searched, and it was afterwards ascertained that they carried away above two millions sterling. This great abstraction the General had not expected, though he was willing they should go forth with comfort and even splendour.

In the fortress, proof was obtained that Sobdar and Mohamed, the Ameers who had not surrendered as being absent from the battle, were equally guilty and treacherous as the others. It was they who had concerted the attack on the Residency, Mohamed had been engaged there, and the followers of both were at Meeanee, although the masters kept away, and now pretended amity : they were therefore constituted prisoners.

Previous to the battle, and after it, the country south of Hydrabad was in commotion ; the British coal stations and depôts had been plundered ; officers and servants were killed, or driven with their wives and children to fly for life, losing all their property. Small guards and escorts were destroyed generally, or escaped down the river, but one sergeant with a few sepoys fought his way up the Indus so manfully as to draw forth the public applause of the General, who promoted him. The communications, above and below Hydrabad, were thus intercepted for all but the armed steamers, Roostum's nephew, Ali, acting from Shah Ghur, cut those on the side of Jessulmere, while Shere Mohamed's gathering force did the same on the side of Cutch. The army was thus isolated. But the greatest difficulty was to deal with the captive Ameers.

To treat them generously and secure the troops from their treachery was impossible. This shall be made manifest ; because advantage has been taken of the intricate and generally unknown state of affairs which intervened between the battles of Meeanee and Hydrabad to calumniate Sir C. Napier. It was a short but a terrible period of danger, and nothing but his intrepidity, coolness and energy, could have preserved the army. " *We shall Cabool him,*" was the confident cry of the Ameers, inside and outside his camp.

" *Yes, he will be Cabooled*," was the exulting echoing cry from the faction at Bombay. And because Sir C. Napier would not suffer his army to be Cabooled, according to the predictions and wishes of that sordid set, his character has been maligned, and his actions misrepresented in India and in England.

He was however, happily relieved at this time of difficulty from the burthen of Outram's presence. Having evaded the first battle by asking for a detachment, having delayed the second battle by false counsel, that person now, when another action became inevitable, returned to Bombay on pretence that his political functions had ceased. Sir G. Arthur, strangely and erroneously supposing that Sir C. Napier acted by the advice of a military council, told Outram, truly, that as a soldier he should have remained when a battle was at hand. He offered to return, but when all danger had passed away; he could only come for mischievous intrigue, and the General refused to have him again. Then he went to England, to work evil against the interests of those whose dangers he had not shared, and to calumniate the man who had befriended him against the just anger of Lord Ellenborough.

The treatment of the Ameers was at first a perplexing question : were they prisoners of war, or deposed Princes? This difficulty was resolved on the 12th of March by the following Governor-General's proclamation, annexing Scinde to the British territory. The Ameers were to be sent as captives to Bombay.

" The battle of Meeanee entirely changed the position in which the British Government stood with respect to the Ameers of Scinde. To have placed confidence in them thereafter would have been impossible. To have only exacted from them large cessions of territory, would have been to give them what remained as the means of levying war for the purpose of regaining what was ceded. Foreigners in Scinde, they only held their power by the sword, and by the sword they had lost it. Their position was evidently different from that of a native Prince succeeding a long line of ancestors, the object of the hereditary affection and obedience of his subjects. They had no claim to consideration on the grounds of ancient possession, or of natural prejudice. Certainly they had none arising out of the goodness of their government. To take advantage of the crime they had committed to overturn their power, was a duty to the people they had so long misgoverned. It was essential to the settlement of the country to take a decided course with respect to the Ameers; and the justice of dethroning them being clear, that decision was announced."

When this was made known, the General expressed his satisfaction.

" I had no prejudice," he said, " against the Ameers. I certainly held their conduct as rulers to be insufferable; but as individuals I felt pity for them. I thought them weak Princes, whose folly had brought them into difficulties. It was this feeling that made me return to them their swords, for assuredly I was not insensible to the honour it would be for a private gentleman to possess the swords of so many Princes, surrendered to him on the field of battle: and I believe by all the rules and customs of war their swords were mine. This was an undoubted proof of my feelings then. Since then I have seen their real character developed; and I do think that such thorough-paced villains I never met with in my life. Meer Sobdar is even worse than the others. He certainly had five thousand men in the action. I doubted this at first, as he was not there in person. Being now assured that your Lordship will occupy the country, I can act decidedly, and I shall have cover for my troops very soon. I executed the murderer of the Parsee, putting a label on his breast, to say he was not hanged for fighting with us, but for murdering a man who was a prisoner. The villagers are coming back to their villages. I believe that the country is gradually growing quiet. The proclamation has already produced effect."

This character of the Ameers was just, and it was impossible to treat them with respect, because their power to effect mischief was still very great. The six who had surrendered on the field had been at once placed in a large pleasant garden of their own, close to the entrenched camp.

There they occupied pavilions containing all luxuries; they had an unlimited number of attendants, and free intercourse with the city and the country. Sobdar, Mohamed Khan, and the two Hoosseins were at first treated as friends. When their delinquency was discovered, Sobdar and Mohamed were sent to this garden, the younger Princes remained in the fortress, but all were allowed their usual luxuries and numerous attendants. This arrangement, which greatly augmented the difficulty of guarding them, was made at Outram's desire, his last pernicious meddling being to implore the General so to lodge them!

It was now ascertained that the Ameer Shahdad had caused the murder of Captain Innes. That unfortunate officer's boat had been grappled and dragged to the bank by some Beloochees; they stripped him naked: when they were tearing off his linen, he shivered and pleaded hard to save it. "I am ill," he said, "the water is very cold, leave me my shirt." The reply was a sword stroke which sent his head flying into the river. Shahdad, when taxed with this crime denied it, but the actual murderer was by the other Ameers given up, and he, glorying in the deed, said he acted by Shahdad's orders. "I did it," he exclaimed, "and I would do it again: hang me." He was hanged, and it was the General's design to hang Shahdad also on the highest tower of Hydrabad in sight of Shere Mohamed's army, but Lord Ellenborough with misplaced lenity forbad the execution.

While the Ameers were thus gently used in confinement, their women remained in the zenanas, strongly-built palaces, presenting six separate citadels within the great fortress of Hydrabad. They were scrupulously respected, and no man of the British army entered the women's apartments; but it was soon discovered that the Ameers had, under the name of attendants, also left eight hundred robust Belooch warriors of the Talpoor race within these zenanas, which contained arms complete for the eight hundred, sword, shield, pistol, and matchlock. These men were constantly going back and forwards to the garden of the Ameers, to the city, and to the camp of Shere Mohamed. If one of them was stopped or questioned, a cry that the women would starve if their attendants were molested was immediately raised; and it was impossible with any human feeling to reduce these fierce fellows to obedience, because they openly threatened to cut all the women's throats on the instant, and fight their way out. They were capable of both actions, and no great effort was necessary; for Shere Mohamed's army was within a few miles, the British garrison was but four hundred strong, and had both to guard the outward ramparts of the fortress, which was of great extent, and to watch the six separate zenanas within.

In the garden the Ameers adopted a similar course of policy. Under the name of attendants they gathered five hundred stout Beloochees, all armed with large knives, many with sword and shield; and they were continually sending some of these men to the British camp to spy out the disposition and number of the troops, and then to Shere Mohamed to give him intelligence. They arranged a plan also for a concerted attack by his army on the fortress and camp from without, while their Beloochees should fall upon the garrison from within, their intercourse with him being incessant, almost every hour, and they were so confident as scarcely to conceal their treachery.

Outside, Mohamed, called *Shere* or the Lion, had, the spies said, forty thousand men; but they went plundering, a long way and his force varied. He was by public rumour charged with horrible crimes, matricide amongst them; but he did not disgrace his cognomen in the field. Advancing within ten miles of Hydrabad, and being deceived by Sir C. Napier's feigned timidity, and real difficulties, he openly boasted that he would " *Cabool him.*" This boldness again put the whole country in commotion. The hill tribes, always eager for spoil, prepared to descend on the plains. Mir-Allee, Jam of the Jokeas, the most powerful chief of Lower Scinde, instead of protecting the däks, for which he was paid, intercepted them, and menaced Kurrachee. The military stations of Jerruck and Vikkur were plundered.

Meanwhile the reinforcement coming from Sukkur by land, was exposed to a sudden attack by the Lion, which

would have forced the General to follow him, leaving his
camp in danger and confusion. A more critical situation
could scarcely be. There were only four hundred men in
the fortress; the field force reduced by battle and sickness
was less than two thousand, and had to guard not only the
camp, hospitals, magazines and steamer station, but the
Ameers' garden, the enclosing wall of which was more than
a mile in circuit. Hence the troops were of necessity separated in three bodies, the fortress being four miles, and the
garden half a mile from the camp. The Lion, with from
twenty-five to forty thousand brave men was but ten miles
off, and in constant communication with twelve hundred in
the garden and fortress; the reinforcements from the north
were on a hazardous march, the stations to the south
broken up or invested; the hill tribes were gathering in
arms to descend on the plains; the communications with
Cutch, Joudpore, Jessulmere and Kurrachee were cut off,
and those with the mouths of the Indus and Sukkur entirely
dependent on the armed steamers.

The captive Ameers were taking active advantage of
their conqueror's generosity. They continually despatched
emissaries to excite their feudatory chiefs and allies to continue the war; they kept the Lion informed of all that
passed in camp; and organized their own Beloochees in the
garden and in the fortress to fall on the garrison of the one,
and the hospitals of the other, when the Lion, according to
a concerted plan should attack the British. To cover these
schemes, and, using their own expression "*throw dust in the
eyes of the General,*" they continually made false complaints
of outrage and violence being offered to them by the officers
and soldiers; one of the outrages being the taking away
knives and other weapons from their attendants: for as
there were no women there that was done.

At first the General admonished them mildly upon the
extreme audacity of prisoners thus making war; and upon
the impudent falseness of their complaints. He spoke in
vain, and the following curious example of unflinching
mendacity will illustrate their characters. Before their
attendants were disarmed, Sir C. Napier, accompanied by his

P

staff, entered their garden to remonstrate against the number
of Beloochees they had gathered there, his license for attendance being restricted to Hindoos and household slaves. Arrived at their pavilion, which was immense, being formed by
hanging canvass from the surrounding trees, he found the
whole space within crowded with Beloochees, whose robust
bodies, fierce air, and peculiar features could not be mistaken. Outside stood two hundred more, all well armed,
and they pressed around him and his officers so rudely, that
the latter, expecting violence, closed together for defence.
Yet with this menacing proof of the fact, the Ameers expressed the utmost surprise at his remonstrances, exclaiming
with one voice—"What people! What Beloochees! We
have nobody here but a few Hindoo servants! No Beloochee
ever enters this garden!" Then it was he caused these
people to be disarmed, and the Ameers complained of it as
an outrage!

Long this treachery was borne, lest the remedy should
be attributed to revenge for the cruelty designed against
himself; but when danger to the army pressed, he wrote
thus in answer to one of their usual insolent and false
complaints :—

" I have received your letter this day. You must recollect that your intrigues with Meer Shere Mohamed give me a
great deal to do. I am also much surprised by the falsehoods
which you tell. I will no longer bear this conduct; and if
you give me any more trouble, by stating gross falsehoods,
as you have done in your two letters, I will cast you in
prison as you deserve. You are prisoners, and though I
will not kill you, as you advised your people to do to the
English, I will put you in irons on board a ship. You must
learn Princes, that if prisoners conspire against those who
have conquered them they will find themselves in danger.
Be quiet, or you will suffer the consequences of your folly.
Your friend, Meer Shere Mohamed, has prevented the letter
from the Governor-General as to your fate from reaching me ;
his soldiers intercept the däks. He is a very weak man, and
will soon cause himself to be destroyed; and so will you, unless you submit more quietly to the fate which your own

rash folly has brought upon you. I will answer no more of your letters, which are only repetitions of gross falsehoods that I will not submit to."

Finally, seeing their intrigues were continued, when the Lion was come so close that a battle became inevitable, he placed them on board the steamers, but not in irons.

This letter was condemned in Parliament, as an unheard of ferocity towards captives. Napoleon and his rock had no doubt passed entirely from memory. It was stigmatized as wanting in chivalry! The chivalry of a waiting woman's romance it may have wanted, not the chivalry of common sense; nor yet the chivalry of madness, for even the Knight of La Mancha gives no warrant for such frothy sentiment. The man who fights and fails is at the mercy of his vanquisher, to kill or spare. Civilization leads men to spare, yet with the condition understood, that the man thus taken to mercy, relinquishes further hostility. He is not to practise against the safety and honour of those who have granted him life; he is not to profit of the victor's generosity, by plotting against the army under whose protection he exists. Such acts take away the character of prisoner, substituting that of spy, traitor, and assassin, and death is the proper punishment. Sir C. Napier's letter therefore, was not ferocious, it was generous, considerate, and merciful. To have shot them would have been but justice.

But they were "Fallen Princes"—"Illustrious victims" —"Friends of all the political agents who preceded Sir C. Napier"—"Oppressed weeping sufferers"—"Dignified in misfortune, domestic, and deeply attached to their relations." In such gentle pity-seeking accents was their fate bewailed, by men whose only sympathy sprung from discontent at being by Lord Ellenborough debarred plundering the Scinde revenues, under the names of collectors, secretaries, political agents, and other forms of the Directors' nepotism. Such in substance was the constant cry of the daily press in India, and a portion of that in England; such was the declamation in the House of Commons, and at the India House, and in the pages of the Directors' nameless scribbling sycophants.

But what was their real character as rulers?

They governed by the sword. The Beloochees were their troops; the Scindees and Hindoos their victims. Up to their defeat at Meeanee, any Beloochee might kill a Scindee or Hindoo for pleasure or profit with impunity; and this license was widely exercised, especially where women were concerned.

They dealed largely in slave trading, both as importers and exporters.

To form hunting grounds they had laid waste in sixty years more than a fourth of the most fertile land in Scinde; and to form one of these preserves, even for a child, they would depopulate villages with less compunction than an Englishwoman smokes a hive of bees.

They extracted revenue and money from merchants by torture and mutilations. They forced labouring men to work for them at a tenth of their just wages; and more often than not cheated them of that pittance. When Scinde became British scarcely could a handicraft man be found: all had fled to other countries.

They restricted commerce, oppressed merchants and traders, and repelled strangers lest they should tell the Scindians that such inflictions were unknown save in Scinde, the most fertile and most miserable country of all Asia. Finally they stopped one of the great water courses, derived from the Indus, purposely to destroy the neighbouring country of Cutch which had been irrigated by it.

" The oppressive nature of their government is possibly unequalled in the world," said Sir Henry Pottinger.

" It is an iron despotism," wrote Sir Alexander Burnes.

" They have all the vices of barbarians without their redeeming virtues," was the observation of Mount Stuart Elphinstone.

Outram called it a " Patriarchal Government."

But God did not form the teeming land of Scinde with all the germs of fecundity, nor spread the waters of the Indus to bring them forth with plenteousness, merely to support the brutal Ameers in luxury: they thought so, but his arresting and avenging hand was laid upon them at Meeanee.

As private men they were even more hideously wicked than as sovereigns.

They filled their zenanas with girls torn from their homes, and permitted all their great men to do the same. How were those girls treated? It would suffice as an answer, to say, that when the Ameers fell, not one woman, old or young, mother, wife, or concubine, would follow them to Bombay, so much were they detested. And reason there was for that hatred. They and their Sirdars, and followers, perpetrated such horrid iniquities that the women could not but shrink from such contamination. If suspicion crossed the mind of a Beloochee, he sought no proof, but made the father or mother hold the daughter by the hair while he cut her throat, or hacked her to pieces with a sword. The slightest quarrel, or disobedience, or even reluctance shewn, was provocation for cutting off the miserable girl's nose or ears with a knife.

The Ameers killed all their illegitimate children; and, not unfrequently, their female legitimate offspring. This has with shameless effrontery been denied, even in Parliament. But Dr. Burns, who resided at Hydrabad, as court physician, thus confirms the information acquired on that head by Sir C. Napier. "*I may here remark, that it is the custom of the Court of Scinde to put to death all children born to the Princes by slave women. The butchery which this horrid cruelty engenders must be shocking, and I was assured that one member of the family alone, had consigned to the tomb no less than twenty-seven of his illegitimate offspring!*" And how did these monsters destroy? First they gave potions to procure abortion; if those failed, they sometimes chopped the children to pieces with their own hands immediately after birth; but more frequently placed them under cushions and sat down, smoking, drinking, jesting about their hellish work, while the helpless creatures were being suffocated beneath them! Nor was this the limit of their abominations. With inhuman cruelty they chastised what they deemed the poor women's offences, such, perhaps, as weeping over their slaughtered infants. Nusseer of Hydrabad, reputed the most humane of the pernicious brood, had a whip expressly to correct the women; the lash composed of two lengths of twisted brass wires! It is no fable! The usage is certain, the whip is in the General's possession, and not the least prized of his trophies — it tells him how excellent a deed it was to put his foot upon the ruffians' necks!

Such were the Ameers as Princes; such as fathers and husbands. Were they better as relations and friends?

It has been shewn how they put Roostum's interests forward, protesting to Outram, that pity for that Talpoor patriarch was their ground for resisting the new treaty; and how Outram pretended to believe them. When they went forth in arms, they had their furnished palaces and gardens behind them; he came to the field after a long flight and a sojourn in the desert ; his all was carried on camels, was taken and lost, when on the false alarm the captured camp had been fired. Thus Roostum was without personal resources, and when sent to the garden the other Ameers refused him any aid. There he stood, eighty-five years of age, his white beard streaming, his head bared in the sun of Scinde, without food, without attendance, without cover, without a carpet to lie down on, without a change of clothes —and he was sick also. He stood, a suppliant at the door of the other Ameers' gorgeous pavilion, which was filled with every convenience and luxury that their near palaces could supply, yet no man asked him in, none would let him enter! When he prayed for shelter none proffered him help, none gave him clothes, or money, or food; they would not even lend him utensils to cook with, or a carpet to kneel on for his prayers. He was on the point of perishing when the General and his staff furnished him with a tent and carpets, with clothes, cooking utensils, food, and money taken from the prize funds. Here then was ample proof that not for Roostum's sake had they gone to war.

But how had that old Ameer borne himself towards his own family? His brother, Ali Moorad, was a child when their father died. He was left by that father to Roostum's care and protection, and to prevent dispute a will was written in the Koran which stated and defined each son's share, but

Roostum and another adult brother fraudulently dispossessed
Ali Moorad of his patrimony. When grown up, being a
man of energy, he assembled a force and demanded his
rights. This was in 1838; he was too formidable to be resisted; but Roostum, making solemn promises to restore his
villages and having contracts to that effect written in the
Koran, induced Ali, a generous man for an Ameer, to disband his troops after a victory, and then laughed at him as
a dupe. When the Auckland treaty was ratified, this dispute
was referred by virtue of that treaty to the Anglo-Indian
Government for decision, and the award, being in favour of
Moorad, perhaps kept him true to the alliance.

It was with a full knowledge of their faithlessness, their
horrid government, and still more horrid practices, that Sir
C. Napier designated the Ameers as thorough-paced villains,
and expressed his satisfaction that they were deposed. But
it was said their subjects loved them, fought for them to
death! The Beloochees fought for them indeed; that is
they fought for their pay, and for plunder, and because,
being fanatics, they hated the Feringees as unbelievers.
That they fought for love of the Ameers is false, and this is
the proof. Roostum's sons and nephews remain at large, to
the number of perhaps thirty; they have not ceased to solicit
the mountain tribes on the right bank of the Indus to commence a new war, yet have never been able to rouse a man
to battle. Many of those wild fellows have indeed come
down to rob in the plains according to their ancient customs,
but none to fight for the fallen Princes.

If the fighting tribes had taken arms to restore the
Ameers' dynasty, it would not have been pertinent to the
matter. The Beloochees were the soldiers of the Ameers,
the Scindians their subjects. As soldiers the first fought
nobly, being by nature brave and emulous of military reputation; but they had no attachment for their cowardly
Princes, who cared for them as little as they did for the
miserable Scindian whom they killed or mutilated with cold
cruelty. Of this there is proof. Amongst all the men who
fought at Meeanee only three were taken alive, and they
were badly wounded. They had been carried along with the

British sufferers to the hospital on the Indus, close to the Ameers' garden; but no attendant speaking their language could be found, and Sir C. Napier, interested in their fate, personally requested of the Ameers to send a native. No! He then ordered them to do so, and they sent a person with a promise of three halfpence daily! The second day he said he could not live on that sum, but the Ameers answered, "It is too much, we have no money." The man therefore abandoned his charge, and the poor wounded fellows were entirely taken care of by English soldiers! Yet faction laments over the patriarchal Princes, and calumniates the man who has enhanced even the glory of England by their fall.

CHAPTER V.

SHERE Mohamed, when he first heard of the battle sent a false deprecatory message to the victor; the answer would have been the charging shout of the British cavalry, if Outram had not, as before noticed, prevailed on the General to let him substitute a foolish epistle, which produced no effect. The Lion soon learned from the captive Ameers the weak state of the army, and was now menacing the camp, having concerted the following plan.

The eight hundred Talpoors in the fortress were to fall on the weak garrison from within, when the Lion's right wing attacked from without. If the army came up to succour the garrison, the Lion's main body would meet it, while a strong detachment should join the Beloochees in the garden, and storm the camp.

This was well conceived: but barbarian plans are seldom executed with precision, and to shew how the Lion failed, the operations on both sides must be exactly traced.

On the 3rd of March Sir C. Napier thus addressed the warring Ameer:—" Prince, you wrote to me, and said you had not joined in battle against the English. I believed you, and told you to disperse your troops, and that you would be safe. Had you done so you would have been in no danger; but instead of this, you are rallying the defeated Beloochees; you have increased the number of your troops; and unless you come to my camp at Hydrabad, and prove your innocence, I will march against you and inflict a signal punishment."

On the 13th the spies first reported the Lion's numbers to be forty thousand. Sir C. Napier would not credit this. He has not much money he said; he has not much water; he has not much ammunition: how then can he have assembled forty thousand men? It seemed incredible; yet it

was so, and again he was compelled to lament his own folly
in attending to Outram's pernicious suggestion. But his
reinforcements were coming, and meanwhile he adhered to
his plan of tempting the Lion to approach close. Yet,
though willing to give the Ameer a long day, he never designed to delay beyond the 24th of March, because from
that time until the unendurable heat, would scarcely suffice
to win a victory and capture Meerpoor and Omercote.
Hence, with a greatness of mind which distinguished all his
acts in this memorable campaign, he resolved, if his reinforcements were delayed, to seek the enemy even with the
few troops at his command, and fight him, though more than
twenty to one.

Shere Mohamed, judging this caution to be the effect of
fear, soon approached closer, and ravaging the country
around, carried off the camels of the army from their pas-
tures: thus he excited great hopes amongst the Belooch
race, terrified the Scindians, and gave himself the air of a
conqueror. Nevertheless, when he had concerted his plan of
attack with the captive Ameers, he, from pride, or it might
be latent fear, sent, on the 18th of March, vakeels to the
British camp with an insolent offer of terms, saying—" Quit
this land and your life shall be spared, provided you restore
all you have taken." The vakeels entered the camp, and
delivered their haughty message just as the evening gun was
fired. " You hear that sound; it is my answer to your
chief. Begone!" And with that stern observation he turned
his back on the envoys. Next day he received a shocking
proposal to assassinate the Lion; it came from the Ameer's
own brother! Indignant and disgusted, he instantly sent
information to Shere Mohamed, bidding him beware of the
treachery, but at the same time repaid his insolent message
with the following warning:—

" I will make no terms with you, except unconditional
surrender, and security for your person, such as the other
Ameers have received. We were at peace with you; we
made no war with you; you have made unprovoked war
upon us, and have cut off our däks. If you do not surrender
yourself a prisoner of war before the 23rd instant I will

march against you." These proceedings delayed the execution of the Lion's concerted plan, and then the General's
combination drew his attention another way. He was then
at Ali-ka-Tanda, a few miles from Hydrabad with twelve
thousand men, having detached eight thousand to Dubba on
his right; and five thousand to Khooserie on his left, in pur-
suance of the project already described. (Plans 3, 5.) He
was confident of .storming the fortress and camp, and though
the battle between were lost he judged his final success
certain; because the British, weakened and having lost
their camp, their stores and steamer station, must retreat by land in the heat. In fine he had ably modified the
Ameers' original plan of warfare, and would, as he boasted,
have " *Cabooled the British*," if a shallow political agent like
Outram had been in authority instead of a skilful general.

Before the 16th some recruits and six months' provisions,
money and ammunition came to the camp from Kurrachee,
and at the same time the 21st regiment of sepoys arrived
from Sukkur down the Indus. The fortress was at that time
repaired, and the entrenched camp completed. On the 19th
Major Stack's column, coming by land, was computed to be
within a few marches: he had eight hundred sepoy infantry,
three hundred Eastern horsemen, and Leslie's battery of
horse artillery, and his junction was looked for on the 22nd.
Therefore it was that the General fixed the 23rd for submission when he replied to the Lion's insolent message.

He was however uneasy for Stack's safety because the
Lion's army was between the camp and that officer, and might
crush him on the march. The affair was critical, and was
rendered dangerous by unauthorized meddling.

On the 21st, Stack having reached Muttaree, a long
march from Hydrabad, was met by a cossid or native messenger, bearing orders to force his marches. But the Lion
had notice of his approach, and designing to fall on him the
22nd, had in the night moved with his whole army to Dubba,
thus relinquishing for the moment his original plan. The
two Commanders were thus pitted for a trial of skill—nearly
all the chances being however for the Ameer, who had only to
mass his troops and make a night march of a few miles,

whereas the English General, with scattered troops, very inferior in numbers, had many objects to guard. His combinations were therefore more complicated, and more subject to accidental disturbances, which were not wanting.

Major Clibborne, charged with the secret intelligence, hearing of the Lion's movement, sent, without informing the General, a cossid to Stack, bearing this message in a small quill.

" Halt, for God's sake ! You will be attacked by at least forty thousand men to-morrow."

Stack, having just before received the General's orders to march steadily onwards, was perplexed, and amazed withal at the enormous force assigned to Shere Mohamed. He sent the cossid back instantly with the quill and message, demanding positive orders, and the man, happily passing through the enemy, reached the camp when the General was entertaining a great body of officers in his tent. The affair was momentous. The vicinity of Shere Mohamed, his numbers, his arrogant boasting and message, his known intercourse with the captive Ameers, the force which those Princes had in the garden and fortress, and the many at their command who were lurking in the city and the neighbouring villages awaiting the hour of battle—these were matters known to every follower of the army, and had caused great disquietude ; the reinforcements were looked for with anxiety by the troops, and even by the officers, and great uneasiness prevailed.

Clibborne's interference was very untoward. If Stack should halt, the Lion having ten miles start might crush him before succour could arrive. If the General marched in force to his aid the fortress and camp would be endangered, because the Lion's movement might be only a feint : nor would it be wise to give him an opportunity of falling upon either column separately in march. It was essential therefore that Stack should force his marches to get as near Hydrabad as possible before he was assailed. All these considerations rushed upon the General's mind when the cossid brought back Clibborne's message, and being very uneasy about the bad moral effect, he instantly adopted a happy expedient, which for the scholar will recall the jest of Hannibal before the battle of Cannæ. Reading the note aloud to his guests, Sir C. Napier added

with a pencil " *Clibborne's men are all in buckram. Come on !*"
Thus amended he sent it once more to Stack. The joke
took, was repeated in camp, and confidence was restored.

He had yet to save his detachment. Clibborne's news
was confirmed in the night. There were three places where
the Lion could fall on Stack with advantage. These were
Muttaree, Meeanee, and a place a few miles nearer to Hydrabad, between Loonar and Bagayet. (Plan 5.) The first was
unlikely because of the distance, and Stack would soon
advance.; but Meeanee and Loonar were distant from each
other, and the precise combinations required would not suit
both places. Which was to be chosen? One of those scin-
tillations of genius which indicate the strength of the fire
within, determined the line of action. "Muttaree is distant,
the plain of Meeanee is covered with the bleaching bones of
chiefs and warriors; the Beloochees are superstitious, they
never will go there—Loonar will be the place of action, there
I will march."

But he did not neglect Muttaree. The enemy was on the
eastern bank of the Fullaillee, whose windings would compel
a circuitous march, whereas his own line was straight; wherefore he sent Captain McMurdo with two hundred and fifty
Poona horsemen, to feel for the Lion on the road to Muttaree,
and if the way was open to join Stack and confirm the order
to advance. McMurdo reached Stack on the morning of the
22nd, on which day Jacob was sent with the Scinde horsemen
along the same road, and the General followed at a short
distance with the Bengal cavalry and some guns, being supported at a later period by all the infantry.

This succession of columns was a mastery in the art.
The report of the Lion's march had been somewhat vague,
and no sure intelligence of his real numbers could be obtained.
The country, though flat, was covered with houses, gardens,
shikargahs and nullahs, where thousands of men might be
concealed : no extended view could be got. The hospitals,
magazines and camp, if uncovered, might be surprised, because the Lion had men enough to overwhelm Stack and leave
sufficient force in ambush behind : it was known that five
thousand men had been so placed at Khooserie, and there was

no certain report of their withdrawal. Hence McMurdo had been first detached; for the General expected the Lion's spies would exaggerate that officer's numbers, and if he met the Belooch army his sudden appearance and supposed strength would delay their movement against Stack; that would disclose the Lion's real position and give time for the main body to support McMurdo. But if, as really happened, the road was clear, a resolute officer with a body of good horsemen would be added to Stack's force and enable it to push on boldly. Meanwhile the head of the army would be approaching Loonar, and the perilous separation of the troops rapidly diminished, while the rear would still be able to turn and aid the camp, if it was attacked.

Stack marched at eleven o'clock on the 22nd from Muttaree, and, as the General had anticipated, crossed the field of Meeanee without seeing an enemy; then passing the Fullaillee, he entered a plain, having that nullah, which there took a sudden bend towards Hydrabad, close on his left. He was however so intent on a rapid junction with the General, the head of whose column was now only four or five miles from him, that disregarding other considerations he managed his operations imprudently.

His line of march lent his left flank to the enemy, especially near Loonar, where the opposite bank of the Fullaillee had a thick wood, in which the Lion lay perdue. Stack's baggage should therefore have filed on the reverse flank of the column, and well in advance; his infantry and guns should have kept togethef, covered by the cavalry towards the Fullaillee. All this was easy on a wide plain having no obstacle save a small transverse nullah crossing his front. Stack pushed forward his guns, followed with his cavalry and infantry in mass, and left his baggage behind straggling, so that when his cannon had passed the nullah in front the rear of the baggage had scarcely quitted Meeanee several miles behind: thus tempting the enemy.

When the long column of sumpter animals approached Loonar, the Belooch matchlock men crossed the Fullaillee from the wood and opened fire, while heavy masses appeared in movement, some supporting this attack, others menacing the flank of the troops ahead, one large body evidently meaning to cross the front and cut the column off from Hydrabad. In this crisis McMurdo, who happened to be in rear with only six Poona horsemen, charged and beat back the matchlock skirmishers, sending at the same time to Stack for aid. The Beloochees were reinforced and renewed the attack, but McMurdo kept them at bay for three-quarters of an hour; the troops he had asked for then came up, and he drove the enemy back over the Fullaillee and thus saved the baggage.

Meanwhile Stack, with extreme negligence or ignorance of war, had continued his march. Wherefore McMurdo, still fearing for the baggage column, left Lieutenant Moore to protect it as he could and galloped ahead to obtain aid. The guns were then across the transverse nullah and he could scarcely obtain leave to take two back, but placing those in a flanking position he raked the enemy's masses and stopped the attack. The Belooch column which had menaced the head of the march also halted, because Stack, at last sensible of his error, now drew up in order of battle. Jacob's cavalry soon after came in sight, the baggage closed up, and the march recommenced, but the troops did not reach the camp until midnight much exhausted with fatigue.

Had the Lion persisted in his attack the baggage must have been taken, and his military vigour was at the time undervalued; but the true cause of his forbearance afterwards became known and did honour to his chivalry, if not to his policy. He saw a great number of women with the baggage and stopped the attack, saying, "The English General treated our women very generously at Hydrabad and I will not let his women suffer now." He thus lost the baggage: but he would not have prevailed against the troops, for there were five hundred cavalry, a battery of horse artillery, and eight hundred infantry: all good troops. Moreover Jacob was close at hand with five hundred more cavalry, and the General scarcely three miles behind Jacob: the combination was therefore perfect.

Sir C. Napier was desirous to find Stack closely engaged, for his troops were excellent, and the Lion would soon have

been placed between two fires, and thrown into confusion.
The vicissitudes of war are proverbial, the decisive combat
was yet to be fought.   Shere Mohamed had calculated that
Stack could not reach Loonar before the 23rd, but the forced
marches imposed on that officer brought him there the 22nd,
the Lion's reckoning was thus falsified, and his chivalric
respect for the women perhaps somewhat enforced.

On the British side difficulties were now abated, and
Fortune began to pour out her gifts in double handfuls.
After the battle of Meeanee, Sir C. Napier had played his
game so cautiously, had so suddenly dropt from his heroic
daring, that he appeared to his enemies sunk in sloth and
fear, and they began to despise him, as he wished them to do.
The Lion thought a final sweep certain, being unconscious
that his adversary's drift was to make him waste his treasure,
and so render a battle decisive of the fate of Scinde.   Pride
misled him and the captive Ameers, and their confidence
being accepted as the warrant of success by their Beloochee
subjects, numerous independent bands traversed the country
only intent on plunder during the short time they expected
the war to last.

They spread terror far and near.   On the day of the
skirmish at Loonar, a convoy of three hundred camels,
coming from the coast and escorted by a hundred sepoys,
was assailed near Tatta ; and at another place, Agha Khan,
a Persian prince, of whom more shall be said hereafter,
being then wandering about Scinde and friendly to the
British, was assailed and had, after a fight, to fly with only
thirty horsemen out of two hundred to the entrenched camp.
Thither also came some of Ali Moorad's Beloochees, but the
rest of his forces he kept in Upper Scinde to enforce his authority as Rais—for many chiefs and killedars, expecting the Lion
to win, refused obedience, and in some cases fought him with
success.   These commotions were formidable, but the English
General had now perfected his preparations.   He had secured
his hospitals with entrenchments, had repaired the fortress,
had reopened his communications, obtained supplies for six
months, and brought his reinforcements happily into camp.   He
had baffled his principal adversary in the field, filled him with

false hopes, wasted his treasure, rendered him hateful to the Scindian people from the plundering of his bands, and by enticing him close to the British position he had saved his own soldiers long marches to obtain a good field of battle. That battle he was now fiercely eager for: the snake had cast his slough!

His first design was to fight on the 23rd, but Stack's troops were too much fatigued, and he waited yet a day. This delay was happy, for reinforcements were coming by water down from Sukkur, and up from Bombay and Kurrachee, and, though resolved not to wait for them he longed for their arrival. In this state of mind, being at breakfast on the morning of the 23rd with his principal officers, and revolving in his thoughts the operations for the next day, he suddenly exclaimed, "Now my luck would be great if I could get my other reinforcements from Sukkur, from Kurrachee or from the mouth of the Indus; but it cannot be, they will not be here for a week, and I will not let the Lion bully me any longer, I will fight him to-morrow." Scarcely had he spoken, when an officer looking out exclaimed, "there are boats coming up the river." All rushed forth, and, lo! the reinforcements from Bombay were entering the port behind the camp! "There are more boats—a fleet coming down the river," cried out another officer, and in the direction he pointed to, a grove of masts was discerned towering above the flat bank of the Indus: they brought the reinforcements from Sukkur, and these simultaneous arrivals added to the army five hundred good recruits, store of entrenching tools, and two eight-inch howitzers, with a detachment of artillery men; much needed, for previous to this fortunate event there were only three artillery officers to command sixteen guns scantily manned.

The recruits were thrown into the fortress, the garrison of old soldiers was added to the field force, and a new order of battle was organized. These arrangements were made by seven o'clock in the evening, when the whole force was drawn up in front of the camp to give the principal officers a lesson to their commands; for the brigades were under majors, the regiments under captains, and the staff had scarcely a man

Q

above three and twenty years of age. Full of fire and courage and zeal and devotion they were, but unpractised in the duties of their stations.

His wish was to put sick men and stores in the fortress and augment his fighting force with their guards, but had no carriage to transport them from the camp. He however, in contempt of chivalry, put the captive Ameers on board the steamers, and having organized his convalescents, Ali Moorad's men, and Agha Khan's followers, in all eighteen hundred men, confided his camp to them. In fine he mistrusted Fortune just so much as to unite all his available strength for striking, and yet prepared for disaster while seeking victory. He knew her to be capricious, that the crisis was dangerous, but the hour of battle had struck and he was again the heroic soldier of Meeanee.

Just as his line was formed in the evening, the vakeels of Shere Mohamed again entered the camp. They came to spy, but pretended to bear the Lion's last summons —" The British army was to yield or be destroyed." Silently the General led them along the front of his line, and then turning, told them to report what they saw. At that moment another vakeel came, and eagerly sought a conversation. All these envoys repaired to the head-quarter tent, where with great ingenuity they sought to learn the General's intentions, prolonging their efforts through half the night; but then, overwhelmed with fatigue, he dismissed them with the following letter and a recommendation to hasten or he would be with their master before them. " If the Ameer, Meer Shere Mohamed, chooses to meet me to-morrow as I march to attack him at the head of my army, and will surrender himself a prisoner without other condition than that his life shall be safe, I will receive him. If the Belooch chiefs choose to accompany him, I will receive them on condition that they swear obedience to the Governor-General: then they may return to their villages with their followers, and all their rights and possessions shall be secured to them."

This done, he lay down at two o'clock, to rise at four for battle.

CHAPTER VI.

AT break of day five thousand men were under arms, eleven hundred being cavalry with nineteen guns, five of which were horse-artillery. Two guns were assigned for defence of the camp, seventeen for the field, and the march commenced. Hydrabad was kept on the left because the spies reported that the Lion had resumed his original position at Ali-ka-Tanda and Khooserie, and the movement was directed against the latter place. But in the night he concentrated his army at the village of Dubba (Plan 6) where he had before entrenched a position, and this being soon discovered by scouts sent towards Khooserie, the march was directed diagonally in front of Hydrabad upon Dubba, which was eight miles north-west of that city.

In one compact mass the infantry and guns moved, the cavalry scouting ahead and on the flank; for so thickly was the whole country covered with houses, gardens, shikargahs, and nullahs, that fifty thousand men might be in position without being discovered at half a mile distance: even where the level was open, the nullah banks were so high, that a horseman could not look over.

During the march despatches from Lord Ellenborough arrived, by the only post which had not for two months been intercepted. They conveyed thanks to the army for Meeanee, expressed in glowing terms, and assurances that honours and rewards would mark that victory. Prompt to apply all moral incentives, the General instantly made this known to the troops. Then arose a shout of exultation, for hope swelled the soldier's heart when he found that honest service was acknowledged; and again arose a shout for the General who had named the private soldier as well as the officer in recounting heroic deeds. These were cries of victory which made the General's heart swell in return.

Ten miles were now passed over, and still the exact situation of the enemy was unknown, when suddenly an emissary came with information that the Lion was with his whole force two miles on the left. The direction of the column was instantly changed. The irregular horsemen went forward at a rapid pace; the General galloped ahead, and in a quarter of an hour found himself on a plain in front of the Belooch army. Far and wide it stretched. The whole plain was swarming with cavalry and infantry, and yet he could not see above half the real numbers, nor get any distinct view of their order of battle. There were, however, more than twenty-six thousand fighting men before him, with sword and shield and matchlock, and they had fifteen guns, eleven being in battery. Two lines of infantry were entrenched, and a heavy mass of cavalry was in reserve.

Their right rested on the Fullaillee, the bed of which, though generally dry, had at that point a large pond of mud protecting the flank, and beyond it was a thick shikargah, which prevented the position being turned, except by a wide movement.

The front was covered by a nullah twenty feet wide and eight deep, with the usual high banks, which were scarped so as to form a parapet. Behind this, the first line of infantry was posted, extending on a slightly waving trace for a mile, in a direction perpendicular to the Fullaillee. From thence it was prolonged another mile in the same line to a wood, which was occupied, and appeared to be the left flank of the position. It was not so however. Another nullah, scarped like the first, went off from thence in a diagonal direction to the rear, forming an obtuse angle with the first line, and there the left of the enemy's army was really posted, for the wood only contained an isolated body thrown forward as if for attack.

Thus the true front extended from the right for one mile perpendicularly to the Fullaillee, presenting what may be termed the right wing and centre to an attack; but the left wing, behind the second nullah, refused and masked by that ditch, was covered also by the prolongation of the first nullah covering the right and centre, and by the wood, which was again covered by several smaller nullahs.

All the cavalry were behind the left in one great mass ; and behind the right wing, close to the Fullaillee, stood the village of Dubba or Naraja, filled with men and prepared for resistance by cuts and the loopholing of the houses.

But this was not all the defence.

Between the first line of the right and centre and the village of Dubba was a third nullah, forty-two feet wide and seventeen feet deep, the bank scarped and prepared like the first. Both of them had, however, one or two ramps for the purpose of advancing or retreating, which proved of singular service to the British in the fight.

This third and largest nullah extended to where the smaller one, covering the left wing, went off diagonally, that is to say a mile, but no further; and was planted thickly with the second line of the Belooch army. The Lion's guns also were ranged behind it, with the exception of one, placed on a mound to the right between the two lines, and, raking the bed of the Fullaillee.

The Lion had also scarped two smaller nullahs at a considerable distance behind the left and centre of the position, apparently to protect his rear, or to give himself a new front if he should be turned; and having cleared the low jungle in front of his line, in that faultless position resolutely awaited the attack. But good a soldier as he may be called, a better and braver than he ruled in the fight. This was the African slave, Hoche Mohamed Seedee, who, if his first name be correct, was not unlikely the son of some Abyssinian attached to the French army in Egypt. His vigorous exhortations had urged the Ameers to war ; his genius had principally directed the operations at Meeanee ; and now, true and loyal to his captive master Sobdar, who, though wicked and oppressive to others, had been generous to him, the dark hero displayed all his magnanimity. Standing with his brother Seedees the foremost in the fight, when he could not conquer he and they died sword in hand without a backward step.

The march of the British force, being diagonal to the

front of the Belooch army, brought the head of the column, left in front, near the right of the enemy, and the line was immediately formed on the same slant, the cavalry being drawn up on the wings, the artillery in the intervals between the regiments : thus the right was somewhat refused, though not in so great a degree as the enemy's left.

At first the General was very jealous of the wood menacing his right. It was occupied, he could not tell whether by many or few ; but his spies positively assured him that five thousand of the best men were ensconced on some part of the line, with design to rush out when the British should advance. From the wood he expected this counter attack, and pushed the cavalry of his right wing forward, partly to cover his flank, partly to make the enemy shew his order of battle more clearly. His own position was meanwhile delicate and dangerous. The plain on which he stood was not large, and the Fullaillee, making a sudden bend, wound round his rear, while on all other points of the circuit, save the gorge by which he had entered, was a network of nullahs, amidst which his compact column, opposed to the multitude of Beloochees, seemed at first like a wild beast within the closing circle of an eastern hunt. Yet the bend of the Fullaillee in his rear was no disadvantage, being dry, it furnished a reserved line of defence.

He could not see the whole of the Lion's position. He made out that, notwithstanding their deep method of drawing up their swordsmen, they outflanked him by more than half a mile on his right, and still had their cavalry in reserve ; but the double lines and nullahs containing their centre and right he could not see ; neither could he ascertain that Dubba was occupied: it appeared empty. He could not examine their line closely without crossing the Fullaillee, and riding through the shikargah on the other side ; but here, as at Meeanee, he feared to give time for reflection and comparison of numbers, lest it should smother the warlike fire kindled by the despatches. His were not national troops. The rough European stood by the meek gentle sepoy of Bombay, the small lean Mahratta, marched beside the large-limbed man of Bengal ; the regular cavalry

charged with the wild horsemen, the fanatic Mahomedan
levelled his musket between the Christian and the Idolator.
But all acknowledged the bonds of discipline; and better
still, for the moment, were enthusiastic from the contrivance
of their General.

When the line was formed, the left being advanced, was
under the Belooch cannon and several men were killed:
one shot nearly grazed the General's leg; but the flight of
the balls betraying the elevation of the guns the wing
was thrown back in safety.

To make out the enemy's position more exactly, the
engineer Waddington, assisted by two Lieutenants, Brown
and Hill, rode straight to the centre of the Belooch line,
and then along the front to the junction of the centre with
the left, being always under a sharp fire of matchlocks.
They thus forced the enemy to shew two-thirds of his position; but the third nullah was not seen, nor was the wood
made to speak plainly. Several ramps for passing the two
nullahs were discovered by these intrepid officers and indicated for the artillery.

While this daring exploit was going on, Sir C. Napier
observed many Beloochees, troubled as he thought by the
sudden appearance of the British army, hurrying from their
left towards the village of Dubba; and so hidden were their
lines in the two nullahs covering that village, he also thought
they had neglected their right, and were hurrying to repair
the error. Hence he at once put his own troops in movement, advancing here as at Meeanee in the echellon order,
with the 22nd leading, from the left. He hoped to seize
the first nullah and the village before the enemy could reach
it. His judgment was at fault, yet the promptitude was
admirable, and the attack, though founded on a mistake,
could scarcely have been amended with better knowledge.
But while thus rapid of execution, he did not fail to provide
for all contingencies that could be foreseen.

The wood on his right he viewed with peculiar jealousy;
the close manner in which the Beloochees were there posted,
convinced him they were the select division appointed to
break out upon his flank. From the wood therefore as from

Pandora's box all evil might come, and to watch it he placed
the Scindian horsemen and 3rd Bombay cavalry, under
Major Stack, in advance, with orders to oppose whatever
came out. This would give time, if he was so assailed
before he could pass the nullah in attack, to throw back all
the infantry on the right of the 22nd into a new position,
between the Fullaillee and the village of Chilgheree. There
he could fight on the defensive with the sepoys and cavalry
of the right wing, while with the 22nd, the horse-artillery and
the cavalry of the left wing, he continued the attack on the
enemy's right.

At nine o'clock the battle commenced.

Leslie's horse-artillery, pushing forward, made a slant
march for the junction of the point where the first nullah
fell into the Fullaillee, on the enemy's extreme right; he
thus got a partial view of their centre, and a complete view
of their left: there he halted at intervals to rake, but still
rapidly gained ground towards the extreme right. The rest
of the artillery, following in succession by batteries, likewise
obtained raking positions, crossing their fire with the horse-
artillery, so that the bullets tore the thick masses of the
enemy's infantry in a terrible manner; but previous to this
Lieut. Smith, thinking of his duty and not of his life, with
desperate valour rode foremost and alone to the bank of the
first nullah and ascended it. He sought for a place where
his guns could pass, and found death! the nullah was filled
with Beloochees, and "*there the hero fell.*"

Meanwhile the 22nd, followed by the sepoy regiment,
presented only a diagonal front to the hostile line of fire,
while the Bengal and Poona horsemen, on the left wing,
moved in column close to the Fullaillee, to support Leslie
and meet any sudden rush. Soon it was found that the
nullahs and the village had not been neglected. The men
seen hurrying towards them were rushing to reinforce the
dark hero, Hoche, who had filled them with men, and at
the head of his brother Seedees awaited the attack, resolved
to win or perish. Their matchlocks and the single gun on
the hillock behind them played incessantly, and the march
of the 22nd was marked by the dead; half the light company

went down by fire from the first nullah, and beyond it
the second and greater one was seen more strongly lined
with men, while the village became suddenly alive with
warriors, whose matchlocks could also reach the advancing
line.

Now the General saw that he had undervalued the Lion's
skill, and that the rush of men towards the village and right
wing had been a fine military impulse to strengthen that
flank. He had neither time nor means to countercheck
them, and, as generally happens even with the greatest
captains, had to remedy his error by courage. Hence with
the foremost of the 22nd he rode, meaning in person to
lead the charge, when suddenly came a horseman from the
right, to tell him all the cavalry of that wing was charging.
Then concluding that the wood was vomiting forth its am-
bushed warriors, and that his flank was turned, he desired
Major Poole of the 22nd to lead the attack on the nullah,
and went at full speed to the right. The report was
correct. The cavalry of the right wing was madly charging
across the minor nullahs covering the enemy's left; not
because the Beloochees from the wood had moved, but that
seeing numbers of the enemy still hurrying in apparent
confusion towards the centre, the horsemen, thinking it a
panic, had gone headlong down upon their left wing. Stack
had thus uncovered the flank, and exposed the whole army
to a defeat, if the wood had really been filled with the
Belooch division appointed for the counter stroke.

It was a great error, but could not be remedied. The
whole body of cavalry was at full speed, dashing across the
smaller nullahs, the spurs deep in the horses' sides, the
riders pealing their different war cries, and whirling their
swords in gleaming circles—there the fiery Delamain led the
gorgeous troopers of the 3rd cavalry, there the terrible
Fitzgerald careered with the wild Scindian horsemen, their
red turbans streaming amidst the smoke and dust of the
splendid turmoil. For a moment the General gazed, at first
with anger, then with admiration, and seeing no indications
of mischief from the wood while the redoubling thunder of
his artillery called him to the left, trusting all to fortune

and courage he went back with such speed as to reach the
22nd at the moment it was rushing to storm the first nullah.

Riding to the first rank he raised that clear high-pitched
cry of war, which had at Meeanee sent the same fiery
soldiers to the charge. It was responded to with even
greater ardour; for here no check occurred, though the
danger and difficulty was greater. Lieut. Coote first gained
the summit of the bank, and tearing a Belooch standard
from its bearer waved it in triumph while he reeled along
the narrow edge, fainting from a deep wound in his side.
Then with a deafening shout the soldiers leaped into the
midst of the swordsmen; and they were no sluggards to
deal with, for there the black hero· Hoche and all the
Seedees fought—and there they fell!

Murderous was the fire of the British guns and musketry, and the bayonet clashing with the sword bore back
the bravest and strongest Beloochees, or levelled them in the
dust, until the struggling crowd was forced into the second
and deeper nullah, where with desperate fury the fight was
renewed, as if the previous struggle had been as nothing.
But still with conquering strength, and wasting fire, and
piercing steel, the 22nd forced its bloody way through the
dense masses, being well supported by the sepoys of the
25th, who, striving on its right, kept pace and stroke in this
terrible conflict. Soon the victorious troops passed the
second nullah, pressing with undiminished fury on the rear
of the retreating swordsmen until they reached the village
of Dubba, where the Lugarees and Nizamanees, two of the
most warlike tribes of Scinde were well entrenched in the
houses, and once more contended for the victory. The two
regiments, thus opposed, immediately lapped round the
nearest point of the village, while the cavalry of the left
wing turned the place, partly by the bed of the Fullaillee,
partly by passing the nullahs. Galloping round the left
of Dubba they got a view of the plain beyond, where the
cavalry of the right wing were now seen driving the
Beloochees, horsemen and footmen, before them in scattered
bands. Leslie's horse-artillery, also came up, having passed
the nullahs with the cavalry by the aid of Henderson's

sappers, who had worked slopes down the bank in the midst of the fire. Dubba, thus isolated, was left to the infantry, and was soon surrounded; for the other regiments of the line, seeing the 22nd and 25th across both nullahs on the left, Stack's cavalry victorious on the right, and the enemy in their own front fearfully smitten by the guns, which never ceased to ply their masses with sweeping discharges; seeing all this, the other regiments rushed vehemently forward, crossed the nullahs, and bringing up their right shoulders continued the circle from the position of the 25th, lapping further round the village. In this charge the 21st sepoys stabbed every Beloochee they came up with, whole or wounded, calling out Innes! Innes! at every stroke of death they dealt. Thus hundreds died for the crime of the villain Shahdad.

From the speed of this advance some confusion ensued, and a Belooch field magazine exploding, killed all around the General as he was striving to restore order, he alone remaining unhurt, although his sword was broken in his hand and his clothes singed. Strongly and fiercely the enemy still fought, but they were finally driven from the village, and joined the other retreating masses; yet there was nothing like flight amongst the footmen: slowly and sullenly they retired, some going off to the desert with the Lion, the greater number making for the Indus, hoping to pass that river; but the victorious cavalry of the right wing intercepted and drove them in heaps towards the wilderness. Meanwhile the Bengal and Poona horse, under Major Storey and Captain Tait, were by the General in person, after forcing his way through Dubba at the head of the infantry, led against the retreating masses, putting them to the sword for several miles: not without loss to themselves, for the brave Captain Garrett and others fell.

The Scinde horsemen pursued on a parallel line more to the right; and there Fitzgerald and Delamain actually got sight of the Lion's elephant and camel, on one of which he was retreating: in a few moments he would have been taken or slain, but Colonel Pattle, second in command, rode up, and thinking perhaps the dispersion of the cavalry too great, stopped the pursuit. It was the third great error of the day. The two first were however happy errors, this was a misfortune—the Lion escaped to renew the war.

When the General returned with his cavalry from the pursuit, the infantry met him with loud cheers, thus proclaiming their admiration of his conduct in this battle, which lasted three hours and was very bloody. Hoche and three great chieftains, two of them Talpoorees, the other a Murree, fell on the field. The victors lost two hundred and seventy men and officers, of which number one hundred and forty-seven, more than a third, were of the 22nd regiment. The vanquished lost five thousand, and would have suffered still more but for the untimely halt of the cavalry on the right. Eight hundred bodies were lying in the nullahs and at Dubba; and all the villages and lanes beyond the latter place were so filled with dead and dying that the army encamped where it stood. All the fallen warriors were of mature age, grim-visaged men and of athletic forms: the carcass of a youth was not to be found.

Two thousand archers, coming to join the Lion, were too late for the fight and dispersed, and no judgment could be made of their value in battle. The weapon seems however to be in use. Shere Mohamed's own bows of painted horn were afterwards taken at Meerpoor, and a Belooch archer, of Ali Moorad's force, attended the General as an orderly during the battle, but he gave no specimen of his skill. Seventeen standards, and fifteen guns, eleven taken on the field and four next day, were the trophies of the fight, and, contrary to all expectation, there were thirteen wounded prisoners. Three only had been found alive at Meeanee, and this slight approach to mildness gave the General infinite satisfaction, for the ferocity on both sides had pained him deeply: the Beloochees would neither take nor give quarter, and the British troops would shew no compassion.

Here, as at Meeanee, surprising feats of personal prowess were displayed. Four or five fell beneath the iron hand of Fitzgerald, whose matchless strength renders the wildest tales of chivalry credible. And again the hardy vigour of McMurdo was displayed in three successive combats, hand to hand, with champions who had the advantage of shields to aid their swordsmanship. Two he slew in succession, but the third, with an upward stroke sheered him from the belly to the shoulder, and the well-driven blade would have gone to the viscera, if McMurdo's blow, falling first, had not cleft the man to the brows and thus abated his stroke, which nevertheless gave a terrible wound.

Three other officers, Wilkinson, Nixon, and Thompson also displayed surprising personal prowess; but the most remarkable exploit of the fight was performed by a sepoy, who was seen by the cavalry fighting in the nullah alone against five swordsmen, and slew them all!

Near the village, a chief retiring with that deliberate rolling stride and fierce look, which all these intrepid fatalists displayed in both battles, passed near the General, who covered him with a pistol, but then, remembering Meeanee, where in the midst of their warriors no hand had been raised against him, he held his hand. A fruitless generosity, for a sepoy of the 21st instantly killed him with the terrible cry of blood! blood! Innes! Innes!

This battle, fought thirty-five days after Meeanee, and within a few miles of that field, bears three names, Dubba, Naraja, and Hydrabad. The first from the village, the second from the plain, the third from the city near which it was fought. The last is the one inscribed on the colours and medals of the soldiers by whom it was won.

Prompt as the English General was for the battle, he was still more to render it a decisive one.

Having gathered his wounded and arranged for their transmission to Hydrabad, he wrote his despatch, reorganized his army, and having ascertained that the enemy's retreat was towards Meerpoor, in eight hours he was again on the march, resolute to take all that Fortune would give. The desert was before him, the Lion's force was still four to one, and it had two fortified towns, Meerpoor and Omercote on which to rally. The mercury stood at 110° on the day of the battle, and the heat was hourly augmenting; the troops had marched twelve miles to find the enemy, had fought for four hours and only rested eight, if that can be called rest when they had to gather the wounded, to receive fresh ammunition, and to cook within the time. But all this was disregarded by their General when he found himself greeted with cheers wherever he moved, and remembered Cæsar's saying that " nothing was done while aught remained to do." Nor were his hopes baffled by his men's weakness, for notwithstanding their fatigue and the withering heat they advanced twenty miles without a halt.

During this march they passed two strongly intrenched positions previously prepared by the Lion, but his warriors were too dispersed to rally on them in time. This was the first reward of energy, and next day the Poona horse were at the gates of Meerpoor, forty miles from the field of battle! Thus pressed, the Lion abandoned his capital, and carrying with him his treasure and his family, fled to Omercote. The gates of Meerpoor were immediately opened by the people, for being all Hindoos and Scindians they welcomed the victors as deliverers. It was well fortified, and stored, and had it been defended could scarcely have been besieged, for the hot season was coming on apace, and the Indus on the rise for inundation. An escalade would have been a desperate matter against Beloochees, and there were no ladders; the chance of blowing in the gates was small; and failure must have been ruinous for so weak an army. The Lion would then have quickly gathered a new force, all the hill tribes, and those of the plain on the right bank of the Indus, would have taken arms, and they could still produce sixty thousand fighting men. In the Delta also, the peculiar Ameeree of Shere Mohamed, swampy, unhealthy, intricate, and having many forts, a partisan warfare had already commenced; and it would, if a check had been given to the British, have gained such a head, that more than one campaign and twice five thousand men would have been required to put it down. But Hoehe was dead, and the Lion, though a stout warrior, was not equal to the crisis.

Abashed by the rapidity and vigour of his opponent, Shere Mohamed fled with diminishing forces in all haste; but swift as his flight was, his pursuers were not far behind. Even while taking possession of Meerpoor, the Scinde horsemen and the camel battery of Captain Whitlie were laid on his traces, and were supported with the 25th sepoy infantry under Major Woodburn. The General remained at Meerpoor with the rest of the forces, not from fatigue of body, though he had endured much, but from that cautious skill which characterized all his operations. For the line of march upon Omercote furnished little water, and he pushed on his troops at first only by small bodies and in succession, rather that he might not affront Fortune than with strong hope of gaining the place, which he knew to be well fortified and well stored.

Meanwhile having to fear the inundation of the Indus in his rear, he kept his main body in a central position, ready to regain Hydrabad with the artillery if the waters continued to rise; and to reinforce his vanguard at Omercote if the Indus kept down.

But to understand the nicety of his operations, it must be remembered that nearly the whole of Scinde is a dead flat, and all the cultivated districts near the Indus and its branches present a network of nullahs, artificial or natural. These water-courses are from six inches to sixty feet deep, broad in proportion, and when the Indus overflows become streams, rivulets, and rivers, most of them impassable for guns and cavalry, and many impassable for infantry without bridges. On the other side Omercote had eleven guns mounted, and its own garrison besides the men accompanying the Lion: wherefore Sir C. Napier trusted more to the moral effect of victory and rapidity than to force, and did not choose to risk the loss of that power by sustaining a check in person. Acting therefore by his lieutenants, he wrote thus to the Lion four days after the fight: " Ameer, I offer to you the same terms as before the battle; the same terms as those given to the other Ameers; what those terms will be I cannot tell you, because I have not yet received the orders of the Governor-General, but I am sure he will treat them generously. However, I, being his servant, cannot tell what the orders of my master may be. I promise to you your life, and that your family of women shall be respected as those of the other Ameers have been. I advise you to surrender. There is no dishonour in being defeated in battle. To try and defend Omercote is foolishness. I can batter it down in a day, and destroy all within it."

This letter sent by a camel rider, he expected some benefit from; but he was not so elated as to risk the danger of the inundation in his rear for the uncertain chance of getting the town; wherefore, though he menaced it with his irregular cavalry and camel battery, the portion of his army most capable of moving in the desert, he supported them very cautiously with his infantry and the rest of his artillery, and his troops placed in succession at different posts, were equally ready to close up and assault Omercote, or fall back to escape the inundation.

Reports soon arrived from both sides. " The river was rising before its time, and with unusual rapidity." " Omercote would not open its gates." Then orders were issued for a retreat. Nevertheless all hope of winning the city of the desert was not resigned. Lord Ellenborough, as noticed, had two months before extended his command to the troops of the Bombay Presidency quartered in Cutch. Now exercising that authority, the chief officer at Deesa was ordered to move from the east upon Omercote, and to aid that movement a new combination was to be arranged at Hydrabad, but unexpected events intervened. The order to retreat reached Whitlie when twenty miles from Omercote, and at the same moment that officer heard that the Ameer had quitted the place: hence he resolved to await further instructions, and found in Lieutenant Brown a young man ready to go for them.

He had before distinguished himself, and now rode the forty miles to Meerpoor without a stop, borrowed one of the General's horses, and back with the same speed, bearing orders to attack Omercote! Eighty miles he rode under a sun whose beams fell like flakes of fire, for the mercury stood above 130°! Passing the supporting infantry in returning he pushed them forward, and on the 4th of April Omercote opened its gates, the garrison retiring to a small interior fort. Major Woodburn soon got up with the 25th sepoys by forced marches under great difficulties, and then the citadel surrendered.

Omercote was thus reduced ten days after the battle, though a hundred miles distant and in the heart of the waste! This was the third advantage forced from Fortune, and it was a great one—the desert was no longer a refuge for the Lion, who fled with a few followers northward. " There" said his conqueror, " he may wander for a time; he may even collect another force; but he cannot base a warfare on sand, he must come sooner or later to the cultivated districts, where he will be met by the British." The event justified the prediction.

These operations could not have been successfully conducted without astonishing exertions and resolution, illustrating the character of the troops. On one of the long marches, which were almost continual, the 25th sepoys, nearly maddened by thirst and heat, saw one of their water-carriers approaching; they rushed towards him, tearing away his load, with loud cries of Water! water! At that moment, some half-dozen exhausted soldiers of the 22nd came up and asked for some; at once the generous Indians forgot their own sufferings, and gave the fainting Europeans to drink. Then they all moved on, the sepoys carrying the 22nd men's muskets for them, patting them on the shoulders and encouraging them to hold out: they did so for a short time, but soon fell, and it was found that those noble fellows were all wounded, some deeply! Thinking there was to be another fight, they had concealed their hurts and forced nature to sustain the loss of blood, the pain of wounds, the burning sun, the long marches, and the sandy desert, that their last moments might be given to their country on another field of battle! Their names have been recorded by their grateful General; but what will that avail them, when that General himself has been reviled and calumniated for leading them to battle at all, and Lord Ellenborough driven from power for honouring and protecting such soldiers!

It was a grand and touching spectacle to see those poor men displaying such heroism, while their young officers, full of fire and intelligence, gathered about their veteran leader, to offer that hardihood which no fatigue could break down, that resolution which no danger could appal, that nervous

R

strength and courage in battle before which no enemy could stand—yet acknowledging that none amongst them endured more labour of body and mind than he, their aged chief. His victories were indeed not lightly gained, nor was his the generalship that required hundreds of camels from the public service to carry his personal luxuries; he did not direct the marches from a palanquin, appearing only when the battle was commenced. Five camels, purchased at his own cost, carried all the baggage and records of his head-quarters; and all day the soldiers saw him on horseback engaged with field objects, while his staff knew that far in the night he was engaged in the administrative duties. Seldom did he sleep more than five hours. But none could know the extent of deep and painful meditation, which amidst all this activity and labour enabled him to judge clearly of affairs, and organize with so much simplicity the means of winning those glorious battles and conquering so great a kingdom.

When Woodburn's success was known, orders were sent by camel riders to stop the march of the troops from Cutch, a small garrison was placed in Omercote, the army was again concentrated at Meerpoor, and the tide of good fortune continued to rise. From information received from the natives, it had been calculated that the inundation would permit operations in the desert until the 15th of April; and on that chance the troops had pushed so boldly against Omercote. The sudden, unexpected, rapid rise in the river, suspended, as before noticed, the attack on that fortress, and induced the order for retreat; it was then even feared the guns of the army must be left in Meerpoor until means could be prepared to bridge the nullahs. But when Lieutenant Brown arrived the river had begun to fall as rapidly as it had before swelled, and such false indications of the periodical overflows are not uncommon: Hydrabad was, therefore, easily regained, and on the 8th the General was in the palace of the Ameers, master of Scinde, having in sixteen days, with five thousand men, defeated more than twenty-six thousand in battle, captured two great fortresses, and marched two hundred miles under a Scindian sun!

CHAPTER VII.

LORD ELLENBOROUGH now appointed Sir C. Napier Governor of Scinde, and independent of the Presidencies; enjoining only the abolition of slavery, yet giving a wide discretion as to the time and mode. He also conferred honours and rewards upon the troops, thanking them with expressions of deep feeling, evincing his grateful admiration of their heroic services. " The army of Scinde" he said, " has twice beaten the bravest enemy in Asia, under circumstances which would equally have obtained for it the victory over the best troops in Europe.

" The Governor-General regards with delight the new proofs which the army has given of its pre-eminent qualities in the field, and of its desire to mitigate the necessary calamities of war by mercy to the vanquished.

" The ordinary expression of thanks would ill convey the extent of the debt of gratitude which the Governor-General feels to be due to Sir C. Napier, on the part of the Government, the army, and the people of Hindostan.

" To have punished the treachery of protected Princes; to have liberated a nation from its oppressors; to have added a province, fertile as Egypt to the British empire; and to have effected these great objects by actions in war unsurpassed in brilliancy, whereof a grateful army assigns the success to the ability and valour of its general; these are not ordinary achievements, nor can the ordinary language of praise convey their reward."

Thus speaking to, and of, brave men in humble life, Lord Ellenborough shewed that he knows the heart of a soldier, and how it beats: but the appointment fell like a wet blanket on the sordid hopes of the Bombay authorities and civil servants, who looked to Scinde as a fine field for the accustomed rapine of the Company's Government.

Their anger broke forth in abuse of Lord Ellenborough and Sir C. Napier, and by their newspaper organs they endeavoured to destroy the conquest which they were not allowed to profit from. Henceforth Sir C. Napier was, both in words and deeds, treated as a public enemy. Outram's journey to England and his slanders against his General there, was a part of these factious proceedings, which were instantly adopted and encouraged by the Directors in Leadenhall-street.

The captive Ameers, eleven in number, including three of their sons, were transferred to Bombay; the murderer Shahdad being separately and strictly confined, a slight punishment for the death of Captain Innes. And now the women proved how inhuman and brutal the Ameers were in their domestic habits. Not one female in the zenanas would accompany them into captivity, though it was not devoid of luxury and state: abhorring their former masters they desired to rejoin their families. The lash of Nusseer's brass-wire whip, said to be mild compared with the punishments of the other Ameers, was not forgotten, and with one accord the women demanded leave to return to their homes. It is impossible to conceive a more entire and destructive condemnation of those " fallen Princes" and their " patriarchal rule," for the condition of Scindian women in their own families is never agreeable or safe, and the soldier was then abroad.

By the departure of these vile tyrants, for whose fall no Beloochees expressed sorrow, while all the Scindians and Hindoos openly rejoiced, Sir C. Napier was left free to act as he thought fitting, in civil as well as military matters. With respect to the war, the principal subject of his anxiety was the Lion's operations. Emaum Ghur, having been with a far-reaching policy destroyed, he had no rallying point in the waste nearer than Shah Ghur on the frontier of Jessulmere, where the son of Roostum still maintained a small force, and from thence menaced Ali Moorad. But the last had an army, and British troops were, on the side of Roree, ready to support him and intercept the Lion if he fled to that quarter. Meanwhile several great chiefs proffered submission. They were not treated alike.

Wullah Chandia, whose tribe was the most powerful but one on the right bank of the Indus, proffered his salaam the day Omercote surrendered. He had led ten thousand warriors from the hills, and was close in rear of the British at Meeanee, though too late for that battle. His tribe was less lawless than the Booghtees, and Dhoomkees and Jakranees, who were his neighbours, and with whom he was often at feud, and the General, anxious to conciliate him, thus accepted his submission. "I honour you for your obedience to the Ameers of Hydrabad, but God has decreed that they are to rule Scinde no more. The British Government is now master; serve it faithfully as you have done the Ameers, and honour and respect will be shewn to you. But mind what I say, keep your own side of the river. Woe to the mountain tribes that cross the Indus."

Relying on this message Wullah met Ali Moorad in conference, but that Ameer, with barbarian habits, seized and sent him to Hydrabad. The General instantly rebuked Moorad severely, set the Chandian free, restored his arms, and made him a present. Touched by this, Wullah swore that he would always be true, and he was so to his death, without fault or failure.

Meer Mohamed, one of the Talpoor Sirdars, who had plundered Jerruck before the battle of Hydrabad, also demanded terms: the reply run thus:—

"Give back to Agha Khan the plunder you took from Jerruck, and make your salaam. I will pardon you then and be your friend, and your jagheers shall be respected."

To the Jam of the Jokeas, whose conduct had been disloyal and insolent, he wrote menacingly. That powerful chief, scarcely acknowledging the supremacy of the Ameers though their feudatory, was eighty years of age, yet of strong body and vigorous mind, had great reputation as a predatory leader, and was a very superb robber! His country, partly on the plains westward of the Delta, partly in the lower ridges of the Hala mountains was very strong; and during the war he had menaced Kurrachee, though the entrenched camp there was occupied by two thousand fighting men with a fine field battery, one of the regiments being the

British 28th! From this it may be known, that if Sir C.
Napier brought his army triumphantly through all dangers,
it was by the exercise of unusual sagacity and vigour, amidst
embarrassments which would have overwhelmed an inferior
man. The Jam had only seven hundred warriors, yet Colonel
Boileau suffered him to invest his camp, until the battle of
Meeanee taught the barbarian who was master. Then, half
submissive, he merely asked protection for some ladies of his
family who had fallen into the victor's power : and he continued to menace Colonel Boileau until the battle of Hydrabad. Incensed at this, and that he should have been allowed
to insult a British force greater than that which strewed the
plains of Meeanee with carcasses, the General ordered Boileau
to make a sally, whereupon the Jam fled, and Sir C. Napier
sent him the following missive :—

"You have received the money of the British for taking
charge of the däk; you have betrayed your trust, and
stopped the däks; and you have also attacked the troops.
All this I forgive, because the Ameers were here, and were
your old masters. But the Ameers are now gone from
Scinde for ever. They defied the British power, and have
paid the penalty for so doing. I, being Governor of Scinde,
am now your immediate master. If you make your salaam
and promise fidelity, I will restore your lands and former
privileges, and the superintendence of the däks. If you refuse, I will wait till the hot weather is gone past, and then I
will carry fire and sword into your territories, and drive you
and all belonging to you into the mountains; and if I catch
you I will hang you as a rebel. You have now your choice.
Choose!"

The Jam yielded, but his barbarian pride would not bend :
entering Boileau's camp at the head of his armed followers,
he pushed even into his room with six of his grim attendants, displaying the insolent airs of a conqueror rather than
the submissive demeanour of a man obnoxious to the anger
of a victorious General. He soon discovered his error, when
a single officer delivered the following message from that
General!

"Come here instantly. Come alone and make submission, or I will, in a week, tear you from the midst of your tribe and hang you." To back this menace, a select body of cavalry and guns were ready to march; but the Jam obeyed, and with such dread, as to entreat the British agent at Kurrachee, whom he had until then oppressed by insolence, to accompany him as an intercessor. He was pardoned, and the lesson induced several chieftains, fugitives or still in arms, to offer submission; they were treated so frankly that the conqueror's clemency and liberality spread widely, that even Meer Mohamed Khan of Kyrpoor, and another Mohamed, a great Talpoor Sirdar, desired to know what terms they might expect.

To the former, as a dethroned Prince, the General, not being authorized to propose any but unconditional surrender, replied thus :—

" Ameer, I advise you to go to Ali Moorad, and remain with him till the pleasure of the Governor-General be known. I recommend to you to join the other Ameers at Bombay; but till I have the authority of the Governor-General I can promise nothing but personal security."

To the Talpoor Sirdar, who was a brave man, he wrote as follows :—

" I never quarrel with a good soldier. Come and make your salaam, serve the British Government and be faithful; your jagheer shall be safe."

The Sirdar, still feeling doubt, only sent his sword in token of fealty, whereupon, allowance being made for his fears, he was thus reassured.

" Come and make your salaam and you shall receive from the English Government all you held under the Ameers; and I will place the sword which you have sent me again in your hands, that you may fight as bravely for my nation as you did against us when you served the Ameers."

This brave man was conscious that resistance was vain, but being a Talpoor would not desert the Lion then: afterwards when that Prince was irretrievably ruined he submitted, and met with no worse treatment for the delay.

There was still another chieftain to be dealt with. Ahmed Khan, head of the Lugarees, whose dwellings were on the right of the Indus.   His men fought well and suffered severely; but at their head Ahmed had attacked the Residency: he however only obeyed his sovereign's orders, had bravely exposed himself in battle, and was a gallant, generous barbarian, who did not fear to trust his conqueror.   The latter could not promise the Governor-General's pardon, but he would not hurt him, and answered thus:—

"I honour a brave soldier, but have no authority to forgive you.   You attacked the residence of the British Envoy, your Princes themselves accuse you.   The Governor-General is in wrath at this insult, and has ordered me to make the Ameer Shahdad and yourself prisoners.   I must, therefore, appeal to the Governor-General, and I will plead your cause with him.   I hope to gain your pardon; but I will not pledge myself to anything which I may not be able to perform.   If you come and reside here, I will receive you until his Lordship's pleasure be known; and if he refuses pardon I will give you forty-eight hours to depart unmolested."

This pardon he finally obtained.

Notwithstanding the second battle, the country, especially in the Delta, continued to be troubled by the plundering bands calling themselves the Lion's soldiers.   The followers of the British army also, above fifteen thousand, and all armed, began to rob the Scindees, but were with a rough hand checked by the General, who at once disarmed them. To quell the Beloochee robbers was more difficult: the proper time for dealing with them by the troops had not arrived; but Sir C. Napier soon organized a native police force, and by great activity and vigilance gave protection to the traders and cultivators.   This, and his liberal treatment of the feudatory chiefs and sirdars, produced a surprising quietude, and the character of the new Government was indicated by unmistakable gestures.   Rapid to strike, prompt to pardon, clear and simple in detail, its aim was to produce tranquillity and give the labouring masses security.

Make no avoidable changes, was Sir C. Napier's instruction to the officers entrusted with the subordinate government of the districts into which he divided Scinde— make no avoidable changes in the ancient customs and laws of the land. The conquest of a country is sufficient convulsion for the people, without adding to their disturbances by abrupt innovations in their habits and the usual routine of their social life. Confine your exertions to the correcting of those numerous evils which the late tyrannical government of the Belooch conquerors inflicted on this unhappy land. It will depend upon the Government of Scinde, to make the people hail the coming of the British as a memorable redemption from slavery and oppression, or look upon it with apathy as a mere change of cruel masters.

It was however impossible that so large a territory, governed as Scinde had been by a federation of tyrants, and a dominant race of feudatory chiefs and followers, warriors by profession and used to commotions which it was for their interest to excite — connected also with kindred hill and desert tribes, poor, rapacious, and robbers by national custom, who looked down on the cultivated plains with longing eyes, and had sure retreats, as they thought, in their rocky fastnesses on one side, and their burning arid sands on the other—it was impossible for such a population, to sink at once into quiescence under the rule of a conqueror, whose strength had been tried in only two battles, and then only by a portion of those ferocious warriors. New commotions were naturally expected, and the hope that they would prove fatal to British ascendancy in Scinde filled the hearts of Lord Ellenborough's enemies at Bombay, and in other parts of India, with a treasonable delight which they did not conceal.

The newspaper editors loudly proclaimed the wishes of this infamous faction. The Beloochees were regularly informed by articles, translated and read by the chiefs, which were the strong and weak points of the occupation, of the number of sick, and of those who could carry arms; of the places along the river where the steamers could be assailed with most effect, and precise information was given how to effect their destruction with most certainty. One extract from the *Bombay Times*, edited by Dr. Buist, will illustrate their system.

" The Indus is but a pitiful protection against an enemy

who sweeps over fifty miles at a stretch, who could leave his mountain home in the afternoon, approach the river in the dark, and before morning have a trench and embankment constructed sufficient to protect some scores of matchlock men. A single volley from a position which no musketry or ordnance could touch, might clear the deck of a steamer, and leave the vessel aground, and at the mercy of the enemy before danger was suspected. Should the crew be too strong, or not have been sufficiently reduced by the first fire to prevent their landing to attack their opponents, the fleet-footed Beloochees would have mounted their fleeter steeds and left pursuers far behind before our shot could reach them."

They were also encouraged to profit from these suggestions by assurances of the deep interest in their cause felt by persons of power and influence at Bombay. When the General stopped plundering by his provost-marshals' punishment, the sepoys were invited to rise in mutiny and " put a stop by force to the fellow's breaches of law!" And when an unusual sickness, afflicting the natives as well as the soldiers, broke out, the latter were told that the General was the cause of their sufferings. The information thus given to the enemy was often false, and generally exaggerated, because it was an object with the faction to disgust the people of England with the conquest; and the editors were also so habitually intent on falsehood that truth was often rejected even where it might have best served their villainy. This was notably the case with Dr. Buist, who, surpassing all others in pandering for the faction he served, endeavoured to account for the refusal of the Ameers' women to follow them into captivity, by announcing that the ladies were carried off by the British officers as paramours; an inexpiable offence, which he called on all the Mussulmans of India to avenge! the Indian population of that sect being at the time very inimical to the British power. It was in the following terms this despicable tool assailed the honour of British officers.

" They who three months since were sharers of a palace and in the enjoyment of the honours of royalty, are now the

degraded lemans of the Feringhi! So it is; the harem has
been defiled; the last drop of bitterness has been mingled
with the cup of misery we have given the Ameers to drink:
the heaviest of the insults Mahomedans can endure has
been heaped upon their grey discrowned heads. Let it not
be supposed we speak of this in the language of prudish
sentimentalism. The officers who have dishonoured the
zenana of kings have committed great wrong; but for that,
as for the other evil deeds attending upon so unjust and
cruel a conquest, the Government which ordained it is responsible. We know now, to our shame and sorrow, the
evils which flowed from frailties such as this permitted in
Cabool; and at Hydrabad we may yet discover the heinousness of our sins in the magnitude of our punishment. If
one thing more than all the other wrongs we have inflicted
on them, could awaken in the bosom of each Beloochee
chief the unquenchable thirst of never-dying vengeance, it
must be to see the sanctities of domestic life invaded and
violated as they have been—to see the daughters of nobles,
and wives of kings, living while youth and beauty lasts, as the
concubines of the infidel, thrown aside when those attractions
have departed to perish in their degradation and shame.
This is the first of the black fruits of invasion for which
Britons must blush. We have avoided explicitness on such
a subject; our readers will be at no loss to discover our
meaning:—The most attractive of the ladies of the zenana
now share the tents of British officers! A series of acts of
injustice first introduced to the Scindians the character of
the British Government: what has just been related will
afford them an insight into the virtues and blessings they
may look for from the advance of civilization; the benefits
and honours destined them by the most refined people of the
world. This contrasts well with the reception English ladies
experienced at Affghan hands."

To this accusation, an instant and indignant denial was
published, signed by the General and all the European officers at Hydrabad: not one lady had ever even been seen by
a British officer! When this slanderous falsehood was exposed, Buist contended that the Ameers' women should be

collected by force and shipped to join the Ameers. "They were prisoners," he said, "as well as their lords : they were slaves, and should be made to follow their lawful masters, who had the right, if they had the will, to cut their throats or poison them!"

These calumnies were a part of the intrigues set on foot in revenge. The greatest misfortunes were predicted, and Ali Moorad, because he had not joined the other Ameers to destroy the British, was denounced as a traitor whose atrocities had been rewarded by Sir C. Napier with honours and grants of territory! Yet no territory, no money had he received, and the only honour was an elephant given at his request on condition that he was to pay for it if the Governor-General disapproved of the proceeding. It was prognosticated also that Ali would betray the British as he had betrayed his own family, and that he would join the Lion, whose power was exaggerated and dwelt upon with malignant anticipations of his final success.

" He was no fugitive, he was undismayed, he laughed at the impotent boasting English General; he was a great commander, a heroic Prince; he was gathering new forces in the desert, the advantage of which he well understood. His kindred were joining him from all quarters with the warriors of the hills, in fine all the Beloochees were resolved to support him ; he had crossed the Indus, he was at the head of forty thousand men ; the standard of Islam had been raised, the war had taken a religious turn, the feeling would spread throughout Beloochistan and Affghanistan and the Punjaub ; he was advancing with an irresistible army, was within a few miles of the British, who, few in numbers, sinking from disease, and commanded by an incapable ignorant old man, would inevitably be overwhelmed, and the tragedy of Cabool re-enacted."

Sir C. Napier after the last battle had said, there was reason to believe another shot would not be fired in Scinde— meaning that the Ameers yet at large, would not again dispute the conquest at the head of an army in the field. This expression the faction affected to take in its literal sense, and contrasted it in ridicule with the mighty power and menacing position falsely assigned to the Lion. It was, nevertheless, the result of a sagacious consideration of his enemy's character, the heterogeneous population and the peculiar topography of Scinde. He knew the Lion was the only Sovereign Ameer, still at large, having treasure and influence, he knew the bravest chiefs and most daring swordsmen had fallen, and the spirit of the others cowed. He expected Meerpoor and Omercote to fall, as they did, calculated on the moral effect, and had with a long foresight destroyed Emaum Ghur, leaving the Lion no refuge in the desert. The fugitive Ameer could not collect a formidable army in the waste, though he might rally a few thousand men and become troublesome. Meanwhile the disposition of the Scindees and Hindoos was unmistakable. They clung to the conquerors as children would to a protector, and the Beloochees would not serve the Lion without pay or plunder: the first he could not long furnish, and the second must be got from the Scindees and Hindoos, who would thus be knit more strongly to the British. It was clear therefore that no army able to deliver a great battle could be raised on the left bank of the Indus, north of Hydrabad, and if the Lion could be debarred passing to the right bank the conquest would be established.

But though no formidable force was to be expected on the left of the Indus, partisan warfare was to be apprehended, especially in the Delta, a peculiarly unhealthy intricate district, intersected with nullahs and tormented with jungle and marshes. Already bands had there gathered and it was to be feared that the Lion would throw himself into that quarter, which was his patrimony. There he could prolong the warfor another year, as the Delta malaria could not be braved in the hot season. Sir C. Napier however, thought himself skillful enough to baffle the Lion's attempts to get there; and the Ameer's warfare could not hinder the establishment of a solid government which would satisfy the Scindees and Hindoos without exasperating the Beloochees.

With great vigilance therefore he watched every movement of the Lion in his desert lair, silently and surely surrounding him and predicting with surprising accuracy the spot where he would be taken in the toils which were thus spread.

Chamberlayne's horse, moving from Roree, supported Ali Moorad, who had orders to intercept Shere Mohamed if he attempted to gain the Seik country, or to join Roostum's son at Shah Ghur. Ali dared not be unfaithful; his instructions were precise, Chamberlayne watched him, and the success of the Lion and Roostum's son would be his ruin: but there was no reason to doubt him; the alliance had been a rock of safety: his house was standing when those of the other Ameers were in ruins. .

The Lion's force augmented, not, as the Bombay faction asserted to forty thousand, but to eight thousand, with four guns, and the plunderers in the Delta began to unite in larger masses, and occupied several forts. Some tribes from the south also collected eastward of the Delta, calling themselves the Ameer's troops, and they and the Beloochees were continually exhorted to vigorous warfare by the treasonable Bombay faction speaking through the *Bombay Times*. Debarred of the expected plunder of Scinde as civil administrators, they thought the destruction of the army, which they laboured assiduously and insidiously to effect, would be a poor atonement for the offence; and when the General's courage and genius left them no hope of such a catastrophe they railed thus. " *Alas ! that this man bears the name of Englishman. Alas ! that he is born in the glorious age of Wellington, which he disgraces.*"

To aid Chamberlayne, Fitzgerald, who knew the desert, was sent to the north, and Colonel Roberts was ordered to come down the right bank of the Indus to Sehwan with fifteen hundred men and a battery. His instructions were to seize all boats as he descended, and thus prevent the Lion crossing to the right bank, and the western tribes passing to the left· bank. These movements were combined with others in the south and east, on a plan so vast, yet so profoundly reasoned and vigorously executed as to vie with any of the previous exploits of the war.

Was not that an intrepid general, and a leader of good troops, who could resolve to brave the deadly sun of Scinde in

its utmost force; and when the thermometer stood above 130°
in artificially-cooled tents, to make marches of one hundred
to two hundred and fifty miles—and this to circumvent a
native army wandering without baggage in an unknown
country covered with jungles, and intersected by nullahs
filled at that time with water? Less brilliant in its results,
less obvious in its difficulties and dangers, less imposing
for public admiration than the battles of Meeanee and
Hydrabad, or the march into the desert, it was more complicate in arrangement, and not less heroic in execution, or
decisive in effect. Nor was it a reckless enterprise, undertaken in the pride of command; it could not be rejected
without risking the conquest altogether.

The General was indeed between two millstones: great
loss from heat during the operations, greater loss from sickness afterwards, were inevitable. But if the Lion could throw
himself into the Delta, an insurrectional warfare, longer
operations in the heat, and greater loss of men, or inactivity
until the cool season came round were as inevitable. The
whole country would thus have been delivered to oppression:
the labourer would not dare to till the ground while the
Beloochee was abroad in arms; famine would have followed,
and the whole scheme of government designed to attach the
people would have been delayed. Commotion, horrors and
misery, would have ensued: the hill tribes, those of the plains
westward of the Indus, and those of the desert eastward
would have all taken the field, ravaging and slaying! None
but a man of overbearing resolution and uncommon resources
could win his way through such difficulties.

Shere Mohamed, now called by the natives the " *Jungle
Wallah*," or keeper of the jungle, remained in the wilderness
until the last days of April: then he removed to Khoonhera,
fifty miles north of Meerpoor, and sixty from Hydrabad. He
was driven there to seek water, which became each day
scarcer in the desert as the hot season advanced: he however
came with eight thousand men and four guns, and had other
objects in view. His family were on the right bank of the
Indus, in the Lukkee hills, inciting the tribes there to take
arms, and he desired to be near the river when they should

be ready to cross over. His brother, Shah Mohamed, had also come down, and encamped not far from the right bank with two thousand men and some guns; but with views for his own aggrandizement rather than the relief of the Ameer, who he had before offered to assassinate.

In the north, Roostum's son, had advanced from Shah Ghur, and some slight actions happened between him and Ali Moorad.

In the south, the robbers of the Delta were very mischievous; and eastward of them, five thousand fighting men had taken post in the thick jungle on the Poorana river, forty miles below Meerpoor and Hydrabad, intercepting the communications between those places and Wanga Bazaar, on the road to Cutch.

These simultaneous movements, and the general state of affairs, becoming more critical every day, gave Sir C. Napier great anxiety, but his own plan of counteraction also made progress. Colonel Roberts was in full march to Sehwan; Chamberlayne and Ali Moorad were vigilant in the north. Jacob was at Meerpoor, where the General, under divers pretexts, and as if he merely designed to complete his posts of communication with Omercote, and hasten the repairs and additions to the works of that fortress and Meerpoor, formed a column, consisting of the Scinde horse four hundred infantry and two guns. Ali-ka-Tanda, the connecting fort between Hydrabad and Meerpoor was repaired, and the Lion was thus debarred a passage southward, and his communications with the Delta and the tribe on the Poorana intercepted. Troops were also drawn from Deesa across the desert to watch the Ameer eastward, while the General, having a select body organized for rapid movement, was ready to pounce in person upon him if he should seek to force a way to the south.

Captain Jacob, contrary to orders, now made a movement against the Poorana tribe, but had not firmness to attack, and retired again, thus augmenting the difficulties. At the same time the Lion was reported as about to move to Sukkurunda on the Indus, to cover the passage of the Lukkees, who were said to have collected boats to cross over to him; moreover the Rins, the most powerful tribe of Scinde were in arms and had promised him twenty thousand warriors. These wide combinations menaced evil, and the General immediately sent steamers up the river with orders to destroy the Lukkee boats, and run down without mercy every vessel carrying armed men: a stern order, purposely made public to alarm the tribes on the right bank and abate their desire to aid the Lion. The effect was to discourage the Ameer, and he tried negotiation, demanding terms; but his adversary, resolved to preserve his moral ascendancy replied by the following austere communication.

"In ten days I shall attack you with a larger army than I had on the 24th of March. Troops will come upon you in all directions. I do not wish to kill either you or your people, and I advise you to submit in time to the will of the Governor-General. If not, take your fate. Your blood will be on your own head."

This was on the 2nd of May, but the Ameer, with arrogance and false pretensions, continued to negotiate until the following missive, dated the 6th of May, put an end to his hopes, leaving him only the choice of absolute submission or victory.

"You never disbanded your army, as I desired you to do.

"You sent an insolent letter to me by vakeels; you offered, if I would capitulate, to let me quit the country. I gave your vakeels the only reply such a letter deserved, namely, that I would answer you with my cannon. Soon after that your brother sent to me a letter, offering to assassinate you: I sent the letter to you. In my letter, I told you that you were *a brave enemy*, and I sent you the proposition of your brother, to put you on your guard. I did not say you were *not an enemy*. If your Highness cannot read, you should get trusty people to read for you. Your Highness has broken treaties, you have made war without provocation, and before a fortnight passes you shall be punished as you deserve. I will hunt you into the desert, and into the mountains; if you wish to save yourself, you must surrender in five days."

s

This letter was decisive, and both Commanders prepared for battle. They were not of equal skill. The Lion, though prompt and hardy was not vigilant or long-sighted: the English General was both, and of equal hardihood: his plans were wider, and always he knew how to seize accidental advantages. Thus he had instantaneously turned Roostum's flight from Dejee, and his resignation of the Turban, to profit; thus he marched on Emaum Ghur, forcing Ali Moorad to go with him before he could find an excuse for refusing, and so placed the younger Ameers in rebellion against the Rais. The same promptness brought him to Meeanee before the enemy could collect all his forces, and in that battle taught him how to paralyze the action of six thousand men with a single company. Again, at Dubba, the reading Lord Ellenborough's despatch aloud previous to engaging, and his rapidity after the victory, which gave him Meerpoor and Omercote, were all proofs of his aptitude for war.

To these instances he now added another. Between the four points of Sukkurunda, Khoonhera, Hydrabad, and Meerpoor, the Lion was ensconced amidst nullahs, jungles and ravines, known to him, unknown to Sir C. Napier; but with great exertions the latter got some knowledge of it, and instantly formed a new scheme more concise than his great combination, yet without disarranging it. He put a detachment on board the steamers to land at Sehwan before Roberts could reach that place from Sukkur, and meanwhile prepared to close on Sukkurunda from Meerpoor and Hydrabad, thus encompassing the Lion and driving him into the Indus. To slip between these three columns he must go into the desert: then, by occupying Khoonhera, the only watering place on its edge, he could be forced to return to the Indus, or fly northward to Shah Ghur, where he would be met by the united forces of Ali Moorad, Chamberlayne, and Fitzgerald.

This scheme did not take effect. The Ameer had delayed his march while negotiating, and the caprices of the Indus unexpectedly delayed the British operations. It had twice irregularly overflowed in April, and twice as irregularly subsided. It was now rising a third time with all indication of truth, but the uncertainty chained the army, for the troops might march, to find themselves suddenly cut off from their base by nullahs filled with water; or be prevented from advancing, by swamps through which camels could not pass. In fine no movements could be made until it was known how far the waters would spread, a knowledge denied by the unusual vacillation of the inundation.

While thus fretting on the curb of necessity, Sir C. Napier heard, that the Lion was actually in the cultivated districts, expecting soon to be at the head of thirty thousand men, and had proclaimed his resolution to fight and win, or die sword in hand. He was a brave man, and on a line of more than a hundred and fifty miles of river might draw aid in small bodies from the tribes, which could not be prevented by the steamers. The General's remarks on this new turn of the war were short.

" I doubt the Lion's determination to die on the field; but if he really collects twenty or thirty thousand men I shall be in no hurry to fight him. Let him bear the expense, I can laugh at his attacks from behind my entrenchments on the Indus : I can sally when he retreats : and if the present overflow is the true one, his followers will find it difficult, the waters being out, to disperse when beaten, and I shall make them deeply repent their temerity."

This uncertainty lasted until the 22nd of May, when the spies said, the Lion, unable to raise the Scindian Beloochees generally, was negotiating with the hill tribes of Beloochistan ; and the Lukkees, recovered from the fear of the steamers, had again collected boats where their rocks overhung the river, thus very exactly following the advice given to them by Buist in the *Bombay Times.* To stop them Lieut. Anderson was put, with one hundred sepoys, on board a steamer with orders to destroy their boats and drive themselves from the bank. On the 27th he reached the rocks, from whence a fire of matchlocks was opened and the Captain of the steamer, Miller wounded. He replied with his large guns, and some sepoys being landed drove the Lukkees away; the boats were then destroyed, and the armament steered for Sehwan to meet Roberts and aid his operations : thus the Lion was again deprived of his expected allies.

On the 29th Colonel Roberts reached Sehwan with fifteen hundred men. The communication between the Lion and his brother, and the intercourse with the western tribes, was thus entirely cut off, and the three points from whence the movements to encircle him were to be made attained.

Now let the difficulties overcome be considered. Sukkur was one hundred and sixty miles from Sehwan, Hydrabad was eighty miles from it, and Omercote was a hundred miles from Hydrabad; Shah Ghur was more than a hundred miles from Omercote, and Deesa was two hundred miles: yet all these places were embraced by this vast combination, which was conducted with such secrecy and exactness that the circle was completed around the Lion ere he knew it was being formed, and by marches made under a Scindian sun in the hottest season.! Nor was the secret gathering of the troops at the different points of departure, without disclosing the object, less worthy of notice: it was so managed as to baffle the Lion's spies, and render the mischievous loquacity of the Indian newspapers subservient to the design.

Colonel Roberts's orders were to cross to the left bank of the Indus in the night of the 9th of June, and march towards Khoonhera, upon which point also Jacob was to move from Meerpoor, and the General himself from Hydrabad. Meanwhile Ali Moorad came down towards Lower Scinde, having Chamberlayne's horse in the desert on his left. But on the evening of the 7th, Roberts heard that the Lion's brother, after a successful skirmish with one of Ali Moorad's Sirdars, in which he took some prisoners, had encamped at Peer-Arres, fourteen miles from Sehwan. This opportunity was instantly seized. Roberts marched in the night with four guns, five companies, and a troop of cavalry: when day broke he was three miles from the Ameer's camp, which was at the foot of the Lukkee hills in a large grove. He had taken the alarm, and was retreating, but the cavalry under Captain Walker charged his rear, and put ninety to the sword.

Meanwhile the infantry, reaching the camp, found Shah Mohamed in a close part of the grove with seventeen attendants. At first he was disposed to resist, but seeing the sepoys eager to kill him surrendered. All his cannon, and family collection of matchlocks swords and shields, were taken, but no treasure ; a fact proving his impotence to raise a serious warfare, for the Beloochees do not serve without pay. This enterprise had been undertaken chiefly on the information and advice of a Patan horseman, called Ayliff Khan, one of those eastern adventurers who serve any side for pay. Simple horsemen one day, generals the next, they will aim at a kingdom if occasion offers as readily as at a gratuity. Ayliff guided the column, and in the charge four Beloochees fell beneath his vigorous arm : he is now with his son in the mounted police of Scinde, both being alike distinguished for courage, comeliness, fidelity and skill in arms.

On the 9th Roberts crossed the Indus, on the 10th Jacob advanced from Meerpoor, and the General from Hydrabad, all pointing on Shah-i-Khauta, where the Lion was said to have gone from Khoonhera ; but that chief, taking alarm, retreated not to Khoonhera, but up the river leaning towards the desert. (Plan 3.)

On the 13th, the General, being at Ali-ka-Tanda, heard that Roberts was over the Indus and Jacob would be that day near Khoonhera. Ali Moorad also reported that the Lion, now seemingly aware of Roberts's approach, had suddenly returned again to Shah-i-Khauta, only sixteen miles from Ali-ka-Tanda. Thither Sir C. Napier made a night march with his cavalry and guns, directing some of the infantry to follow as fast as they could. His design was to keep the Lion in check until Jacob and Roberts could close on him, but early on the 14th it became known that the Ameer had again moved to the eastward of Shah-i-Khauta ; he thus indicated an intention to break through to the south, and the General also moved eastward upon Nusserpoor to intercept him. The rest of the infantry had orders to come up from Ali-ka-Tanda, on his right, and communicate with Jacob ; but he had no report of that officer's position, nor any intelligence from Roberts : it was however evident from the uneasy movements of the Lion that both were near.

These marches were generally made by night, the soldiers

keeping under canvass during the day with wet cloths on their heads, yet more Europeans died from heat than would have sufficed to win a battle, and the General's anxiety hourly increased; for the Belooch population was much excited and an insurrection had been prepared, the signal to be the presence of Shah Mohamed. The capture of that Ameer by Colonel Roberts was publicly announced, but the Beloochees were incredulous; wherefore his person being well known, he was exposed to public gaze in a balcony of the Tower of Hydrabad. This was a successful device, but to put down the Lion was the main object, and no obstacle, difficulty or danger could arrest the General. His fatigue of body and mind was indeed so great, that fearing he might drop, he wrote to Colonel Roberts thus— *"Whatever you may hear of insurrection, whatever may happen to me, let nothing divert you from crushing the Lion."*

He had quitted Hydrabad suffering from fever, and in the midst of his movements the däk, long retarded, reached him with the accumulated correspondence of four months from the Governments of Calcutta and Bombay, thus imposing the perusal of and replies to hundreds of letters after long marches when rest was most needful. Nature could not long sustain this pressure.

On the 14th, unable to obtain intelligence of Jacob or Roberts, he halted during the heat, very uneasy, because the Lion was evidently seeking to break the circle, and might succeed; for the columns were not in military communication—a failure, caused by the officer at Ali-ka-Tanda, who neglected his orders. While thus anxious the sound of Jacob's guns boomed in the east, but ceased so abruptly as to give rise to the painful suggestion that he had been suddenly overwhelmed, that the Ameer had broken the circle, had rendered abortive the great operations made with such labour and loss, and would raise the dreaded partisan warfare in the Delta.

While thus oppressed with care, fever, fatigue and want of sleep, Sir C. Napier stepped from his tent and instantly fell from a sun-stroke; around him at the same moment went down thirty-three European soldiers, and most of them died in a few minutes : all in three hours ! The General, caught up and bled instantly in both arms, survived, but the struggle for existence was hard and thus described by himself. " All was anxiety for me, when just as they bled me, a horseman came to say Jacob was victorious, and the Ameer's force dispersed. I think it saved me. I felt life come back."

The Lion had dallied in the cultivated districts until he found the columns were around him, and then desirous to repair his fault by courage had made a dash at Jacob as the weakest. But that officer, while conducting his column along the edge of the desert, had on the 13th, got information of the Lion's march up the river, and of his sudden return, the cause of which he rightly judged to be the approach of Roberts, and therefore pushed on to Shahdadpoor, an advantageous post for intercepting the Ameer. In the night a Bramin servant, deserting from the Lion, reported that he would fall on next morning with ten thousand men and four guns—and, as he said, when day broke the Ameer's army was descried advancing, yet slowly and with hesitation, whereupon Jacob, leaving a guard in his camp, marched out to meet him. With the Lion were eight great Sirdars, most of them Talpoorees, and amongst them a son of Roostum, and the brother-in-law of Nusseer. But he was not bravely supported by any chief save Mohamed Khan, the Sirdar who had before sent his sword to Sir C. Napier. The troops also were disaffected, the greatest part had deserted in the night, and only four thousand with three guns were in line. These he drew up behind a nullah, taking the left, and giving the right, composed of cavalry, to Mohamed Khan. So rough was the ground that battle could not be easily joined, and during a short cannonade that ensued, the Beloochee infantry dispersed before Jacob came personally into action. Their cavalry made a false charge in a cloud of dust, and when that cleared there was no enemy ! No effectual pursuit could be made, yet the rout was entire ; Jacob lost no men, very few Beloochees fell by the cannonade, and the Lion fled with only ten followers.

Sir C. Napier's operations were thus ended without loss

in action; but more than sixty officers and soldiers died from sun-strokes, and a greater number afterwards from sickness: peace was however attained. " *We have taught the Belooch, that neither his sun, nor his desert, nor his jungles, nor his nullahs can stop us—he will never face us more.*" Such was his summing up; and in truth those desperate fatalists, who had at Meeanee and Dubba dashed with sword and shield like demons on the serried bayonets and rolling fire, fighting as if life were to them a burthen, now suffered nature to prevail, and acknowledged the mastery of the British soldier. Their real feelings and particular behaviour in this action were made known afterwards by the Sirdar Mohamed, who commanded the Lion's right. Finding all lost he made salaam, and being well received, the following dialogue took place.

General.—Mohamed, how came it you made such a bad fight with Jacob? Twice you fought with me well, and I honoured you as stout soldiers; I hold you cheap now. You ought to have killed half of Jacob's men, and he had to fire only five or six cannon-shot at you: he had not a man wounded.

Mohamed (laughing).—Why, General, it is just because we did fight you twice, that we did not like the third time. We were afraid of you. But, to tell the truth, I know as little of the fight with Jacob as you do. I commanded the right, the Ameer commanded the left, he had the guns, and I nearly all the cavalry. It was hardly light when I heard the Lion's guns. I thought Jacob was upon him, as there was nothing that we could distinguish in my front. I therefore rode full gallop, expecting to charge Jacob's flank. You know our horrible dust, it was in vain to look for a man, I thought I was followed. I reached the Ameer, he was alone almost. On halting, the dust cleared off and behold! only twenty-five men were with me: I was lucky, had Jacob been there I should have been killed. But all had run under cover of the dust, and so the Lion and I run also, and that is all I know of the battle.

General.—Well, the Lion is a fine soldier; I honour him, and if I could take him, I would do all in my power to get the Governor-General to pardon him and give back his estates.

Mohamed Khan.—The Lion is a fool. After the battle of the 24th we all saw our people would never stand more, and none of us will ever try it again; you are hawks, and we are but little birds. I stood out as long as I could, but we see our folly now, and are your slaves for ever.

General.—But Mohamed, (he was a very strong, handsome, portly man,) how did you get so fat in the jungle?

Mohamed.—I am not fat, I have been too much worked since you drove me into the jungle; now that I am safe and at my ease under you, who treat us all so well, you will see what I shall become!

With this courtier-like stroke the conversation ended. Yet the Khan spoke knowingly and truly, as well as flatteringly; for soon afterwards, four hundred minor chiefs came to lay their swords at the General's feet, relying on his generosity as to their jagheers, and offering their rich weapons as propitiatory presents: every blade was richly sheathed or ornamented, and their value estimated from fifty to two hundred pounds each, a great sum, and a lawful prize of war, belonging solely to the General. Without hesitation he returned them, as he had before returned those of the Ameers, simply saying, " I lose money, but I gain the good-will and confidence of these chiefs."

The Lion escaped to his family, which had remained with his treasure on the right bank of the Indus. Then he went to the Khelat Beloochees, afterwards to the Affghans of Candahar, who promised him aid with barbarian deceit, to gain his money, in which they succeeded. From them he fled to the Booghtees and other predatory tribes of the Cutchee hills, and his warfare became that of a mountain robber. They devastated villages, he became a sharer in their crimes, and Sir C. Napier gave him notice that he should, if taken, share their fate: finally he took refuge at Lahore, and sinking in sloth became fatuous.

When Roostum's son heard of the defeat he abandoned Shah Ghur, disbanded his men, and joined Shere Mohamed in the Booghtee country. This terminated the war in Upper

Scinde, and meanwhile the General tranquilized the Delta by means of his native police. The tribe on the Poorana river dispersed; the roving robber bands, no longer able to call themselves the Lion's soldiers, were readily opposed by the people; and many were taken: those against whom murders could be proved were hanged with labels on their breasts, announcing, that they were executed for those crimes, not for fighting against the British. The effect was great, the principle appreciated; " the Padishaw is just, he does not kill any one for himself," became a saying with the people, and the conquest was achieved !

CHAPTER VIII.

OBSERVATIONS WRITTEN IN 1845.

THE complete subjugation of Scinde, a great kingdom teeming with natural riches, was effected by Sir C. Napier in six months. He thus gave to the Anglo-Indian Empire, a shorter and safer frontier on the West, with command of the Indus, opening a direct commercial way to Central Asia, and spreading through that vast country a wholesome terror of the British arms. All this he did with a force varying from two to five thousand men in the field, and in one campaign, during which, though ill supplied with carriage and delayed by intricate vexatious negotiations, he, in the first three months marched above six hundred miles, constructed an entrenched camp, repaired a large fortress, fought two great battles, defeated sixty thousand enemies, killed twelve thousand, took twenty-six guns in the field, two camps with their baggage, four considerable fortresses, several minor forts, and made eight Sovereign Princes captives!

In the second three months, he marched two hundred and eighty miles, dispersed twelve thousand fighting men in the field, drove another Sovereign Prince, the one of most reputation, a fugitive and a vagabond on the face of the earth, and captured his brother. He received the submission of four hundred feudatory chiefs, some so powerful as to bring twenty thousand fighting men into the field; he repaired Meerpoor and Omercote, erected a fort at Ali-ka-Tanda, and another on the right bank of the Indus to protect the steamers. He formed a military police of horse and foot, and a body of spies upon the Ameers yet at large, choosing them from persons who had suffered in purse or person from their tyranny.

He organized the civil and military occupation and government of Scinde, and with such sagacity, that the first conception and framework has never been disturbed, though he enlarged it by degrees. It was not made with the pride of conquest but with all regard to justice, and it did not violate any of the people's customs or habits which were not opposed to the immutable principles of humanity. Mild it was to all save murderers. But they were many, for the Beloochees had enjoyed such impunity for wrong, that to slay a Scindee man or woman, or drag them into slavery, was an every-day occurrence. For such crimes he had no pardon; but his boast was that in his military operations no man was slain, save in battle, no cruelty was perpetrated, no plunder permitted, no insult offered to a woman! The Scindian people hailed his soldiers as deliverers, while they abandoned their villages at the approach of the ruthless Beloochees.

With what resolution and sagacity he imposed his own system of government on the land shall be told hereafter, in a history of his administration: it has now continued two years, and is not less extraordinary than his military career. In that period he has substituted security, peace, and comparative happiness, for misery, oppression and brutal degradation, has raised the Scindian serf to freedom, and abated the pride of the fierce Beloochee by moral force and just control. He has protected trade, fostered commerce, partially explored the natural resources of the country, and taken measures to draw them forth. Public works, with a view to future prosperity, have been commenced on a great scale, such as the construction of a mole at Kurrachee, which, besides its land approaches, will run two miles into the sea and furnish a secure harbour.

Large and healthful stone barracks for the troops are being erected; the police amount to more than two thousand well-organized, zealous and courageous men; a native battalion of troops has been raised and disciplined; a fighting camel corps has been formed, which has made marches of ninety miles at a time to surprise robber bands; and were it not for the commotions in the Punjaub the General would undertake the charge of Scinde without the aid of a soldier. Finally, although the revenue is drawn from territory, less by Ali Moorad's share than the Ameers possessed, it exceeds their receipts, being raised under a rigidly economical system, executed by young officers of his selection.

All the expenses of the civil and political administration, including the police force, have been defrayed from the receipts, and a surplus of ninety thousand pounds paid into the Calcutta treasury; making with the prize-money half a million derived from this decried conquest in one year—a profit received with complacency by the Directors, who are only inimical to the men whose courage gained it for them. Meanwhile the Scindian labourers cultivate the land, sure of something more than a miserable existence and the handicraftsmen, no longer dreading mutilation in payment of work, are returning from voluntary exile, allured by high wages and ample employment. Girls are no longer torn from their families to fill zenanas, or to be sold for distant slavery; the Hindoo trafficker and the Parsee merchant pursue their vocations with confidence; and even the Belooch warrior, not incapable of noble sentiments though harsh and savage, is content with a Government which has only changed his feudal ties into a peaceful instead of a warlike dependence. He has moreover become personally attached to a conqueror whose prowess he felt in battle, and whose justice and generosity he has experienced in peace.

These great actions have, according to the usual course of human nature, created a desire in small and envious minds to lessen them; and all the ingenuity of petty malice has been exerted to discover errors or to invent them, and promulgate censures. Some of the latter are puerile and ridiculous in the extreme, others plausible for those who know not the motives which determined the choice of measures: the first may be contemned, the second shall be refuted.

The disparity of force at the battles of Meeanee and Hydrabad struck men with astonishment, and the public generally admired the courage and fortitude which could obtain victory against such odds. But self-constituted judges, turning away from the glorious spectacle, proceeded to condemn Lord Ellenborough for furnishing so few troops; and the General for risking the army in such an unequal conflict.

These censures are unfounded. Lord Ellenborough gave more troops than were required, and offered others. Sir C. Napier, therefore, was responsible for having so few troops at Meeanee: but he was not censurable. When he took the field he had strong grounds for believing no war would ensue, and was therefore anxious to save Government an expense it could ill afford. This induced him to send back the Bengal troops; but he used them on their passage skilfully, to save the ceded districts from plunder, to cover the rear of the army from insult, and prevent a partisan warfare menaced by the Ameers. They kept the Bhawal Khan true to his alliance, an object not to be left entirely to his sense of honour when all India was beginning to waver, from the Affghan disasters. And all this was effected while these Bengal troops were advancing slowly to the Upper Sutlege, where, from the falsehoods of the Indian editors, a war appeared more likely to happen than in Scinde.

It has been, however, plausibly said, that war being commenced Sir C. Napier should at any cost have collected his whole force, seeing how numerous the Beloochees were. No man felt this more strongly than himself; but he was governed by necessity, not choice. In Scinde it was then impossible to act with a large force. At certain seasons water could not be got at any distance from the Indus, at other seasons a scanty supply only could be obtained; and there are extensive districts in which it cannot in any season be found sufficiently abounding for an army. On the march to Emaum Ghur only three hundred men could be supplied, when prudence demanded the employment of three thousand; and there, and all through the campaign, the want of numbers and facilities was remedied by genius and hardihood. The chances were all adverse: it was only by great moral qualities success was obtained.

Sir C. Napier commenced his campaign with three thousand men when he had six thousand available; but to use the greater number he must have adopted a different line of operations, have moved slowly, close to the Indus, in one huge unwieldy mass; for his camp followers would not have been less than thirty thousand. The war however required rapid enterprise, with the temporary loss of communications: wherefore suppleness was substituted for numbers.

At that season water was scarce, hardly could three thousand men be supplied at once ; moreover, the country was intricate and unknown, and the General had to grope, as it were, like a blind man for the wells; had he been harassed by the enemy the difficulties would have been very great, because the marches were necessarily determined by the water localities. But in Scinde every season has its peculiar military obstacles. At one period there is no water, at another there is too much ; the heat is unendurable in its climax, and anon, when it cools, intermittent fevers strike down the soldiers by thousands: man was found the least dangerous opponent, and yet the Beloochees were brave, well-armed, fanatical, not deficient in skill, and twenty to one in number !

Sir C. Napier was by circumstances compelled to operate in all the seasons. He had to brave climate, sickness, scarcity of water, and superior numbers, difficult to contend with because they moved without a commissariat, plundering for subsistence, always knowing where water could be had, and able to change their positions without difficulty. They knew also how to conceal the wells they left behind; they would inevitably have baffled a large force, and were only overcome by the cautious though prompt genius of their opponent. These motives for acting with a small force would suffice, but there was another reason even more potent —the want of camels to transport provisions and stores; and if these had been abundant only one regiment could have been added to the field force, without leaving Sukkur and Roree open to an enemy who could easily move round the flanks of the army to attack them unawares.

It has been said the Governor-General should have increased the garrison of those places at once, and sent camels to the field force. He did so soon as it was practicable ; but Lord Ellenborough came out, not to a well-ordered government having command of great resources ; he came amidst disasters and confusion, amidst public poverty both of money and spirit : he came to save, to create, and time was required. Moreover the Ameers' quarrel grew very suddenly to a head: it was unexpected. Ferozepore is forty marches from Sukkur, and had Sir C. Napier waited for reinforcements and camels, he would have been thrown into the hot season, and then the Ameers, with all their forces united, would have defied and insulted the British Government, have made new combinations with the Brahooe-Beloochees, the Affghans, the Seiks, and the Mahrattas of Gwalior, and the warfare of the latter was not found easy even as an isolated event.

It was impossible to avoid war with the Ameers, and as the crisis was vital, there was a necessity to strike boldly and promptly. The army was undoubtedly ill provided, and the risk great; but the English General, conscious of ability, put aside all difficulties with this remark. " If a man is afraid to undertake that which the public good imperiously demands till everything in his army is perfect, he had better try any trade rather than war, because the very nature of war prevents everything from being perfect."

When the result justified his daring, he thus epitomized his campaign. " I did everything I could to maintain peace with the Ameers, but I resolved to force their bands to disperse, as I was ordered. I considered the troops I took with me able to coerce the Ameers, and they were so."

They would not have been so under a man of less genius and resolution. Yet he did not provoke the danger, he only confronted it heroically. When he marched against Kyrpoor from Roree, the Upper Scinde Ameers were not united with those of Hydrabad; nor with the Lion. Separate negotiations were going on with each; and though a secret concert for a general war was known to exist, the constant inebriety, the unsettled policy, and the clashing personal interests of the different broods, made it doubtful if they could act with a timely unity. The General therefore judged, and truly, that when Ali Moorad broke from those of Upper Scinde, the latter could be coerced before the others could come to their aid.

Again, when the whole military power of Scinde was being collected around Hydrabad, Sobdar's and Mohamed

Khan's protestations of amity, joined to those of the young Hoossein, deceived even Ali Moorad, who assured the General, and in good faith, for his own interest was involved, that they might be depended upon.

Then came the treacherous proposal from Sobdar to send five thousand men, with secret orders to fall on their own countrymen during the battle, giving reason to suppose that all the Ameers' forces would not take the field, and that a like result would be obtained in Lower as in Upper Scinde. It was only when this, apparently well-founded hope failed, that the astounding discrepancy of force became apparent, and called forth the heroic energies of the leader, and his gallant troops.

The two great errors, namely, the detaching men at Outram's desire the night before the battle of Meeanee; and refraining from an attack on Shere Mohamed the morning after that battle, have been noticed. It has been shewn that they sprung, not from want of judgment in the General, but from yielding against his judgment to the importunities of a man for whom he had at that time a friendship, at a moment when the intrepid defence of the Residency falsely claimed by Outram, had touched his feelings.

So difficult an art is war, that it has been, with something of hyperbole, designated as a series of errors, even when exercised by the greatest captains. No great captain was ever quite satisfied when calmly considering his own exploits; perhaps, because the fiery spirit and energy, so conducive to success in action, being then quiescent, extraordinary daring appears rashness, even to the man by whom it was displayed. It shocks the cold reasoning faculty, which always seeks perfection by a cautious, circumscribed process; whereas the sudden impulses of genius belong to a higher intelligence, impervious though inexplicable, and vouchsafed to few.

Sir C. Napier blamed the precipitancy of his own attack at Dubba. He thought he should have employed an hour or two to examine the enemy's position more exactly from the flank, as well as on the front. Passing with some cavalry across the bed of the Fullaillee on his left, he could from thence have seen the whole of the Beloochee right and

T

centre, and would thus have discovered the double nullah, and the great numbers posted there, and in the village of Dubba; and with that knowledge would have made his principal attack at the junction of their left wing with the centre.

This self-criticism is just, but the enemy's numbers were so great, and his position so strong, that delay might have affected the enthusiasm of the troops; moreover the spies affirmed that the Lion had prepared a counter attack, which might have happened while the General was on the other side of the Fullaillee, the armies being within cannon shot of each other.   Here then the impulse of the moment was probably more valuable than the conclusions of an after examination.

The battles of Meeanee and Dubba were astonishing exploits : the victor's despatches did not do them justice. When that of Meeanee was written all was confusion; officers and soldiers were oppressed with fatigue; heat, dust, and a false alarm in camp after the battle, conjoined with severe bodily pain from a broken hand, weighed on the writer. The Adjutant-General Wyllie was too badly wounded to be disturbed, there was no field return ready, and Sir C. Napier taking the last morning state of the army from his desk, more than a week old, hastily gave the force there set down as the number engaged. Nothing could be more erroneous. Outram's detachment, the sick of the last ten days, and the baggage guard, were thus all reckoned as good fighting men in the field.   When the true returns were afterwards made up, the total of sabres and bayonets, exclusive of Clibborne's grenadiers, who were scarcely engaged, did not exceed seventeen hundred and eighty !

With respect to the enemy's force the error was greater.

The surest of the spies said the number before the battle was forty thousand, while others said thirty-five thousand, and one reduced it to twenty-two thousand : this last number was, from modesty, adopted in the absence of sure proof to the contrary. But subsequently, formal authenticated muster rolls of the tribes, made out for the Ameers, were found. These gave only twenty-five thousand eight hundred and sixty-two men, bearing sword and shield; but there were two strong tribes, numbering together twelve thousand fighting men, which joined on the very morning of the fight, and were not in the muster rolls : thus the whole force coincided with the report of the best emissary. The English General therefore fought with one to eighteen, not effeminate reluctant Hindoos without discipline and having ten thousand of their cavalry in secret league with their opponents ; not a rabble more ready from the beginning for flight than battle, as at Plassey, but strong valiant warriors, fanatics, wielding sword and shield with terrific power, giving no quarter, asking for none—men habituated to war, skillful after their own mode, and so intrepid, that six thousand died under shield, and the remainder retired, amazed rather than dispirited, broken, not subdued. Six thousand was the number assumed by the conqueror : but the Ameers, who were allowed to bury their dead, said eight thousand.

Here may be noted a remarkable resemblance between the English General's operations and those of the Macedonian conqueror two thousand years before, in the same country. In Williams' *Life of Alexander*, a work which, with some errors of conclusion, arising from the author's want of military knowledge, is the best digested account of that wonderful man, the following passages occur :—

" Alexander received information that the Malli and Oxydracæ, two powerful and free states, were preparing to give him a hostile reception, and dispute the passage through their territories. . . . The plan agreed upon by the two nations was, for the Malli to send their warriors down the river and make the territories of the Oxydracæ the scene of war, for the former looked upon themselves as sufficiently protected by a considerable desert. . . . Alexander marched laterally from the left bank of the Acessines, and encamped near a small stream which skirted the western edge of the desert. . . . There, after a short repose, he ordered them to fill their vessels with water, and marching the rest of the day and all night, with the dawn arrived before a Mallian city which had no fear of being attacked thus suddenly from the side of the desert. The Malli fought resolutely, but the passage of the desert had taken them by surprise, and entirely deranged the plans of the chief who had conducted their warriors down the river."

Substitute the Ameers of Upper and Lower Scinde for
the Malli and Oxydracæ, and the native plan is the same ;
while the march to Emaum Ghur is a repetition of Alexander's operations, with this difference, that he was only five
days in the desert, and the English General was eighteen.

The campaign ended, as it begun, in the mazes of the
Ameers' deceit and falsehood, aided and abetted by a cabal at
Bombay, whose discontent at being debarred by Lord Ellenborough of expected official plunder in the new conquest, was,
and continues to be, evinced with all the rancour and vulgar
vehemence belonging to sordid minds deprived of anticipated
profits.   Had Lord Ellenborough annexed Scinde to the
Bombay Presidency all would have been well; lean relations
and dependents would have been fattened, and the two or
three years required so to fatten them, would have given
Scinde back to the Beloochees with the loss of a British
army.

Scarcely had the Ameers reached Bombay, when the
newspaper organ of this unprincipled cabal commenced lamen-
tations over the " fallen patriarchal Princes." Their virtues,
their dignity, their generosity were extolled, the iniquity
of overthrowing them was denounced. The deposed Princes set
their names and seals to petitions, concocted at Bombay and
bearing unmistakable signs of their origin. These men, Mahomedans, few of whom can either read or write, were made to
interlard their statements with appeals to the doctrines of
Christianity, which they had, they said, learned from history
and books!   Appeals also to the principles of the English
Government which they had acquired a knowledge of in the
same manner, and they prated about the Queen of Sheba !
Each Ameer signed separate statements, designed for the
Queen, the Governor-General, and the Governor of Bombay ;
and these were multiplied with such alterations and additions
as it suited their European prompters to dictate. Ranging
over all their past intercourse with the British Government
they may be thus epitomized :—

" The Ameers, always sincere friends of the British
Government, had willingly become its subjects at the demand
of Lord Auckland, and, as such, were faithful.   There was

no cause of complaint against any of them, yet they had been treated with a violence and oppression exceeding any thing recorded in history. They had accepted and signed all the Auckland treaties, and never violated an iota of any one of them. They had, though feeling deeply the injustice of it, accepted and set their seals to Lord Ellenborough's new treaty; yet they had been, in disregard of that act of submission, attacked and deprived of their dominions. Sir C. Napier's arrival in Scinde was the signal for perpetrating every species of iniquity against them, helpless innocent Princes as they were, reposing without care or suspicion of evil, with quiet confidence in the British Government.

" Astonishment and grief overwhelmed them at first, when they found their gentleness and dutiful behaviour no safeguard from oppression.

" In their anguish they pleaded for mercy, but it was denied, and then their Belooch subjects and friends, enraged at the sight of their misery, assembled in arms and could not be restrained from attacking the British army, though they, the Ameers, had, with wonderful zeal and perseverance sought to restrain their fury; and they would in truth have succeeded, if Sir C. Napier had not, with unexampled violence, seized Hyat Khan and the other Murree chiefs while passing through his camp. Negotiations were then going forward, but this iniquity rendered fruitless the efforts of the Ameers to repress the national phrensy, which was excited, not so much by the injustice and harshness practised against the Ameers of Hydrabad as by the cruelty exercised towards the aged Roostum, whose desolate condition neither the other Ameers nor the Belooch warriors could bear. He had been misled, deceived, tricked out of his possessions by the insidious English General, and by his false brother Ali Moorad, who drove him forth, at eighty-five years of age, a wanderer in the desert.

" The attack on the Residency, and the battle of Meeanee, were results of the natural generous indignation of the Beloochees. The first was commenced without orders, conducted without chiefs; the Ameers had strenuously exerted themselves to prevent the accident. At the battle of Meeanee the Ameers were forced to appear by their warriors, but their intention was not to fight; they were in the camp to prevent others from fighting; and they thought they would even then have succeeded in this humane project, if the English General had not attacked the moment he came in sight, killing some and forcing others to run away. But he could claim no triumph, because he had attacked and killed, not enemies but Queen Victoria's subjects, seeing the Ameers had long considered themselves as her people.

"After the battle the Ameers entered Sir C. Napier's camp, not as captives but as friends. They delivered their swords to him indeed, but he returned them, saying to Nusseer in particular, ' I give you all praise. In twenty-five days your affairs shall be settled, and you will be restored to Hydrabad with all your dignity and rights.' To their astonishment, after this voluntary promise given, the English General entered Hydrabad a conqueror, and as it were by storm, plundering houses, breaking into zenanas, robbing the women by violence, even of their ear-rings and other ornaments, causing them to rush out of their secret apartments to save their lives, and thus exposing them to the gaze of strangers, an abomination and an insult not to be endured by Mahomedans. Every article in the palaces, even to the peculiar family arms of the Ameers, things of no real value, yet dear to them as heirlooms, were made spoil of, and the original treaties and certificates of alliance with England were carried off with the plunder. Servants of the palace, men of high rank and respectability, were made prisoners without cause, and their houses plundered, and especially one, named Meerza Khoosroo, who former Ameers treated as a child, was in wantonness of cruelty tied up and flogged until he fainted. In fine, unparalleled horrors were perpetrated."

These accusations, repeated and varied, formed the substance of the memorials; but Sobdar and Shahdad added circumstances peculiar to their cases. The first stated, " That he had been the known particular friend of the British Government, in contradistinction to others. That he took no part in the battle, nor in the attack of the Residency. That after Meeanee he remained in his palace, confident in the good will of the General, who could have no fault to find with him and indeed owed him favour, since he had strenuously opposed the wishes of those turbulent Beloochees, who, when returning from the battle, desired to defend Hydrabad and the fortress. Yet all his merit had not saved him from captivity or from plunder ; his women had been insulted, his servants maltreated. Never since the English had become masters of India had such disgrace and oppression, and tyranny, been experienced towards any friend of Government."

And then he, a Mussulman, appealed in the name of Jesus Christ for redress ! thus betraying the real authors of his shameless memorial. He, who pretended he had no control of the Beloochees that attacked the Residency ; he who claimed favour because he was not at Meeanee, thus casting aside the declarations of his brother Ameers as to their innocence of hostilities ; he, this Sobdar, had nevertheless offered just before the battle, to place five thousand of his warriors in the Belooch ranks with orders to fall on their own countrymen during the action ; he had control over them for that treachery, none to prevent them attacking the British ! But ample proof was obtained that he had urged the attack on the Residency, and had sent his warriors to fight at Meeanee, where hundreds of them perished, while he, coward and traitor, remained in his palace to profit from whatever might happen. In truth he expected victory, like all the other Ameers, and sent his men because any lukewarmness would have been his ruin if the battle was gained. The other Ameers cared not for his poltroonery, but they had his former fallings off from them to avenge ; and as he was a " *Soonee*," while they were " *Sheas*," religious fury would have conjoined with political revenge.

The Ameer, Mohamed Khan, who had been wounded at the attack of the Residency, complained, that though, like Sobdar, he was the peculiar friend of the British, had sent no men to fight, and was in no way concerned in the disturbances, he had, nevertheless, been plundered, and made captive in a more degrading manner than the other Ameers had been. For while residing in the fortress he was suddenly seized, thrown on an elephant without attendants, and so carried off to the garden of captivity. He also had learned from books and histories, that oppression was not allowed by the Christian religion.

Shahdad's case was even more piteous. He was a lonely captive, yet he had always been a friend, and had nothing to do with the attack on the Residency. He had restrained the Beloochees at that time; he had harangued the other Ameers on the folly and wickedness of such a proceeding, and, after Outram's retreat, he had prevented the Lugarees from pursuing the boats up the river. Finally, he had no part in the murder of Captain Innes.

Such were the shameless memorials concocted for those degraded beings by their infamous coadjutors at Bombay; and hard they prayed not to be sent out of that capital, feeling truly that at a distance the game of interested calumny could not be so conveniently played.

Three of these memorials, namely, those of Sobdar, Nusseer, and Mohamed, were sent by the Bombay Government to Sir C. Napier; and they reached him while engaged in his last operations against the Lion, just two days before he was struck down by the sun: he thus noticed them to Lord Ellenborough:—

"I send your Lordship three complaints against us, with the replies of the accused. I think it my duty to make no answer (except to your Lordship) to accusations which I know to be concocted by a hostile party at Bombay. There are several other complaints, each of several sheets of foolscap, and gross impudent falsehoods all. I have not answered them, but when I have a little leisure I shall send them with the necessary remarks. After your Lordship has seen my defence I will burn it, if your Lordship pleases, or re-word it, for the facts are as I state. Your Lordship will, I am sure, make some allowance for a man absolutely wearied out with their incessant unblushing downright falsehoods. As to going minutely into a disproof of all their gross assertions, I could easily do it, but I must give up my command, and request a permanent establishment; for every disproof of their assertions would be immediately followed by another volume of lies."

But notwithstanding his fatigue and anxiety and illness,

and the accumulation of business suddenly imposed on him
by the arrival at once of four months' communications from
two Governments, he did send refutations of the Ameers' calumnies, complete and irrefragable. Those calumnies were,
as he had foretold, then repeated, and sent to him by the
Bombay Government, purposely to irritate him; but he refused to receive any more, and desired they might be sent to
Lord Ellenborough. But as their aim was neither truth nor
justice, nor the public interest, nor any thing decent or
honourable, they were, notwithstanding the complete exposure
of their falsehood transmitted to England by their concoctors,
to influence the Directors, and with the hope of influencing
Majesty: the only effect hitherto, however, has been to display the baseness and knavery which originated them.

It has been shewn that Outram's expedition to burn a
skikargah saved him from the dangers of Meeanee ; and that
he voluntarily quitted the army before the battle of Dubba,
leaving Sir C. Napier with a lowered opinion of him both as
a diplomatist and an officer; yet he still bore the name of
friend, and the assurance, not coldly expressed, of the
General's esteem. After a short stay at Bombay he proceeded to England, openly professing his obligation to the
man who had risked the Governor-General's displeasure to
get him restored to a public situation in Scinde ; yet when
he obtained access to the Ministers and the India House, he
secretly stated that the Ameers were to the last moment
willing to submit, and there was no necessity for hostilities—
that he could himself have attained the peaceable termination of the difficulties, if he had not been restrained by the
General, who had moreover misled Lord Ellenborough, by
withholding certain notes of conferences held with the
Ameers of Hydrabad, by Outram himself, and copies of
which he now gave to the secret committee: in fine, he repeated the falsehoods of the Ameers' memorials, so exactly,
as to prove that he had aided in concocting them.

Astonished at these revelations from such a source, the
Ministers became apprehensive that Sir C. Napier's victories,
instead of being worthy of honours and rewards, would be
found crimes subversive of England's reputation for justice

and good faith. That reputation was not indeed very high for those virtues in the East, but the Government, disturbed by this intelligence, suspended all notice of the victories. No rejoicing guns announced, no public thanks graced the conquest of a great kingdom, and battles almost without parallel in history, were passed over in gloomy silence. A whispered accusation had more weight than those great exploits!

Outram, who had evaded the battles, who had been the direct cause of the only military errors committed, and whose counsel, if followed, would have destroyed General and army, thus intercepted the Government's acknowledgment of the dangers and glories which he had not shared. And English journals, taking for guides the foul Indian press, laboured to extol him and to depreciate Sir C. Napier, asserting that Outram ought to replace the General as the abler man! This was what he aimed at, but his swelling pretensions soon collapsed: he returned to India, and after having declared that he disdained to fill any office under Lord Ellenborough, accepted, meekly, an inferior political one, in an obscure province, which he had held twenty years before.

Sir C. Napier has governed Scinde with the same energy and ability he displayed in the conquest. Widely spread is his fame as a General, widely as an Eastern ruler: his name is known and his warfare dreaded throughout central Asia. Distant barbarian Princes seek his friendship, for they cannot separate the idea of sovereign power from great exploits in war. A curious proof of this has been furnished by two embassies.

The first from Yar Mohamed of Herat, whose nephew, being sent with credentials to the Bombay Government, turned aside to offer them and presents to Sir C. Napier. He was advised to go on to Bombay, and did so, but was there insulted. Scarcely had he quitted the camp, when another Prince, sent by the Khan of Khiva, whose dominions touched on the Aral Sea, arrived in the camp, sent also with presents direct to the conqueror of Scinde. He had made his journey with great difficulty and danger, delivered his credentials and thus spoke:

" The Khan of Khiva hates the Russians, and the Bokhara Ruler, and the man of Herat. Why do you English of whom it is said, you will avenge even the death of a dog, suffer tamely the massacre of your army at Cabool? If you will attack the Affghans the Khan will assist you. If you will attack the man of Herat and the Ameer of Bokhara from the east, the Khan will attack them from the west, and success will be certain."

Such is the renown of Sir C. Napier in Central Asia. With twelve thousand selected troops he could gibbet the murderer of Bokhara over the graves of Connolly and Stoddart. The glory he has gained by arms and policy is too bright to be obscured by the foul breath of insidious maligners. The morning sun which lights up the mountain's brow raises malignant vapours from the marsh at its base, but the midday sun disperses them.

Outram's notes were sent by the Secret Committee to Lord Ellenborough. He had never seen them before, and required an immediate explanation. He soon got it, and so full, so complete, that all doubts as to where censure should fall were instantly dissipated. Far from furnishing ground for belief that peace might have been preserved, Outram's accusatory notes only proved how egregiously he had been deluded by the Ameers. The withholding of them from the Government, to whom they were not addressed, was accidental; but in a public view the General thought them of no importance, Outram's weakness of judgment and want of penetration being apparent to him at the time, and more completely exposed by subsequent events. In justice to himself, however, he now sent other communications which he had received from Outram, and had designedly withheld, from a generous reluctance to lessen him as a public man in the opinion of Lord Ellenborough.

Among these defamatory notes was Roostum's account of his intercourse with Sir C. Napier as to ceding the Turban; but Sir C. Napier's letter to Outram, contradicting Roostum's statement, and exposing its falsehood was withheld by Outram, and the Government was thus led to believe the General had coerced that Ameer. And while thus treacherously retentive, he had reported that Sir C. Napier, by treaty, pledged himself to give Ali Moorad wide lands and revenue. Hence along with a demand for explanation as to Outram's notes, Lord Ellenborough required also, an account of this pledge and treaty, of which he had not before heard. Neither had Sir C. Napier! It was one of Outram's many figments!

The General's exposition of these falsifications was so complete, that both the English and the Eastern Governments were more than satisfied; and Lord Ellenborough recorded, by a formal minute of Council, the strong sense entertained of Sir C. Napier's conduct and the astonishment felt at Major Outram's delusions!

The English Ministers then moved for the thanks of Parliament to the gallant troops and their leader, declaring in glowing language the great qualities of the man whose honour they had before doubted on the secret report of a factious tool. The Duke of Wellington's encomiums on the occasion, amply and forcibly expressed and with a nice discrimination, shewing that he had critically judged the operations, may be considered as history and fame.

Outram's slanders were thus dispersed. But though the Sovereign and the Parliament have accepted the policy of Lord Ellenborough and the military exploits of Sir C. Napier, as honourable augmentations for England's glory, anonymous calumniators, encouraged by faction, still labour to lower the fame of those brave and worthy men, misrepresenting the judgment of the Queen and Legislature, as one founded on expediency, in scorn of justice, whereas it was founded on the expediency of justice, as the following slight summary will prove.

It was inexpedient and unjust to invade Affghanistan, and that invasion made it expedient, though unjust, to coerce the Ameers of Scinde; but both being done by Lord Auckland's Government, with hypocrisy superadded, the result was imminent danger to the Anglo-Indian Empire. His successor had to save it, and to do so it was expedient and just that Lord Ellenborough should insist upon the exact maintenance of existing treaties, and should punish any violation.

The Auckland treaties were unjustly imposed, but accepted by the Ameers without protest. They had profited from them, and claimed the merit, not only of adhering to them but of having been eager to accept them; both claims false, yet proving the validity of the treaties, which, however, they grossly violated. It was, therefore expedient and just to punish those violations and to insure future faith by new conditions.

The Ameers accepted the new treaty, signed it, and next moment attacked the British troops. They were defeated, and it became expedient, just, wise, and benevolent, to put an end to their horrid rule. Expedient, because they were faithless in peace and war; benevolent, because the well being of their people was thereby secured. It was wise, because it was benevolent and just, and because it promoted civilization and commerce in barbarous countries.

Who has suffered by it? The Ameers only! The very persons who had offended. To remove such brutal treacherous tyrants, having a well-grounded right to do so, was worthy of England's greatness. The conquest of Scinde is therefore no iniquity. The glory of the achievement is a pure flame kindled on the altar of justice.

APPENDIX.

I.

THE trustees of the British Museum, through their secretary Mr. Forshall, have denied ever giving directions to cut the statue of Sesostris, or any other statue in Egypt, for the ease of transport. Such directions may however have been given without their knowledge by subordinates — my statement was derived by Sir C. Napier from Dr. Abbot of Cairo, whose collection of Egyptian antiquities is so well known to travellers.—W. NAPIER.

II.

LETTERS FROM SIR C. NAPIER.

16th January, 1843. I found the Ameers and our Government in the position which a treaty made by Lord Auckland placed them. I had no concern with its justice, its propriety, or any thing but *to see it maintained.* I found that all the politicals had gone on, from the beginning, trifling; sometimes letting the Ameers infringe the treaty without notice, at others pulling them up, and then dropping the matter: in short I saw it was a long chain of infringement, denial, apology, pardon, over and over. I therefore resolved not to let this, which old Indians call " *knowing the people,*" go on; and I wrote to the Ameers, saying, I would not allow it to continue; they of course continued their game and I, as I had threatened, reported the infringements to Lord Ellenborough, who agreed with me, that their irritating, childish mischievous secret warfare and intrigue should not continue. And as letters from the Ameers were intercepted, proposing to other powers to league and drive us out of Scinde, Lord Ellenborough thought, and I think justly, that a new treaty should be entered into, which he sent me. I had laid before him the proposal, and I think my treaty was a more fair treaty, at least a more liberal treaty than his; but I do not, as far as I have been able to consider it, think his unjust. Mind, I always reason upon affairs as Lord Ellenborough and myself *found them.* I cannot enter upon our right to be *here at all,* that is Lord Auckland's affair. Well! I presented the draft of the new treaty. The Ameers bowed with their usual apparent compliance, but raised troops in all directions. These I was ordered by the Governor-General to disperse. To disperse irregular troops, they having a desert at their back and four hundred miles of river to cross and run up the mountains; and all this with their chiefs swearing they submitted to everything to get me into the *hot* weather, when I could not move, and thus cut off all our communications at their ease, was no trifle. In short it was to attack a " *Will-o'-the-wisp.*" Every man is armed to the teeth, and armies of great strength could assemble and disperse like wildfire.

Sukkur, 16*th and* 17*th December,* 1842. I am ordered to take a considerable portion of the territory which belongs to the Ameers or Princes of Scinde, who have been plotting to turn us out by a simultaneous attack in concert with various allies: there are many of these princes, some are with us, some adverse. *My object is to save bloodshed.*

I have cut off the communication between the Ameers and the ceded districts and their town of Roree. So I shall effect what I am ordered to do, and, unless they attack me, no blood will be spilled. I can produce a war in two hours if I like it, but I want to prevent it and trust in God I shall. I am the only man in camp who does not wish for war with the Ameers, and their own peasantry detest them and are longing for us. But still they collect great numbers of Beloochees and other warlike tribes of the mountains: these robbers form their armies, and their deserts are difficult, and there are great jungles in the deserts. So it is necessary to be careful. A very little rashness might invoke disaster for my small army : and as it is, I have near nine hundred sick with fever. I shall move across the river in three days. I am only waiting to arrange the defence of my camp here against the tribes from Larkaana, who, it is said, mean to attack it the moment I move over to Roree and am engaged with the Ameers. If they do it will be worse for them ! I feel I am their master in every thing but numbers. How our troops got defeated by these tribes is to me inconceivable !

March, 1842. I mourn over the whole thing. I hate bloodshed. I did all I could to prevent it as my conduct will prove, and as every officer in this army knows ; for they used to say, " The General is the only man in camp who does not wish for a battle." The Ameers are the greatest ruffians I ever met with, without an exception ; however I have only obeyed my orders.

III.

ON THE AMEER ROOSTUM.

Sir C. Napier to Major Outram, 11*th February,* 1843.

Roostum's plea of being sent to Ali Moorad by me is a shallow affair, because, in the first place, he sent a secret message (by Moyadeen, I think Brown told me) to say he was to all intents a prisoner in Kyrpoor, and that he tried to send away his family, and was obliged to bring them back after they were on the road, and that he would escape and come to my camp. Brown knows all this matter. The messenger said, he, Roostum, would do whatever I advised. My answer was, " Take your brother's advice — go to him, and either stay with him, or *I will escort you to my camp.*" His flying from his brother's camp proves that he was not a prisoner. His not flying to mine, proves either his *duplicity* or his *imbecility.* I believe the latter, but imbecility is not a legitimate excuse for Rulers ! I have only to deal with his acts. He played you the same trick. He even now stands

v

out! He cannot say Ali Moorad still influences him! I believed he did at first, but he does not *now*; and I am half inclined *now* to doubt the former fact, though I did not do so at first. But as I said, the intrigues of these people are nothing to me; only I will not let his cunning attempt to cast his conduct on my advice pass. He went *contrary* to my advice, and now wants to make out that he went *by it*.

December 1843. Outram told me what a fine fellow Ali Moorad was; how frank and open, and a thorough friend of ours; adhering to his treaty honestly, as indeed he has done up to this moment. Well! I was quite new to them all, and one night, 18th of December, 1842, a secret message came to me from Roostum, to say, he was a prisoner among his family, and they forced him to act against the English; he begged of me to receive him in my camp, for he was helpless. I wrote to him the above letter [given in the text, chapter VI, advising him to go to his brother, &c. &c.] He did go to his brother, and then would not see me! I really know not what I am found fault with for. He did not take my advice, he only took a part. Now if I advised him to take a seidlitz powder, and he drank only the *acid* powder, he could have no right to complain that I gave him a pain in his belly. But this is exactly what Roostum did. He went to Ali Moorad as I advised; but he neither remained with him as I advised, nor came to me as I advised. He made over everything to Ali Moorad and then fled, and proclaimed that he was forced! The formal way in which he made all over to Ali has been proved in detail, and is in the hands of Government: it was also submitted to the Mahomedan College by order of the Governor-General, and the College pronounced it perfectly correct in all particulars.

Now, why did not Roostum meet me? If he was forced as he pretends, why not tell me? " Oh!" said Outram, " he was afraid. Ali Moorad made him think you were going to put him in prison." My answer was, "Why should he think so? There was not the slightest motive; but if he did fear it at Dejee, that was no excuse for his not meeting me when I overtook him on the march to

Emaum Ghur. When I had force to seize him and all that
were with him ; and when instead of doing so I sent you,
Outram, his friend of four years, to invite him to come to
my tent, and you returned with his two sons, and brought
me a message, that he was so *tired* he could not come himself. He could have no fear then." To this Outram said,
" Oh! Ali has bribed all about him." This was nonsense;
he had humbugged Outram.

Well! after Emaum Ghur, Outram again met him on
the road to Kyrpoor, and he agreed to meet Outram there
the next day to discuss the treaty, but was again *so tired* that
he advised Outram to ride on and he would follow early next
morning. Off went Outram, duped ; and the moment he was
out of sight, Roostum ordered his baggage to be packed, and
marched that night with all his treasure and seven thousand
men, who he had kept out of sight of Outram, and also two
pieces of cannon ; and he never stopped till he got to Khoonhera, sixty miles from Hydrabad, where he had land, and a
fort, which he held until I captured him! Here you see my
conduct was all clear.

I wished to have *one* man to deal with, instead of a *dozen*,
and that dozen in the hands of an old fox, Futteh Mohamed
Ghoree, the sworn enemy of the English, and working to
form a coalition to fall on us with Beloochees, Affghans, and
Seiks united, to the number of two hundred thousand men ;
I having but seven thousand in Scinde, and those divided
between Kurrachee and Sukkur, five hundred miles asunder!
I wished the younger brother to be the minister of the
other, the Mayor of the Palace, the King being an imbecile
old fool, full of useless cunning and in the hands of a clever
knave and some six or seven violent young men. When I
found Roostum had resigned the Turban to his brother I
was opposed to it; because, at first, I thought it would produce war, and I sent to Ali Moorad to advise him not to
take it. His answer was, " he could not give it up; that
it had been solemnly given by his brother with all legal
formality, and he neither could nor would give it back." I
had in the mean time reflected upon the matter, and was
convinced Ali was right. It made the matter a decided one,

whereas the old idiot would constantly, by his cunning tricks, prevent Ali doing what was necessary. Thinking it was voluntary, I offered no opposition, but sought a meeting with old noodle to ascertain from his own lips that it was voluntary.

I never advised him to give up the Turban, I consented to it because I thought it would prevent bloodshed : indeed, it mattered little whether I consented or not, for it was done before I knew of it, and Ali Moorad refused to undo it at my request. He proved right ; for, as the sequel shewed, Roostum would have bolted, and used his power as "*Rais*" against us with some appearance of justice. I mean, that holding the Chieftaincy he could have sanctioned acts which might have embarrassed us ; for the Mahomedans think much of whoever holds the title. . . . . The more this question is discussed about Roostum the better, because my conduct was quite honest. I advised Roostum to be *guided* by Ali Moorad. I never forced him to do anything. I never advised him to give up the Turban, when I heard he had I tried to prevent it, and when I could not prevent it I sought an interview with him, to be certain the old man had not been forced or ill used by Ali. But he fled of his own free will. This is the whole story.

I was very much afraid of the old man being killed in the attack of Kyrpoor if the people defended it, and I knew this would be vexatious, and give a handle for abuse of all sorts from the infamous Indian press, than which the whole world cannot produce one more rascally. Besides, I pitied the old man. I thought he was the victim of his son, who wanted to get the Turban against all law and right, and who, for aught I knew, might kill him on purpose in the row ! They are capable of this, any one of them.

Ali Moorad to Sir C. Napier, October 9th, 1843.

Meer Roostum Khan, a week before he granted me the Turban and territory, importuned me to accept them, saying, that none of his sons appeared qualified to possess the Turban and rule the country; and that I should therefore take possession of the Turban and territory from him. He deputed to me at Kote Dehuj, his eldest son Meer Mohamed Hoossein, Meer Nusseer Khan, Futteh Ghoree, Peer Ali Gohur, and certain other confidential persons to solicit me earnestly to accept the Turban and territory. At last he came in person, bound the Turban with his own hands and of his own accord around my head, made the entry in the Koran of his having granted me the whole of his country, sealed it and ratified it with his seal and signature, and thus distinctly made over his country to me.

How is it possible then that I should have used coercive measures to obtain possession of the country, since I had not even preferred a request to obtain it?

Note by the Secretary to the Government of India,
August 30th, 1843.

Sir C. Napier adverts to the legal bearing of the deed under which Meer Roostum abdicated in favour of Meer Ali Moorad.

It had been represented to Sir C. Napier, that every chief is master of his own property, none of which can be entailed; that the will of the possessor decides who is to have the land; that if he gives it to his children, he may, in virtue of his paternal power, revoke that gift; but that if he gives it to a chief who is his equal, and over whom he has no paternal power, the deed is final.

It is quite correct that every person is master of his own property, and that there can be no entail:—he may give it to whom he chooses. The gift, when possession has been obtained by the donee, is complete. It can, however, be cancelled under certain circumstances; but one of the barriers to cancelling a gift, is relationship within the prohibited degrees. A gift therefore to a son cannot be cancelled any more than to a brother.* If made to a person

* Vide Macnaghten's *Principles of Mahomedan Law*, chap. v. par. 13, p. 51; Hamilton's *Hedaya*, vol. iii. p. 302.

not a husband or wife, nor within the prohibited degrees, it may in certain cases be cancelled.

Sovereign power is not however considered property according to the Mahomedan law, nor is it regulated by the laws which govern the transfer of property, whether real or personal, for there is no distinction between the two. The legal title to sovereign power amongst the orthodox Mahomedans of the Soonee sect, rests upon the election of the chiefs or people ; but, as there are few Sovereigns who could bear to have their titles subjected to this test, much ingenuity has been exercised by lawyers to accommodate their system to modern usage. The accompanying opinions by the doctors of the Mahomedan college of Calcutta are a fair specimen of the kind of arguments which can be brought forward. There is no reason to suppose the opinions to be otherwise than sound and correct. It is customary to refer to the law officers of the Sudder Dewanny Adawlut, when a legal opinion is wanted ; but there is only one such officer now entertained in the court, and the post happens at the present time to be vacant. By referring to the college, the unanimous opinion of ten doctors has been obtained : some of them are very able men, and all of them are well informed on the subject.

It will be seen that the opinions given lead to the same result as was represented to Sir C. Napier, though there is no ground for the possible distinctions which were supposed to exist. The abdication of Meer Roostum is complete and irrevocable ; the assumption of the power by Meer Ali Moorad is also complete, and recognized by law.

J. THOMASON.

Questions and Answers respecting the legal effect of the transactions between Meer Roostum and Ali Moorad.

Ques. 1.—The ruler of a country died and left his country and forts to his sons. They divided the country and forts amongst them, and each obtained full possession of his own portion. After a time, one of the sons gave, and made over to his brother, his country, forts, and power. In this case, can the donor recall his gift of country, forts, and power?

Ans.—The donor cannot recall his gift, because, when he has once removed the country, and power, and forts, from his own control, and made them over to his brother, he is necessarily divested of all authority, and becomes one of the subjects of the state. Thus no option of recalling his gift remains. Such is ruled in the books, but God knows what is right.

Ques. 2.—What proof do you adduce that the ruler of a country cannot legally retract his gift to his brother, of his forts and country, and that he becomes thenceforward one of the subjects of the Government?

Ans.—There are two foundations of all authority and kingly power,—

1st. The consent of the nobles and chiefs to the supremacy of any one.

2nd. Obedience to his orders, in consequence of the establishment of his power and his supremacy. It is thus laid down in the Buhur-oor-rayik, in the chapter on Judicial Decrees, and in the Kazee Khan, in the chapter on Apostacy. "A king obtains his power by two means :—first, by consent to his accession, and this consent must be on the part of the nobles and chiefs of the nation ; and, secondly, by the obedience of the people to his orders, from fear of his power and superiority. But if men consent to his accession, and yet no obedience is paid to his orders, from his inability to enforce them, he does not become a king. If, on the other hand, he become king by common consent, and then turn oppressor, still, if his power and authority be confirmed, he cannot be deposed, for if sentence of deposition were passed, he would yet remain king by his power and strength, and the sentence would be ineffectual ; but, if he have no power and authority, then he would be deposed." Now, since in these troublous times discord is the common practice, and union is seldom procured, therefore the learned men of later times have agreed upon this, that in the present day, power and supremacy is the test of kingly authority. It is thus laid down in the Fatawa-i-Alumgiri and the Khuza-nutool-Mooftiem, in the chapter on Judicial Decrees, " and in our time authority depends on superiority; and we do not inquire whether kings be just or unjust, because all of them seek after temporal power."

It is gathered from the drift of the question, that the ruler in question was actually possessed of power and supremacy; and whereas he gave over to his brother his country and power and forts, and divested himself of his supremacy and dignity, with all their attendant circumstances and pomp, and made these over to the donee, it follows that this gift and transfer could not have been made, without the deposition of himself. Thus necessarily the donor becomes completely deposed, and this may be gathered from a remark of Hunavee upon a passage in the Ushbah. The passage in the Ushbah is to the following effect : " A king died, and the people consented to the succession of his minor son. It is necessary that the affairs of the administration be made over to a regent, and that this regent consider himself a dependent on the son of the king, on account of the superior rank of the latter. Now the son is the king ostensibly, but the regent is king in reality." Upon this passage Hunavee has remarked, " The object of this arrangement is to meet the necessity for a renewal of the administration after his coming of age, for this cannot (legally) take place, except when the ruler has effected his own deposition, because a king cannot (legally) be deposed, except by his own act."

The ruler who makes the transfer, and is thus deposed, becomes one of the subjects of the realm : and this is established by a passage in the Hedaya, on the resignation of a judge,—" On account of the resignation, the power reverts to the people, and therefore he no longer retains the option of recalling his resignation."

MOOHUMMED WUJEEB, *First Professor, Mahomedan College.*

MOHUMMUD BUSHIRUDDIN, *Second Professor, Mahomedan College.*

NOOROOLLUCK, *Third Professor, Mahomedan College.*

MAHUMMUD IBRAHIM, *Fourth Professor, Mahomedan College.*

ABDOORUHREM, *Professor of Indian Law and Regulations.*

GHOOLAM HOOSSEIN, *First Assistant.*

MAHUMMUD MUZHEER, *Second Assistant.*

HUBEEB-OOL-NUBBEE, *Third Assistant.*

UJEEB AHMUD, *Moulvee of the Law Examination Committee.*

HUMUD KUBEER, *Secretary to the College Committee.*

IV.

Sir C. Napier on conversations between himself and Major Outram.

Outram.—" Ali Moorad is by far the best of the Ameers. I wish you knew him. He is good looking, a frank open manner that you cannot help liking. I wish you could see him, you would be pleased with him. At first he was quite opposed to us, and would have made war against us if the other Ameers had joined him, however seeing it was of no use to oppose us, he joined the alliance with us, and is the only one who has never given us cause of complaint. I am sure you will like him."

Napier.—I believed all that Major Outram said as far as a certain point ; that is to say, that Ali Moorad was a superior description of barbarian ; but I had too much experience of barbarian chiefs to have much confidence in the best of them. They may be naturally very superior men, but the best of them is, and must be under control of the petty chiefs who surround them ; and however strong their own minds may be, the physical force which these petty chiefs command is too powerful to be resisted, and consequently, however naturally honest the great chief may be, you can never be sure of any engagement you enter into with him being fulfilled; unless that engagement involves the good wishes of the minor chiefs, or that you have power to force both him and them to a steady line of conduct. I therefore could not altogether confide in Major Outram's admiration of Ali Moorad: but it so far influenced me as to make me believe that he was the best among the Ameers of Kyrpoor to hold the rule in Upper Scinde.

Outram.—" The great agitator and cause of all opposition to the English is a scoundrel named Futteh Mohamed Ghoree. I have tried to catch this old villain, but he is such a cunning fox, that there is no discovering any fact which I can lay hold of. But allow me to put you on your guard against him, for he is the secret mover of all the breaches of treaty and insults that we have received from the northern Ameers: the Syud Mohamed Shurreef whom I caught with so much trouble was merely one of this old villain's emissaries."

Napier.—These observations of Major Outram, I considered as the result of long experience in the petty politics of Scinde. I scarcely knew Major Outram then, but his public character and position gave me a right to confide in his opinion. I therefore assumed upon his authority, that Ali Moorad was the man to look to, and Futteh Mohamed Ghoree, the man to be watched in any transactions I might have with the Ameers. *It is curious, that within a month or six weeks of this time, Ali Moorad being then Rais, and Futteh Mohamed Ghoree a prisoner, there was no term of abuse too strong in Major Outram's opinion for Ali Moorad! and the Major asked me to let Futteh Mohamed Ghoree loose! having himself before told me that this man ruled Meer Roostum; that he was the bitter enemy of the British, the most intriguing and dangerous man to our interests in all Scinde!* This dangerous man he would have had me let loose at the most critical juncture of affairs that ever existed between us and the Ameers; namely, at the moment of my return from Emaum Ghur, when I had summoned a general meet-

ing of the Ameers of Upper and Lower Scinde, personally
or by their vakeels, to discuss the new treaty : the question
of peace or war being in the balance ! Futteh Mohamed
ruled the majority of the Ameers of Kyrpoor, and yet
Major Outram wanted me to let him loose ! If Major
Outram wanted to secure our having war, such a step was
likely to accomplish it. I positively refused to agree to it,
and was in utter astonishment at Outram being so short-
sighted as to propose it, which he did at the request of
Meer Roostum !

Now let us consider how the elevation of Ali Moorad
to the Turban took place.

First, I will give two extracts from Major Outram's
letter to the Government of India, dated 21st April, 1842.

1st Extract. " Even were not right so clearly in Ali
Moorad's favour, I should have been loth to advise the attempt to dispossess him in favour of any other party of what
he now holds ; for it could only be done at the risk of considerable disturbance, Meer Ali Moorad being by far the most
powerful, influential, and able of all the Upper Scinde
Ameers ; on which account, so far from wishing to weaken
his power, I would consider it politic to strengthen him, at
least by our countenance and guarantee to such a degree as
will induce his assuming the chieftainship in Upper Scinde
without opposition on the demise of Roostum Khan."

2nd Extract. " My opinion is that it would be both just
and politic to support Meer Ali Moorad : the public recog-
nition of whom, and investiture with the Turban, by the
British representative when Meer Roostum dies, most probably would at once put an end to the intrigues of other
parties for that distinction; and at any rate Meer Ali
Moorad would not be likely to require further support, than
merely the countenance of the British Government. Whereas,
as he would not under any circumstances relinquish what he
deems his right, and is powerful enough to maintain his own
cause against the power of the other party, we should have to
support the latter with troops did we espouse their cause."

Major Outram here speaks of the death of Meer
Roostum, but his resignation of the Turban, whether to Ali

Moorad or to his son Hoossein Ali, was the same thing: it was the cessation of Meer Roostum's wear of the Turban.

My mind being imbued with the substance of this letter and Major Outram's conversations, made me accept with pleasure an invitation from his Highness Ali Moorad, to meet him at Roree. After some time had passed in general conversation in the Dhurbar, his Highness invited me to retire with him and his vakeel into a private apartment of the tent. Lieutenant Brown was with me, and the following conversation took place:

Ali Moorad.—" My brother Meer Roostum is about to give the Turban to his son Meer Mohamed Hoossein. By the laws of Scinde, if he dies, I inherit the Turban. If he abdicates he can only legally do so in my favour—he has no right to pass me over, and place the Turban on the head of my nephew. I am willing to obey him, but I will not allow him to give the Turban to any one else—what I want to know from you General, is, if we quarrel, do you mean to assist Meer Roostum or not? I am determined to assert my right. I have force enough to do so if you will be neuter, but at any rate—I am determined to maintain my right by force of arms whether you agree to it or not."

Sir C. Napier.—I will certainly give you assistance to take the Turban from your *nephew*, but not from your *brother*. By treaty we are obliged to support the Ameers in their respective rights, one against the other. My duty here is to maintain the treaties, and you may be sure of my doing so in your case in all lawful rights.

Ali Moorad.—" That is all I want. I wish my brother to keep the Turban, and I will obey him; but I will not allow him to give it to any one else.

" I have great affection for my elder brother. I am ready at all times to obey him, and I always have obeyed him, but he has become so weak and vacillating that if you go into his room and make any arrangement with him, however important it may be, he will change it all, if the next person that goes in thinks fit to propose another scheme. Now, as Futteh Mohamed Ghoree is always with him, and always making war upon me, I am obliged to defend myself, not against my brother but against Futteh Mohamed Ghoree, who controls him in every thing. I am determined not to let Futteh Mohamed wear the Turban, and I will not obey his orders. I am much stronger than my brother's family. I beat them lately in battle. Every body knows I can take the Turban if I choose by force, but I don't want it: I wish my brother to remain chief."

Embued by Major Outram with a good opinion of Ali Moorad, of whom all the English with whom I conversed at Sukkur held the same opinion, I gave credit to what he said, because I knew the mischievous character of Futteh Ghoree, and the imbecility of Roostum was proverbial. Soon after, a message arrived from Roostum, claiming my protection against the intrigues of his own family; this offered an opportunity of having one man to deal with, instead of a faction with which it was impossible for a civilized government to deal, and into whose intrigues, with due respect to Major Outram and his predecessors, I considered it undignified for a great government to enter, and from the first I determined not to enter into them. I was resolved, when there was a breach of treaty, whether great or small, I would hold *all* the Ameers responsible, and would not be played off like a shuttlecock, and told *this* was done by one Ameer, *that* by another, and so have a week's inquiry to find out who was responsible for aggression; for I at once saw, on arriving at Scinde, that this hide and seek, shifting responsibility, was the game which the Ameers had been playing. The proposal of Meer Roostum to come into my camp offered me an easy remedy for this evil, and having adopted the high opinion of Ali Moorad entertained by Major Outram, I had no hesitation in recommending his brother to seek his protection and be advised by him: but it must be borne in mind as a matter of first importance, and one upon which the gist of the thing depends, that, while advising Roostum to be guided by his brother, I, having suspicion, despite the high character given by Major Outram of Ali Moorad, that some intrigue *must* be going on, gave Meer Roostum not only the option of coming, but an invitation to come to my camp, and to put himself under my protection. I use the word *must*, because it is utterly impossible for me to believe that any Eastern divan can act without intrigue.

By my advice to Roostum, which was not given until asked, I offered to him the honourable and powerful protection of the British Government. This he did not choose to accept. He went to his brother, and then he fled from that brother with his usual vacillating imbecility, an imbecility I believe to have been, produced by his long habits of drunkenness; for he is said never to be sober after mid-day. That this flight was caused by Ali Moorad, as Major Outram affirms, I do not now believe. I have neither seen nor heard of any thing to make me believe it. He deceived Major Outram twice in the same manner, if not oftener. Thus, when he promised to meet Major Outram at Kyrpoor next morning, but walked off to the south with a large armed force and his treasure, he could not have been influenced by Ali Moorad, who was then far off with me in the desert. He had played me the same trick on my first arrival at Sukkur, long before there was any question of a new treaty and when Ali Moorad could have no interest to prevent our meeting.

When I heard he had resigned the Turban to Ali Moorad I disapproved of it, and Mr. Brown will recollect my sending Ali Moorad's vakeel back to him with this message. I even recommended him to return the Turban and act as his brother's Lieutenant. His answer was the deed had been executed in due form, before all the Moolahs or Priests, and it was impossible to alter it. I had nothing to reply. I had no business to interfere with the private arrangements of the Ameers. I was authorized to give advice when asked. I was obliged by existing treaties to give protection to any Ameer whose rights were invaded by another; but I was not called upon to originate a complaint when none was made to me, and especially in a case, which, whether originating or not in family intrigue, had a result so favourable to my own Government and useful to that of the Ameers. I therefore did not interfere between Ali Moorad and his brother. The proofs that he was voluntarily elected by Roostum were laid before me. I sought to have an acknowledgment that it was a voluntary act from Roostum's own lips, but he pertinaciously avoided meeting me; nor was Major Outram able to bring about a meeting afterwards. I believe it was his own family prevented the meeting; they were afraid he would confess to having voluntarily given up the Turban. Evidence of their complete power over him from beginning to end are not wanting in every transaction that I have had with him since I have been in Scinde.

As to Ali Moorad's conduct, I do not believe Major Outram can give proof of any thing he alleges against him; all his allegations are general, there is nothing specific. If the not joining his family in their breaches of treaty be betraying his family, it is clear that he has betrayed them; but I know of no other act of treason against them. Ali Moorad may be any thing Major Outram chooses to accuse him of being, but there must be something specific and accompanied by proof. I have heard of neither. We will even suppose, what I do not admit, though I suspected it at the time, that Ali Moorad bullied his brother into ceding the Turban and his estates; he, Ali Moorad, guaranteeing a due and dignified maintenance to Roostum. We will suppose this, and change the position of the individuals. Suppose Roostum an English gentleman of a large fortune, eighty-five years of age, perfectly imbecile, incapable of managing his estates. Ali Moorad is his legal heir; those who are not his heirs try to deprive him of his inheritance. What would the law of England do? I imagine it would give him the guardianship of the estate and of the old idiot, under certain restrictions. Well! what the law of England would have done for him Ali Moorad did for himself and by his own power!

However upon these matters Major Outram, or Major anybody, may form their own opinions, they are indifferent to me; but Major Outram had not a right to tell Sir George Arthur, that I had given power and riches to Ali Moorad, and had caused the war, because there is no foundation for such an erroneous assertion; and by giving his notes of a conversation with Meer Roostum and the other Ameers at Hydrabad, in which I am represented, and certainly by implication made to have forced Roostum into his brother's

power, and to the surrender of the Turban and all his territory, without accompanying such notes with my denial of
the circumstance, I do consider Major Outram to have acted
very unjustly towards me, if Major Outram did so; of which
however I have no proofs, except hearing of his notes being
in the hands of high and influential authorities without any
notice being taken of my contradiction. All this I am determined shall be cleared up.

V.

The falsehoods published by Outram, and ignorantly
repeated by Lord Jocelyn in the House of Commons, as to
Roostum's cession of the Turban, are peremptorily disposed of in the following letter written by Roostum to his
son at the time he resigned the Turban. It was only made
known in 1850 before a Commission appointed to inquire
into a charge against Ali Moorad. Roostum here acknow-
ledges that he was a free agent, for he speaks only of
persuasion not of force, and if he could have withheld any
territory he could have retained all.

Meer Roostum Khan, to Meer Mohamed Hoossein. 17th
Zekaght, 1258. A. D. 20th *December,* 1842.

[*After compliment*]—According to the written directions
of the General (Napier), I came with Meer Ali Moorad
to Dejee-ka-kote. The Meer above-mentioned said to me—
" Give me the Puggree (Turban of Rais) and your lands, and
I will arrange matters with the British! By the *persuasion*
of Meer Ali Moorad Khan I ceded my lands to him; but
your lands, or your brothers', or those of the sons of Meer
Moobarick Khan, I have not ceded to him; nor have I ceded
the districts north of Roree. An agreement to the effect,
that he will not interfere with those lands, I got in the hand-
writing of Peer Ali Gohur, and sealed by Meer Ali Moorad,
a copy of which I send with this letter for you to read.

Remain in contentment on your land, for your districts, those of your brothers, or of the heirs of Meer

Moobarick Khan (according to the agreement I formerly wrote for you), will remain as was written then, and Meer Ali Moorad cannot interfere in this matter.

Dey Kingree and Bashapore I have given to Peer Ali Gohur in perpetuity; it is for you to agree to it. My expenses and those of my household are to be defrayed by Meer Ali Moorad.

[*True Translation.*]   (Signed) JOHN YOUNGHUSBAND,
Lieutenant Scinde Police.

Sukkur, 14th May, 1850.

The letter, of which the above is a translation, was given to me by Meer Mohamed Hoossein.* It bears the seal of Meer Roostum.

(Signed) JOHN YOUNGHUSBAND.

Sir C. Napier to Ali Moorad, December 1842.

Meer Roostum Khan voluntarily went to your Highness's fortress of Dejee; he there publicly and formally placed the Turban on your head. He then wrote solemnly in the sacred Koran, that he had given to you the Turban of the Talpoors.

When I heard of these things, I asked permission to wait upon the Ameer, to speak with his Highness as to the new treaty, and to hear from his own lips that he had given up public affairs to your guidance. What was the course pursued by his Highness? He abandons your roof, he flies from me, he places himself at the head of those Ameers who have been intriguing against the English, and who have, as you inform me, collected bands for the purpose of resistance to the authority of the Turban. This is strange conduct in the Ameer. The only course for me to pursue is to advise your Highness publicly to proclaim to the Scindians, that you are the legitimate chief of the Talpoors; to call on the other Ameers to obey you as such and to dismiss their armed followers. If they refuse, I will disperse them by force. To

* Roostum's son.

W

those Ameers you will preserve their lands, but no fortress
shall be held in Upper Scinde but by your Highness's
Killedar.

To the same, January 14th, 1843.

I understand from Major Outram, that he thinks your
Highness has not clearly understood what has been inter-
preted to you, which makes me greatly regret not being
able to speak with your Highness myself, that I might
make myself understood by your Highness personally.
The next safe thing is to put my meaning into writing.
The Governor-General has ordered me to support your
Highness as the lawful possessor of the Turban. As Rais,
your Highness has certain privileges and certain lands,
which appertain, not to the individual, but to the Turban.
These must be given to you with the Turban, but the
rights and possessions of the other Ameers must be maintained, as prescribed in the draft of the new treaty; and
I endeavoured from the first to have it explained to your
Highness, that no portion of their estates can be transferred to
you. If they resist the arms of the Company in war, and if
a shot be fired by them at the troops under my command,
then I have orders to take all their estates, in the name of
the Company, and they would not be made over to your
Highness; at least such, in my belief, is the intention of the
Governor-General. I hope, therefore, that your Highness
will explain to your relations, what great loss of power and
territory would fall upon the Talpoor family, if any of them
commit hostilities upon the troops under my orders.

To the Governor-General in Council, August 16th, 1843.

By reference to my letters and proclamations, it will be
seen that I promised to preserve to all the Ameers their
rights. If Roostum had legally bestowed upon his brother
Ali Moorad, all his, Roostum's lands, I should have held
myself pledged to support that gift in the discussion of the
details of the treaty. If Meer Roostum had not done so, then

would his Highness in that discussion have rejected the claims of Ali Moorad, and I should have felt bound to support his Highness Meer Roostum. I more than once repeated to their Highnesses Ali Moorad and Roostum, that all should be supported in their rights and possessions. My letters and proclamations to this effect are before your Lordship in Council; but I never attended to the details of private transactions, the time for which had not arrived.

In one of the letters to Major Outram, I proposed, even after insult had been offered to me by the Ameer Roostum, to receive him with every honour and attention, whenever he pleased to come to my camp. From first to last, I sought a meeting with Meer Roostum. I made every effort to succeed. Once I sent Major Outram into the Ameer's camp, it was close to mine; he persuaded Outram that he was tired, and would not come. This was all a trick, as I well knew at the time. I was always baffled by the Ameer himself, not by the intrigues of Ali Moorad, as the Major believes, but, as I assert, by the Ameer himself, which finally changed the opinion I originally entertained, that Roostum's flight from Dejee was caused by his brother. I became satisfied that his flight was a voluntary act of the old Ameer's concocting. He is full of duplicity. This, subsequent events have proved. He fled in like manner from Outram.

By the above your Lordship and Council will perceive three important things:—

First. That I made every attempt to ascertain from the Ameer himself, whether or not he had voluntarily made over the Turban to his brother, and I was invariably foiled by the Ameer himself.

Secondly. That I considered the lands given over, exclusive of those belonging to the Turban, as a mere private transaction, with which my Government had then no concern; that it was an affair for after consideration in discussing the details of the treaty.

Thirdly. That I was, without a choice, obliged by treaty to acknowledge Ali Moorad. It was the Ameer Roostum, not I, that had given him the Turban. But I was very glad that it was so, for it was evident, that the Ameer Roostum's conduct made it almost impossible to negotiate with him. I could not trust him; and Major Outram, who was his personal friend, was duped by him.

It may be worth remarking, that before Meer Roostum made over his Turban and lands to Meer Ali Moorad at Dejee, he had placed all those lands and the forts in the hands of his son and out of his own power, (see his letter, a translation of which I enclose.) This shews that he was casting discord amongst his relations, for it is evident, that he had virtually made his son the Rais as Ali Moorad averred, and said he would not submit to it; all this shews the duplicity of this Prince.

To the same, September 29th, 1843.

In reply to your Lordship's letter of the 4th instant, I am again obliged to dissect Major Outram's letter. The sentence to which your Lordship refers is contained in the Major's letter of the 24th Jan. I shall take certain sentences and examine them:—

Major Outram.—" Assigning to Ali Moorad what has been pledged to him, viz. one-fourth of the remaining territory of Upper Scinde as his perquisite as Rais, besides one fourth as co-heir of the former sovereign, Meer Sohrab."

What has been pledged to Ali Moorad? By law Meer Ali Moorad became Rais. By law certain revenues are attached to the Turban. The laws of his family and country are pledged to him, and he is pledged to them to perform the duties of the chieftainship. I know of no other pledges.

When his Highness Meer Ali Moorad told me he would never interfere with his brother's chieftainship, he added, that he would not allow him to place the Turban on the head of his, Roostum's, son. " It is," said he, " either my brother's during his life, or mine if he chooses to resign it, but it cannot be placed on the head of my nephew. This shall not be, for I have force sufficient to prevent it; what I want to know is, whether you will interfere with me or not? " This is the substance of our conversation. My answer to the

Ameer was distinct. It admitted of no equivocation; it entered into no treaty; it gave no pledge. The substance was—" By the existing treaties of 1839, the British Government is bound to support the Ameers in their rights. You have a right to the Turban; the existing treaty obliges me to support you, and I will support you."

Your Lordship will perceive that I merely assured his Highness that I would support the treaty, and this assurance was in a casual conversation. But Major Outram's words imply that some treaty had been entered into by me with Ali Moorad, and, as I know nothing beyond what I have stated above, I must leave it to Major Outram to explain his own meaning.

Major Outram.—" And as you are bound, I understand, to make good to Ali Moorad his share."

I know not what Major Outram understood, or did not understand, but I was bound to nothing, neither to Ali Moorad, nor any other Ameer.

With regard to the claim of Ali Moorad to part of the territory ceded to Bhawalpore, all that passed between me and his Highness here follows :—

Conversing during the march to Emaum Ghur, the Ameer told me that he possessed one or two villages in the midst of the territory ceded to Bhawalpore, but he added, throwing up his head, " they are trifling things, and the Governor-General is welcome to them." I replied, " if your Highness has any possessions in that territory the Governor-General has not been aware of it, and when the details are arranged any loss of this kind will be made good to you. The new draft treaty does not contemplate depriving your Highness of any part of your possessions." This is all that passed, and as nearly as I can recollect, the interpretation was in the above words. It is not impossible that a similar conversation may have passed more than once between Sheik Ali Hoossein (Ali Moorad's vizier) and myself; indeed, I am sure this must have been the case, for I find a pencil memorandum on Outram's letter, saying, that the moonshee, Ali Ackbar, informed me that the village, or pergunnah, in question, was in value from 40 to 50,000 rupees; and the Secretary of

Government, Mr. Brown, informs me he thinks the value does not amount to more than 30,000 rupees at the utmost.

Major Outram.—" By a late treaty."

What treaty Major Outram alludes to I know not. I have already said that *treaty, pledge, or promise*, entered into by me, *there has been none*. I know that before I arrived in Scinde, Meer Ali Moorad and his family were at war ; a battle had been fought, in which he defeated his brother Roostum and the rest of his family. Roostum, I believe, gave himself up to Ali Moorad on the field of battle. The general opinion that I heard at the time I arrived was, that Meer Roostum and his family had behaved ill to Ali Moorad. However, the latter made it up with his brother on the field of battle, and some family compact may then have been entered into, but that such was the case I do not know, nor did I ever hear that any such compact had taken place. I have been driven to this conjecture in my endeavour to account for Major Outram's expression, " *By a late treaty.*"

Finally, my Lord, I never gave, or promised, a farthing of money or an inch of land to his Highness Ali Moorad, although Major Outram seems to think, from his letters, and from what I have since heard of his conversations at Bombay, that I piled riches and power upon the Ameer ! I made him one present, it was an elephant; your Lordship confirmed the gift ; and to shew your Lordship how very cautious I have ever been in giving what is not my own property, I took a pledge from his Highness that if your Lordship disapproved of my giving the elephant, he was to pay for it, for as I take no presents I am too poor to make them myself. Ali Moorad's conduct appears to have been loyal from first to last, both to his family and to the British Government. It is obvious that this was his interest, but with his motives we have nothing to do. The fact has been as I state, and had the Talpoors been ruled by the advice of his Highness they would now have been in the full enjoyment of their sovereignty.

VI.

TOUCHING OUTRAM'S NOTES OF CONFERENCES WITH THE
AMEERS.

[The notes are to be found in the Parliamentary Papers on
Scinde; the substance has been given in the narrative of
Outram's diplomacy at Hydrabad.]

The Governor-General to the Secret Committee,
June 13th, 1843.

These notes I never read until I saw them to-day. I
know absolutely nothing of what may have passed between
Major Outram and the Ameers, while he was acting as
Commissioner under Sir C. Napier for the settlement of the
details of the treaty, to which the Ameers had generally
given their assent.

Sir C. Napier to the Governor-General.

Hydrabad, July 11th, 1843.

I have to acknowledge the receipt of your Lordship's
letter, dated 14th ultimo, which arrived here yesterday,
inclosing notes of conversations held by Major Outram with
the Ameers, and with their vakeels, between the 8th and 13th
February last.

The notes of the meeting with the Ameers, on the 12th
of February, were probably sent to me, but I did not receive
them.

The notes of the meeting on the 8th February, I received
on the 11th; these I could not forward to your Lordship,
because, after the 13th, our communications were intercepted; but the enclosed copy of a letter to Major Outram
shews that I intended to do so, although I did not think it
necessary, as we were on the eve of a battle, which I knew
could not take place if the Ameers were honest and spoke the
truth. After the action, the Ameers placed my small force

in so much danger, by their intrigues with Meer Shere Mohamed, that I never thought more of Outram's " minutes," till I received your Lordship's present letter.

Recurring to that period : as it seems that Major Outram has sent his statement to the Government, it is incumbent on me to shew what weight was due to his judgment on that occasion ; and what weight also was due to the assertions of the Ameers, that they wanted to keep the peace with us ; for upon their sincerity depends any value which may be supposed to attach to their conversations with Outram.

I shall, for the present, confine my remarks to the period between the 8th and 12th of February.

Major Outram had been deceived by the Ameers. On the 10th and 11th February, he sent two letters to me, following each other, by express; these letters contained three important things :—

1. A request that I should halt the troops.

2. A request that I should go in person to Hydrabad.

3. The information that the Ameers had dispersed all their troops.

Now, my Lord, it so happened, that the moment when Major Outram wrote the above, 25,862 fighting men were, a portion of them strengthening their position at Meeanee, about six miles off, and the others were round Major Outram's house, preparing to attack it.

Ten thousand men of the Chandia tribe had crossed the river, and were coming down the left bank of the Indus, in my rear ; 7000 of Meer Roostum's men were within thirty miles, in rear of my left flank at Khoonhera, and were about to march on Meeanee ; 10,000, under Shere Mohamed, were marching from Meerpoor ; and in the mountains on the right bank of the Indus, thousands more were preparing to come ; so that I had, as my spies correctly stated, 25,000 men in my front, and 25,000 more marching upon me in all directions, and these without reference to the tribes gathering in the hills, and all these, as the Ameers affirmed to Major Outram, perfectly beyond their control. Yet Major Outram sent me two letters in one day, to assure me that the Ameers had dismissed all their troops, and asked me to let him give them a pledge that I would not march. Thus, in a most perilous position, would the Major's advice have completely shackled my movements, and placed my small army beyond the power of being saved, except by a miracle.

In examining the foregoing facts, let me draw your Lordship's attention to two very important points :—

1. That the Ameers did not want to have peace, that they were confident of victory, and had accurately calculated the day I should arrive at Meeanee, namely the 17th February ; that they knew that they could not assemble their full force of 50,000 men, till the night of the 17th or the morning of the 18th of February. Therefore all their diplomacy of dissimulation, procrastination, and protestation, was put in force to deceive Major Outram and obtain a pledge that I should halt, if only for a day. I think he would have so pledged himself, had I not positively forbidden him to give any pledge without my consent.

That this was the real motive of the anxiety exhibited by the Ameers to suspend my march, if only for a day, is made more apparent by the fact that there was no advantage to be gained by delaying the signature of the draft Treaty. On the contrary, to sign this draft would enable the Ameers at once to discuss and formally to protest against any and every part of it, while it would relieve them at once from the presence of our troops ; but they were confident of victory, and wanted to fight. There were 25,000 men to be obtained by one day's delay in my arrival at Meeanee ; and if the Ameers could have gained a week, it would have brought us into the hot season, which they thought would paralyze my movements, and finally destroy the troops— they were in a great measure right.

2. Had I been persuaded to believe in the jesuitical protestations of the Ameers, I should have betrayed the British arms.

Now, my Lord, when I considered these matters, I saw that I could place no faith in the truth of the Ameers. Their "conversations" (Outram's) appeared to me to be so much waste-paper.

But this was not all. Outram had asked me seriously to go to Hydrabad alone, and recommended me to send my troops to Meerpoor. My throat would have been cut, of course; and the troops having lost their General, and having been removed forty miles from their line of communication, viz. the Indus, would have been placed as follows:—

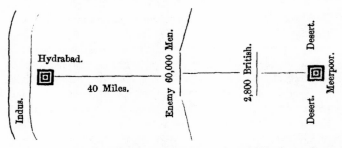

From this position they would very quickly have been pushed into the desert, and there every soul must have perished; even victory could not have saved them, they could never have regained the river, harassed by a repulsed but hourly increasing force for forty miles, a force more than twenty times their own numbers before the battle.

As Major Outram seems to have forwarded his notes, I think he ought also to have forwarded my denial of Meer Roostum's assertions.

This does not appear to have been done, so I take the liberty of sending herewith a copy of my letter; being indeed the same letter in which I acknowledged the receipt of the conversation with the Ameers on the 8th of February.

Though much harassed by the unavoidable labour, which attaches to the command of a young and inexperienced force suddenly assembled, I am not aware that I left anything unreported to your Lordship that I considered of importance; but, in case of accident, I have all my letters to the Ameers copied, as well as my proclamations, together with any letters to Major Outram, which bear on the subject; indeed, I believe, all I have do so. These will enable your Lordship to shew the English Government, that I did

all but sacrifice the honour of our arms to maintain the
peace, for which I believe that both your Lordship and
myself were as anxious as Major Outram or any other
person."

The Governor-General in Council to Sir C. Napier.

Calcutta, August 7th, 1843.

We have all read with the greatest interest your Excellency's letter of the 11th ult., communicating certain
explanations, with respect to your correspondence with
Major Outram immediately before the battle of Meeanee,
and with respect to the position of your army at that period.

We cannot but feel that it is to your penetration and
decision your army owes its safety.

Major Outram's confidential letter to you, of the 11th of
February, he had intended to send by a servant of Meer
Roostum, who was then betraying him by a false statement
of his force at Khoonhera; yet that letter contained a suggestion, which, if communicated to Meer Ali Moorad, might
have added him to the confederacy against us.

On the 15th of February, Major Outram observed, that
his despatches of the last few days would have led you to
expect, that his earnest endeavours to effect an amicable arrangement with the Ameers of Scinde would fail; yet, on the
previous day, the Ameers had affixed their seals to the
treaty, a proceeding usually viewed in the light of an amicable arrangement, or at least, an arrangement intended to
preclude hostilities, not immediately as in this case to pre-
cede them.

Sir C. Napier to the Governor-General.

Hydrabad, July 13th, 1843.

I was much vexed at myself for not having sent Major
Outram's notes of his interview with the Ameers, because I
received them on the 11th of February, and the post was
open to the 13th, as I find, by a long letter written to your
Lordship on that day.

We were all hard-worked at the time, and I recollect thinking that, as a battle would take place, or peace be made in a few days, (if Major Outram's assertions were correct,) the face of affairs would change. I therefore delayed sending this paper, till I heard of the Ameers having signed the draft treaty. I had however made preparations for sending the notes of Outram's meeting to your Lordship, for I have just found among my papers, a copy of that paper prepared for transmission to your Lordship, and with it I find my private notes made on reading it. I had by that time discovered, that there was a party resolved to support the Ameers through thick and thin.

I received Outram's notes on the 11th, I must have made these notes that evening. The copy, occupied as every one was, could hardly have been ready before the evening of the 12th. I required much time each of those days to be alone in uninterrupted reflection, upon the conflicting information sent me by Major Outram, and the reports of my spies. It was impossible to "*jump at conclusions.*" Major Outram's character and local experience, gave great weight to his assertions, yet they were diametrically opposed to the statements of the scouts. The fate of the force, perhaps much more, depended on my decision ; few men could go through more anxiety than I did during those days, lest disgrace should fall on the British arms through my agency. The papers found on the Murree chiefs, and their arrest, had occupied all the 12th nearly, and decided my opinion. There remained little doubt of the way in which Outram had been duped. I thought it essential that the copies of the letters found on the Murree chief Hyat Khan should be sent to your Lordship, in case of any misfortune befalling the troops. I still hoped for the promised treaty, and must have intended to send that and the notes on the interview together. On the 14th all communication was at an end, and my whole time occupied by preparations for meeting the enemy, endeavouring to ascertain where he was, what were his intentions, our proper direction of march, for our guides were either treacherous or frightened to death. The Ameers and their falsehoods passed from my head ; their

armies alone occupied my attention. The march upon an
enemy of such force, was alone so engrossing, that really if
I had thought these papers important, which I neither did,
nor do now, I could not have attended to them. If they
produce annoyance, or throw difficulties in your Lordship's
way, very deeply do I regret that I forgot to send them
after the battle.

The Governor-General in Council, to the Secret Committee,
August 14th, 1843.

Sir C. Napier has entered at some length into a justifi-
cation of his proceedings previous to the battle of Meeanee.
In doing this, he has placed upon our records a mass of most
curious and interesting matter, which we regret that it was
not in our power to lay before you at an earlier period. We
strongly feel that it was to Major-General Sir C. Napier's
penetration and decision that our army owed its safety; and
we are astonished at the extent to which Major Outram
suffered himself to be deluded by the Ameers.

We transmit for your consideration, certain memorials
which the ex-Ameers have addressed to us from Scinde; but
we consider it unnecessary to make any observations upon
them. Sir C. Napier's indignant refutation of the calumnious charges brought against himself and the gallant troops
whom he commands, will be sufficient to satisfy you that the
Ameers are without truth.

Remarks on Letter from the ex-Ameers Roostum Khan and
Nusseer Khan of Kyrpoor to the Rt. Hon. Sir Robert
Peel, dated 17th August, 1844.

THE AMEERS WRITE—

"In the meantime Mr. Ross Bell was appointed Resident and arrived at Sukkur, part of our kingdom, and aided
my younger brother, Meer Ali Moorad, in seizing four or
five inhabited villages of my country, which I had presented
to my nephew Meer Nusseer Khan."

REMARKS.

On the division of Upper Scinde by the deceased Meer Sohrab Khan, he, to prevent future disputes, wrote in his Koran, detailing exactly the shares of his three sons, Meers Roostum, Moobarick, and Ali Moorad Khan. By this deed the villages alluded to were granted to Ali Moorad Khan. During the minority of this Meer the villages were by deceit taken possession of by his brothers in 1838. Ali Moorad assembled a force to recover the villages he had been unjustly deprived of. Roostum Khan persuaded him to disband his force, solemnly promising by writing in the Koran to cause the restoration to Ali Moorad of the villages. This promise Roostum Khan broke. On the British troops being located in Scinde the matter in dispute was, according to treaty, submitted to the Political Agent, Mr. Ross Bell, who after due enquiry adjudged the case in favour of Ali Moorad. That decision has been approved of and confirmed by the Rt. Honourable the Governor-General of India.

(Signed)   E. J. BROWN,
Secretary to Scinde Government.

THE MEERS WRITE—

" After about seven days, on the 16th of Zil Kadur, 1257 Hegira, Captain Brown came to Kyrpoor, and said, ' If you agree to seal the treaty good ; if not, the English army, which is now at Pultun, near Roree, will march on Kyrpoor to-morrow and plunder it.' Under this threat he compelled me to seal (sign) the new treaty ; he also told me I was to be guided in all parts of my conduct by the advice of my younger brother, Ali Moorad, which I would find for my advantage."

REMARKS.

There is not one word of truth in this. I was deputed on the occasion referred to by Major-General Sir C. Napier to take a letter to Meer Roostum and Nusseer Khan at Kyrpoor, calling on them to give a direct answer whether they would sign the new treaty, which had previously been offered for their acceptance. They detained me more than two hours, endeavouring to persuade me to enter into a discussion of the details of the treaty. I gave them but one answer throughout, viz. that I had no authority to enter into any such discussion, that I was the bearer of a letter to them, and that I required their reply, yes or no — and that if they would not give it I should leave for Sukkur without it. They eventually gave me a reply stating their willingness to sign the treaty.

I need hardly remark that at this period no British troops had passed the Indus from Sukkur. Ali Moorad's name was not once mentioned in the conversation.

(Signed)   E. J. BROWN,

Secretary to Scinde Government.

VII.

OUTRAM'S DIPLOMACY.

Sir C. Napier to the Governor-General.

Hydrabad, July 3rd, 1843.

A private letter from Bombay informs me that a letter received from * * *[a], says he " considered the destruction of Emaum Ghur, as a more flagitious act than the attack upon the Residency."

As nothing would give me more pain than having done anything which might expose your Lordship to attack, it is necessary for me to furnish proofs that I have not done so.

1. Emaum Ghur, with all other fortresses in Upper Scinde, belonged to the Turban, or " Rais."

2. His Highness Ali Moorad was Rais by the law of Scinde, and Meer Mohamed was in rebellion against him.

3. His Highness accompanied me to Emaum Ghur. On our arrival, he proposed to destroy the fortress, but afterwards seemed doubtful whether he would do so or not.

[a] Name unknown.

I wrote to his Highness to convince him of the necessity of that measure.

4. He consented, and I enclose to your Lordship his Highness's reply, authorising me to destroy Emaum Ghur.

5. His Highness himself fired some of the guns, and once or twice threw shells into the fort, so that I was fully borne out in what I did by the owner of the fortress. I could legally have done the same thing under the like sanction in the middle of England, and this without adverting to the breaches of treaty and preparations for war everywhere carrying on by the Ameers against us.

Another charge against me I find to be, that my " continued march upon Hydrabad, in despite of the advice of Major Outram, was that which forced the Ameers to war." I certainly did reject Major Outram's advice, because I soon saw that he was grossly deceived by the Ameers. I had several proofs of this, one or two of which I now feel it right to state to your Lordship.

1. Major Outram, being at Hydrabad, sent me two (three my journal says, but I can find but two) despatches by express, on the 12th, to assure me that the Ameers had not any armed men except their usual personal attendants, and that these were not more numerous than Indian Princes of their rank would move with in time of profound peace. At that moment the army of the Ameers was assembled at Meeanee, only six miles from Hydrabad, and were preparing their position! At the moment he was writing these despatches to me, his house was surrounded by 8000 Beloochees (who had eight pieces of cannon) preparing for their attack on him, the 15th February.

2. Major Outram wrote to ask me to go to Hydrabad alone to meet the Ameers.

3. He proposed my sending my troops to Meerpoor.

Had I allowed myself to be guided by Major Outram, my own throat and his, and the throats of all with us, would probably have been cut, and the army left without a leader at Meerpoor, forty miles from the river, which formed our line of communication by steam with Sukkur and Bombay, and with the friendly territory of his Highness Ali Moorad which extended south as far as Nowshera: when thus isolated, the army would have been attacked by 60,000 men, pushed back upon the desert, and there have miserably perished.

As Major Outram had lived many years at the Court of Hydrabad, and every one spoke of his " great local knowledge of the Ameers, and of this country," while I was a perfect stranger to both, I might well have been excused (supposing anything can excuse a general officer for losing an army) had I allowed myself to have been guided by Major Outram; and his advice was pressed upon me with all the zeal inspired by honesty of purpose, added to an ardent disposition. But my spies brought me intelligence that 30,000 men were in my front; some said 40,000. I concluded that these spies exaggerated numbers, but it was clear to my mind that the Beloochees were above 20,000 men, and in sufficient numbers to make them believe that their victory would be certain. Therefore I argued that Major Outram's report was wrong, that he was deceived, and ignorant of what was passing about him. His proposal to march the troops to Meerpoor, made me think he understood very little of war; I therefore paid no attention to his suggestions. I put all my sick and treasure on board a steamer, and resolved to attack the enemy; if we were beaten we had plenty of provisions, and with our backs to the river and the steamers, (for retreat would have been disastrous,) I would have entrenched myself till reinforcements arrived. I had full confidence in the troops, and little feared an undisciplined multitude; but still the game was not an easy one, and I have shewn that, had I taken Outram's advice, as I am reproached for not having done, a second Cabool massacre would probably have taken place.

One would have imagined that the attack on the Residency would have, at least, opened Outram's eyes to the treachery of the characters he had to deal with. Not a bit; he joined me on the 16th at Muttaree, and still wanted me to delay my attack for a day! yet, six hours' delay would have added 24,000 men to the forces of the Ameers at Meeanee. It is true I had no positive information of this at

x

the moment; but I was sure of it from the letter I found on the Murree chief, Hyat Khan, whom I had seized. In this letter the Ameers pressed the Murrees to join on the 9th. Now, I knew these barbarians would not leave their villages while the feast of the Moharem lasted, it was to finish on the 11th, and therefore I guessed how fast they would gather after that day, and resolved not to lose an hour. If my conduct be attacked in the House of Commons, I think the foregoing statement will be sufficient defence. I am not conscious of having erred in rejecting Major Outram's advice.

Outram's answer will be, " there would not have been war." The Ameers answered this on the 15th; but suppose not; was I to place the army at their mercy, to spare or destroy as they pleased? Their mercy! I have it in proof, that about the time Major Outram kept assuring me of their pacific feelings and disposition towards us, they had sent orders along both banks of the Indus to their people, " to kill every Englishman, woman and child, they could lay their hands upon." We should have received the tender mercies of the Affghans in the Tezeen Pass,—the mercy which Outram would have received himself but for my forebodings, and sending him the light company of the 22nd regiment.

Meer Ali Moorad to Sir C. Napier. January 12th, 1843.

I have received your letter pointing out several reasons why you think it would be better to blow up Emaum Ghur. As far as the value of the property goes, I am quite indifferent; and I fully concur with you in the reasons which make it necessary to destroy it. Therefore, considering me joyfully willing, by all means blow up the fort and consider me always your well-wisher.

VIII.
Sir C. Napier to Major Outram.

Hydrabad, 22nd July, 1843.

My dear Outram,

1. Before I proceed to discuss other things, I shall begin by observing, that in one of your letters, you twice remark,

that you had only received a short note from me. Now the
only letters which I have received of yours which I have not
answered, are those dated the 8th and 29th of March; the
first (with a letter from Lady Napier about the same date,
and yours describing your visit to Mahabuleshwar,) I only
received a few days ago!!! so it is idle to refer to any
letters but those actually received.

2. I could not reply to your letter dated 20th, sooner;
that of the 29th, reached me as I was going out against
Shere Mohamed; that of the 8th, I have only had a few
days. If I had not a sincere regard for you, I should have
no anxiety at all! However, I shall state all that has passed,
and you must judge how far you consider yourself right or
wrong. I am placed in a situation where in my own defence
I am obliged to state all that passed between the 3rd and
12th of February. I am attacked both in public papers and
private letters, and I am accused of forcing on the war, because I did not allow myself to be advised by you to halt,
but am said to have attacked the Ameers after they had
signed the treaty; and about four days ago I had a letter
from Lord Ellenborough, saying that he had received from
the Secret Committee, printed notes of conversations between
you as Commissioner, and the Ameers, and asking if I had
ever heard of these conversations; and expressing his surprise at now hearing of them for the first time. At the
same time private letters have said that I am supposed to
have intercepted reports made by you, and which ought to
have gone to the Governor-General.

3. How these notes came into the hands of the Secret
Committee I do not know, nor do I the least care; but the
results are these :—*First*. That Lord Ellenborough evidently
attaches importance to them; and as I never sent them to
him, I appear, till he gets my explanation, as if I concealed
what passed from his Lordship for the purpose of forcing the
Ameers to battle. *Second*. That Sir George Arthur also
attaches importance to these papers, in consequence of his
conversation with you and their own contents, for he sent
them to Lord Fitzgerald. *Third*. That the Secret Committee attach importance to these notes because they have

not only sent them to Lord Ellenborough, but caused them to be printed! My position has therefore this appearance, that I intercepted most important papers, which, had they reached Lord Ellenborough, might have prevented the war; or, that even if I had been induced by your advice to halt and act differently from the way in which I did act, the war would not have broken out; and worse, (if any thing can be worse,) that I betrayed Lord Ellenborough who had placed unbounded confidence in me, and given me the utmost possible support in every way. This was the position in which the letters from Lord Ellenborough and Sir G. Arthur must have placed me in my own and their opinion, and this the position in which the printing of those notes, if they become public, must place me in the opinion of the world. Now it is quite clear that if such was the state of the case, I might perhaps be allowed to lay claim to courage, and to some degree of military skill, because success will generally give a man so much credit; but assuredly I could never pretend to honour, to humanity, or to be trusted with the slightest diplomatic transaction: in short, I should deservedly be execrated as a resolute scoundrel, who had sacrificed every thing to military glory, and turned a deaf ear to the supplicating cry of injured and betrayed Princes. This would be my position in face of the public, supposing that there be a word of truth in the whole story. That there is not, it was necessary to shew to Lord Ellenborough and my friends.

4. I therefore directly answered Lord Ellenborough thus. *Firstly.* That I had only received *two* of the conversations, and I believed that the third had been intercepted. *Secondly.* I sent him the copy of those notes, prepared on purpose to send to his Lordship with the probable reasons why they were not. *Thirdly.* I forwarded to his Lordship your demi-official letters, between the 8th and 13th of February, (first examining them to see that they contained nothing private.) *Fourthly.* I told him that my reasons for not halting were, that I knew the assertions contained in those conversations to be false as respected anything I had done, especially Roostum's assertion, that I had made him give himself up to Ali Moorad; and that I thought, when you shewed that

assertion to Sir G. Arthur, you should also have shewn him my contradiction of it, (perhaps you did?) *Fifthly.* That your wanting me to halt, and twice in one day and once in another, telling me the Ameers had dispersed their forces, when I knew they had not, convinced me you were deceived by the Ameers; that your wanting me to go to Hydrabad without my army added another proof to my conviction that they had deceived you, and finally, that your proposing to me to march to Meerpoor completed the proofs. *Sixthly.* That the important letter I found on the Murree chief Hyat Khan, coupled with my secret intelligence and a comparison with the Ameers' anxiety that I should halt, proved to me, past all hesitation or doubt, that they were only trying to gain a day or two, that they might bring 50,000 men to Meeanee instead of 25,000: our subsequent knowledge of events leaves this a matter of history. Therefore, had I halted I should have lost the army, unless saved by a miracle; and if the force had marched to Meerpoor and lost its line of communication with the Indus, it would equally have been destroyed. Now you, a Major, without much experience of war, may well be excused such errors; but I as an experienced General officer could have no excuse, and should be very justly condemned. For these reasons I stand acquitted for not attending to your advice. *Finally.* I have told his Lordship my reason for being silent, and not keeping him informed on these matters with that exactness which I did on all others. The reason was, I thought it would injure you in his Lordship's opinion; and that I was anxious to avoid. Afterwards I gave that up, because it was evidently out of the question; so that when, not long ago, he wrote to tell me he heard you were going to apply for employment again in Scinde, I told his Lordship I was sure you were not going to apply, for that our ideas of the politics in Scinde were so adverse, that our working together was impossible.

Now, my dear Outram, whether it has been you or your friends that have pushed this matter ahead, I know not; but it has been done, and I necessarily have defended and will defend my conduct. " *It has been done,*" as * * * * * * * * * * * * * * * * very justly says in a letter to me, speaking of the attacks of the press, " *to attack Lord Ellen-borough through you.*" All this has passed within a few days, except the attacks upon me in the papers (especially the *Bombay Times*). They have long been at work, but I did not condescend to defend myself against them, nor indeed had I time.

Having now told you all that has passed, I shall refer to your letter dated 20th March. You are angry that Lord Ellenborough did not thank you for your exertions during the short time you were Commissioner; and you say you are sure I reported to him all your exertions. My answer is that I did no such thing. I studiously avoided mentioning your name to Lord Ellenborough, as I was well aware that my appointing you Commissioner was contrary to his opinion : from all you had told me I judged this. You were not his selection, and I have heard that he was surprised at hearing that the papers, without contradiction, held you up as having powers in Scinde. If any one had to thank you it was me, and I did so in my despatch. As to your political exertions they failed; my advance is said to be the cause of that failure; to thank you for them would have been to condemn myself. Now I entirely differed with you except in your wish to prevent blood being shed. We even there differed in our motive; I did it from humanity alone, thinking the war policy of Lord Ellenborough perfectly just; you wished to keep the peace because you thought the policy unjust, and, as you said to me, " every drop of blood shed you thought was murder." Of course, in despite of such feelings, you exerted yourself as you were bound to do after accepting the office; but I confess I see nothing in that which particularly calls for public thanks! Suppose that the Ameers had made peace, and no battle taken place, should I have thanked you, or expected Lord Ellenborough to thank *me ?* Certainly not; I should have expected no such thing; my view of thanks is that they are only to be given for great success in battle, or for a long series of brilliant civil service. I confess I cannot see how it casts the slightest reflection upon you; but I think your wishing to moot the question is injudicious. I did all I could to avoid the question being brought forward;

but it has now been done, and we must both abide the public
judgment, for assuredly I never will allow it to be even
hinted at without a flat contradiction that I led Lord Ellenborough into error—that I deceived him, that I was unequal
to the high position in which her Majesty had placed me as a
General officer. Even the affection of a brother should by me
be swept away in a question involving my honour and military
character: if you were wrong it was an error of judgment;
if I was wrong it was either a criminal sacrifice to a thirst of
military glory, or a total ignorance of my profession.

This brings me to another matter. The violence of a
party against Lord Ellenborough at Bombay, leads it I hear,
to say I made my promised account of the defence of the
Residency, and that Lord Ellenborough " burked it." This
is false, I did mean to make it, and I do mean to make it,
but I never said when, nor can I *now!* I have not time to
devote *at least* two days to make a good dissertation on the
defence of outposts, and give the Residency as an example in
all its details. You know the heat here, and that the operations I have carried on, military and civil, since the capture
of Hydrabad, preclude all work which is not absolutely necessary, but I nevertheless do mean to write the essay on the
defence of the Residency when I *can.*

I assure you that this business of defending my conduct
has given me more pain and annoyance than anything that
has happened to me in Scinde.

Believe me to be, my dear Outram,

Yours truly,

(Signed)   C. J. NAPIER.

I beg of you not to mistake me; I neither do nor have a
right to object to your defending both the cause of the
Ameers and your own exertions; nor am I at all worried at
any one else defending them. I only mean to say that *I must
defend myself;* and if the public take a different view, if
it pronounces that you were deceived, it has not been my
doing, but that of those who have placed me on my
defence.*

* Outram's reply to this letter caused Sir C. Napier to renounce his
friendship.

IX.

Sir C. Napier's Observations on the Ameers' Memorials.

Hydrabad, June 12, 1843.

The complaints of the Ameers form a tissue of false-hoods. I will answer them seriatim, meeting assertion by assertion, for to send documentary proofs would take up a volume.

1. Complaint of Meer Mohamed Khan.

The Ameer may have, and did acquiesce in, and I believe signed all the treaties with the English; and in common with the other Ameers violated their provisions. The Ameers formed one Government, and must be responsible collectively. The proofs of their violations of treaties are in the hands of the Governor-General, signed by Major Outram.

The Ameer says he submitted to the draft treaty. This is exposed by the answers to three plain questions :—

First Question. Who solemnly signed the new treaty in full Dhurbar?

Answer. Meer Mohamed Khan.

Second Question. Who attacked the residence of my Commissioner, (sent in the sacred character of diplomatist,) with the intention to massacre the said diplomatist and all that were with him?

Answer. Meer Mohamed Khan.

Third Question. Who, in full Dhurbar, insultingly tore the signed treaty to atoms, the treaty to which the traitor had affixed his name and seal, for the purpose of blinding the diplomatist and securing his destruction?

Answer. Meer Mohamed Khan.

" None of the Ameer's servants went by orders to fight," but they did fight, and our comrades were slain by those servants. I utterly disbelieve the fact, that he did not order his servants to fight, but he was bound to prevent his troops from fighting against his ally: as he did not do this he must take the consequence.

The falsehoods stated against Lieutenant Brown and Major McPherson, are answered by those officers with the truth and simplicity becoming English gentlemen. Colonel Pattle is away.

Does the Ameer suppose, that when he and his compeers had received their just punishment by force of arms, the lost lives of our soldiers and the cost of the war were to be cast out of sight as matters of no value, and their traitorous Highnesses be allowed to keep all their forfeited treasures? Assuredly not!

The Ameer proceeds, "I have spent my life in serving the Government." I deny the assertion : I refer to Major Outram's letter to Sir John Keane; I refer to Major Outram's book; I refer to a mass of documents against the Ameers that I forwarded to Lord Ellenborough, which were delivered to me as authentic by Major Outram and verified by his signature.

2. Meer Sobdar's complaint.

I always thought Meer Sobdar was a faithful ally. He was greatly favoured by the new draft treaty, and his position among the Ameers raised by the increased revenue he would have received; but the cloven foot of duplicity and cowardice was soon displayed. His Highness' vakeel, named Outrai, met me on the march to the south; he assured me of his master's good wishes; that he would send 5,000 men into battle with the other Ameers, and on a signal turn and traitorously fall upon those troops, while I was so to arrange it, that my soldiers were not to attack those of his Highness. The wretched duplicity of such conduct was disgusting. Had the force that I commanded been worsted in battle, Sobdar's 5,000 men would have been fresh, unattacked and untouched during the combat, and they would mercilessly have cut the British up, to clear themselves from the charge of treason to their friends if secrets should transpire. If, on the other hand, we were victorious, no doubt the troops of Meer Sobdar would have fulfilled his engagements by the merciless slaughter of his flying countrymen. My answer to this insidious and abominable proposition, was, " Tell your master, that my army has no fear of the Beloochees, and does not need the aid of traitors. I consider his Highness as our good ally, and, as a friend, advise him to keep his soldiers in Hydrabad, for if I should meet his 5,000 men in the field of battle, I would assuredly fall upon them." His Highness sent 4,800 men into the field at Meeanee, where they fought us manfully.

The Ameer Sobdar says, " no sepoy in my service fought in the recent battle by my orders." This hypocritical quibbling is of a piece with that of the Ameer Mohamed. The answer is, " your chiefs lie dead at Meeanee by the side of our men whom they slew : and for this your Highness must answer, or the responsibility of Government for the conduct of its subjects must become a farce and a by-word among men."

Had Meer Sobdar been found in this fortress at the head of his 5,000 soldiers, and that none of them had fought at Meeanee, I should have respected him as an ally. In proof of this, I offer the respect which I paid to Meer Shere Mohamed, whose dislike to us has been inveterate from first to last. I well knew he was our enemy. I knew that he had arrived within six miles of Meeanee with 10,000 men, when the defeat of the Talpoors made him rapidly retrace his steps ; and he wrote to me a letter, assuring me that he had never passed his frontier (which was a falsehood), and requesting me to say how he was to be treated. Major Outram, who was with me at the time this letter arrived, assured me that this Ameer would be quiet if I would only shut my eyes upon his premeditated aggression.

By my desire Major Outram wrote to the Ameer, and I consented not to notice his misconduct. I thought Major Outram's knowledge of the man would give a tone to his letter, and insure the best chance in my power of making peace : but my hopes were vain. Major Outram was deceived in the intentions of Meer Shere Mohamed, and the battle of Hydrabad was the result.

On arriving at Hydrabad, I discovered that Sobdar's men had been in the battle of Meeanee, and I saw no good reason, why his hypocrisy should shelter him from the fate which attended the more manly delinquency of Nusseer

Khan : that hypocrisy had not sheltered us from his matchlocks at Meeanee.

Meer Sobdar states that he signed the treaty offered by
Lord Ellenborough, and that he has it still. Yes! But
Meer Sobdar signed a duplicate treaty, which was put in
possession of Major Outram, according to the rules of diplomacy. Meer Sobdar, in dark council with the other Ameers,
had resolved to massacre Major Outram, and above a
hundred British officers and soldiers that were with him.
The Ameers made an ostentatious pretence of protecting him
in the evening, knowing that he was to be slain next morning.
They had bribed the moonshee of Major Outram to steal and
deliver to them the treaty signed in full Dhurbar, and in full
Dhurbar they tore it in pieces. Was this an action to restrain,
or to encourage their Beloochee chiefs? How absurd then
was their assertion to Major Outram the evening before, that
they could not protect him. But suppose this assertion to
be true, what does it prove? Why, that Princes who cannot
protect accredited agents (invited by themselves to their
capital) from being massacred by their troops, are mere
chiefs of brigand bands, and must be put down by any
civilized government that has the power.

The Ameer says, " that from the time the English became masters of India, never was such disgrace, oppression,
and tyranny offered to any sincere friend of Government."
The answer to this is easy ; sincere friends of Government
don't send 4,800 men to cut British soldiers' throats. Moreover, no disgrace was put upon him, except that of being
defeated in battle, in which it was disgraceful to him that his
troops should have joined ; no oppression and tyranny except
being made prisoners, the natural result of such battle ; and
as to being plundered, nothing was taken beyond what is the
usual prize of the victorious Government ; nothing was pil-
laged, everything is in the hands of the regular prize agents
and ready to be accounted for to her Majesty.

3. Complaint of Meer Nusseer Khan.

If friendship be taken into consideration, I beg to say,
from the beginning up to the day of the battle of Meeanee
everything was wanting on Meer Nusseer Khan's part : and

on arriving at Hydrabad in the month of September, hearing from Lieutenants Gordon and Mylne, then political agents, that the petty insults and breaches of treaty were frequent, my first act was to put a stop to them, and I wrote a distinct letter to the Ameers to that effect. Had they guided themselves by my letter, they would have been, unfortunately for humanity and the Scindian people, still on their thrones at Hydrabad; but they continued to break certain articles of the treaty, and I reported them to the Governor-General, as I told them I would do.

The Ameer says that no attention was paid to his questions relative to shares in the port of Kurrachee. The decision of these minor details was entrusted by me to Major Outram; but instead of meeting Major Outram to enter into the discussion of them, the Ameer endeavoured to cut that officer's throat. It was therefore very natural that no attention was paid to his questions.

The Ameer says, " Meer Roostum Khan was sent to Hydrabad without asking us or our agents." Meer Roostum Khan had promised to meet Major Outram at Kyrpoor. Major Outram mounted his camel, and went to Kyrpoor, and the Ameer mounted his camel and went off the other way to Hydrabad—an insult to my Commissioner, and through him to me, that I am convinced was concocted by the other Ameers, in whose power Meer Roostum was from first to last. The Beloochees of the Murree tribe were seized on the road. " These two things," says the Ameer, " exasperated the Beloochees, and the consequence was slaughter and bloodshed." The last was quite true: twenty-five Murree chiefs were arrested passing near my camp, into which they were brought fully armed; they imagined that I was to be the dupe of a got-up story, that they were going to demand payment of wages due by the Ameers. They were all chiefs of the Murree tribe, and I took the liberty of examining their persons, as well as of taking away their arms. The chief of the Murrees, named Hyat Khan, was one of them. In his pocket I found a letter from the Ameers, summoning the clan to arms; every male that could muster sword, or shield, or spear, or matchlock. They were to meet the

Ameers at Meeanee on the 9th of February; it was therefore, very natural that I should seize the Murree chiefs; and
I then gave orders to my outposts if such parties presented themselves, immediately to cut them down.   The
Ameers are much mistaken if they fancy English officers are
so easily duped; and nothing but my determination not to
shed a drop of blood before a declaration of war, prevented
my ordering these twenty-five Murrees to be cut to pieces,
for they gave sufficient provocation to have been charged
by Jacob's horse; but that officer, having my orders, saved
them.

The Ameer says he fixed his seal to the new treaty;
yes, he did so in the evening of the 14th, and in the morning of the 15th, tore it with contumely in open Dhurbar.   The
Ameer says he sent a guard of favourite nobles to protect
Major Outram—it was very evident that there was no occasion to murder Major Outram in the evening, when
they intended to destroy him, and all who were with him,
next morning.   They knew that by murdering him in the
evening, his party would immediately retreat to the steamers
and get away, and they would have lost the pleasure of murdering upwards of 100 Englishmen by the premature assas-
sination of one.

But the Ameer at last determined to fight, "having become indifferent about life; and he went forth to battle."
It seems, however, that when he heard the British guns, his
love of life returned, and, instead of rallying his troops, he
ran away.

The Ameer proceeds to say, that he had not more than
7,000 horse and foot in the battle; whom they belonged to I
don't know, but I have the sealed and verified returns in my
possession of 25,862 fighting men on the field of Meeanee.*
The words attributed by the Ameer to me, when I returned
him his sword on the field of battle, are utterly false.   The
Ameer proceeds to say, " as long as Major Outram was there,
everything went on well;" as if Major Outram had the power
in any way to interfere with his treatment.   Major Outram

· * There were above 35,000 fighting men.

had no power whatever in Scinde, or over the Ameers, and I had given the charge of the Ameers to Lieutenant Brown, the accusation against whom, together with Lieutenant-Colonel Pattle and Major McPherson which immediately follows this sentence, has already been answered by those gentlemen.

Meerza Khoosroo Beg was not beaten, nor was anybody else; but, being in a passion, he seized Major McPherson (who had neither said nor done anything to him) by the throat, and of course, was instantly made a prisoner.

The following falsehoods are again stated by the Ameer: 1st, he says the fortress was plundered. It was not plundered, it was completely protected from plunder. The treasure it contained was regularly taken possession of for the Government by the prize agents. The Ameer is right when he says the fort was neither besieged nor taken by storm; but it would have been both, had not the terrors of the battle frightened its owners into an unconditional surrender. It was not visited under pretence of seeing, it was taken possession of by right of conquest; and it was done gradually and carefully in order to prevent the ladies of the zenana being alarmed or seen by the troops; but for this delicacy I would have entered the fortress at the head of the troops.

The Ameer again says, " after granting quarter, making peace, promising satisfaction, and agreeing to restore the fort," &c. That we granted quarter is true, nobody was either injured, or even insulted after the fight was over; but the " making peace " is a falsehood; " promising satisfaction," another; and " agreeing to restore the fort," a third; what remains of the complaint is an accumulation of falsehood.

(Signed)　　C. J. NAPIER.

Sir C. Napier to the Governor-General in Council.

Kurrachee, October 27, 1843.

I have the honour to enclose to your Lordship some more information relative to the conduct of the ex-Ameers. I hope it may not prove unsatisfactory, because the further the inquiry is pushed the more will the treachery of the

Ameers become apparent. I could have sent this information last February or March, had I chosen to spend my
time in the employment suited to a chief of police receiving
depositions. But at the period in question I had not the
power of drawing up above 1,500 men in order of battle;
no reinforcements had yet been received; 20,000 men under
Shere Mohamed were within a march of my camp; we
were in the midst of an insurgent population, warlike and
well armed; I had the magazines and hospitals full of
wounded men to guard on the banks of the Indus. I had
six sovereign princes in my camp, intriguing as hard as
they could to arrange an attack upon my camp by overwhelming multitudes. I had a large fortress to guard;
this fortress was three miles from my camp, and I had an
immense treasure to guard. I was obliged to respect the
zenana in the fortress, to the hazard of the regiment in the
fortress (which regiment had suffered greatly in the battle,
and could not muster above 400 men); for in these zenanas were about 800 powerful Beloochees, well armed, and
the zenanas full of arms. I well knew the treachery of the
Ameers, or I should not have been so unjust as to use the
terms I applied to them in my despatch after the battle of
Meeanee.

*Memorandum of a conversation between Meer Gholam Shah,
Meer Fuzzil Ali, Meer Bijjur, and Lieutenant Rathborne,
relative to the part taken by Meer Shahdad in the attack on
the Residency, on the 15th February, 1843.*

Yesterday evening, about half-past five o'clock, I called
on Meer Gholam Shah at Gholam Hoossein Ka Tanda. He
and his brother, Fuzzil Ali, received me. I mentioned
to them that I wished to have some conversation in their
presence with Meer Bijjur, their cousin, whose house adjoins
theirs. The Meers, Gholam Shah and Fuzzil Ali, are
nephews of the ex-Ameer Meer Mohamed, their mother
having been his sister; and Meer Bijjur is brother-in-law of
the ex-Ameer Meer Shahdad, his sister being Meer Shahdad's wife.

When Meer Bijjur arrived, which was within a few minutes, I requested that we might be private, and then a conversation took place nearly word for word as follows; the parties present being the above-mentioned Meers, my moonshee, Meerza Jan, and myself.

Myself.—Meer Bijjur, you joined in the attack on the Residency; by whose order, or at whose instigation, did you do this?

Meer Bijjur.—I joined in that attack by order of Meer Shahdad.

Myself.—Have you any objection to stating how that business commenced, and what part Meer Shahdad acted in it?

Meer Bijjur.—I will tell you willingly. The way of it was this; but first I must explain how we three Meers, now conversing with you stood. I was in the service of Meer Shahdad; Meer Gholam Shah was in the service of Meer Sobdar; Meer Fuzzil Ali was in the service of Meer Mohamed. Well, as you know, for some days before the attack on the Residency there had been a great deal of unpleasant discussion between the Ameers and Major Outram; but at last, on the evening before the attack, Meer Nusseer Khan moved out with his forces to Meer Futteh Ali's garden, on the road to Meeanee. He moved in the evening, the other Ameers remaining in the fort. The night he moved out a large assemblage of Belooch Sirdars took place at his Dhurbar: but what was done I do not know, as I was not there. The next morning, as I was going as usual to make my salaam to Meer Shahdad, I saw great crowds of Beloochees, and heard they were going to attack the Residency. I went on to Meer Shahdad's. On going into the Dhurbar, Mutakum Moonshee also came in, and said the Beloochees were ready to start and attack the Residency, when Meer Shahdad who was all prepared for battle, jumped up and said he would go forthwith and head them. He desired me to go with him. I had my sword with me as usual, but no shield or matchlock, and was quite unprepared for fighting, but of course I obeyed. I then learned that Ahmed Khan Lugaree had been detached with seven or eight thousand men to attack the Residency, by orders given him the night before by Meer Nusseer Khan.

Myself.—What! By order of Meer Nusseer Khan?

Meer Bijjur.—I understood it was by his order, given overnight at the garden, but I cannot speak positively as I was not there. However, there were the men ready to start. Meer Shahdad was proceeding to put himself at their head, he ordered me to accompany him, and I did so. I had very few men with me, and sent a messenger to Meer Gholam Shah, who was with Meer Mohamed Khan, to tell him what was going on and beg him to persuade Meer Shahdad to desist. Meer Gholam Shah spoke to Meer Mohamed, and he sent a confidential servant, who came to Meer Shahdad, and told him, that the business he was engaged in was a mad one, and prayed him over and over again to desist.

Meer Gholam Shah.—Yes, I was not in Meer Shahdad's service, but living as I did near the Residency, I had had much intercourse with the gentlemen there: I had seen enough of the English to be pretty sure that they would beat us, first or last, if we went to war with them; and I knew, when they did beat us they would deeply revenge the murder of their envoy: besides I thought is disgraceful to murder defenceless people. I therefore begged Meer Mohamed to send an order to stop Meer Shahdad, whose hot-headed proceedings would bring eventual destruction on us all; a confidential person was then sent to Meer Shahdad, but the latter replied, he had sworn to do the business and would go on with it. He added that the attack was all arranged, and that Ahmed Khan Lugaree was going with his followers; that he had sworn to act through thick or thin with Ahmed, and would place himself at the head of the force.

Meer Bijjur.—Well, after this there was an end of remonstrance, and Meer Shahdad, with myself and the rest of the party, started for the Residency, and when we arrived there Ahmed Khan led forward the people to the attack, while Meer Shahdad with myself and other attendants re-

Y

mained on horseback under a clump of trees out of reach of the fire till all was over: we then returned, and joined Meer Nusseer Khan at Meeanee. That is all I know of the matter. The truth is, though I was Meer Shahdad's brother-in-law, I was never consulted by him—his power was lodged in the hands of servants and others.

Meer Gholam Shah.—Meer Bijjur has given a true statement of the transaction.

Meer Fuzzil Ali.—Yes, that is all true.

Meer Gholam Shah.—May I ask why these inquiries are now made? Meer Bijjur has made his salaam, and we hope the past, as then promised, is forgiven.

Myself.—I can have no difficulty in telling you. Meer Bijjur has made his salaam and has been forgiven, and there is not the slightest intention of molesting him for what is past. The cause of my questioning him is this :—Meer Shahdad now states that he never headed the party that attacked the Residency, that it was the Belooch Sirdars who insisted on attacking it, and that the purpose for which he went was to remonstrate with them and save the garrison.

Meer Bijjur.—Why this is notoriously untrue; every one who was with the party knows it to be so. What influence the boasting of Beloochees may have had in procuring the order for the attack I know not; I dare say it may have had a good deal, for they talked loudly of what they could do : but Meer Shahdad headed the party as I have said, voluntarily, against the remonstrances and orders of Meer Mohamed; he attended throughout the fight, and after driving out the English, rode with us over to Meeanee, went up to Meer Nusseer Khan, and saluting him said, " Good fortune attend you, I have gained the day."

Myself.—What! said this to Nusseer Khan?

Meer Gholam Shah.—Meer Bijjur speaks truth; Meer Shahdad, on his return from the Residency, rode up, as Meer Bijjur says, to Nusseer Khan's tent, and entering it, said, " *Meer Sahib Moobarick, Meer Futteh Khia.*"

Myself.—I thank you for this explanation.

Meer Gholam Shah.—We have stated all we know and

this truly.   I have never spoken an ill word of the Ameers to you, because they were our sovereigns and relations, but as you now question us we have spoken the truth.

Myself.—I have also, as you know, avoided a topic which I thought must be painful to you, but it was my duty to make this inquiry, and I thank you for the readiness with which you have answered me.

After some further short conversation on general subjects I took my leave.

A. B. RATHBORNE,
Collector and Magistrate, Hydrabad.

October 22nd, 1843.

N.B.—The above conversation took place on the 21st inst., I made the original memorandum of it on the 22nd, but on reading it over to the moonshee, he differed as to one point; this was, whether it had been said that Meer Mohamed sent a man to Shahdad to call him, and *himself remonstrated with him;* or, whether the *man* merely conveyed the remonstrance, as now stated. I sent the moonshee to Meer Gholam Shah to ascertain which was the correct version, and in his interview he elicited from him the following important additional admission :—

Meer Gholam Shah, on the morning of the attack, also waited on Meer Sobdar, *who desired him to join in the attack also.* Gholam Shah replied, that he was not going to put himself under the orders of an inexperienced child like Shahdad, especially as he thought the business a bad one; but if Meer Sobdar chose to go himself, he would, as in duty bound, accompany him. *Meer Sobdar then laughed, and said that would never do.*

This morning Meer Gholam Shah and Fuzzil Ali called upon me, and I took the opportunity of reading over to them the above conversation, taken down on the 22nd inst. which they said was quite correct : on this occasion the moonshee was not present, and on both his aid was not required.

A. B. RATHBORNE,
&c., &c.

24th October.

*Evidence given by Peer Budroodeen, Moosahib, or confidential
servant of the ex-Ameer, Sobdar Khan of Hydrabad.*

Question.—On what day did the army of the Ameers
leave Hydrabad, and where did it encamp?

Answer.—On the 6th of February, 1843, the troop
under the command of Gholam Mohamed Komriewalla and
Meer Khan Mohamed Talpoor (Khananie) went out and encamped in the Babool jungle near Meer Futteh Ali Kebah.
The two chiefs then returned to Hydrabad, and told Nusseer
to get all in readiness for battle.   Afterwards the force collected there, and chiefs, as they arrived, remained there.
On the evening of the 14th of February, 1843, Meer
Nusseer Khan moved out and joined this force.

Do you know what strength the force was?

I did not count them, but it was well known that it
amounted to 30,000 strong.

That was on the 14th of February.   What did this force
do next day?

In the morning an order was issued to plunder Major
Outram's dwelling.

Who gave this order?

I know not.

What number of men went to the agency for that purpose?

Nine or ten thousand men.

Who commanded this party, and what chiefs accompanied it?

Meer Shahdad commanded the party, and by him the
order was given to plunder the agency.   Meer Nusseer of
Kyrpoor; Jehan Mohamed; Meer Khan Mohamed; Gholam
Mohamed Komriewalla; a Nizamanee chief, whose name I
forget; Ahmed Khan Lugaree; Meerza Bakur, and other
inferior chiefs, accompanied him.

When this party reached the agency who commanded it,
and what orders were given by him?

Meer Shahdad Khan commanded, and he gave these

orders " if the troops fight kill them, but if they run away
never mind ? "

When Major Outram quitted the agency what did the
Scinde troops do ?

They plundered all the property left and burnt all the
buildings. They then joined Meer Nusseer Khan at the
garden, and Meer Shahdad and the afore-mentioned chiefs
said, " We have gained a victory; Major Outram has fled,
and we have plundered his property ; our party have behaved
most bravely." Meer Shahdad sent a man, whose name I
forget, to give the news of his victory to Meer Sobdar Khan
in the fort, and to inform him that Major Outram had fled.
Meer Sobdar, on hearing this, answered, " You have done
ill : if with 8,000 men you have been unable to destroy 100
men, what will you be able to do in front of the General's
army ? "

This was on the 15th of February. What then occurred ?

On the evening of the 15th of February, Meer Nusseer
Khan moved from his garden and took up a position at Lunar,
half a coss from it ; on the evening of the 16th he reached
Meeanee ; next morning the battle took place.

In the battle of Meeanee what was the strength of the
Ameers' force ?

Some say 40,000, and some say 35,000.

How many of Sobdar's men were in the battle?

With Iktyar Lugaree 4000 ; with Mohamed Khan Tora
300 ; with other chiefs subject to Meer Sobdar Khan there
were 500 men.

How many men of Meer Mohaed Khman's were there in
the battle?

I know not, but every soul he could collect was there.

Was Meer Sobdar in the battle, and what other Ameers
were there?

Meers Sobdar and Mohamed Khan were not in the battle.
Except these two all the Ameers of Upper and Lower Scinde
were there.

Such being the strength of the Ameers' force on the 17th
of February, had the battle been delayed for two or three days
more, to what extent would they have been reinforced?

It would have increased to 50,000 or 60,000 men.

Did Meer Sobdar send information to the General that troops were collecting at Hydrabad?

On the night of the day on which the General reached Sukkurunda, Meer Sobdar called me and said, "Take two days' food and drink and proceed by the jungle to the General's camp; tell him if he comes quickly it is well, but if he delays the force here will greatly increase." Jemada Couza said, "Budroodeen is a great man, if he goes it will be well known, and you will get a bad name, it will be better if some one else is sent." I afterwards heard that orders were given to Syud Abbis Ali Shah, and a Cazee, to proceed to the General's camp and beg of him to come quickly.*

At this time, the 10th of February, 1848, Meer Sobdar was a friend of the British, when did he become hostile?

I do not know.

When did the Ameers commence collecting troops?

When Meerza Khoosroo wrote from Nowshera to the Ameers, "The General is bent on war, so get ready." When the Meerza returned to Hydrabad the order for collecting troops was given.

Had this collection commenced before Major Outram reached Hydrabad?

The collection of troops had commenced before Major Outram reached Hydrabad.

Had the Ameers gained the victory what would have been the fate of the British troops?

Every soul would have been massacred.

Budroodeen having read over his evidence, declares it to be correctly recorded, and applies his seal to it 22nd October, 1843. Mohamed Moyadeen is witness that Budroodeen gave this evidence, and that he declares it to be correct.

Evidence given in my presence this 22nd day of October, 1843.

E. J. Brown.

* These men never came to me.—C. J. N.

X.

Section 1.

Reply to the Accusations of the Ameers, Sobdar Khan, Nusseer Khan, and Mohamed Khan, by the Officers accused.

Major McPherson, Prize Agent.

The assertion of the three Ameers, that I entered the fort with the view of seeing it, is erroneous on their part. I accompanied the troops to take possession of it, and to see the British standard hoisted on its tower, which was done on the 21st of March, 1843. No outrage was committed, no zenana approached, and sentries were placed to prevent any one approaching them. Notice was given when the men would mount the tower, that the ladies might retire, and not be overlooked; and people were only admitted on the tower at a certain time, lest the ladies should be annoyed. During that day, as prize agent, I collected treasure to a considerable amount, principally in gold. No zenana was ever entered by me, or any British officer, during the time they were inhabited by the ladies; but I have taken treasure from those vacated. No female of any description was ever suffered to be ill used at any time. As for taking the ladies' jewels from them, I positively deny it; in many instances they were sent out for me to take, but I, as well as my colleagues, invariably returned them again, as being their personal property. I have never heard of any of the ladies of the zenana being ill used, or even seen; and I can safely assert, the complaint made is a gross falsehood on the part of the Ameers. That we the prize agents took money, jewels, swords, &c. &c. from the empty houses is certainly the case. To do so was the duty of the prize agents.

(Signed)   P. McPherson.

Captain Blenkins, Prize Agent.

After the perusal of three letters respectively from Meer Nusseer Khan, Sobdar Khan, and Meer Mohamed, I beg to state that the whole therein contained, as far as I have any knowledge, or which relates to myself, or any other of the prize agents, is entirely without any foundation. They, the Ameers, never experienced anything but the greatest kindness and consideration from us. They were repeatedly told that we did not wish the ornaments of their women to be given, or any other property which belonged to them; and in several instances when proffered, I have myself sent them back to their owners; so did the other prize agents: we had no idea of intruding on the ladies, nor did we ever intrude on their zenanas; and we had strict orders from the Major-General to keep perfectly aloof from the dwellings of the women.

W. BLENKINS.

Captain Bazett prize agent, Lieutenant Brown commissioner, and Major Reid commanding the troops in the Fort, made similar statements; the contradictions are to be found in the supplement to the Scinde Parliamentary Papers, together with the Ameers' memorials.

Sir C. Napier to the Governor-General, May 9th, 1843.

The whole of the women of the Ameers refused to accompany them, and are here. They say they have no means of subsistence. This is said to be untrue. I positively forbade their personal ornaments of gold and jewels to be taken from them by the prize agents; but whether they carried out treasure or not, I cannot say.

[They carried away two millions sterling!—W. N.]

SECTION 2.

Contradiction of the falsehoods promulgated by Dr. Buist, of the " Bombay Times."

Sir C. Napier to the Governor-General, May 16*th,* 1843.

An infamous article appeared in the *Bombay Times* of the 6th instant. The whole is one lie from beginning to end. The officers of this army are extremely indignant. The article is headed " The Ladies of the Ameers' Zenana."

My reason for troubling your Lordship on the subject is, that you might have thought some outrage had been committed, and the case amplified. My Lord, there has not been a single irregularity ; nor is there a woman, much less one of the ladies of the zenana, in any officer's quarters, nor do I believe any one of these ladies has ever been seen by an officer of this army.

At a general meeting of the Officers of the Scinde Field Force, stationed at and near Hydrabad, held with sanction of His Excellency Sir C. J. Napier, K.C.B., Governor of Scinde, and commanding the forces in Scinde, to take into consideration the measures that should be adopted to refute a certain calumnious article which appeared in the *Bombay Times* newspaper of- the 6th May last, headed, " Ladies of the Ameers' Zenana," it was unanimously resolved :—
That an address to His Excellency the Governor of Scinde be drawn up and circulated for the signature of the officers of this force, expressive of their indignation at the unfounded and injurious calumnies contained in the abovementioned article, soliciting the protection of His Excellency, and requesting his permission to make their sentiments more generally known, by circulating copies of this address to the Indian press for publication.
The following address was then drawn up and agreed to—

Address of the undersigned Officers of the Scinde Army, stationed at or near Hydrabad, to His Excellency Major General Sir C. J. Napier, K.C.B., Governor of, and commanding in Scinde.

Sir,—We, the undersigned officers in the army, serving under your Excellency's command, have seen with indignation an article in the *Bombay Times* newspaper of the 6th May last, closely affecting our honour, and tending to degrade us in the eyes of our friends and country. The article in question is headed " The Ladies of the Ameers' Zenana," and concludes in the following terms :—

" Where are they now ?   They, who three months since,
were sharers of a palace and in the enjoyment of the honours
of royalty, are the degraded lemans of the Feringhi! So it is,
the harem has been defiled ; the last drop of bitterness has been
mingled with the cup of misery we have given the Ameers to
drink, the heaviest of the insults Mahomedans can endure
has been heaped upon their grey discrowned heads.   Let it
not be supposed we speak of this in the language of prudish
sentimentalism ; the officers who have dishonoured the zenana
of kings have committed great wrong; but for that, as for
the evil deeds attending upon so unjust and cruel a conquest,
the Government which ordained it is responsible.   We know
to our shame and sorrow the evils which flowed from frailties
such as this permitted in Cabool; and at Hydrabad we may
yet discover the heinousness of our sins in the magnitude of
our punishment. If one thing more than all the other wrongs
we have inflicted on them could awaken in the bosom of each
Beloochee chief, the unquenchable thirst of never-dying
vengeance, it must be to see the sanctities of domestic life
invaded and violated as they have been ; to see the daughters
of nobles, and wives of kings, living while youth and beauty
last as the concubines of the infidel, thrown aside when their
attractions have departed, to perish in their degradation and
shame.   This is the first of the black fruits of invasion for
which Britons must blush.   We have avoided explicitness on
such a subject : our readers will be at no loss to discover our
meaning :—the most attractive of the ladies of the zenana
now share the tents of British officers.   A series of acts of
injustice first introduced to the Scindians the character of
the British Government: what has just been related will
afford them an insight into the virtues and blessings they
may look for from the advance of civilization ; the benefits
and honours destined them by the most refined people in the
world.   This contrasts well with the reception English ladies
experienced at Affghan hands."

We beg to assure your Excellency, from our own knowledge and inquiry as to facts, that the grave charges contained
in this extract against the officers under your command are
utterly without foundation, and that not a single instance of

ill-treatment or disrespect to the inmates of the Ameers' zenana has ever come to our knowledge. Having expressed to your Excellency our deliberate conviction that the whole of the statements in the extract complained of, are unfounded in truth, we respectfully solicit that you will be good enough to take such steps as you may deem advisable to clear our characters thus aspersed in the eyes of our military superiors and comrades, and of our friends and countrymen in India and in Europe; and that, with the same end in view, you will kindly permit us to circulate copies of this address to the Indian newspapers for publication.

We have, &c.

Hydrabad, 10th May, 1843.

(Signed.)

C. Waddington, Comdg. Engr. Bombay Engrs.

P. McPherson, Major, M. S.

Edward Green, Acting Asst. Adjt. General.

E. J. Brown, Lieut. Engrs. and Commissioner.

W. Brown, Fort Major.

A. Gibbon, Assist. Surgeon, Post Master.

M. McMurdo, Lieut. Acting Asst. Qr. Mr. Genl.

H. J. Pelly, Lieut. Persian Interpreter.

F. Cristal, Bt. Capt. A. D. Judge Advocate General.

D. Erskine, Lt. Artillery.

John Lloyd, Major Arty.

H. Gibberne, Bt. Capt. Arty.

J. S. Unwin, Bt. Capt. Arty.

T. F. V. Outlaw, Lt. Madras Sappers and Miners.

J. P. Nixon, Lieut. 25th Regt. N. I.

A. Boileau, 2d Lieut. Madras Sappers and Miners.

T. Studdert, Lt. Fd. Engr.

J. A. Wood, Lieut. 20th Regt. N. I.

D. Carstairs, Capt. 6th Regt. N. I.

C. G. Bazett, Capt. 9th Light Cavalry.

C. P. Leeson, Lieut. 25th Regt. N. I. Supt. of Police.

W. Ward, Assist. Surg. 12th Regt. N. I.

A. B. Rathborne, Lieut. Collector and Magistrate.

W. Blenkins, Capt. 6th Regt. N. I.

J. P. Leslie, Bt. Major, 1st Troop H. A.

G. Hutt, Capt. Artillery.

J. G. Petrie, 2d Lieut. Arty.

D. Gaye, 2d Lieut. Arty.

A. Rowan, Capt. H. A.

W. S. Hatch, 2d Lieut. Arty.

W. J. Whitlie, Capt. Arty.

W. J. Milford, Bt. Capt. 9th Light Cavalry.

H. C. Plowden, Lieut. Adjt. 9th Lt. Cavalry.

C. Turner, 9th Light Cavalry.

W. B. Wemyss, Capt. 9th Light Cavalry.

J. R. Snow, Lieut. 9th Cavalry.

A. T. Wylly, Lieut. 9th Bengal Lt. Cavalry.

J. H. Thomson, Cornet, 9th do.

M. B. Stone, Cornet, do.

M. Hyle, Assist. Surgeon.

H. A. Balmoyn, Cornet, 9th Light Cavalry.

J. H. Firth, Cornet, 9th do.

P. F. Story, Major, do.

C. Buckle, 3d Rt. Bombay, Lt. Cavalry.

M. Stack, Major, do.

R. R. Younghusband, Lieut. 20th Regt.

W. Collum, Assist. Surg. 3d Light Cavalry.

T. P. Taylor, Lieut. 3d Light Cavalry.

F. F. Forbes, Lieut. 3d Lt. Cavalry.

R. B. Moore, Lieut. do.

E. F. Moore, Cornet, do.

T. Eyre, Capt. do.

C. Delamain, Capt. 3d Lt. Cavalry.
F. S. Oldfield, Lieut. do.
H. Mackenzie, Lieut. do.
C. T. North, Lieut. Bombay Engrs.
T. Pownall, Lieut. H. A.
R. Henderson, Bt. Capt. Madras Engineers.
A. Woodburn, Major, 25th Regt.
G. H. Robertson, Lieut. do.
G. Mayor, Lieut. do.
T. Follett, Capt. do.
J. Jackson, Capt. do.
A. Wright, Assist. Surg. do.
H. Grice, Ensign, do.
E. Glennie, Lieut.-Adjt. 25th Regt.
E. Lowrie, Ensign, do.
A. J. Thompson, Lieut. Provost-Marshal.
A. P. Barker, Lieut. 21st Regt.
H. Farrell, Lieut.-Col. do.
W. C. Wilkinson, Lt. Adjt. do.
F. S. Stevens, Capt. do.
E. A. Green, Lieut. do.
E. S. Leathes, Ensign, do.
M. J. Battye, Lieut. do.
W. J. Merewether, Ensign do.
J. M. Younghusband. Lieut. 8th Regt.
H. Fenning, Lieut. 21st. Regt.

E. L. Scott, Ensign, 21st Regt.
J. P. Laurie, Ensign, do.
G. W. West, Ensign, do.
H. J. Carter, Assist. Surg. do.
W. J. Brown, Major, 8th Regt. N. I.
A. Thomas, Capt. do.
J. McKenzie, Assist. Surg. do.
A. S. Hawkins, Capt. 8th Regt.
C. Brasnell, Ensign, do.
S. J. Dalzell, Ensign, do.
R. T. Reid, Major, 12th Regt. N. I.
E. J. Rusell, Lieut. do.
I. Fisher, Capt. do.
W. Lodwick, Lieut. do.
W. T. Holbrow, Ensign, do.
A. Y. Bease, Ensign, do.
O. Clarkson, Capt. do.
Jas. D. B. Forest, Ensign, do
W. J. Soppitt, Ensign, do.
J. B. D. Carter, Lieut. do.
C. M. James, Ensign 6th Regiment N. I.
J. Dalrymple, Surg. 9th Light Cavy.
W. Ashburner, Lieut. Adj. 3d Lt. Cavalry.
E. G. Malet, Capt. do.
G. Allender, Staff Surgeon.
James Down, Lieut. 12th Regt. N. I.

(*True Copy.*)

P. McPHERSON, *Major.*
Military Secretary.

Hydrabad, July 25th, 1843.

Gentlemen,—Your address has given me great satisfaction. I concur in every word, and confirm every statement it contains.

We are accused by Mr. Buist, the Editor of the *Bombay Times*, of disgracing ourselves, our profession, and our country, by the most infamous conduct towards the women of the zenana; and I am, personally, held up to public scorn as the immediate cause of such scandalous conduct.

You have protected your character, collectively and individually, by exposing this unprovoked and unparalleled calumny; and it is right the public should know that, so far from offering these ladies any insult, no officer of this army has even *seen* a lady of the zenana.

But the officers whom I have the honour to command, are of the same class of high-minded gentlemen which compose the rest of the officers of the Queen's and Company's service; the calumny, therefore, applies to the character of the whole military profession—all will feel the insult!

This calumny is intended to make England look down upon her armies with horror and disgust; and when I consider the bad climate in which we are now serving; that dangers and privations surround us; that we have put forth our best energies to serve our sovereign and our country, and to gain the approbation of our friends; that all have served with reputation, and some of us grown grey in undishonoured arms; that many of our comrades have lately fallen in battle, and by disease, and that all are ready to fall; when I consider these things I say I am at a loss to account for the feelings which induced Mr. Buist (if it be true that he is an Englishman, deliberately to make the groundless fabrication which he has put forth to the world.

Gentlemen, your reputation and mine are inseparable, and I assure you that my best exertions shall be united with yours, to defend our private character as gentlemen, and our military character as soldiers.

I have, &c.   (Signed)   C. J. NAPIER,

Major-General and Governor of Scinde.

(*True Copy.*)   P. McPHERSON, Major,

Military Secretary.

[This infamous libel was written by Dr. Buist.]

XI.

Names of Officers mentioned in the Despatches as being distinguished in the battles of Meeanee and Hydrabad.

Lieut.-Colonels. Pennefather.—Pattle.

Majors. Poole.—Jackson.—Teasdale.—Lloyd.—Mac Pherson.—Waddington.—Wyllie.—Storey.—Stack.—Leslie.—Reid.—Brown.—Woodburn.

Captains. Garrett.—Meade.—Tew.—Cookson.—Tucker.—Conway.—Whitlie.—Hutt.—Blenkins.—Henderson.—Tait.—Delamain.—Jacob.—Willoughby.—George.—Jackson.—Stevens.—Fisher.

Lieutenants. Smith. — Coote. — Wood. — Harding. — Phayre.—M'Murdo. —Pelly.—Boileau.—Outlaw.—Thompson.—Younghusband.—Leeson.—Brennan.—Brown.—Rathborne.—Hill.—North.—Battersby.—Leeson.—Fitzgerald.
Surgeons. Dalrymple.—Bell.
Moonshee. Ali Ackbar.

Names of Officers killed at Meeanee.

Majors. Jackson.—Teasdale.
Captains. Cookson.—Tew.—Meade.
Lieutenant. Wood.

Wounded.

Lieut.-Colonel. Pennefather.
Major. Wyllie.
Captains. Tucker.—Smith.—Conway.
Lieutenants. Plowden. — Harding. — Phayre. — Bourdillon.
Ensigns. Firth.—Pennefather.—Bowden.—Holbrow.

Officers killed at Hydrabad.

Captain. Garrett.
Lieutenant. Smith.

Wounded.

Lieutenants. Pownoll.—Tait.—Chute.—Coote.—Evans. —Brennan.—Bur.—Wilkinson.—M'Murdo.
Ensign. Pennefather.

Names of men of the 22nd Regiment who concealed their wounds, received in the battle of Hydrabad, and marched with their Regiment the next day, thinking another battle was at hand.

John Durr. — John Muldowney. — Robert Young. — Henry Lines. — Patrick Gill. — James Andrews. Wounds not severe.

Sergeant Haney. Wound rather severe.

Thomas Middleton.—James Mulvey. Severely wounded in the legs.

Silvester Day. Ball in the foot!

Report sent by Sir C. Napier to the Governor-General, of non-commissioned Officers and men who had particularly distinguished themselves at the Battle of Meeanee.

From Major-General Sir C. J. NAPIER, K.C.B., to the Right Honourable LORD ELLENBOROUGH, Governor-General of India, &c. &c.

Hydrabad, 2nd March, 1843.

My Lord,—I beg leave to send to your Lordship reports made by my order; that while the memory is fresh, distinguished deeds may be put on record. The great results of this battle have made me anxious that those who were so conspicuous in the hour of trial should be known to your Lordship. Their devotion to their duty was very honourable to them.

In the case of the brave drivers of the two batteries I am sure your Lordship will do them justice, and I beg especially to recommend them to your Lordship's protection.

I have, &c.,

(Signed)   C. J. NAPIER, *Major-General.*

From Captain G. Hutt, Commanding Field Battery, to the Adjutant of Artillery, in Scinde.

Camp, near Hydrabad, 23rd February, 1843.

Sir,—With reference to Division After Orders of yesterday, I beg permission to bring to the notice of the Major-General, the general steadiness and good conduct of the drivers of the battery under my command, throughout the action of the 17th, particularly of three men (*Drivers*—Uggar Khan, Bahadoor, Mahadoo), who brought up the howitzer first in action on the right of the line, under a very heavy and destructive fire, with a degree of coolness and steadiness that could not be surpassed, though two of their horses were dangerously wounded.

I would not presume to bring these men to notice were they enlisted, or treated as fighting men ; but as they are still considered as mere followers, men whose families receive no pension in the event of their death, or themselves if disabled by wounds, I beg to submit the case to the Major-General, as a strong argument in favour of those, on whose courage and conduct the very existence of the battery must often depend.

I have, &c.,

(Signed)   GEO. HUTT, *Captain,*

Com^{dg.} Field Battery.

From Major P. F. Story, Com^{dg.} 9th Light Cavalry, to Lieutenant Pelly, Assistant Adjutant-General.

Camp, Hydrabad, 26th February, 1843.

Sir,—In forwarding the accompanying Roll, for the information of the Major-General, I have the honour to request you will inform him, that I have had the greatest difficulty in selecting these men, where all behaved so gallantly, and nearly equally well.

I have, &c.,

(Signed)   P. F. STORY, *Major,*

Com^{dg.} 9th Light Cavalry.

Roll of native commissioned and non-commissioned officers and privates of the 9th Bengal light cavalry, who particularly distinguished themselves in action with the enemy, on the 17th February, 1843.

Camp, Hydrabad, February, 1843.

Subadar. Shaik Bekr Ally—Had his horse severely wounded in the chest, led his men in a most gallant manner, and was very active in re-forming them for a second attack.

Subadar. Shaik Emam Bux—Engaged with two troopers in taking a Standard planted near some guns, and which was most bravely defended by the enemy.

Jemadar. Khoman Sing—Carried the Standard of the 1st squadron (Queen's colour), and was very zealous and active during the whole action.

Havildar. Shaik Emam Bux—saved the life of his officer, Shaik Emam Bux, (subadar,) and his conduct was conspicuous during the day.

Havildar. Shaik Golam Hussain — Strongly recommended for great gallantry during the charge.

Naick. Bucktawer Sing — Behaved most gallantly during the whole day.

Troopers. Birma Deen, Golam Russool—These two men were equally engaged with the subadar in taking the Standard, which was so nobly defended.

Trooper. Sewdial Sing—Singly rushed into a walled enclosure and killed one of the enemy, who had several times fired from it with effect.

Trooper. Mootee Sing—Saved the life of his officer, Captain Garrett.

Trooper. Gungah Sing—Killed after a long and severe personal conflict with one of the enemy, when no assistance was at hand.

Trooper. Beharee Sing—After being severely wounded in the wrist, and his horse also in two places, cut down his adversary.

Trooper. Fyzoolla Khan—Behaved gallantly throughout, and cut down his enemy after a severe personal conflict.

Trooper. Hussain Ally—Strongly recommended for great gallantry during the charge.

Trooper. Nasser Ally — Behaved with great gallantry during the charge, and was severely wounded.

(Signed)   P. F. STORY, *Major*,
Comdg. 9th Light Cavalry.

From Major J. H. Poole, Commanding 22nd Regiment, to the Assistant Adjutant-General, Scinde Field Force.

Camp, Hydrabad, 24th February, 1843.

Sir,—In reference to No. 2, After Division Orders of the 22nd instant, I called upon the captains and officers commanding companies, to furnish me with the names and acts of individuals under my command, who had especially distinguished themselves in the action of the 17th instant. The officers generally assert that they feel difficulty in making selections, where the conduct of every man of the companies was so satisfactory. In so general a field of action and persevering exertion, I equally feel at a loss, where to draw a distinction; but it may be proper to mention the names of private James O'Neill, of the light company, who took a standard whilst we were actively engaged with the enemy, and Drummer Martin Delaney, who shot, bayoneted and captured the arms of Meer Whulle Mohamed Khan, who was mounted, and directing the enemy in the hottest part of the engagement. When all the regiment behaved with enduring coolness and intrepidity, I hope the particular circumstances of these two cases will exonerate me from the imputation of doing injustice to all the brave soldiers of the regiment, by particularizing them.

I have, &c.

(Signed) J. H. POOLE, *Major,*
Com^{dg.} 22nd Regt.

From Major S. Clibborne, Com^{dg.} 1st Grenadier Regt. N. I., to Lieutenant Pelly, Acting Asst. Adjt.-Genl., Hydrabad.

Camp, near Hydrabad, 24th February, 1843.

Sir,—Agreeably to Division Orders of the 22nd instant, I beg to bring to the especial notice of Major-General Sir C. J. Napier, K.C.B., the names of the following officers and men of the 1st grenadiers, who distinguished themselves by zeal and gallantry in the action of the 17th February.

Lieutenant Johnstone, who cut down a Beloochee, and

saved the life of a sepoy who had bayoneted this Beloochee, but was overpowered in the life struggle. .

Subadar Major Kooshall Sing, and Subadar Esseree Pursaud, likewise privates Sunkur Misser and Kadaree Powar, who were conspicuous throughout the day for their zeal and gallantry.

I have, &c.

(Signed)   S. CLIBBORNE, Major,

Com^{dg.} 1st Grenadier Regt. N.I.

From Major N. R. Reid, Commanding 12th Regt. N. I.
to the Acting Assistant Adjutant-General.

Scinde and Beloochistan,
Hydrabad Fort, 25th February, 1843.

Sir,—With reference to No. 3 of the Division Orders, dated the 22nd instant, I have the honour to transmit, for the purpose of being laid before the Major-General, a nominal Roll of non-commissioned officers, naicks and privates, in the 12th regiment, N. I., who have been reported to me by the officers in command, and in charge of the companies to which they belong, as having particularly distinguished themselves in the action of the 17th instant.

I take this opportunity of recording the gallant conduct of the late Captain and Brevet Major Jackson, who fell at the head of the grenadier company, in a personal conflict with several of the enemy. The other officers, Lieutenant and Brevet Captain Meade and Lieutenant Wood, who were killed, were also most conspicuous when they fell, in cheering on their men at one of the most critical periods of the action. To the other European officers I am also much indebted for their gallant conduct and example throughout the day; but to Lieutenant and Brevet Captain Brown, the only mounted officer with me in the battle, in a particular degree I beg to place on record the deep gratitude I must ever feel for the assistance he afforded me, as well as my admiration at the gallantry he displayed in cheering the men throughout the conflict, at every part of the line where the resistance was most hot and determined.

I have, &c.

(Signed)   N. R. REID, *Major,*
Commanding 12*th Regt. N. I.*

Nominal Roll of those men in the 12*th Regiment, N. I., who distinguished themselves in the action of the* 17*th Feb.* 1843.

Fort Hydrabad, 25th February, 1843.

1 Havildar Dutram Tewaree,
1 Naick Bhowanee Sing,
2 Naick Allum Sing,
1 Private Shaik Adjum,

Wounded, in gallantly defending Capt. and Brevet Major Jackson.

(Sd.)   B. D. CARTER, *Ens. in charge of Gr. Company.*

1 Havildar Oomrow Sing,
1 Naick Lall Khan,
1 Private Mathadeen 1st.
2   „   Booree Aheer,
3   „   Seetul Lohar.

I heard these men cheering on their comrades after a slight check, and saw them most forward in the action.

(Sd.)   G. FISHER, *Capt. Com$^{dg.}$ 5th Company.*

1 Havildar Bugwan Sing,
2   „   Thackoor Ram,

Behaved gallantly, urging the men on, and foremost in the action.

(Sd.)   W. F. HOLBROW, *Ens. in charge 8th Company.*
(True copy.)   (Sd.)   W. BROWN, *Capt. Adjt.* 12*th Regt. N. I.*
(Sd.)   N. R. REID, *Major, Com$^{dg.}$ 12th Regt. N. I.*

From Capt. J. Jackson, Com$^{dg.}$ 25th Regt. N.I., to the Assistant Adjutant-General, in Scinde and Beloochistan.

Camp, Hydrabad, 25th February, 1843.

Sir,—Agreeably to Division Orders of the 22nd instant, I beg to bring to the especial notice of Major-General Sir C. J. Napier, K.C.B., the following officers of the 25th regiment, N. I., who particularly distinguished themselves, by zeal and gallantry, in the action of the 17th of February, 1843.

The whole of the sepoys behaved so well, that I consider it would be invidious to make any distinction.

Lieutenant Marston, grenadier company, who cut down two of the enemy, single handed, in front of the line.

Subadar Major Nund Ram, who, though wounded, remained with his company throughout the action.

Subadar Russall Sing, grenadier company, who shot three men, and cut down one, and shewed great zeal in encouraging and leading on his men.

Jemedar Bappoo Sawunt, light company, who cut down one man. I have, &c.

(Signed)   JOHN JACKSON, *Captain*,
Com$^{dg.}$ 25th Regt. N. I.

From Captain J. Jacob, Com$^{dg.}$ Scinde Irregular Horse, to the Acting Assistant Adjutant-General.

Scinde and Beloochistan,
Camp, near Hydrabad, 23rd February, 1843.

Sir,—With reference to Division Orders of the 22nd instant, I have the honour to request that you will bring to the notice of Major-General Sir Charles Napier, K.C.B. commanding in Scinde and Beloochistan, that throughout the battle fought on the 17th I received the most essential service from my Acting Adjutant, Lieutenant Russell, whose steady, cool, and daring conduct on the occasion mainly contributed to the good behaviour of the corps I have the honour to command, especially while it was exposed alone for nearly two hours to a heavy fire of artillery, in a most trying position for an irregular sepoy corps, which, until a few months before that day, had, since it was raised, been always dispersed in small detachments, and the men of which had, with few exceptions, never been engaged in any but skirmishing fights. I am also greatly indebted to this officer for the promptness with which he assisted me in the very difficult task of reforming, after charging through the enemy's camp, when the men were excited to the highest pitch, and when their services were required to repel an unexpected attack on the rear guard.

I also request that you will have the kindness to bring to the notice of the Major-General, the excellent conduct of Russuldar Surferaz Khan, Jemedar Alladad Khan Nawab, and Duffadar Mhobut Khan. The good conduct of these three native officers was most conspicuous throughout the day, and particularly on one occasion, when the regiment was moving over ground rendered nearly impassable by watercourses, hedges, and deep cuts filled with thorns and lined by matchlock-men; in advancing at the gallop over these obstacles so many falls took place, that more than fifty of our horses were lying on the ground at once; this occurred under a very heavy fire from the village and nullahs on the right of the enemy's line, and on this occasion, the native officers above mentioned, re-formed their men, and restored order in a style which was deserving of my highest admiration. I do not mention Lieutenant Fitzgerald, my second in command, as I have already brought that officer's services to the notice of the General.

I have, &c.

(Signed)　　　　J. JACOB, *Capt. Arty.*
Com^{dg.} Scinde Irregular Horse.

XII.

Extract from a private Letter of Sir C. Napier, touching the Operations against Shere Mohamed, in June 1843.

18th July.

I am very ill; I had an apoplectic fit, from the sun, when out on the 13th of June last. I had before had the fever, and was very ill recovered, when I went out, and my tent was 132°. The sun struck me down, and I was, I believe, the only man of many who were so stricken that was not dead within three hours, and most of them in a few minutes. The doctor was with me in a minute and bled me, put my feet in hot water, wet towels round my head, and so I was got right; but I have never been right since. Such terrible weakness that I cannot write a letter without lying down; a sickening feel comes over me that is quite indescribable. The doctors tell me I must give myself holidays! I ask them how? If I take one day's rest, I must work double tides the next! How can I take rest? That is beyond their power to answer; I *know* I want it as well as they can tell me, but let them tell me who is to answer, perhaps, *one hundred letters* which at times come in at once, from Bombay, Calcutta, Delhi, or Agra. In short, it is impossible, without I quit this for ever, to have rest; and I feel unable to go on. Even this letter to you knocks me up! Yet 20 sheets of letters on stupid nonsense await at my elbow! There are two reasons why I cannot get rest. There is no one to do the work. 2nd. It is impossible to go away, we are locked up for five months by heat and the monsoon. This world is one of suffering, and he who believes it to be only a sojourn makes up his mind to its roughs and smooths; besides, who is to prophecy? I may in a week be quite well! The weather is cooling, the peace of Scinde is secure. I yesterday heard from the north, and the only chief left in arms has fled over the Indus, with a dozen of followers; and his troops dispersed! I think I feel better already. Tran-

quillity is now *certain*, the want of that weighed hard
upon me, as I felt my last point of personal strength
was to surround Shere Mohamed on the 14th, as I did.

There he was, and
though he was a bad
soldier to let me pin
him up; yet like a good
one, he slapt at Jacob,
who was the weakest,
and tried to get to
the desert, where he
would not fear me, in-
deed the few Jacob

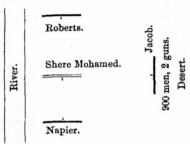

had could hardly find water ; poor Shere Mohamed's men
would not look us in the face. The 24th March took the
heart out of the whole of these wild tribes ; and they fled,
4,000 and three guns, before 900 and two guns ! Jacob did
not fire a shot but with his cannon. I wanted to go north,
to rout out Mohamed Ali, but am too weak, and this fretted
me ; now he is disposed of, and all is quiet, I shall throw as
much work as I can upon others, which with the cool weather
will, perhaps, set me up.

My position was a terrible one from 17th February to
22nd March. I had hold of river, fortress, and town, three
miles off, Ameers prisoners, immense treasure, and 40,000
men as all accounts stated, gathering upon me; a large
hospital, and to guard all these 2,500 men at the most,
including officers ! And besides all this, the anxiety about
the brigade which I had at all hazards ordered to push
double marches to Hydrabad from Sukkur; and to protect
which, had the enemy ventured to march against it, I must
have pursued with 2,000 men at most, an awkward number to
follow 40,000 ! as I heard, and then believed. At last my
brigade arrived, and at the same time reinforcements from *up*
and *down* the river all arrived on the 23rd and joined. At 7
in the evening I manœuvred the whole in divisions, at 2 in
the morning I dismissed an ambassador who arrived to demand
my surrender, and told him to make haste home for I would
be at his heels. I then lay down for two hours, half dead

with fatigue, marched at 4 with 5,000 men, and gave my friend Shere Mohamed such a hiding as he little expected. They will never again fight. All their chiefs have come in and laid their swords at my feet. The whole country is quiet, and rejoicing at being rid of the tyrants. You never saw such a magnificent country, but a wilderness. The collectors have made the calculation, every cultivator paid two-thirds nearly of his produce to the Ameers, rigidly exacted. They have held the country fifty-eight years, and it is nearly ruined. Do not fancy the Belooch is the Scindian. ——— says, "I wish you had not been opposed to people fighting for their independence." How they do blunder in England! Oh! no, we have fought for the *liberties of the people!* Even the Belooch himself is glad, now he finds he is not dispossessed of his conquest, but has only got a good master for bad ones."

THE END.

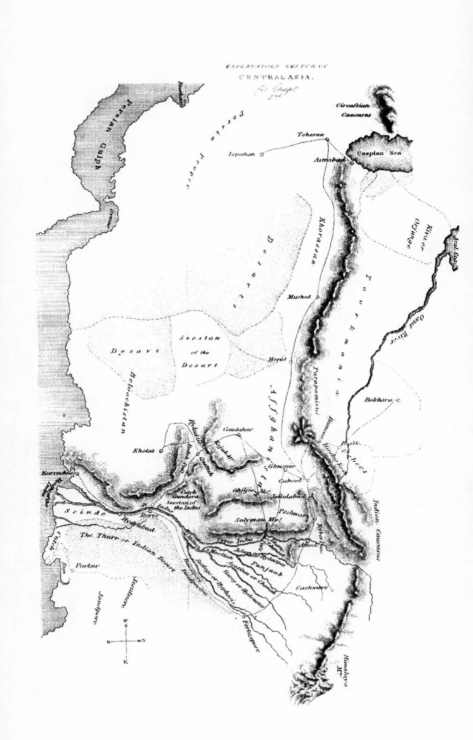

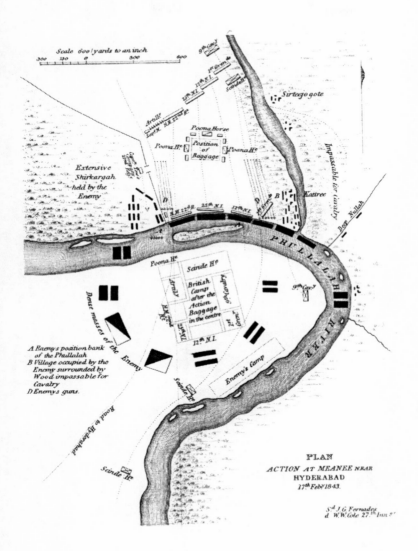

Scale 600 yards to an inch.

9th Cav.y

1st Gren.s

17th N.I.

22nd N.I.

Scinde H.e

Sirteejo gote

Artill.y
Sap.M. H.M. 22nd R.

Poona Horse

Poona H.o   Position
of
Baggage   Poona H.o

Extensive
Shirkargah
held by the
Enemy

Kattree

Impassable for cavalry

D

H.M.22nd R. 25th N.I. 12th N.I. D   B

Dur. Nullah

PHULLALAH

Poona H.o

Scinde H.e

British
Camp
after the
Action.
Baggage
in the centre

9th Cav.y

Cav.yPicq.t

Army   12th N.I.

H.M.22nd

12th N.I.

RIVER

Enemy's camp

Dour masses of the Enemy.

A Enemy's position bank of
the Phullalah.
B Village occupied by the
Enemy surrounded by
Wood impassable for
Cavalry.
D Enemys guns.

Road to Hyderabad

Scinde H.e

Scinde H.e

PLAN
ACTION AT MEANEE NEAR
HYDERABAD
17th Feb.y 1843.

S.d J.G. Fernades
d. W.W.Cole 27th Inn.s.

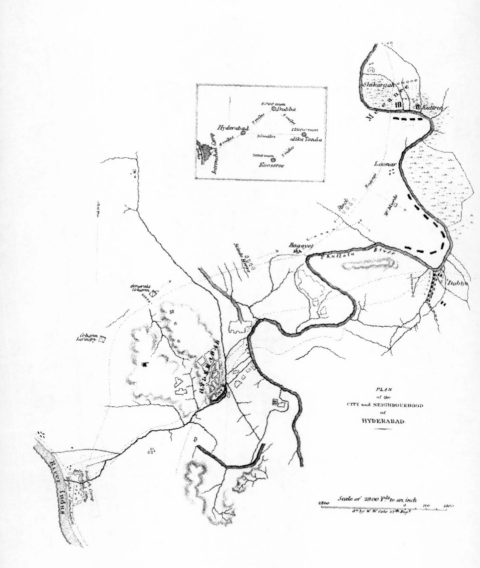

PLAN
of the
CITY and NEIGHBOURHOOD
of
HYDERABAD.

Scale of 2800 Yds to an inch

Drn by W. W. Coke 27th Regt

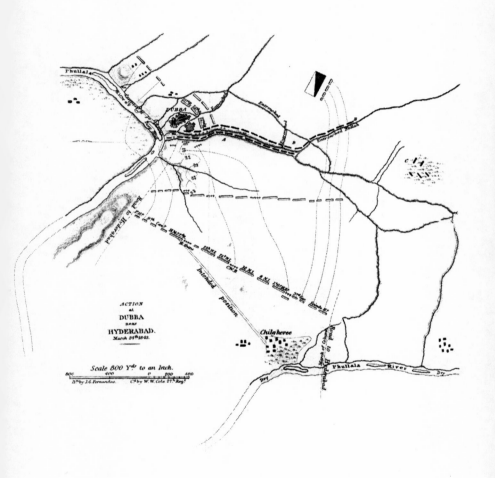

ACTION
at
DUBBA
near
HYDERABAD.
March 24th 1843.

Scale 800 Yds to an Inch.

Drn by J.G. Fernandes.   Cd by W.W. Cole 27th Regt.

Printed in the United Kingdom by
Lightning Source UK Ltd., Milton Keynes
139291UK00001B/60/A